Comenius: A Critical Reassessment of his Life and Work

By the same author

Imagination and Religion in Anglo-Irish Literature, 1930–1980
Martin Buber's Philosophy of Education
Tolstoy and Education

Comenius

A CRITICAL REASSESSMENT
OF HIS LIFE AND WORK

Daniel Murphy

Fellow of Trinity College, Dublin

IRISH ACADEMIC PRESS

This book was set
in 11 on 12 Ehrhardt by
Carrigboy Typesetting Services for
IRISH ACADEMIC PRESS LTD
Kill Lane, Blackrock, Co. Dublin

and in North America for
IRISH ACADEMIC PRESS LTD
c/o ISBS, 5804 NE Hassalo Street, Portland, OR 97213

© Daniel Murphy 1995

A catalogue record for this book is
available from the British Library.

ISBN 0-7165-2537-2

Printed in Great Britain by
Cambridge University Press, Cambridge

For we are not born for ourselves alone.

Comenius, *Pampaedia*

I have said that all the endeavours of my life hitherto were similar to the care of Martha for the Lord and his disciples; motivated by love, indeed, for I am not conscious of anything to the contrary. For cursed be every hour and every moment of whatever labour spent on anything else.

Comenius, *Unum Necessarium*

Comenius was concerned for practical Christianity, for Christian love, but active, effective love. To this ideal he devoted his whole life.

Thomas G. Masaryk, *Johannes Amos Comenius*

The whole of life is a school.

Comenius, *Pampaedia*

Every man has inborn in him the desire to know.

Comenius, *Via Lucis*

He regarded education and educational methods as part, and indeed the principal medium, of the general culture both of the nation and of mankind as a whole.

Thomas G. Masaryk, *Johannes Amos Comenius*

He was the first great democrat among educational thinkers.

Eduard Beneš, *The Teacher of Nations*

Three centuries later the world still suffers misery and chaos because Comenius, the man with the message of universal brotherhood in knowledge and love failed. . . . Today we need more than ever the faith of Comenius in the talents latent in man.

Oskar Kokoschka, 'Comenius, the English Revolution, and our Present Plight'

Tempus erit, quo te Comeni, turba bonorum,
Factaque, spesque tuas, rota quoque ipsa colet.

Wilhelm Leibnitz

CONTENTS

PREFACE

In a work such as this, with its exceptionally complex research requirements, one is necessarily dependent on various people for advice, guidance
and practical assistance. I have been most fortunate in the extraordinary
generosity I have received from a number of individuals and would like
to express my gratitude to them for all they have done for me in the
years while the work was in preparation. I do so while making it as clear
as I possibly can that they are in no way responsible for any of the views
I have expressed in the work and are not to be held accountable for any
of its faults or blemishes.

My greatest debt is to Dr Jana Švecová of the Faculty of Education at
Charles University in Prague. She provided me with valuable source-
material, assisted me with translations from Czech, and, in addition to clar-
ifying numerous points in relation to the writings of Comenius, arranged
interviews for me with some of the most eminent Comeniologists in
Czechoslovakia during several visits to that country.

Amongst those whom I had the honour to meet as a result of her inter-
ventions were two leading figures in Comenian scholarship: Professor
Radim Palouš, Rector of Charles University, and Dr Dagmar Čapková,
author of numerous papers and monographs on Comenius, completed in
the course of an entire lifetime devoted to the study of his work.
Professor Palouš received me in his office in the historic Carolinum in
Prague and shared with me his vast knowledge of Comenius, giving me
particularly illuminating insights on the latter's writings on higher education. Dr Čapková invited me to her home in Prague where she entertained
me most hospitably and talked with me for several hours on numerous
aspects of the life and work of Comenius. I am deeply grateful to them
both and will always treasure my memories of their inspirational per-
sonalities, their kindness, wisdom and generosity.

Here at home I have been very kindly assisted by my late colleague in
Trinity College, the Moravian born literary and scientific scholar, Dr
Petr Skrabanek of the Department of Community Health. As well as helping me with translations from Czech and providing me with important
source-material, Petr enlightened me on many aspects of Czech history,
philosophy and literature in the course of several informal lunchtime
conversations, all of which greatly helped to deepen my understanding of
the ethos and spirit of Bohemian culture. Like all his friends and admirers,

I was deeply shocked by his tragic and untimely death in June of this year and regret that I did not have the opportunity to thank him appropriately for all the assistance he has given me.

On my first visit to Prague in 1991 I had a wide-ranging interview with Professor Jiři Kotasek, Dean of the Faculty of Education in Charles University, which enabled me to grasp some of the complexities of Czech education and to appreciate the continuing relevance of Comenius to all developments in education in his country. Others with whom I have since discussed Comenius include Dr Mirka Vaňova, Dr Maria Třeštikova and Dr Milan Kunkus. I thank each of them sincerely for their friendly and illuminating conversations.

I owe a special word of thanks to my three daughters, Ms. Fidelma Murphy of the Escuela Inglesa in Almeria, Spain, Dr Deirdre Murphy of the Faculty of Medicine, University of Oxford and Dr Nuala Murphy of the Collège de France, University of Paris, for securing important source-material for me and for assisting me with translations from French, German and Spanish texts.

I would like to thank Professor Valentine Rice, Director of the School of Education in Trinity College, for his friendship and support over many years. Thanks are due also to my colleague, Patrick Wall, for morale-boosting companionship during two of my trips to Prague.

I would like to acknowledge the financial assistance I have received from the Arts & Social Sciences Benefaction Fund in Trinity College, which made it possible for me to undertake several highly fruitful research visits to Central Europe while the work was in progress.

I am greatly indebted to the staffs of the J.A. Komenský Pedagogical Museum and Library (Státní Pedagogická Knivovna Komenského) in Prague, the Bodleian Library in Oxford, the Libraries of the University of Cambridge and the Institute of Education of the University of London. I particularly wish to thank the library staff of Trinity College for efficiently meeting my numerous demands on inter-library loan and other services. I want to say a special 'thank you' to the Keeper of Readers' Services, Mrs Eileen McGlade, for all the assistance and advice she has given me through the years. I deeply appreciate her lady-like courtesy and efficiency and, like all regular users of the Library, am full of admiration for her vast knowledge of its bibliographic and technological complexities.

I would like to express my gratitude to the Secretary of The Department of Higher Education & Educational Research, Ms Mary Pat O'Sullivan, for assistance with word-processing and with the layout of the text. Thanks are due also to Dr Michael Adams, Martin Fanning and the staff of Irish Academic Press for seeing the work through the final stages of publication.

Most of all, I want to thank my wife, Margaret, for consistent encouragement and support at all stages during the preparation and completion of the work.

INTRODUCTION

Our state should never again be an appendage or a poor relation of anyone else. It is true we must accept and learn many things from others, but we must do this again as their equal partners who also have something to offer. Our first president wrote: 'Jesus not Caesar.' In this he followed our philosophers Chelcicky and Comenius. I dare to say that we may even have an opportunity to spread this idea further and introduce a new element into European and global politics. Our country, if that is what we want, can now permanently radiate love, understanding, the power of the spirit and ideas. It is precisely this glow that we can offer as our specific contribution to international politics.[1]

So wrote Václav Havel, the President of Czechoslovakia, in his New Year Address to his people in January 1990. He was speaking in the aftermath of the fall of the communist regime and was welcoming the emergence of the newly independent Federal Republic of the Czech and Slovak peoples. Only once before, during almost five hundred years of colonial domination, had Czechoslovakia enjoyed control over its own affairs. That was in the period between World Wars I and II when the country was led by Thomas G. Masaryk, whose words are cited by Havel in his Address. From 1526 to 1918 the country languished under Hapsburg rule and, following the brief period of self-government between the Wars, was to experience even more repressive domination under Communist rule from 1948 until the electrifying events of November 1989. The words of Masaryk, as quoted by Havel, point to the spirit of freedom that remained latent in the national consciousness of the Czech and Slovak peoples throughout these years of colonial rule. That spirit, which was inherently Christian in character—as indicated by Masaryk's slogan, 'Jesus not Caesar'—could be traced to the emergence of the Moravian Church in the middle decades of the fifteenth century and, as Havel indicates in his speech, was sustained by the leaders of that movement through the centuries of foreign rule. It is this tradition which is the focus of the present study.

The traditions of Moravian Christianity were made known to the world through the writings of one of that movement's most prominent members, Jan Amos Komenský or 'Comenius'. In his writings the tradition is given expression in a body of liberal educational thought that has deeply influenced European education down to the present time. The intrinsically Christian character of those writings—their embodiment of the special synthesis of faith and freedom which was the hallmark of Moravian Christianity—will be the particular concern of the present study. It will be argued that most of the previous studies of Comenius's educational thought have failed to emphasise its essentially religious orientation. As might be expected, many of the studies produced in Czechoslovakia itself in recent decades strongly reflect the materialist orientation of the communist ideology and fail to give due attention to the religious foundations of Comenius's thought.[2] There are notable exceptions to this—such as the work of Dagmar Čapková[3] and Jiřina Popelová[4]—but Czech scholars, in most instances, have concentrated on the supposedly secular body of pedagogy that they abstracted from Comenius's work as a whole, without indicating its dependence on the religious convictions that are all-pervasive in his work. Ironically, a similarly secularist spirit pervades much of the work produced on Comenius by western scholars. This is true especially of the interpretations of Jean Piaget[5] who, writing mainly from a pragmatist standpoint, fails to identify the central importance of the ethico-religious aspects of Comenius's thought in the determination of his theories of learning and teaching, and seriously misinterprets the latter as a result.

Pragmatist thinkers generally tend to see him as the first in a line of 'progressive' educators, the latest and most influential of whom is the American writer, John Dewey. The affinities between Comenius and Dewey are obvious but superficial and are ultimately misleading. Both stood for a learner-centred or heuristic pedagogy, both stressed the importance of learning through individual enquiry and discovery, both condemned coercive methods of enforcing classroom discipline, both stressed the need to make knowledge meaningful by relating it to the individual experience of the learner. But such similarities serve merely to conceal the fundamental differences that exist between them. There are profound differences between Comenius and Dewey regarding the priority to be accorded ethico-religious values in education, the nature of experience, its relation to the spiritual and the transcendental, the formative role of the teacher, the design, structure and content of the school curriculum, the importance of literacy, the role of the arts and the sciences—all of which can be traced to the affirmation by the first, and the rejection by the second, of the teachings of the Judaeo-Christian scriptural tradition.

It is contended in the present study that from the time of Comenius, or not long afterwards, there emerged two strands of educational thought, both of which shared a common commitment to the principles and ideals of learner-centred education. The first of these strands includes educators such as Comenius himself, Oberlin, Pestalozzi, Froebel, Novikov, Pirogov, Tolstoy and Buber—all of whose works deeply reflect their origins in the cultural traditions of Christianity and Judaism. The second, which begins with Rousseau and reaches maturity with Dewey, stands in marked contrast to the first, by virtue of its advocacy of learner-centred ideals within the framework of a philosophy which is predominantly secular in character. Two previous volumes by the present author—*Martin Buber's Philosophy of Education* and *Tolstoy and Education*[6]—explored the educational writings of two significant figures within the first of these traditions and sought to identify the distinctive character of the educational theories that were drawn from it. It was contended that the liberal educational theories advocated by Buber and Tolstoy derive their strength from their integration of the spiritual, moral and cultural ideals of education within the framework of an essentially religious tradition, while progressive-pragmatist theory, it was argued, evolved as a secularised system of ideas that was distorted, culturally and morally, by its abstraction of a body of pedagogic theory from its roots in the Judaeo-Christian tradition. Unlike the Comenian tradition, the latter, it was suggested, is inherently flawed by its inability to accommodate the spiritual and religious, as well as the cognitive, affective and imaginative, needs of the individual learner.

The present study therefore completes a trilogy, being the third in a series of works on educators who share a common liberal-religious philosophy and who, as it happens, also share a similar Slavic ancestry. The series has been completed in reverse chronological order: proceeding backwards in time from the work of the twentieth century Polish-Jewish educator, Martin Buber, to that of the nineteenth-century Russian educator, Lev Tolstoy, and therefrom to the work of the seventeenth century Czech educator, Comenius. All three of them offer highly radical interpretations of the Judaeo-Christian tradition and their educational writings are deeply imbued with this.

Buber, like Comenius and Tolstoy, saw the promotion of individual freedom as central to the whole educational process but, again, like both of his predecessors, he saw freedom not as the end of that process but as a means to a higher objective: the fostering of the universal human potentiality for love. 'Freedom in education is the possibility of communion,' he declared.[7] His conception of the nature of the educational process was profoundly influenced by the interrelating objectives implied in this statement. He conceived of the whole relationship of teacher and learner as a co-intentional dialogue, requiring voluntary and authentic reciprocation on the part of each—a conception that was deeply at variance with the authoritarian model of teaching that had dominated European education for centuries. Within that context of dialogue he identified the primary aim of education as the cultivation of faith and ethical responsibility in a spirit of active love, seeing both as being illuminated profoundly by the received traditions of moral and religious truth, while being nurtured in a spirit of freedom, deriving authority finally from the dictates of conscience alone. For this, as for all other modes of educating, he advocated a learner-centred pedagogy, designed to ensure that learning could progress as a free and independent activity, while he fully recognised the need for decisive intervention by the teacher to ensure it was also developed effectively and purposefully.

Tolstoy's work lies similarly in the Judaeo-Christian cultural tradition and shares the special synthesis of faith and freedom that characterised Buber's interpretations of its teachings. He too, as I sought to demonstrate in *Tolstoy and Education*, has been widely misrepresented as an educational innovator belonging in the progressive movement from Rousseau to Dewey. In my book I have argued that Tolstoy's educational writings can only be properly understood in the context of the Christian convictions that motivated all his activities—whether as educator, novelist, social theorist or religious reformer. From these convictions emerged a mature conception of learning and teaching that can be traced back to the liberal learner-centred tradition initiated by Comenius. Like Comenius, Tolstoy successfully matched the directional role of the teacher to the individual needs of the learner; he insisted that learning be conducted freely and spontaneously, while also ensuring that all children had the fullest possible access to their cultural heritage. Above all, he stressed the all-embracing importance of the Christian message on love, seeing this as the heart of the whole educational process, the ideal to which all its activities were to be subordinated.

Comenius stands, therefore, as the seminal figure in a movement that has been given expression in a modern context by Tolstoy and Buber. Like them, he too advocated a radical reconception of the meaning of the Judaeo-Christian heritage, emphasising its inherent simplicity, its affirmation of individual freedom in matters of conscience and faith, its radical teachings on justice and peace. Like Tolstoy's, his was a remarkably pure version of scriptural Christianity, close to the teachings of the Apostles and the early Fathers, unencumbered by dogmatic or rationalistic theology, and characterised above all by the spirit of tolerance and love. The radical character of his religious message holds a powerful attraction in itself for twentieth century educators, apart altogether from the extraordinarily original educational theories to which it gave birth. A common spirit of radicalism interpenetrates both. The present work will focus therefore both on the nature and content of his religious beliefs and on the pedagogic philosophy that he derived from them.

Comenius, as was indicated previously, was a Slavic educator, and has much in common with educators in that tradition from Novikov and Pirogov to Tolstoy and Buber. It seems especially appropriate that a reappraisal of the writings of a Slavic educator be undertaken at the present time, given the widespread reassessment of the traditions of Eastern Europe that is now occurring. The author of a recent study, *Lenin's Tomb*, has spoken of 'the return of historical memory' as the greatest achievement of the Gorbachev years and sees it as the main fruit of the policies of *glasnost* and *perestroika* that he promoted.[8] In the case of Comenius research has been greatly assisted by the publication in English of several of his major works in the course of the past decade. Since 1986 all seven volumes of the *Consultatio* have appeared in English, thanks to the labours of the Scottish scholar, A.M.O. Dobbie. Of particular relevance to the present study are the *Pampaedia* (1986), the *Panglottia* (1991) and the *Panorthosia* (1993).[9] Earlier studies of Comenius have drawn only minimally on the *Consultatio*—the work has been available to scholars in its Latin version only since 1966[10]—yet it is a vital source for the full understanding of his educational ideas. The present study has benefited enormously from this wider availability of Comenian texts and has drawn extensively on all of them for its analysis of Comenius's educational thought. The work quotes extensively from all the primary sources. There are two main reasons for this: firstly, it was considered essential to authenticate interpretations of Comenius directly from his own words; secondly, since some of the primary texts (such as *The Great Didactic* and the *Orbis Pictus*) are not currently in print, it was felt that students of Comenius would benefit from having as much direct access to this material as possible.

The present study begins with a portrait of Comenius as a professional educator. The idea of the teacher as 'exemplar' is one of the foremost themes in his writings and it seems appropriate therefore to begin a study of his work with a profile of his own personal exemplification of the role and responsibilities of the educator. All his life was devoted to the cause of education, both as teacher and educational theorist, and both kinds of activity were wholly complementary. Many of his most innovative theories originated in his own experience as a teacher and these innovations were validated in turn in the concrete conditions of classroom experience. The events of his life are reviewed in some detail, therefore, to exemplify his commitment to the cause of education, to demonstrate the range and extent of his activities, and to chart the gradual evolution of his ideas on educational reform over a period of more than fifty years.

Comenius's ideas, while being remarkably new in themselves, and while being deeply at variance with the educational customs and practices of his time, were nonetheless the product of many different influences and had deep roots in various cultural and theoretical traditions, some of which were of recent origin, others of which had dominated European education for centuries. Four main strands of influence are identified in his work and these are examined in some detail. The predominant influence on his writings, and the source of all their major insights, was the Moravian Christian movement that emerged in Bohemia shortly after the Hussite Reformation in the early years of the fifteenth century. That movement had spread throughout the whole of Bohemia by the time of Comenius. It remained the main source of all his convictions from his childhood to the end of his life and was the decisive influence on his educational thought. Secondly, the Lutheran and Calvinist movements also led to significant reforms in education and these profoundly influenced Comenius's ideas as well. Thirdly, the classical-humanist tradition was still a significant force in education in the seventeenth century and Comenius assimilated much of this in his writings, especially in the revised form in which it had been reinterpreted by writers such as Erasmus, Vives and Montaigne. Fourthly, Comenius was heavily indebted to the new movement in scientific realism that he encountered through Bacon, and he drew much of his pedagogic theory from the writings of prominent figures in that movement, particularly Ratke, Andreae and Alsted.

All these elements were merged successfully by Comenius in a liberal pedagogic philosophy, the central feature of which was its effective blending of authority and freedom in a manner unprecedented hitherto in the history of educational thought. The principles of that pedagogic philosophy are explored in detail in a further chapter. The pedagogic, curricular and institutional reforms that Comenius considered essential for the realisation of the ideal of universal education are explored in depth. Particular attention is given to the doctrine of learning through experience, the principles of effective and systematic teaching, and issues such as the promotion of individualised learning, the structuring and sequencing of curriculum-content, the design of school textbooks, the integration of learning activities, the importance of play—on all of which he offered original and far-seeing insights and for the advancement of which he provided detailed and systematic guidance in works such as *The Great Didactic* and the *Pampaedia*.

Comenius insisted at all times that the primary objective of education is the moral and spiritual formation of the individual person. All his ideas were subordinated to this all-embracing principle. Accordingly, a further chapter explores his thinking on ethico-religious education. Given the radical character of his Christian beliefs—his emphasis on the primacy of conscience and individual responsibility, his pacifism, his advocacy of religious tolerance and ecumenicity, his impassioned commitment to social reform—his ideas in this whole field have a distinctly modern relevance and challenge many of the approaches to ethico-religious education currently advocated by the institutional churches. His application of the methods of his learner-centred pedagogy, and particularly of the doctrine of learning through experience, to the whole sphere of ethico-religious education has a deep relevance to contemporary concerns and provides some challenging, and eminently practical, ideas for the promotion of moral and spiritual education at a time when an all-pervasive secularism presents apparently insuperable obstacles to its advancement.

The two remaining chapters explore some further areas of educational thought in which Comenius is seen to have made significant and original contributions. He saw linguistic growth as the key to his ideal of universal education—as the medium through which learning potentiality could be developed in every child. He challenged the Latin-dominated approach to language teaching generally in fashion at the time, insisting that education should begin with mastery of the mother-tongue, proceeding therefrom to the attainment of competence in a range of non-vernacular languages. Here again his approach was learner-centred, being focussed on the fostering of language growth through the individual experience of the learner. His ideas on the role of motivation in language learning, the place of sense experience, the centrality of oral-aural development, and the role of the textbook, were especially far-seeing and enlightened. He produced some of the most popular textbooks ever employed for language teaching; the most famous of them, the *Orbis Pictus*, remained in use for three centuries after it first appeared.

The final chapter deals with Comenius's ideas on adult and higher education. Emphasising the need to make provision for education on a lifelong basis, he devised a pedagogy appropriate to the needs of adult students and a curriculum that was designed to guarantee them access to their heritage of knowledge and culture throughout the whole of their lives. He envisaged a particular responsibility for adult educators in the promotion of religious tolerance and in the fostering of the spirit of peace—both areas in which his thinking remains highly relevant to the needs of the present time. Equally relevant is his thinking on higher education, particularly his warnings on the dangers of excessive specialisation and his advocacy of the ideal of liberal learning. Each of these issues is considered in detail. A concluding section offers an assessment of the importance of Comenius's ideas for the modern age and evaluates their significance in the context of contemporary moral, religious, social, educational and political concerns.

JAN AMOS KOMENSKÝ, 1592–1670
A BIOGRAPHICAL PORTRAIT

1. EARLY YEARS IN BOHEMIA, 1592–1628

Jan Amos Komenský, better known to the world as 'Comenius', was born in Southern Moravia on March 28, 1592. The name 'Komenský' was derived from 'Komné', the name of the place where the family had originated. For many years controversy has surrounded the precise location of his birth-place, the towns of Komné, Nivnice and Uhersky Brod all claiming to have some associations with his childhood. His habit of signing his name, 'Nivnicensis', during his school years, is seen by some scholars as providing confirmation that he was born in Nivnice, a small town in South Eastern Moravia, close to the Hungarian border.[1] Sixteenth century Moravia was part of the Kingdom of Bohemia, having been ruled by a Hapsburg monarch since its noblemen invited Ferdinand I to become King in 1526. The country was to remain under Hapsburg domination until the end of World War I. At the time of Comenius's birth it was embroiled in the religious turmoil that had begun with the Hussite Reformation of the early fifteenth century. This was shortly to engulf the whole of Europe in the catastrophic events of the Thirty Years' War.

Jan Amos was the youngest of five children. His father, Martin Komenský, owned a mill in Nivnice and an estate near Uherský Brod. The family were devout members of the Church of the United Brethren, a Protestant sect that had broken from the Hussite movement, under the leadership of Peter Chelčicky, in 1457. Their lives were characterised by a simple piety which was based on their reverence for the scriptures and an almost literal interpretation of the meaning of the Biblical text. Tragedy struck the Komenský family when Jan Amos was ten years old. His parents and two of his sisters, Ludmila and Susanna, died in rapid succession, probably as a result of a plague. His upbringing, and that of his two surviving sisters, Margaret and Catherine, was entrusted to guardians, Jan being sent to live with his aunt in the nearby town of Strážnice. Here he received his elementary education which, he recalled later in his allegory,

The Labyrinth of the World and the Paradise of the Heart, was harsh and brutal, its hallmark being the repeated infliction of physical punishment on the young pupils. In *The Labyrinth* he speaks of the 'fists, canes, sticks and birch-rods' by which the pupils were beaten—'on their cheeks, heads, backs and posteriors till blood streamed forth and they were almost entirely covered with stripes, scars, spots and weals.'[2] In *The Great Didactic* he deplores the destruction of childhood happiness that occurred in the inhuman conditions of these schools:

> How many of us there are who have left the schools and universities with scarcely a notion of true learning! I, unfortunate man that I am, am one of many thousands, who have miserably lost the sweetest spring-time of their whole life, and have wasted the fresh years of youth on scholastic trifles. Ah, how often, since my mind has been enlightened, has the thought of my wasted youth wrung sighs from my breast, drawn tears from my eyes, and filled my heart with sorrow! How often has my grief caused me to exclaim: Oh that Jupiter could bring back to me the years that are past and gone![3]

At the age of sixteen Jan Amos was sent for his secondary education to the Latin School at Přerov, at that time under the direction of the Unity of Brethren. 'For, losing both my parents while I was yet a child, I began, through the neglect of my guardians, but at sixteen years of age to taste the Latin tongue', he recalled later. 'Yet', he said, 'by the goodness of God that taste bred such a thrift of desire in me that I ceased not from that time by all means and endeavours to labour the repairing of my lost years.'[4] Though he was critical of the teaching methods then in use in the Latin schools—the excessive emphasis on rote learning, the monotonous repetition of grammatical rules, the severity of the disciplinary methods that were employed—he was generally happy at Přerov and was greatly fulfilled by the education he received there. Inspired by the example of Jan Lanécky, its benign and erudite Rector, he developed a deep love of learning, particularly of the scriptures. During these years he changed his name to its Latinised form—Johannes Amos Comenius—as was customary at the time for members of the educated classes, and decided to devote his life to the promotion of the Christian faith.

On the completion of his studies at Přerov, Comenius went to the Reformed Gymnasium at Herborn in Nassau to undertake further study with a view to being ordained a pastor in the Church of the United Brethren. The Herborn school was favoured by the Brethren because of its strong Calvinist leanings, whereas Charles University in Prague—which would have been more convenient for them—was a strongly Lutheran institution in the Hussite, Neo-Utraquist tradition. Comenius was enabled to go to Herborn through the support he had been given by

Rector Lanécky and by Count Carlos el Viejo de Zerotín, the Vice-Regent of Moravia, a generous friend of the Unity Church, to whom he had been introduced by Lanécky. The Herborn Academy had been founded in 1584 and had about 400 students at the time Comenius studied there. It had earned a good reputation in a number of fields, such as theology, philosophy and languages, and had several notable scholars on its staff. They included Wolfgang Ficinus, the Rector, who was a well-known philosopher, Johann Fischer (Piscator), the great Biblical exegete, and the theologian and educationalist, Johann Heinrich Alsted.

The latter two, both of whom were Calvinists, significantly influenced Comenius' thought on religious and educational issues at a crucial stage in his formation. Under their influence he formed a lifelong belief in the supreme authority of the scriptures. He was strongly attracted also by Alsted's educational writings, particularly by his *Encyclopaedia Scientiarium Omnium* which pointed him towards one of the fundamental principles of his own educational writings, the unity and integrity of all knowledge—a principle to which he gave expression subsequently in his widely proclaimed pansophic teachings. From Alsted also he gained important insights into the methodology of language teaching, being particularly impressed by Alsted's view that the acquisition of a second language might be more easily achieved through the medium of the mother-tongue. The latter became the cardinal principle of Comenius's theories of language teaching and was developed in a series of language manuals that remained standard texts in European schools for centuries afterwards.

Comenius spent two fruitful years at Herborn, at the end of which he presented two Latin disputations which were published by the school press. Since Herborn was not a chartered university and did not have the authority to grant degrees, he left the institute without a qualification in 1612. Following a short sight-seeing visit to Amsterdam, he entered the University of Heidelberg, another major institute of Reformed learning, on June 19, 1613. Here, under the guidance of another famous Biblical scholar, David Pareus, he completed his theological studies. Pareus was a leading figure in a movement committed to uniting all the Protestant sects of the time in a common brotherhood of Reformed Christians. In his *Irenium*, published in 1614, he urged Lutheran, Calvinist and Bohemian Protestants to come together at a general synod and to find ways of resolving their theological differences. Comenius was profoundly impressed by the irenic ideals of Pareus, as became evident in his work for ecumenical unity in later years. After a year at Heidelberg he returned to Prague in the Spring of 1614, having walked the entire distance on foot to conserve his meagre resources. From Prague he travelled to Přerov to take up a teaching appointment at his old school, still under the guidance of Jan Lánecky, by then a Bishop in the Church of the United Brethren.

Almost immediately he embarked on a prodigious programme of literary activities, beginning with a Latin textbook and a Czech-Latin dictionary for school students. He commenced work also on his projected sixteen volume *Encyclopaedia Universitatis Rerum*, the first of its kind in the Czech language and the forerunner of a number of similar projects he was to undertake in later years. Only a fragment of this latter work has survived. In April 1616, at the age of twenty-four, he was ordained a priest at a synod in Žeravice, following which he served as a pastor in Olmütz for two years. Amongst his ordained confrères was his childhood friend from Stražnice, Nicolas Drabík, under whose influence Comenius developed a lifelong interest in religious mysticism as well as a susceptibility to visionary 'prophecy' that became a source of acute embarrassment both to himself and the Brethren in later years. Little is known about the two years Comenius spent at Olmütz. Two years later, in 1618, he was appointed pastor of the parish of Fulneck, a town close to the Moravian-Silesian border. Though the inhabitants of Fulneck were predominantly German and Catholic, there was a strong presence of Brethren there, most of whom lived in the surrounding countryside. Shortly before his appointment, Comenius had married a Hungarian, Magdeline Vizovská, with whom he set up home in Fulneck. As well as being pastor, he also took up duty as Rector of the local school. He took a keen interest in community affairs in the town, one of his projects being the promotion of bee-culture, a practice that was unknown throughout this region of Moravia at the time. He wrote a number of works on religious and social issues in those years. Amongst them was his *Letters to Heaven*,[5] a work in which he exposed the social inequalities existing in Moravia at the time. He also published a short history and map of Moravia, as well as a study of the doctrinal differences separating the Protestant and Catholic Churches since the Reformation.

With the outbreak of the Thirty Years' War the whole of Bohemia was plunged into turmoil, its inhabitants being inevitably caught up in the long-threatened conflict between the major powers of Europe that finally erupted into full-scale war in 1618. The Hapsburg Emperor, Matthias, who had come to power in Bohemia in 1611—largely through the support of the Protestant nobles—ruled the country subsequently through the Catholic Regents he had appointed to represent him in Prague. Following repeated acts of discrimination against Protestants— the prohibition of religious services, the confiscation of churches, discrimination in the provision of schools—the nobles drew up a list of their grievances for presentation to the Emperor in March 1618. When the Regents refused to transmit their petition to the Emperor, they were thrown from the windows of Prague Castle on March 23, 1618. The imperial armies, under the command of Count Tilly, marched into Bohemia to suppress the ensuing revolt of the Protestant nobles. At the

Battle of the White Mountain near Prague on November 8, 1620, the Protestant insurgents were massively defeated by the imperial forces. Their leaders were executed publicly in the Old Town Square in Prague on June 2, 1621. These events put an end to all hopes of re-establishing an independent Czech nation (until its brief revival three centuries later at the end of World War I) and it resulted in a mass exodus of Protestants from Bohemia as they sought refuge in countries throughout Europe sympathetic to their religious beliefs.

Moravia suffered greatly from the invasion of the imperial armies. Fulneck was devastated by Spanish troops, and most of the city was burned to the ground. Comenius's home was destroyed and, when he managed to secure his books in the city hall, this also was destroyed, on the orders of the Capuchin Friars who had come to Moravia to convert the 'heretics'. He himself went into hiding, while his wife and two children sought refuge at her mother's home in Přerov. Here two years later all three of them succumbed to a pestilential plague that had spread throughout the region in the aftermath of the war. In his grief at the loss of his family Comenius sought the assistance of his former benefactor, Count de Zerotín. The Count invited him, together with twenty other Moravian pastors and their bishop, Matthew Konečný, to stay indefinitely at his estate at Brandýs in North Eastern Bohemia. During the three years he spent at Brandýs Comenius translated the Psalms into Czech, as well as writing a number of religious treatises, including *Impregnable Fortress*[6] and *The Sorrowful*[7], two works in which he sought to evoke the plight of the vanquished Protestant communities. He urged them to accept their misfortunes in a spirit of Christian resignation. It would be best, he told them, 'to accept everything—happiness and unhappiness, joy and sorrow, laughter and weeping—from His hand with thanksgiving.' In this passage from *The Sorrowful* he vividly evokes the scale of the catastrophe that had befallen the Bohemian nation:

> Woe is to us on all sides: a cruel, bloody sword is destroying my dear homeland; castles, fortresses and strong cities are conquered; towns, villages, splendid houses and churches are plundered and burned; estates are robbed, livestock is taken and killed; the poor populace is subjected to suffering, torture, and here and there even murder and capture. For many maddened nations have for the fourth year come upon us like clouds, and there is still no hope of peace, so that it would seem that everything will perhaps soon be turned into a desert. . . . And the most painful of all is that the truth of God is oppressed, the pure services of God are stopped, the priests are driven out and thrown into prisons. Many were either cruelly put to death or were mockingly driven out, and not a few (of whose number I, unhappy, am one) are miserably in hiding for the fear of human fury.[8]

In these years he also wrote *The Labyrinth of the World and the Paradise of the Heart*,[9] an allegory modelled on Bunyan's *Pilgrim's Progress*. The *Labyrinth* has been described as 'the greatest and most celebrated work of the period in Czech literature'[10] and has been compared to the great classics of mystical literature, such as St Augustine's *Confessions*, Thomas a Kempis's *Imitation of Christ* and the anonymously authored *The Cloud of Unknowing*. It was completed in 1623 and dedicated to Count de Zerotín. A highly autobiographical work, inspired partly by the writings of Johann Valerian Andreae whom Comenius had met at Heidelberg, it describes its hero's pilgrimage through the world as he seeks self-fulfilment in a variety of intellectual, artistic and worldly pursuits, but everywhere finds only deceitfulness, unhappiness and despair. As he contemplates the imminent prospect of death, he hears the voice of Christ calling to him in prayer and realises that the contentment that he seeks can be found only in the soul's quest for union with God. A contemporary Czech writer has given this assessment of the qualities that have attracted readers of *The Labyrinth* through the centuries:

> The mind of the reader is held spellbound by the charms of the composition: behind the allegorical covering he discerns actual life illumined by many-sided experiences and scourged by effective satirical comments; our interest is increased by autobiographical confessions and illusions. A rare vividness and a sense for significant detail, which is frequently accompanied by lively dramatic power, often cause the literary man to predominate over the meditative philosopher and the devout disciplinarian who consistently pursues his tendencious, religious idea. The reader allows himself to be carried away by the powerful phantasy, profound wisdom, personal modesty and lofty ideas of the zealous writer who values the moral worth of the individual more highly than everything else. We experience the author's compassion for human beings in their apathy; we feel his ardent love for his neighbour; we respect his deep religious feeling, for which the reader is prepared in the second part, and we enjoy our intellectual treat. The 'Labyrinth' is written in fresh, vivid, pithy language, and every phrase and expression reveals aptly the Czech spirit. Long after Komenský's death, his consolatory work was extremely highly valued by his exiled fellow-countrymen. In the period of the Czech national revival, the language of the 'Labyrinth' was taken as a model of pure Czech.[11]

In September, 1624 Comenius married his second wife, Maria Dorothea Cyrill, the daughter of his fellow-pastor, John Cyrill, later to become Senior Bishop of the Unity of Brethren. By this time Count de Zerotín had come under increasing pressure from the authorities in Prague to expel the pastors from his estates, and he had little choice but to ask them to leave. For some time they hid in the caves and fastnesses of the Giant Mountains near the Bohemian-Silesian frontier, eventually finding refuge on the estate of Jiri Sadowski at Slaupna. Here Comenius wrote the *Centrum Securitatis*,[12] a work in which he endeavoured to explain issues such as the nature and purpose of existence, and man's relation to the world and to God, through images that might render them comprehensible to the common reader. At a conference held in Doubravice in March 1625 the Brethren concluded they had no choice but to leave the country and decided to seek refuge with the Bohemian exiles in Poland. Comenius and another of the pastors were sent to Leszno to seek permission both from the Brethren and from the Lord of the city, Count Raphael Leszczynski, for the pastors to come and settle there.

On the way they visited the village of Görlitz in Lusatia, where the mystical writer, Jacob Boehme, had died the previous year. Comenius was deeply interested in Boehme's writings and had been particularly attracted by the insights into the nature of God and the structure of the universe that Boehme had developed in his *Mysterium Magnum* which had been published three years before. At Leszno Comenius was assured that the Bohemian Brethren would be warmly welcomed by their Polish confrères. Returning to Bohemia, he spent some time with friends at Branná near Jilemnice, and subsequently spent short periods in Berlin and the Hague. On his journey to Berlin he met a prophet-visionary, Christopher Kotter—one of many such that he met in the course of his life—who foretold a speedy end to the sufferings of the Protestants of Europe. However, by a decree of the Hapsburg Emperor, issued on July 31, 1627, all the people of the Kingdom of Bohemia were ordered to accept the Catholic faith or to leave the country permanently. Protestants living in Bohemia itself were instructed to go to Poland, while those living in Moravia were ordered to live in Slovakia. Comenius and his fellow pastors, though themselves natives of Moravia, decided to abide by the arrangements they had made to settle in Poland. Accompanied by his wife, his father-in-law, John Cyrill, and another prophet-visionary, Christina Poniatowska, Comenius set out for Poland in the Spring of 1628 and took up residence in Leszno, where he was to spend the next twelve years of his life.

2. EXILE IN POLAND, 1628–1641

While staying on the estate of Jiři Sadowski at Slaupna, Comenius and his colleague, John Stadius, had helped with the education of the three Sadowski children. This practical involvement in teaching turned Comenius's thoughts once again to the subject of pedagogic reform. His interest in the subject was further strengthened when, together with some of the other pastors, he walked from Slaupna one summer afternoon to visit the nearby castle of Wilcitz. In the castle library he found a copy of the *Didactic* of Elias Bodinus which fired his enthusiasm once again for the whole subject of school pedagogy. On his arrival at Leszno he immediately began work on what was to become *The Great Didactic*, his systematic exposition of the principles of classroom pedagogy. Written initially in Czech, Comenius postponed its publication until his expected return to Bohemia, a prospect that was never fulfilled, despite the optimistic prophecies of his two visionary associates, Kotter and Poniatowska. The Czech version did not, in fact, appear until two centuries later (it was published in Prague in 1849) but a Latin version, which Comenius prepared in 1637 on the request of Count Leszcynski, was published with his *Opera Didactica Omnia* in 1657.[13]

But while *The Great Didactic* did not appear for many years after his departure from Leszno, all of Comenius's educational activities from the early 1630s were guided by the principles enunciated in it. The basic premise of the work was that education should be modelled on the natural development of the child, with instruction proceeding from the known to the unknown and all learning being related directly to the everyday experience of the pupil. Comenius insisted that all school activities be conducted initially through the medium of the mother-tongue and that they be graded systematically in accordance with each child's ability and rate of development. He laid particular emphasis on the value of children's play but insisted also that all school activity be systematic and orderly and that the spirit of disciplined learning be fostered constantly. He advocated the abandonment of the barbaric methods of discipline that were currently practised in schools. These were the practical aims of the educational process: its ultimate and all-encompassing goal was to be the religious and moral development of the pupil. All his initiatives in educational reform—his experiments in teaching methodology, his imaginatively designed textbooks, his theories of school discipline, his ventures into adult education—were all guided by this overriding concern to promote the ideals and values of the Christian faith. In this he shared common convictions with later reformers such as Pestalozzi and Tolstoy, while differing profoundly from others such as Rousseau and Dewey

Comenius envisaged a four-stage process for the years of conventional schooling. The first stage was to be the school of infancy, embracing the first six years of the child's life. The main objective of this stage was to be character training, the fostering of vernacular proficiency, basic sense training, and the promotion of piety and moral responsibility. From this the child would proceed to the vernacular school where s/he would be taught a basic curriculum consisting of the 3Rs, singing, Latin and another language. Both the school of infancy and the vernacular school were to be open to all children, irrespective of their social class, sex or religious creed—the schools were to be universal, compulsory and free. The Latin school, catering for the 12–18 age group, would provide an education in the classical curriculum—Latin, Greek, Hebrew, mathematics, the sciences, the fine arts and the useful arts. The fourth stage envisaged was that of university education which would cater for an elite body of students in the 18–24 year age group, and would be linked closely to the world of professional training.

Shortly after his arrival in Leszno, Comenius was appointed co-rector of its Gymnasium. This provided him with an excellent opportunity to test out his pedagogic theories in the practical conditions of the classroom. His immediate concern was to effect improvements in the teaching of Latin. Latin was still the chief subject in the curriculum and it was vital that it be taught well. Deeply disillusioned with conventional methods of teaching the language, he devoted three years to the preparation of a textbook suitable for beginners. The *Janua Linguarum Reserata*,[14] which appeared in 1632, was the first work to be issued by the new Leszno printing house which the Brethren had founded with equipment they had brought with them from Moravia. The approach adopted in the *Janua* was partly inspired by Bodinus's work, its basic method being the promotion of linguistic proficiency through the comprehension of words and phrases related to the experiences of everyday life. All language learning, Comenius declared, should be grounded in experience, and the growth of linguistic fluency should go hand in hand with a full understanding of the 'things' which the language signified. His work represented a radical departure from the methods then in use, which were based primarily on the study of literary uses of Latin and were largely unrelated to the experience of the pupil. This was true particularly of the text most commonly used in the schools of the time, the *Janua Linguarum* of William Bathe (or Bateus), an Irish Jesuit who was Rector of the Irish College in Salamanca. In the *Continuatio*, where Comenius gave an account of the publication of his own *Janua*, he made some disparaging comments on Bathe's work. (The reference to Irish *monks* can probably be explained by the fact that Bathe was assisted by his brother, John, and by another Irish Jesuit, Father Stephen White.)

> It came to pass, therefore, that my little work was published in the year 1632, with a slight change of title. For I had been advised by some one that there was already extant such a book containing the whole of the Latin language, called *Janua Linguarum*—the work of Irish monks; but when I had seen it, I perceived it to be written without orderly arrangement of the materials, inasmuch as the vocabulary of the whole language (and that broken up in sundry ways)

was contained within no more than twelve hundred sentences. 'This,' said I, 'is something different.' They, however, (i.e. the two Governors of the College at Leszno), advised that it should be called *The Gate of Tongues Unlocked*, or the *Seminarium* (*Seedplot*). And so it was published at Leszno; and soon afterwards (in German and Polish versions) at Dantzig, at Leipzig also with the addition (bestowed by the professors) of a new epithet AUREA; which epithet was afterwards retained in other editions, translations into all the European languages being added; with a success wholly unhoped by me, nor even imagined in dream.[15]

Closely following his own principle of a careful sequencing of subject-matter to facilitate efficient and ordered learning, Comenius set out his material sequentially in a series of graded textbooks. The first was the *Vestibulum*, intended as an introductory text for beginners. This provided 1000 commonly used words which were presented in easy sentences, side by side with translations in the vernacular—which were placed in adjoining columns. The second text was the *Janua* itself, which consisted of about 8000 Latin words, again presented in simple sentences. The third text was the *Palatinum* or *Atrium*, an anthology of poetry and prose from the great classical authors. The final text was the *Thesaurus*, a further collection of excerpts from scientific and literary sources.

Almost immediately following its publication, the *Janua* was widely acclaimed as signifying a major advance in the teaching of Latin. It was translated into several European languages—Polish, German, Swedish, Greek, English, French, Spanish, Italian and Hungarian—and further versions appeared later in Arabic, Turkish, Persian and Mongolian. 'It was accepted with much applause and unanimously approved by the learned as the true and most genuine way of teaching the languages,' Comenius wrote in *A Reformation of Schools Designed in Two Excellent Treatises*.[16] The *Janua* became the standard textbook for Latin throughout Europe and America and remained so for centuries to come. It was even adopted by the Jesuit schools which had previously been using the text produced by Bathe, a member of their own order. One educator wrote to Comenius from Königsberg, 'We are accomplishing miracles here with the aid of thy golden textbook.'[17] The editor of the *Dictionaire Historique et Critique*, published at Rotterdam in 1697, wrote: 'Had Comenius written no other book than this he would have rendered himself immortal. The work was reprinted countless times, and was translated into I know not how many languages. There are several polyglot editions. I do not doubt that Comenius speaks sincerely when he admits that the success of the work surpassed anything that he anticipated . . . '[18] (There were some exceptions to this chorus of adulatory tributes, amongst them the poet, John Milton, who dismissed the work with a brief contemptuous reference in his *Tractate on Education*.)

In the three years during which he was preparing the *Janua*, Comenius also introduced some radical· innovations into the work of the Leszno Gymnasium. Originally founded as a preparatory school, it had been given full gymnasium status in 1624. It was completely remodelled to bring it into harmony with Comenius's ideas and, under his direction, became known as one of the best of its kind in Poland. The daily programme of activities was carefully regulated: students rose early and attended lessons in a broadly based curriculum for up to five hours each day. A strong emphasis was placed on piety and self-discipline. Comenius encouraged his students to keep notebooks in which they were asked to record their observations on all matters that interested them in the course of the day. This was in keeping with his belief that learning should be related closely to individual experience. As well as specifying the time that was to be devoted to formal learning, he made provision also for regular periods of recreation, a key principle in his pedagogic philosophy being the necessity of combining work with play to ensure the balanced and harmonious development of the pupil. (Dancing, however, was strictly forbidden. 'The dance,' he declared, 'is a circle whose centre is the devil!').[19] The years he spent in the classroom at the Leszno Gymnasium provided Comenius with the practical experience that proved to be a vital ingredient in his pedagogic writings, their skilful blending of theoretical and professional insights being their primary attraction for educators.

Meanwhile he assumed additional responsibilities as part of his priestly ministry. On October 6, 1632, at a synod held in Leszno, attended by priests from Poland, Silesia and Hungary, he was elected a Bishop of the Unity Church. He was also elected Secretary of the Commission responsible for issuing treatises in defence of the Church's teachings. Additionally, he was given responsibility for the supervision of students preparing for ordination to the priesthood. Shortly after his election, he edited the Czech version of the Constitution of the Unity Church, as well as providing a Latin version of its text. He collaborated in writing *The History of the Persecutions of the Church in Bohemia*[20]—an important study of the evolution of Protestantism before the Thirty Years' War—and translated Bishop Lewis Bayley's *The Practice of Piety*[21] from the original German.

In these years Comenius devoted much of his time to promoting religious ecumenicity, seeking to foster better relations between the different confessional sects. In *The Labyrinth of the World and the Paradise of the Heart* he had castigated the sects for their bigotry and fanaticism and had called on them to find ways to resolve their differences. He now wrote a new work, *Haggaeus Redivivus*,[22] in which he outlined a plan for the union of all the Protestant Churches. He urged them to abandon names such as 'Hussite', 'Lutheran' and 'Calvinist' in favour of the common name of 'Christian.' 'For the saying of Our Saviour is forever valid, that every kingdom divided against itself shall perish, and house shall fall upon house,' he warned. 'So is similarly the warning of the Apostle that if ye bite and devour one another, take heed that ye be not consumed one by another,' he cried.[23] He stressed the essential indivisibility of Christian truth, dismissing the different interpretations of the scriptures by the various Churches as 'mere misunderstandings.'[24]

These viewpoints were further elaborated in *The Way of Peace*[25] where he condemned purely rationalist explications of the scriptures, arguing that all doctrine should be defined in accordance with the literal meaning of the Biblical text. He advocated a return to the simplicity of the early Christian Church, and while warning against excessive ceremonialism, suggested Christians should be free to adopt any rituals they chose for their services, so long as they were not 'superstitious or idolatrous.' On the vexed question of the Communion rite—a major source of conflict between the Churches—he argued it did not matter whether it was represented as a commemorative service or a ritual re-enactment of the sacrifice of Christ. The important thing, he declared, was that it be conducted in a spirit of faith and love. He also took a strictly non-dogmatic stance on the problematic issue of predestination—a matter of particular concern to his own Church. He argued that inner piety was far more important than religious orthodoxy and that it was more appropriate to pray for wrong-doers in a spirit of Christian forgiveness than to judge them harshly in accordance with dogmatic precepts. A true ecumenist (a rare being in the difficult conditions of seventeenth century Europe), he concluded that the issues separating the Churches were not *essential* matters of faith, but derived from varying interpretations of the scripture texts to which they all owed a common allegiance and loyalty.

In the midst of all this, Comenius's thoughts were turning to a new educational project that was to become the basis of his thinking on the nature of knowledge and on the kind of curricula that should be taught in schools and higher educational institutions. As early as 1630 he had begun work on a projected synthesis of science, religion and the classical disciplines into an integrated scheme of knowledge he considered appropriate for the conditions of a post-Renaissance society. (The material was published in a work called *Theatrum Universitatis Rerum*.)[26] This was the genesis of the pansophic ideal of universal knowledge. He was encouraged in this work by an Austrian Baron, Ludwig Wolzogen, at that time living as an exile in Poland. Wolzogen had been deeply impressed by the *Janua* and had urged Comenius to extend the innovative principles he had developed in the area of language pedagogy into the wider sphere of the curriculum as a whole. This resulted in the production both of the *Janua Rerum Reserata (The Gate of Things)*[27] and shortly afterwards the *Pansophia Prodromus*, which was included as part of *A Reformation of*

Schools and published in London, with the assistance of Samuel Hartlib, in 1639.[28] The impact of the *Prodromus* was immediate and dramatic. 'Every corner of Europe is filled with this pansophic ardour,' wrote John Tassius, Professor of Mathematics at Hamburg, in a letter to Samuel Hartlib. 'If Comenius were to do no more than stimulate the minds of all men in this way he might be considered to have done enough.'[29]

Pansophism was a humanist concept first encountered by Comenius during his studies at Herborn. The idea of the integrity of all knowledge can be traced back to the Greeks—particularly to Plato and Aristotle— and various attempts had been made through the centuries to design an encyclopaedia of universal knowledge which would demonstrate this. Attempts to construct such a work had been made, for example, by Vincent of Beauvais in 1264 and by two contemporaries of Comenius in the early seventeenth century, Johann Heinrich Alsted and Peter Laurenberg. (Laurenberg's work was actually entitled *Pansophia*.) The idea had been given powerful stimulus by two works of Francis Bacon which greatly influenced Comenius—the *Magna Instauratio Scientiarum* and the *Novum Organon*. Comenius himself had become deeply interested in science, largely through Bacon's influence, and in 1633 had published a treatise on physics, *Physicae ad lumen divinum reformatae synopsis*,[30] in which he sought to reconcile the worlds of religion and science. In his pansophic writings he sought to integrate the findings of the new sciences with the traditional disciplines of knowledge, particularly with the scriptures which he regarded as the ultimate source of all wisdom. He aimed to demonstrate the organic unity of knowledge which he felt was insufficiently recognised in contemporary curricula. He particularly complained of the fragmentation of knowledge occurring in textbooks generally in use in schools and colleges:

> Metaphysicians sing to themselves alone, natural philosophers chant their own praises, astronomers dance by themselves, ethical thinkers make their laws for themselves, politicians lay their own foundations, mathematicians rejoice over their own triumphs, and theologians rule for their own benefit. Yea, men introduce even into the same field of knowledge and science contradictory principles whereby they build and defend whatever pleases them, without much troubling themselves about the conclusion as derived from the premises of other men.[31]

Comenius's pansophic project differed in two important respects from previous attempts to construct an encyclopaedia of universal knowledge. Firstly, it was essentially Christian in conception, being a cohesive integration of all knowledge around the central truths of faith. Its focus was the revealed word of the scriptures and the heritage of Christian truth handed down through the centuries. Secondly, its methodology involved an inductive progression from the familiar world of experience to the more complex orders of knowledge and truth—a process in which it particularly reflected the influence of Bacon and the realist movement. 'There can be no knowledge without nature,' Comenius declared. 'Knowledge emulates nature; knowledge imitates nature; knowledge is the daughter of nature.' And crucially, he added this qualifying statement: 'There can be no nature without God; nature emulates God; nature is the daughter of God; nature imitates God.' He sought, therefore, to facilitate orderly, systematic learning, through his emphasis both on the inter-relatedness of all knowledge and on the natural progression from known, familiar experience to the unknown spheres of abstract and symbolic thought. What he proposed would nowadays be described as a comprehensive curriculum, a harmonisation of different types of knowledge within the unifying framework of religious faith, combined with a learner-oriented pedagogy designed to ensure its effective implementation in whatever conditions in which it was introduced.

The *Prodromus* received a qualified welcome at the time of its publication, one of its readers being René Descartes who was introduced to it by a Franciscan priest, Marinus Mersenne. While welcoming its emphasis on the organic unity of all knowledge, Descartes complained, however, that Comenius had confused philosophy with theology and had failed to recognise the spirit of free enquiry which he (Descartes) saw as the cornerstone of philosophic thought.[32] Some of the Unity priests complained, from a different standpoint, that Comenius had confused 'matters divine' with 'matters human' and they demanded that he be prohibited from teaching because of the heretical character of some of his pronouncements.[33] He was asked to explain the project to the assembled Brethren at a Synod specially convened at Leszno, at which, however, he was eventually exonerated from all blame and his work received the full approval of the Unity Church. The controversy led him subsequently to publish his *Explanation of Pansophy*,[34] in which he stressed the Christian character of the whole scheme even more than previously. He declared he had sought to 'epitomise those books of God—Nature, the Holy Writ and human conscience.'[35] His aim, he said, was to make the scriptures more widely known, showing them as the key to an understanding of nature, capable of opening up its deepest mysteries, and leading man ultimately to the contemplation of eternal life. Once again he stressed the essential unity of all truth: philosophy, he said, was incomplete without knowledge of religious truth; religion was inadequate without the insights of science. Most importantly, he proclaimed his belief that all men should have access to the riches of pansophic knowledge and that all have the capacity to benefit from the truly comprehensive education it could provide. Thenceforward, the promotion of this ideal became the all-consuming purpose of his work for educational reform.

Samuel Hartlib, the son of a Polish, German-speaking merchant from Elbing, was a scientific scholar who developed a deep interest in the cause of interchurch union as a result of his association with the theologian, John Dury, whom he met in the late 1620s. Dury, the son of a Protestant Minister from Leyden, had been educated at Oxford, where he became interested in promoting unity amongst the Christian Churches. Expelled from Sweden on the orders of Queen Christina, who disapproved of his work for evangelical union, he planned to come to London to continue his ecumenical activities there. Hartlib, whose mother was English, had himself moved to London in 1628. At Cambridge University he met some students who had been sent there by the Unity Church, and through his contacts with them came to know of Comenius's writings. Full of enthusiasm for the *Janua*, which had just been published, he began to correspond with Comenius in 1632. As he learned of the hardship and poverty in which the members of the Moravian community were living in Poland, he offered them financial assistance and undertook to support their religious activities. (Amongst the projects he undertook to finance was the publication of the *Prodromus* at Oxford in 1637, as was mentioned in the previous section.)

Hartlib became deeply involved in Comenius's educational activities and planned to found a college in England where the ideals of pansophic learning could be promoted. Being deeply influential in academic circles—the fact that Milton had addressed his *Tractate on Education* to him is a measure of his standing in literary and scholarly circles at the time—he wrote to various individuals requesting assistance for the pansophic project. One of his colleagues, the German scholar, Joachim Hübner, wrote to Comenius in December 1638, outlining their plans for the founding of the college and seeking his advice on the teachers that would have to be recruited. Comenius responded enthusiastically, assuring them of his support and urging them to take the necessary measures to ensure it would be an 'all comprehensive college.'[36] John Gauden, an Anglican clergyman, later to become Bishop of Worcester, was one of the strongest supporters of the project. On November 29, 1640 he addressed the House of Commons on the topic, 'The Love of Truth and Peace'. In the course of his Address he urged the members to invite John Dury and Comenius to come to England so that the members could 'see and weigh their noble and excellent designes.' These were the words of his Address:

> Here give me leave by way of short digression, in so greate and publique an Assembly, to recommend to your favour, the noble endeavours of two greate and publique spirits, who have laboured much for truth and peace, I mean Comenius and Duraeus; both

famous for their learning, piety and integrity, and not unknowne, I am sure, by the fame of their works, to many of this honourable, pious and learned Assembly.

The one hath laide a fair designe and foundation for the raising up of a Structure of Truth, Human and Divine, of excellent use to all mankinde, for the easiness and exquisiteness of attaining the true knowledge of things.

The other hath long studied, and with greate pains endeavured and wel advanced the peace and unity of the reformed churches (a blessing that cannot be purchased at too deare a rate) whereunto he hath the suffrages and assistance of many leisured Divines, and some of our owne, especially the renowned Bishop of Salisbury, as you may see in his letters to him, and in his late tractate, *De pace ecclesiastica* &c. But, alas, both these noble plants (to the infinite shame and reproach of the present age, to the losse and detriment of the future) are like to wither to a barrenness for want of public encouragement and aid to go on in so noble, greate and usefull undertakings. I leave it to your Wisdomes, at your leysure to consider, whether it were not worthy the name and honour of this State and Church to invite these men to you, to see and weigh their noble and excellent designes: to give them all publick aid and encouragement to goe on and perfect so happy works which tend so much to the advancing of truth and peace.[37]

The invitation to Comenius and Dury was issued in the Spring of 1641 by a group representing both Houses of Parliament, the Commons and the Lords. It included John Williams, Bishop of Lincoln, Bishop Davenant of Salisbury and Archbishop Ussher of Armagh. 'Come, come, come, it is for the glory of God: take counsel no longer with flesh and blood,'[38] Hartlib wrote to Comenius. Deciding to delegate his responsibilities at the Leszno Gymnasium to his co-rector, Comenius prepared to make a short visit to London. Recalling the episode in later years, he said he had gone there 'for the propagation of the Gospel among the heathen, for a fresh opportunity had been very happily made for sowing the seed'[39]—a reference to plans then under the way by Church bodies in England to spread the Gospel amongst the Indians in the American colonies. After a difficult voyage across the North Sea, he arrived in London on September 21, 1641. He described his first impressions of the city in a letter to his friends in Leszno:

This corner of the world has much that differs from other countries, and is worthy of admiration. What interests me most are those matters which concern the glory of God and the flourishing state of the Church and the schools. . . .

I. The eagerness with which the people crowd to the services on Sundays is incredible. London has 120 parish churches, and in all of them—of those which I visited I affirm this as an established fact—there is such a crowd that space is insufficient. . . .

III. A large number of the men and youths copy out the sermons with their pens. Some thirty years since (in King James's reign) they discovered an art which has now come into vogue even among the country folk, that of rapid script (tachygraphia) which they call stenography. . . . For this they employ symbols (characters) signifying whole words, and not single letters of the alphabet.

Almost all of them acquire this art of rapid writing, as soon as they have learned at school to read the Scriptures in the vernacular. It takes them about another year to learn the art of shorthand. . . .

V. They have an enormous number of books on all subjects in their own language. . . . There are truly not more bookstalls in Francfort at the time of the fair than there are here every day. Bacon's work *De Scientiarum Augmentis* has recently appeared in English.[40]

Comenius probably stayed with Hartlib at his home in Aldgate, on the East Side of London, near the Tower. Hartlib bought him a new suit of clothes, 'in the fashion customary among English divines.' Both Comenius and Dury were entertained ceremoniously at a formal dinner, hosted by Bishop Williams, in the course of which the latter urged Comenius to bring his family to England with a view to settling there permanently. He offered him an annual stipend of £120 from the state treasury. Comenius's observations of the tour were included in one of his last works, the *Continuatio*, published in Amsterdam in 1669, the year before his death. It includes the following vivid description of the dinner hosted by Williams:

> But on the next day came Hartlib, telling me that my presence was no longer unknown, and that he was bringing me a tailor who would make me at once new clothes in the fashion customary among English divines. Scarce was the suit ready, when it was announced that we were invited by the Bishop of Lincoln, a mighty patron of the pansophic study, to dinner. And into his presence I was taken by Mr Dury (who had arrived before me) and Hartlib. Being asked by the Bishop whether I had brought my family with me, I answered, that neither had it been my desire to do so, nor would it have been easy. He then asked me, after leading the others into an inner room apart, why the business had not been managed otherwise, and he ordered that it should be arranged with me that I should have my family fetched: there could be no other course, he said. As for provision before aught was publicly voted, I should

receive from him £120 sterling a year, and others would contribute more. Dury and Hartlib now came forward, certain noble lords in the meanwhile having come in unto the bishop, and began to treat with me on these matters, persuading me not to oppose good counsel. I answered I was not my own master, since I was of that Church in which none hath sole disposition of himself: I must deliberate with myself and with my friends &c. After dinner the Bishop proferred me his right hand, placed ten James pieces into mine, at which so large a bounty I greatly marvelled.[41]

Comenius wrote to his confrères in the Unity Church, describing the offer that had been made to him. They were undecided on the question of whether he should settle in England, but his wife, he recalled later, 'abjured him with tears that he should not take her, unacquainted with the foreign language, so far away from the company of the exiles.'[42] In these circumstances he decided not to live in England permanently. When Parliament reassembled in October he appeared before a Commission set up to consider his project to found a college of pansophic learning. He was advised that the House intended to assign 'a college with its revenues, whereby a certain number of hard-working men, called from all nations, might be honourably maintained either for a term of years, or permanently.'[43] Three existing colleges were considered as suitable for the project—Savoy, Winchester and Chelsea—the latter being the preferred choice of the Parliamentary Commission. Founded in 1607 as a 'spiritual garrison, with a magazine of all books for the purpose, where learned divines should study and write',[44] Chelsea College seemed ideal for the purposes envisaged by Comenius. His plans were upset, however, by the outbreak of the rebellion in Ireland in 1641 and by the reports (subsequently shown to be greatly exaggerated) that 200,000 people had died in the violence. Parliament was preoccupied with this issue throughout the winter and was unable to give attention to Comenius's project.

He spent the winter months in London, miserable and lonely, unable to speak the language of the people, and restricted to discussing his plans only with those who were able to speak Latin. He wrote a treatise, *Via Lucis* ('The Way of Light')[45] in which he defined the aims of pansophic learning. The term 'light' in the title of this work signifies the wisdom of pansophic knowledge. This, he said, would be attained through four main methods: through universal books, universal schools, a universal college and a universal language. The first three were already in the process of preparation. With regard to a universal language, Comenius initially envisaged the creation of an entirely new language, easier and more comprehensive than the classical languages which partly served that purpose already. Such a project was, in fact, attempted by Dalgarno, a Scotsman, in his *Lingua Philosophia* in 1661, and by Bishop Witkins, in a similarly elaborate scheme sponsored by the Royal Society, largely on the urging of Comenius, in 1668. In later years Comenius abandoned the idea altogether and saw Latin as offering the best prospect of providing a language of universal learning, comprehensible to the whole of mankind. He did, however, consider that the propagation of universal learning was a wholly realisable ideal in itself. He wrote optimistically in the *Via Lucis* of his conviction that 'the intellectual light of souls, namely Wisdom, may now at length at the approach of this eventide of the world, be happily diffused through all minds and among all people.'[46] Such an ideal would help, he said, to heal intellectual, social, religious and other divisions among men.

In keeping with the pedagogic principles outlined in *The Great Didactic* Comenius insisted that the pursuit of universal learning should be conducted in a manner consistent with the ways of nature, i.e. with the spontaneous, inductive modes of knowing inherent in human consciousness. It should proceed, he said, from the particularities of natural phenomena to the more complex truths of abstract and symbolic thought. 'This work,' he declared 'will be concerned with gathering together the history of Nature with the utmost fidelity and accuracy, for in it, more certainly than in any other quarter, lie the bases of our knowledge and the foundations on which a true and perfect Pansophia can be built.'[47] Accessibility to knowledge was to be the hallmark of the whole enterprise. 'We must on all accounts,' he wrote, 'find some compendium or summary, some means of drawing out the quintessence of authors, so that it shall be pleasant and not impossible or even difficult for any man to learn all that has been decided and agreed on by all authors.'[48] He called for the universal provision of education as a condition for the success of the scheme. Education would have to be provided equally for rich and poor alike. He urged the richer citizens, therefore, to 'bring up with their own boys and girls an equal number of poor children of the same age.'

Comenius particularly emphasised the importance of research in the higher institutions of pansophic learning. Here the influence of Bacon is much in evidence. There was much dissatisfaction with universities at the time, on the grounds that their teaching was frequently sterile and archaic, and was insufficiently informed by new research, unlike the new scientific institutes whose activities were constantly revitalised by the dynamic activities in which they engaged. Bacon had given expression to all this in his *De Augmentis*; in another work, *New Atlantis*, he had envisaged colleges of higher learning similar to what Comenius was proposing at Chelsea. Not surprisingly, Comenius declared that the new pansophic college would be a monument to Bacon—'to whom we owe the first suggestion and opportunity for common counsels with regard to the universal reform of the Sciences.'[49] Most significantly, he saw the whole scheme as a means of bringing people of different religious persuasions together and of uniting them through their common pursuit of the unity underlying all the diversity of human culture. His vision of religious union may have been disingenuous and naive in the conditions of seventeenth century Europe, but he presented it as an aspiration which all Christians should share by virtue of the responsibility towards brotherhood enjoined on them by the scriptures:

> The result of that light which is promised is the conversion of all people to the Church, so that Jehovah shall be King over all the earth. . . . Then the Gospel of the kingdom shall be preached in the whole circle of the world, for a witness to all the peoples, before the end shall come. . . . Then the earth shall be filled with the knowledge of God as the sea is covered with waters. . . . And then there will be universal Peace over the whole world, hatred and the causes of hatred will be done away, and all dissension between men. For there will be no ground for dissenting, when all men have the same Truths clearly presented to their eyes. Nor will the uncertainties of opinions make any man perplexed when all are taught not by men who differ from one another in their opinions, but by God who is the Truth. . . . Thus will be fulfilled Christ's promise concerning the one flock and the one Shepherd.[50]

Comenius's pansophic project had to be further postponed because of the outbreak of civil war in England in 1642. For some time his thoughts were directed to New England and the projected plans by the Brethren to found missions there for the Christianisation of the Amerindian peoples. In *Via Lucis* he referred to these plans and saw himself as having a responsibility to lend assistance to the missionaries in whatever way he could. There is some evidence that at this time he was invited to accept the Presidency of Harvard College, which had been founded five years before. In a nineteenth-century chronicle, *Magnalia Christi Americana*, by Cotton Mather, the event was reported as follows: 'That brave old man, Johannes Amos Comenius, the fame of whose worth hath been trumpeted as far as more than three languages (whereof everyone is indebted to his *Janua*) could carry it, was indeed agreed withall, by our Mr Winthrop in his travels through the low countries, to come over into New England, and illuminate this College and country in the quality of a President. But the solicitations of the Swedish Ambassador, diverting him another way, that incomparable Moravian became not an American.'[51] Some confusion remains about the precise identity of the Mr Winthrop mentioned by Mather. It seems unlikely it was Governor John Winthrop of Massachusetts, since there is no record that he was in England in 1642 or had any contact with Comenius. His son, later to become Governor of Connecticut, *was* in England, however, at this time and may have extended the invitation to Comenius on behalf of his father. The whole affair was recalled by the then President of Harvard, J.B. Conant, in a tercentenary tribute to Comenius in 1942. To Edward Beneš, President of Czechoslovakia, and the Editor of *The Teacher of Nations*, he wrote:

> Harvard University has a peculiar indebtedness to Jan Comenius. According to a persistent tradition, he was offered the headship of Harvard College within five years of its founding; probably he was approached on that subject by John Winthrop Junior, Governor of Connecticut and Overseer of Harvard College, who like Comenius was a friend of Samuel Hartlib. In any case, the great Moravian was looked up to by the founders of Harvard as the principal authority on education in Europe. His improved textbooks were used both in Harvard College and in the early Grammar Schools of New England. In our Library there is a copy of the famous 'Janua Linguarum' with the autograph of one of our Indian students on the fly-leaf.[52]

Comenius rejected the invitation from Harvard and did not engage directly in the missionary work that was subsequently undertaken in New England. His pansophic college did not come into existence until some years after he left England. The Royal Society was established by Charter of Charles II in 1662, twenty years after Comenius had departed. When the *Via Lucis* was published in 1668 it was dedicated to The Royal Society. The Dedication read: 'Blessings upon your heroic enterprises, illustrious Sirs! We have no envy towards you; rather we congratulate you and assure you of the applause of mankind. . . . Moreover, men who shall survey the researches which you have already published and our own "Way of Light", will grant that your distinguished enterprise is itself the fairest part of the forecasts which are made here.'[53] As the Civil War broke out in England, his thoughts turned to a new project he was shortly to undertake as a result of an invitation he received from Louis de Geer, a wealthy Dutch-born industrialist who was deeply involved in various ecumenical and educational projects throughout Europe.

De Geer had provided a fleet of over thirty ships to Sweden to support the Protestant cause in the Thirty Years' War. In 1642 he was engaged by King Gustavus Adolphus to assist in the development of new metallurgical industries in the country. He owned copper and iron mines, together with vast estates, throughout Sweden, while retaining his Dutch (Walloon) citizenship. He had provided funding for the work of John Dury in support of Church unity and it was through him that he learned of the work of Comenius. De Geer invited Comenius to come to Sweden and to undertake a major programme of school reform there, offering to cover all the costs of the project from his own resources. In the meantime Comenius had received a similar invitation from Cardinal Richelieu, on the recommendation of the Franciscan priest, Marinus Mersenne—a remarkable development in view of the profound religious differences between Comenius, a radical Protestant, and Richelieu, one of the most formidable and influential prelates of the Roman Catholic Church. Largely because he felt it would be in the interests of the Bohemian Brethren, and would lead to their eventual repatriation, Comenius decided to accept the Swedish invitation. He sent his friend, Joachim Hübner, to inform Richelieu of his decision. Hübner reported that Richelieu had intended to found a pansophic college in Paris in accordance with Comenius's ideas. The project was abandoned, however, when Richelieu died shortly afterwards.

4. THE ELBING YEARS, 1642–8

Comenius left England on June 21, 1642. Before travelling to Sweden, he visited the University of Leyden where he met the Professor of Oriental Languages, Jacob Van Gool, whose brother, Peter, a Carmelite friar living in Aleppo, had recently translated the *Janua* into Arabic. Recalling the event later, Comenius described how Jacob Van Gool gave him a letter from his brother in which the latter reported that when he had 'half finished the translation' he had shown it to some Muslim friends who were so enthused by the work they immediately set about translating it also into Turkish, Persian and Mongolian. In the letter Van Gool said that his colleagues would like to translate some other works by Comenius into these languages. 'You see,' he wrote, 'how happily your *Janua* opens a gate to the Gentiles. 'I replied,' Comenius recalled later, 'Not unto us O Lord, but to Thy Name be the honour.'[54]

Also at Leyden, Comenius was entertained by Adrian Heerebord, the Professor of Philosophy, and a friend of René Descartes, then living at Endegeest, a short distance from the city. Heerebord arranged a meeting between Comenius and Descartes. The two men met for several hours, discussing their views on a variety of issues before eventually parting amicably and agreeing to respect the differences that existed between them. Comenius describes the meeting in this passage from the *Continuatio*:

> On a certain day it pleased my friends (Master Louis de Dieu, Master Abraham Heydan, Master Kluiget and Heerebord) to bring me into colloquy with Master René Descartes, then living in a charming retreat without the city. We exchanged speech for about four hours, he expounding to us the mysteries of his philosophy, I myself maintaining all human knowledge, such as derives from the senses alone and reasonings thereon, to be imperfect and defective.

We parted in friendly fashion: I begging him to publish the principles of his philosophy (which principles were published the year
following), and he similarly urging me to mature my own thoughts,
adding this maxim: 'Beyond the things that appertain to philosophy
I go not; mine therefore is that only in part, whereof yours is the
whole.[55]

Shortly after this, Comenius left Leyden and travelled to Hamburg where
the City Council invited him to take control of the municipal schools.
Resolving to honour his commitment to De Geer, he declined the invitation of the Hamburg authorities. While in the city he also met the
philosopher, Joachim Jung, at that time Rector of the Hamburg
Gymnasium, who complained of the harm that sectarianism had done
both to religion and education in Prussia. Arriving in Sweden, he went
to Norrköping to meet de Geer. The latter introduced him to Johannes
Matthiae, Bishop of Strengnäs, and former Latin tutor to the Swedish
court, who arranged an interview between Comenius and the Queen.
Subsequently, Comenius had discussions also with the Swedish
Chancellor, Axel Oxenstierna, and with Dr John Skytte, the Rector of
the University of Uppsala. Largely on the initiative of Oxenstierna, new
gymnasia had recently been established at Skara and Växö in Sweden
and at Viborg in Finland. For several days the three men discussed
Comenius's didactic theories and the ideals of pansophic education. As a
result, Comenius was asked to take responsibility for the complete reform
of Swedish education. This would involve a longer stay in the country
and a greater commitment than he had envisaged when he first received
De Geer's invitation.

    Comenius was reluctant to settle in Sweden because of his concern for
his outstanding commitments to his friends in England, together with
his worries about his family and confrères in Leszno. De Geer offered an
annual stipend of 1000 thalers for the support of the Moravian Community
in Leszno (by this time numbering 3 bishops and 94 pastors), together
with a further 400 thalers to cover the expenses of Comenius himself
and his assistants. While recognising the difficulties that would result
from his absence from his community for several years—despite the
munificent support that was offered by De Geer—Comenius nonetheless
agreed to take on the Swedish project. Keatinge, in a biographical essay,
described the dilemmas that he faced in making this decision:

In the history of great renunciations surely none is stranger than
this. We have a man little past the prime of life, his brain teeming
with magnificent if somewhat visionary plans for social reform, a
mighty power in the community that shared his religious ideas, and
an object of interest even to those who may have shrugged their

shoulders at his occasional want of balance. Suddenly he flings his projects to the winds, consigns his darling plans to the dust-heap of unrealisable ideas, and retires to a small sea-side town—not to meditate, not to give definite form to latent conceptions or to evolve new ones, not to make preparations for the dazzling of intellectual Europe with an octavo of fantastic philanthropic mysticism, but—to write school-books for the little boys in Swedish schools.[56]

Comenius's strongest motivation in taking on the new project was his hope that Protestant Sweden would provide support for the realisation of his dearest hope: the return of the United Brethren to Bohemia. That hope had been kept alive by the 'prophecies' of his old friend, Drabík, who wrote to him from Hungary in 1643, reporting his latest 'revelations' on the imminent repatriation of the Brethren. Full of expectation for the fulfilment of these hopes, Comenius moved his family to Elbing, a seaside town in East Prussia, in November, 1642. Elbing was sufficiently close to Sweden to enable him to discharge his responsibilities there, while being close enough also to Leszno to enable him to maintain contact with his community. Here he was to spend the next six years of his life, preparing textbooks for use in Swedish schools. With his collaborator, George Vechner, and several colleagues such as Paul Cyrillus, Daniel Petreus, Daniel Nigrinus and Peter Fingulus—the last named was later to become his son-in-law—Comenius produced a series of texts for the study of Latin in Swedish schools. They included a general work, *The Newest Method of Language Study*, and four graded texts: the *Vestibulum*, an introduction to elementary Latin, *The Fate of Languages*, a revised version of the *Janua*, *The Forecourt*, a text for the advanced study of the language, and *The Treasury of the Latin Language*, a collection of readings from various authors.[57] In those years he also completed two religious treatises, *De Dessidentium in Rebus Fidei*,[58] a work on Christian reconciliation which was published in 1643, and *De Regula Fidei*, published at Danzig in 1644.[59]

Shortly after he settled in Elbing he became involved yet again in the cause of Christian unity. Bartholomew Nigrin, a Lutheran pastor working in Elbing, was deeply engaged in this work and offered Comenius attractive financial inducements in an effort to get him to abandon his educational activities so that he could devote himself fully to his ecumenical projects. Comenius refused to be diverted from his work for educational reform, but lent his support nonetheless to the inter-Church activities being promoted by Nigrin. He wrote a number of treatises on Christian union, suggesting that a general council of all the Christian Churches be convened to promote reconciliation between them. He called on all the different sects—Roman Catholic, Lutheran, Calvinist, Unity, Eastern Orthodox, Armenian, Coptic etc.—to come together and seek to resolve their differences. All the Churches, he said, would have to acknowledge their past failures and inadequacies if they seriously wished to achieve lasting reconciliation.

Such a conference was, in fact, summoned by King Wladislaw of Poland in 1644. Comenius attended the preliminary meeting of the Protestant communities, which had been convened by Prince Janusz Radziwill at Orla in Lithuania in August 1644. He delivered an address at this meeting, in which he urged his listeners to attend the Conference proposed by the Polish King. The main conference opened at Thorn on August 28, 1645. Comenius was one of the delegates representing the Unity Church. The Polish Lutherans were represented by a bigoted zealot, Johann Hülsemann, and by two reactionary clerics from Danzig, Abraham Calovius and John Botsak. Comenius described the latter two as 'those sons of Boanerges who know nothing but to call down fire from heaven upon both the Papists and the Calvinists.'[60] The Roman Catholic delegation was led by an equally bigoted layman, Prince Ossolinski, who presided at the Conference, being the emissary of King Wladislaw.

There was conflict from the very beginning, disagreement having emerged initially over the arrangements for the opening prayers and liturgical services. It was decided that these should be held in separate rooms, thus making visible the depth of the divisions that existed amongst the participants. Comenius is recorded as having made numerous efforts to bring the warring factions together, but generally without success. He particularly concentrated his attentions on Hülsemann, who responded by attacking him for his leanings towards Calvinism. The conflicts between the delegates became unresolvable as the Catholics repeatedly insisted on a total acceptance of their position by the Protestant sects and called on them to return to the fold of the mother Church. Seeing that the Conference could not succeed in its objectives, the King declared it closed on November 21, 1645. Comenius had left it some time earlier when his Swedish patrons communicated their annoyance at his diversion from the school reform programme. Additionally, he himself feared that his perceived association with the Calvinists at the Conference might damage his relationship with the Lutheran Church in Sweden.

His fears on the latter issue proved to be well founded. When he returned to Sweden the Commission on Education enthusiastically approved the publication of his textbooks, but he learned that Abraham Calovius, the Lutheran pastor from Danzig, had written to some Swedish theologians denouncing his pansophic schemes as thinly disguised crypto-Calvinist propaganda. This charge was supported by the Archbishop of Skara who made a speech publicly condemning the spread of Calvinism in Sweden and named Comenius as the person mainly responsible for this. Calovius urged the Swedish authorities to terminate Comenius's position as an adviser on educational reform. Comenius was summoned to a meeting with Oxenstierna at which he was reprimanded for having associated himself so closely with reformist theologians at the Thorn Conference. He was urged both by the Chancellor and Queen Christina to devote his energies exclusively to education in the future. He left the country in October 1646, returning to his family at Elbing with a view to rejoining the Brethren at Leszno.

During the years at Elbing he had worked on a projected seven volume study, *A General Consultation About the Improvement of Knowledge*—now generally known as the *Consultatio*.[61] Two volumes of the work were completed in these years. The most widely known, the *Panegersia*, appealed to scholars, statesmen and churchmen to effect reforms in schools, churches and state affairs with a view to promoting the spirit of Christian brotherhood and a truly universal culture amongst all men. It emphasised the evils of sectarianism, declaring that religion should promote the spirit of love rather than the hatred and persecution frequently fostered by the sects in the name of their own dogmatic versions of Christianity. Comenius spoke of the common bonds of knowledge and culture that are shared by all of mankind and emphasised the need to promote these through education. 'When we build all that is worthy of knowing, of observing and of practising, on the basis of universal ideas, motives and capacity, what is there for philosophy, state and religion to fear?' he asked. 'For on this road that which is good, or true, or safe, can come to no harm,' he declared. The evils of violence, greed and civil strife would be overcome, he said, not through political reforms but through the spiritual reform of mankind. The problem of world peace was essentially one of faith, he said, and would have to be resolved through *spiritual* means—through the self-reform of an authentically rooted faith—before the goals of a truly universal culture could be realised.

Following his return to Elbing, Comenius was invited to settle in Holland by the pastors of the Reformed Church and was offered a quiet retreat at Alkmaar where he could further pursue his pansophic studies. It became essential, however, that he return to his community at Leszno, since two of its senior bishops had recently died and a third was suffering from a terminal illness. On his return to the city on July 31, 1648 he was immediately elected Senior Bishop of the Unity Church. In that same year the Thirty Years' War ended with the signing of the Peace of Westphalia. The Peace was a disastrous settlement from the standpoint of the Unity Church, since Roman Catholicism was proclaimed to be the official religion of the Hapsburg Empire and the Bohemian Brethren were denied the freedom of religious practice that had been guaranteed to German Protestants. This made it impossible for them to return to Bohemia and exile in Poland now seemed their inevitable long-term prospect. The 'settlement' represented the final frustration of the efforts

made by Comenius over a period of twenty five years to bring about the
return of his community to its homeland. He was bitterly disappointed
in particular at the failure of Sweden to fulfil its promise of support for
the repatriation of the Brethren. To the Chancellor, Oxenstierna, he
wrote:

> As formerly my countrymen, suffering for the gospel's sake, were
> cheered to hear through me and others that Thy Highness expressed
> Thyself that we shall not be abandoned, so it is sad for us now to
> hear that ye are abandoning us, indeed, that we are already aban-
> doned at the Osnabrück negotiations. For if we should be excluded
> from the peace negotiations, what avails us that we have looked up
> to you as to our saviours? What avails us that ye are victorious by
> the help of our tears, when ye, having it in your power to give
> liberty to those of us who were rescued, are again delivering us into
> the hands of our persecutors? What avail the solemn treaties made
> with your ancestors and sealed with the sacred blood of martyrs,
> that we are encouraged by you, when ye do not trouble yourselves
> whether our kingdom returns to the confession of the gospel? Ye,
> to whom God granted ability to care for it, are (as the world sees
> and is astonished) that magnet of wondrous strength which does
> not attract but repels iron. . . . In the name of many I write this,
> and touched by their signs I prostrate myself at Thy feet, and
> through thee at the feet of the Most Serene Queen, and the whole
> august Council of Directors, and beg and implore Thee by the
> wounds of Jesus Christ that ye do not abandon us, who are afflicted
> for Christ's sake.[62]

For Comenius himself there was the further tragedy of his second wife's
death which had occurred in the course of the journey from Elbing back
to Leszno.

He now convened a general convention of all branches of the Unity
Church in Poland, Prussia, Silesia and Hungary so that they could
decide their future in the hopeless conditions in which they had been
plunged by the terms of the Peace. At the Convention, which was held
in Leszno, the delegates decided that the Unity Church, by then almost
two centuries old, should not be disbanded but that, wherever its branches
failed to survive, the Brethren should be encouraged to join any evangelical congregation of their choice so that they could continue to practise
their faith as members of a Christian communion. Comenius argued that
in this way they would give witness to the spirit of forgiveness and
brotherhood that had characterised the Unity Church since its foundation. In *The Bequest of the Unity of Brethren* he urged the Brethren to
continue to give witness to the Christian message of love and to adhere

to the simple practice of faith in the manner customary for members of their Church:

> And . . . if even you come to be dispersed . . . and if consequently my order, discipline, succession, and all my church ministrations cease, what are you, the remnants of my priests and people to do? This, my sons, is my advice:
> If any of you preachers who have no congregations of your own to which to minister, are left, serve Christ wherever you can, in any evangelical church which may desire your services. Only walk ye in that simplicity in which I had borne and had nurtured you. Walk in the straight and middle path, neither flattering one party to the disparagement of the other, nor allowing yourselves to be used as partisans in factional strife among parties. But rather make that your care that love and concord and all common good reign in the church.
> But joining a communion in which you find the truth of the gospel of Christ, pray for its peace and seek its upbuilding in good.[63]

Once again he called on the Christian Churches to resolve their differences and to seek to live together in the spirit of reconciliation and love. To the Lutherans he said: 'O, my friends! I, suffering the discipline of the mighty God, teach and exhort you to apprehend that the knowledge of Christ without the following of Christ, and rejoicing in the gospel without the keeping of the law of love on which the gospel is founded, is nothing less than an abuse of the gospel, a sure deception, and an error.'[64] He urged the Calvinists to speculate less about the 'evils of popery' and to direct their efforts to practising the simple piety advocated in the scriptures: 'I admonish thee, therefore, first of all that thou mayest hold to piety and to the disciplining order pertaining thereto with sincere single-mindedness, and that not only in appearance but in reality. Then in method, I admonish thee to more simplicity and less speculation; also to a more discreet discussion concerning God and His most profound mysteries than some of Thy sons were wont to indulge.'[65] He ended the *The Bequest of the Unity of Brethren* with a prayer for his Bohemian fellow-countrymen, now demoralised in their defeat and abandoned by their erstwhile friends:

> Nor can I forget thee, thou Czech and Moravian nation, my native land, now that I take my final leave! . . . I trust God that after the passing of the storm of wrath which our sins have brought upon our heads, the rule of thine affairs shall again be restored to thee, O Czech people!'[66]

These words, a Czech scholar wrote, 'have furnished inspiration to brave
and lonely souls throughout the succeeding dark centuries and to the
hundreds and thousands who fought for Czechoslovak independence
during World War I.'[67]

In one of the passages quoted above from *The Bequest of the Unity of
Brethren* Comenius warns the Calvinists against the disruptive consequences of excessive theological debate. 'For thereby was caused a sore
disruption among themselves and thee,' he wrote. Later in the same
work he condemned the English Puritans for the fanatical zeal with
which they pursued their supposedly Christian beliefs. 'Especially,' he
wrote, referring to their corruption of the reformist faith, 'is this evident
in England, where thy sons, after the terror of wars has subsided, are
making a sad and derogatory exhibition of themselves and have defamed
thy name amongst their fellows by their practice of ever searching for
novelties and never attaining to stable convictions.'[68] When the Second
Civil War broke out in England in 1648, and several other religious sects
found themselves facing persecution from the all-powerful Puritans, he
addressed yet another treatise to the latter, urging them to practise
tolerance and rebuking them for their corruption of Christian ideals.
This work, *Independence, the Origin of Eternal Confusion*,[69] marks a
further development of his thinking on the problems of sectarianism. It
provides some new insights on issues that have proved highly divisive
amongst the Christian Churches through the centuries, especially matters
concerned with ecclesiastical organisation, such as the validity of the
episcopal system, the question of apostolic succession, questions of
authority and discipline, and their interrelation with the freedom of
individual conscience and faith.

5. FINAL YEARS IN HUNGARY AND HOLLAND, 1648–70

In 1649 Comenius received an invitation from Prince Sigismund Rákóczy
of Transylvania to come to Hungary for discussions on the reform of
Hungarian schools. At the same time he was invited to visit a gymnasium in the Hungarian town of Sáros Pátak by its Rector, John Tolnai,
who had heard of his work in England through contacts with Samuel
Hartlib. Additionally, Comenius wished to visit the large Moravian
Community in Hungary who, like the Brethren in Leszno, had lived in
exile since the outbreak of the Thirty Years' War. In March 1650 he set
out from Leszno, travelling firstly to see the Moravian Brethren at
Skalice, a town close to the Hungarian–Bohemian border, not far from
Stražnice where he had studied many years before. During his stay at
Skalice he ordained a bishop for the Unity Church and visited various

communities of Brethren in the region. From there he went to Sáros Pátak to meet John Tolnai and both of them subsequently visited Prince Sigismund who was staying in his summer palace nearby. Comenius had strong affinities with the Prince, by virtue of the latter's support for the Protestant cause in the Thirty Years' War. At the palace he also met the Prince's mother, Susanna Lórántfy, who had promoted various initiatives on school reform in Hungary—largely under the influence of John Alsted, Comenius's professor during his student years at Herborn. She now planned to establish a pansophic school at Sáros Pátak.

Comenius spent several days discussing educational matters at the summer palace in Sáros Pátak, as a result of which the Prince eventually urged him to come and live in Hungary to supervise the proposed reforms. Feeling he should first consult with his family and his confrères at Leszno , Comenius returned there later in 1650. Following his second wife's death, he had remarried some time in 1649, and two of his daughters had also married: Dorothea to Peter Fingulus, Comenius's collaborator on several of his educational and religious projects, and Elizabeth to a young Hungarian called Molitor. Largely as a result of approaches from the Brethren at Sáros Pátak (and the influence exerted on them by Susanna Lórántfy), the Council of the Unity Church in Leszno approved of Comenius's projected stay in Hungary. Together with his son-in-law, Peter Fingulus (his wife and son, Daniel, remained in Leszno), he set out for Hungary in October 1650.

Comenius immediately set about transforming the gymnasium at Sáros Pátak into a major centre for pansophic learning. He laid down a number of conditions for this project, to which Prince Sigismund immediately agreed. He wanted a 'well-built school' with seven classrooms, boarding accommodation for poorer students (some of whom he insisted should be Bohemians), the recruitment of an individual teacher for each of the seven classes, and the provision of a printing press for the publication of textbooks.[70] He was provided with a collegiate building and some adjoining houses that were to be used for boarding accommodation, together with a large garden where outdoor activities could be conducted. He drew up a detailed programme for the project in his *Sketch of a Pansophic School*,[71] envisaging a two stage process, beginning with three preparatory grades in which basic instruction would be provided in Latin, to be followed by four advanced grades in which the whole pansophic range of subject-matter would be taught. He wrote two manuals, *On Manners*[72] and *Laws of a Well-Ordered School*,[73] in which he set out guidelines on the kind of behaviour that was to be fostered in school, in the church, on the playground, and in every sphere of the lives of his pupils.

The school was opened on February 13, 1651. To stimulate interest in the project Comenius had delivered a number of lectures on pansophic learning at the Gymnasium for several weeks beforehand. Almost immediately, however, he faced resistance to his work both from the Rector, John Tolnai, and from the other teachers in the school, all of whom objected to the increased demands that were made on their time. They were also out of sympathy with the learner-centred pedagogy advocated by Comenius. Tolnai, who had links with the Puritans in England, had come to regard Comenius with suspicion, following the publication of *Independence, the Origin of Eternal Confusion*, in which the latter denounced the Puritans for their intolerance of other Christian denominations. He now disagreed with the methods of language teaching advocated by Comenius, particularly rejecting the emphasis he gave to the individual interests and experience of the pupil, as well as his encouragement of story-telling, dramatisation, informal conversation and the use of various forms of play for the fostering of language growth.

Following repeated disagreements with Tolnai, Comenius threatened to leave the school at Sáros Pátak and to return to his community at Leszno. He was persuaded, however, by Prince Sigismund to remain, and Tolnai was ordered by Susanna to co-operate more fully with the reforms. In June 1651 Comenius officiated at the wedding of Prince Sigismund to the daughter of the Palatine Elector and marked the occasion with an Address calling on the Prince and his Protestant allies to secure the repatriation of the Bohemian Brethren. His plans were dashed, however, by the sudden death of Sigismund in February 1654, following which he began once again to reconsider his commitment to educational reform in Hungary. He subsequently appealed to Oliver Cromwell for support for the Bohemian cause, but rejected the offer from the latter to provide lands for the resettlement of the Brethren in Ireland.

Despite the intervention of the Dowager Princess in the running of the school at Sáros Pátak, the conflict between Comenius and Tolnai continued and was intensified by Comenius's repeated insistence on the importance of play in the process of learning. 'My whole method aims at changing the school drudgery into a play and enjoyment,' he declared. 'That nobody here wishes to understand.'[74] He particularly advocated the use of drama as a means of fostering language growth, a method that Tolnai, with his strong puritanical leanings, found especially abhorrent. 'I have also advised from the very beginning that some theatrical plays be introduced, for I have learned from experience that there is no more effective means for the expulsion of mental flabbiness and the arousing of alertness,' Comenius wrote. 'But,' he complained, 'I was told that such playthings (as the producing of comedies in schools) should be left to the Jesuits; that I had been called for serious work.'[75]

Insisting on the validity of his pedagogic beliefs, he soon set about dramatising much of the material from the *Janua* for production by the students at the Gymnasium. The performances, which took place generally in the open air, were highly successful, attracting large crowds of people from the town and its surrounding regions. Gradually the teachers began to acknowledge the value of Comenius's methods—with the conspicuous exception of Tolnai who agreed merely to tolerate activities he regarded as being of doubtful moral validity. Comenius published a new work, *Schola Ludus* ('School as Play')[76] in which he offered a detailed exposition of the methods that might be used to ensure that school learning would always be enjoyable and stimulating. One of his most significant pedagogic works, *Orbis Sensualium Pictus* ('The World in Pictures')[77] appeared also at this time. Essentially a simplified version of the *Janua*, this work used visual illustrations for the teaching of Latin, thus marking an innovation in reading pedagogy that was subsequently to revolutionise the whole process of language teaching and that would contribute significantly to the achievement of mass literacy many years later.

The *Orbis* could not be printed at the Sáros Pátak printing press, as an engraver sufficiently competent to produce the illustrations could not be found. Eventually it was printed in Nuremberg in 1658. In the Preface Comenius defined its guiding principle: 'There is nothing in the intellect that has not first existed in the senses. It is because schools commonly neglect this truth and give the pupils things to learn that they do not understand and which have never been properly placed before their organs of sense-perception, that the tasks of the teacher and the learner are so irksome, and that so little is produced.'[78] The work was widely welcomed as a major breakthrough in language pedagogy. 'Apart from the *Orbis Pictus* of Amos Comenius,' Goethe wrote, 'no book of this kind found its way into our hands.'[79] It proved to be an excellent primer for the teaching of Latin, but subsequently was recognised as a suitable model for the teaching of vernacular languages as well, because of its emphasis on vernacular proficiency as the foundation of all language learning. The work became immensely popular throughout Europe and the U.S., and remained in print until the late nineteenth century. The latest U.S. edition was published in 1887. (At a Conference in Nitra, Czechoslovakia in 1992 a Russian educator advocated the adaptation of some of the principles of the *Orbis* for the revitalisation of contemporary reading pedagogy—a remarkable indication of its originality and enduring effectiveness.)[80]

Though his work at the Sáros Pátak Gymnasium proved to be successful in many respects, Comenius failed to extend his influence beyond its immediate region, and, being somewhat disillusioned with the whole Hungarian venture, decided to leave the country and return to Leszno in 1655. In the school itself he failed to extend the programme he had envisaged beyond the first three classes and never succeeded in launching his grand pansophic scheme. Seeing that a grave problem of teacher morale existed in Hungary—due mainly to the departure of large numbers of teachers for better paid positions—he issued a tract, *Gentis Felicitas*,[81] in which he argued the case for social reform as a pre-condition for educational reform. On June 2, 1655 he delivered a farewell speech in the great hall of the Gymnasium and shortly afterwards departed for Leszno. At this time he learned of the death of his patron, Louis De Geer, and wrote a long letter of condolence to his son, Laurence, in which he paid fulsome tribute to the support he had received from the latter's father during his years in Sweden.[82]

On his return to Leszno Comenius took up duty as Pastor to the local community, following the death of the previous incumbent. Shortly afterwards he was caught up in a tragedy that engulfed the whole of Poland and brought catastrophe of an unprecedented character to the city of Leszno. Charles X of Sweden had invaded Poland in 1655 in support of a group of nobles who had challenged the tyrannical rule of the Catholic King, John Casimir. Amongst the nobles was Bohuslaw Lescynski, the Lord of Leszno, who was supported overwhelmingly by the local Protestants, including Comenius and the Bohemian Brethren. Charles X had entered Poland largely on the urging of George Rákóczy who had sent his ambassador, Constantine Schaum, to the King, requesting Sweden to intervene on behalf of the Protestants. Rakoczy, in turn, had taken this step on the urging of Comenius who had been influenced once again by 'revelations' from Drabík.

As the Swedish troops entered Poland, Comenius issued his *Panagyric on Charles Gustavus*,[83] in which he hailed the Swedish King as 'the liberator of humanity, the comfort of the afflicted, the pattern for kings.'[84] The Polish forces, however, offered unexpectedly strong resistance to the Swedish invaders and inflicted several defeats on them, with the result that Charles was forced to sue for peace. Following the eventual departure of the Swedes, several Protestant strongholds were singled out for reprisal by the Polish armies. King Casimir's soldiers entered Leszno on April 29, 1656 and burned the city to the ground. Large numbers of its inhabitants were tortured and killed while thousands fled, seeking refuge in nearby countries sympathetic to the Protestant cause. Comenius lost all of his possessions. They included all his money—about 3000 thalers or £700 sterling—his entire library, the manuscript of the Czech-Latin dictionary on which he had worked for over four decades, his collected sermons of more than forty years, his refutations of Descartes and Copernicus, and all the drafts of his pansophic writings, many of which by then were nearing completion. 'Had God only spared me the *Sylva Pansophiae*,' he cried, 'all else would have been easier to bear but even this is destroyed.'[85]

The Brethren dispersed in several directions, most of them finding refuge in Hungary, Silesia, Lusatia and Brandenburg. Initially, Comenius went to Silesia where he was protected by a wealthy nobleman, Freiherr of Budova. Money was collected for the support of the Brethren from all over Europe; over 3000 thalers was subscribed in Danzig alone and £30,000 was donated from England, the only stipulation being that some of the money be used for the purchase of Bibles. On the invitation of Laurence De Geer, who undertook to cover all his expenses, Comenius eventually found a home in Amsterdam, where he was to spend the remaining years of his life. There he was joined by his wife and children and his son-in-law, Peter Fingulus. He was warmly welcomed in Amsterdam. His friends collected money to provide him with a new library; the City Council offered him a professorship—which he declined—and undertook to provide him with a salary of 800 gulden a year. De Geer, a passionate admirer of his religious views, provided the finance for the publication of his collected educational writings, the *Opera Didactica Omnia*.

This work, which was written entirely in Latin, was published in four volumes in 1657.[86] The first volume included the didactic writings of the years 1627–42, the second the works written between 1642 and 1650, the third the writings of 1650–4, and the final volume some collected papers on the teaching of Latin from the years 1654–57, together with a critical review by Comenius himself of all his educational writings. The complete work ran to over 1000 pages in length, and contained numerous biographical notes prepared by Comenius on the circumstances in which the collected writings were produced. In the Preface he paid handsome tribute to his new patrons: 'The storm of God which suddenly destroyed my second motherland, Poland, has cast me upon our shores, O Holland! You were long considered a haven of refuge by the oppressed, as well as you, Amsterdam, the pearl among cities.'[87]

Regrettably, Comenius also took on the task of editing the 'prophecies' of his three friends, Drabík, Kotter and Poniatowska, in a volume called *Lux in Tenebris*.[88] This was a huge work of over 1100 pages which he published against the advice of most of his friends, including his son-in-law, Peter Fingulus. The work earned him the contempt of many contemporary scholars, amongst them Nicholas Arnold, a friend of Samuel Hartlib, and a former pupil of Comenius, who wrote the *Discursus Theologicus Contra Comenius*, accusing him of having precipitated the destruction of Leszno by propagating Drabík's predictions of a Protestant victory over the Polish forces. Comenius responded by writing the *Continuatio Admonitionis Fraternae*,[89] an autobiographical review of his life in which he defended all his activities as being motivated by his faith in Christ and his determination to serve the welfare of his countrymen.

He continued to seek support from Protestant rulers for the return of the Brethren to Bohemia. Still trusting in the prophecies of Drabík, he appealed once again to George Rákóczy II, the Transylvanian Prince, to assist the Bohemian cause. 'Behold your Israel, your whole nation is trembling before the Turks, is crying before the Jebusites,' he wrote to the Prince.[90] Nothing came of this appeal and Drabík, who had renounced his prophecies and embraced the Catholic faith, was himself to die a violent death at the hands of the Austrian armies at Bratislava in 1671. A copy of *Lux in Tenebris* was thrown into the fire in which his mutilated body was being burnt.

Side by side with his work for the Bohemian cause, Comenius worked tirelessly in his last years for the promotion of ecumenical Christianity. He published a number of religious works suitable for Christians of all denominations, such as *The Kernel of the Holy Scriptures*, *A Confession of Faith* and *A Church Hymnal*.[91] On the occasion of the Restoration of Charles II he wrote *De Bono Unitatis*, in which he recommended the ecclesiastical polity of the United Brethren as a model to be followed by the English Church. Once again he stressed the organic unity of the whole of Christendom:

> O, you Christian people, dispersed throughout Europe, Asia, Africa, America, and the Islands of the Sea, into so many Religions, Sects, Opinions, and multiplyed different Ceremonies, what else I pray are you now become, but as those bones of Israel in Ezekiel, scattered abroad in the field of the world. O that it would please God to bring on that day, wherein he will put forth his omnipotent power among you: to command that there may be a noise and a shaking, that so the bones may draw near one to another, and come together . . . every one, the one to the other . . . knitting all together, the flesh coming upon them, and the skin covering them over . . . and then the breath come from the four winds, to inspire all that are spiritually dead, that they may live the life of Christ. . . .
>
> Every man seeks after that which he loves, they say. I, therefore, because God had enamoured me with the love: one, of unity, especially that of the Church; two, of order, especially in the Church; three, of settlement, especially of the Church; four, life and vigour, especially of the Church, cannot but be in pursuit of those things with all my desires, and having lost the less, our unity, order, bands, life, I cannot but pray for the greater, even the unity, order, bands and life of the whole people of Christendome.[92]

In further pursuit of his ecumenical ideals Comenius arranged for a translation of the scriptures into Turkish. The work was entrusted to Dr. Levin Warner, who conducted it under the general supervision of Comenius. The project was financed by Laurence de Geer. In the draft preface to the work Comenius addressed the Sultan, Mohammed IV, reminding him that 'all the peoples of the earth were the children of the same God'—that this was the teaching of Moses, Christ and Mohammed. The Koran, he declared, was based both on the Old and New Testaments, and it was fitting therefore that Moslems should be familiar with these texts. . . .[93] In the end Warner's translation was found to be defective and it was decided not to publish it. The whole venture, however, provides important confirmation of Comenius's commitment to Christian-Islamic dialogue and to his vision of an inter-church ecumenicity that extended beyond the Christian fold.

Three years before his death Comenius intervened in the Peace Conference which assembled at Breda in the Netherlands in 1667 to bring the Anglo-Dutch war to an end. The Conference was attended by delegates from England, France, Holland, Denmark and Sweden. Comenius urged the delegates to strive to create the conditions for a permanent peace. In a work entitled *The Angel of Peace*[94] he called on them to send out words of peace 'to all the Christians of Europe and eventually to all the peoples of the whole world that they might cease warfare and prepare a place for the Prince of Peace, Christ, who already desires to bring his message of peace to all the peoples of the world.'[95] Following this he wrote *Unum Necessarium* ('The One Thing Necessary')[96] a beautiful prose-poem in which he restated the theme earlier given expression in the *Labyrinth*: that all worldly hopes are based on vanity and that the soul finds fulfilment only in a life lived in the spirit of Christian love. To the Churches he offered this motto: 'In all things essential unity; in those less needful (which are called additions) freedom; and in all things love to all.'[97] In its very simplicity his own faith had transcended the complexities—and contradictions—of theological orthodoxy, and had enabled him to reach beyond the conflicts in which the Christian Churches had become embroiled.

Details are scarce on the last years of Comenius's life. In 1665 his third wife died, as did his patron, Laurence De Greer, though he was still supported by the latter's brother, Gerard De Geer. His son-in-law and collaborator, Peter Fingulus, died early in 1670, a few months before Comenius himself. At the end of his life his great pansophic project remained uncompleted. He requested his son, Daniel, and a friend, Christian Nigrin, to prepare the work for publication after his death. Nigrin worked on the manuscripts for several years but failed to have them published, despite the urgings of Gerard De Geer. The seven manuscript volumes of what came to be known as the *Consultatio* were eventually entrusted to a German educator, A.H. Francke of the University of Halle. They remained in Halle, virtually unnoticed, for almost three centuries, until they were rediscovered by a Polish-Russian scholar, Dmitri Tschizewskij, in 1935. He made them available for publication to the Comenius Pedagogical Institute in Prague. All seven volumes were published by the Czech Academy of Sciences in 1966.[98]

Comenius died at Amsterdam on November 4, 1670 and was buried at the French Reformed (Walloon) Church at Naarden, a small town on the Zuyder Zee. Some time later his body was removed to a memorial chapel nearby, which is now the Comenius Museum. Shortly before his death he had written the following words in a Dedicatory Epistle, addressed to the people of Amsterdam: 'With Thomas á Kempis, I can from my heart and the bitter lessons of experience say, "I have tried all things, nor anywhere have I found peace, save in a little corner, and a little book."'[99] The words aptly summarise the simplicity of his life and his utter dedication to the ideals expressed in the Christian scriptures. The degree to which he was motivated by those ideals is vividly attested in a short statement from the *Unum Necessarium*: 'I have said that all the endeavours of my life hitherto were similar to the care of Martha for the Lord and his disciples; motivated by love, indeed, for I am not conscious of anything to the contrary. For cursed be every hour and every moment of whatever labour spent on anything else.'[100]

THE CULTURAL AND HISTORICAL ROOTS OF COMENIUS'S EDUCATIONAL THOUGHT

1. MORAVIAN PRECURSORS: CHELČICKÝ TO BLAHOSLAV

They are more like primitive Christians than any other Church now in the world, for they retain both the faith, practice, and discipline delivered by the Apostles. They live together in perfect love and peace. They are more ready to serve their neighbours than themselves. In their business they are diligent and industrious, in all their dealings strictly just and conscientious. In everything they behave themselves with great meekness, sweetness and humility.[1]

So wrote Benjamin Ingham, an Evangelical clergyman from Yorkshire, to his friend, John Wesley, in 1741. He was describing the Brethren of the Moravian Church who were about to establish a community near Wyke in Yorkshire. They had arrived in England, seeking refuge from the persecution and harassment they had experienced all over Europe, following their expulsion from Bohemia during the Thirty Years' War. It was from the traditions of this Church that Comenius derived the main inspiration for all his writings and its teachings constitute the seminal principles of his educational thought. It is appropriate therefore that an examination of the influences that determined the shape and content of his educational theories should begin with a consideration of their origins in Moravian Christianity.

Though the term 'Moravian' was not adopted as the official designation of the Church until 1740,[2] it identifies the part of the Kingdom of Bohemia where it emerged and grew in the middle of the fifteenth century.[3] Originally a breakaway movement from the Hussite Church, it came into being in the disorder that followed the trial of Jan Hus at the Council of Constance and his execution on July 6, 1415. In his sermons at the Bethlehem Chapel in Prague Hus had denounced the Roman Catholic clergy for their materialism and corruption and had charged the Church with encouraging superstitious practices amongst the people. The huge support his movement attracted throughout Bohemia dispersed, however, shortly after his death, and various sects emerged, all claiming to represent his ideals and teachings. The most prominent of them were the Utraquist and Taborite movements, the first of which was distinguished from its parent Church only by the practice of taking communion in both kinds. The other offered a more radical challenge in matters such as the status of the Mass, the doctrine of purgatory, the worship of saints, and the veneration of statues and images. Other post-Hussite movements included the Chiliasts, Adamites and Picards,[4] each of whom advocated reform of Roman Christianity in varying degrees, though with significantly less support from the people than the Utraquists and Taborites. A further group, the Waldenses,[5] who had come to Bohemia from Italy, advocated the practice of a simple form of Christianity, modelled on the example of the Apostles and the Early Christians. The Waldenses were pacifists and lived in accordance with an almost literal interpretation of the Biblical text. Civil strife developed between the various sects, leading to a particularly bitter struggle between the Utraquists and Taborites, as a result of which the latter were defeated in battle in 1434. Shortly afterwards the Utraquists sought reunification with Rome, following which the Compactata of Basle were issued, recognising the Utraquist Church as the National Church of Bohemia.

The Moravian Church emerged from these conditions as a movement whose members were pledged to carry on the struggle for reform that had been initiated by Hus. Its first leader and mentor was Peter Chelčický,[6] a former soldier who had left the army in disgust at the atrocities of war and subsequently embraced the pacifist teachings of the Christian Gospels. Following a close study of the writings of Wyclif and Hus, he issued a series of pamphlets in which he attacked the Catholic Church for its corruptions and denounced its justification of war as a violation of the teachings of the scriptures. Attacking the teachings of the Church on property and wealth, he advocated the complete separation of Church and State and called for a return to the simplicity and poverty of the early Christians. He particularly directed his attacks at the Utraquist Church, charging it with betrayal of the teachings of Hus. Primarily a moral reformer rather than a theologian, Chelčický formed a community of like-minded believers—many of them Waldenses—who pledged to dedicate themselves to a life lived in accordance with the literal teachings of the scriptures. A number of such communities soon spread throughout Bohemia and from them eventually emerged the Church of the United Brethren or the Moravians.

Initially, however, Chelčický and his followers did not break completely with the Utraquist Church and their services were still conducted by Utraquist priests. As a result they attracted considerable support from within the Utraquist Church itself in the early stages of the movement. Amongst those drawn by the new teachings was Jan Rokycana, an Utraquist priest who disseminated Chelčický's writings amongst his congregations at the Thein Chapel in Prague. A nephew of Rokycana, later known as 'Gregory the Patriarch', assembled a community at Kunwald in Eastern Bohemia in 1457. A former monk, Gregory had left his monastery in his disillusionment at the corruptions of the monastic system. At Kunwald he and his followers studied the writings of Chelčický and were joined by reform-minded Christians from all over Bohemia. They included members of all classes of Bohemian society—noblemen, aldermen of the towns, landowners, professors, rich merchants and humble peasants, all of whom were drawn by the simplicity of the lifestyle followed by the Brethren. They built their own cottages, cultivated the soil, practised various trades, and studied the scriptures. The movement had the full blessing of Chelčický, who actively encouraged members to join the community at Kunwald.

Gradually, however, the Kunwald community came to be regarded with suspicion by the authorities in Prague. Though initially it had the approval of the King, the members were soon represented as dangerous heretics, likely to subvert the authority of the Utraquist and Catholic Churches. During a visit to Prague, Gregory and some of the community were arrested and imprisoned and, though eventually allowed to return to Kunwald, they were ordered to rejoin the Utraquist Church or face prosecution by the law. Abandoning Kunwald, they sought refuge in the woods and mountains where they were pursued relentlessly by the authorities. At a Synod held in Lhota in 1467 they decided to break completely from the Utraquist Church and instituted a ministerial Church of their own, under the presidency of Gregory the Patriarch. The new Church was formally designated the Unitas Fratrum, or Unity of Brethren. Its first pastors were chosen by election: the first three were Matthias, Thomas and Elias who were ordained by Michael Bradacius, a Waldensian Bishop. All members took an oath of loyalty to the Church, promised never to accept a civil appointment, and pledged themselves to give up their property and live a simple lifestyle in accordance with the example of the Apostles and the early Christians.

Under Gregory's leadership the movement spread rapidly throughout Bohemia and Moravia, eventually embracing an area of more than 900 square miles. When Gregory died in 1473,[7] he was succeeded as President by Luke of Prague.[8] Like his predecessors, Luke stressed the dangers of sectarian bigotry—a position that was consistently maintained by members of the Moravian Church throughout the course of its history. The conditions relating to ownership of property and the holding of civic offices—which had been enforced strictly in the early years—were gradually modified so that larger numbers were attracted into the Church. Though the movement was largely non-theological in inspiration, its emphasis lying on the simplicity of the Christian way of life rather than on a body of theological doctrine, Luke provided further explication of certain aspects of its teachings, such as the doctrine of justification by faith, the exercise of private judgement and the supreme authority of the scriptures. He wrote a children's catechism and a hymnal and founded a printing press for the dissemination of religious literature. New bishops were ordained, Church courts were set up, and schools were established for the children of the Brethren throughout Bohemia.

Meanwhile the movement attracted the attention of Pope Alexander VI who sent agents to Bohemia in 1507 to investigate its activities. Following their report, the King issued a decree (the Edict of St. James), prohibiting meetings of the Brethren, forbidding their priests from officiating at services, and ordering their tracts and pamphlets to be burned. Once again all those who refused to join the Utraquist or Roman Catholic Church were ordered to leave the country. Several members were arrested, including Andrew Poliwka who was tortured and burned at the stake and George Wolinsky and Bishop Luke, both of whom were imprisoned in Prague. At this time news reached the Brethren of Luther's challenge to the Catholic Church at Wittenberg in 1517. Feeling they had some affinities with the Lutheran movement, they sent two emissaries, John Horn and Michael Weiss, to present Luther with a copy of their Confession and Catechism. Being somewhat cautious, however, about Luther's teachings, and being especially wary of their strong theological orientation, the Brethren continued to model their lives on the writings of Chelčický, ministering regularly to their people, visiting the poor and the sick, teaching in their schools, and working side by side with the peasants in the fields.

By now the Unitas Fratrum had acquired the structures of a fully organised national Church. Its priests were assisted by deacons and acolytes who themselves were preparing for ordination to the priesthood. On ordination they usually adopted the Latinised forms of their names (as did their most famous bishop who changed his name from Komensky to Comenius.) Their services were given over chiefly to Bible readings, with interpretations of the scripture text being offered by the pastors and elders of the Church. Parents were encouraged to instruct their children in the rudiments of reading as early as possible so that they could begin to read the scriptures for themselves. The virtues of honesty and industriousness were extolled, a strong emphasis was placed on equality and the sharing of possessions, and gambling and feasting were generally forbidden. Members guilty of misbehaviour were charged before courts presided over by the elders of the Church and were either reprimanded or, in extreme cases, expelled from the Church. (Comenius was charged before such a court at Leszno, following the publication of the *Prodromus*, in 1639.)[9] The Church detached itself, however, from the theological debates conducted by Lutherans and Calvinists throughout the sixteenth century, their concern being to foster a simple Christian lifestyle modelled on the example of Christ and the Apostles.

In 1532 Bishop Luke was succeeded as Head of the Church by John Augusta, a minister of the Church who had been born in Prague in 1500. Following his election and ordination as Bishop at a great Assembly held in Brandeis in that year, John Augusta issued a Confession of Faith in which he once again outlined the teachings of the Church, finding considerable affinity with Luther on a number of issues, such as justification by faith, the authority of the scriptures and the exercise of personal responsibility. Five years earlier Ferdinand I had become King of Bohemia, thus marking the beginning of a long period of Hapsburg rule in the country, during which the Unity Church was to suffer almost continuous persecution. John Augusta presented the Confession of Faith to the new King who, while disapproving of its teachings, agreed to tolerate the presence of the Church for the time being. By this time the Unity Church had over 200,000 members and over 400 churches spread throughout Bohemia. Its membership included some of the most influential noblemen in the country, many of whom supported the Schmalkaldic League of Protestant Princes which had been formed in opposition to the Emperor, Charles V, in 1546. When the League was defeated at Mühlberg in 1547, King Ferdinand decided to take revenge on the Bohemian nobles. Several of them were executed in Prague in August 1547. Their lands were confiscated, churches were closed and members of the Unity Church were once again ordered to join the Utraquist or Roman Catholic Churches or face expulsion from Bohemia.

Thus began the exodus of Brethren from Bohemia which continued until their final expulsion from the country, following the defeat of the Protestant forces at the Battle of the White Mountain early in the Thirty Years' War. Members left the country in large numbers, most of them travelling in covered wagons, carrying with them their modest belongings, hoping to find refuge in countries sympathetic to the Protestant cause. Initially, they went to Poland where more than forty congregations had been formed by 1570. In that year they assembled at the Synod of Sendomir where they issued a new Confession of Faith and called on all the Protestant communions to come together and resolve their differences. Meanwhile, back in Bohemia, John Augusta had been arrested in his hiding-place in the mountains and confined to prison in Prague. Eventually he was incarcerated in Pürglitz Castle where he remained for sixteen years until his death in 1572. From his prison-cell he issued pamphlets which were smuggled out to communities of Brethren, by now scattered throughout the country. Most were living in Moravia, where frequently they were given the protection of sympathetic noblemen.

Ferdinand I became Emperor in 1556 and was succeeded as King of Bohemia by his son, Maximilian, who proved more tolerant than his father towards the members of the Unity Church. Churches were reopened, services were conducted again, new bishops were appointed, and hundreds of new pastors were ordained. The Church was now divided into three provinces: the Polish Province led by George Israel, the Moravian Province led by John Czerny, and the Bohemian Province led by John Blahoslaw.[10] The Church enjoyed strong support from a number of noblemen, chief amongst whom were Wenzel von Budowa, a Bohemian, and Charles de Zerotín, a Moravian, who proved a generous benefactor to Comenius at a critical period in his life. De Zerotín attracted large numbers of writers and scholars to his estate at Namiest where they held prayer meetings and engaged in Bible study and hymn-singing. (Some significant innovations in the composition of new hymns occurred at this time, involving an imaginative synthesis of Gregorian chant and Bohemian or Moravian folk-song.) Elementary schools were established in villages and towns throughout the countryside of Bohemia and Moravia, classical gymnasia were established in the larger towns, and a theological seminary was founded at Přerau—all mainly through the efforts of the Unity Church. At this time the Kralice Bible appeared. This was a monumental six-volume translation of the Bible in Czech which had been undertaken by six members of the Unity Church at the Castle of Kralice between 1579 and 1593. Generally regarded as a masterpiece of Czech literature, the Kralice text was the first Bohemian Bible to be translated from Hebrew and Greek, previous translations being made usually from the Catholic Vulgate text. A small pocket edition was produced by John Blahoslaw for general circulation. Generally regarded as the Golden Age of the Unity Church, the period was one of exceptional prosperity for Bohemia as a whole and one when its levels of popular education were unmatched in any other country throughout Europe. Significantly, it was at this period that Jan Amos Komensky was born near Uhersky Brod in 1592.

Nominally, however, the Brethren of the Unity Church were outside the protection of the law, ever since the issuing of the Edict of St James, and were still regarded as dangerous heretics by some members of the Imperial Court in Prague. Under the leadership of Von Budowa, a large group of Protestant nobles assembled in 1609 and demanded full religious liberty from the Emperor. The Emperor Rudolph agreed to accede to their demands and issued the Bohemian Charter, allowing freedom of religious practice for the first time in Bohemia. The event was celebrated in hundreds of churches throughout the country. A Board of 24 Defenders—eight of whom were members of the Unity Church—was appointed to ensure that the terms of the Charter were implemented. The Bohemian National Confession was issued, affirming the civic rights of all Bohemian Protestants. At Žeravice the Brethren assembled in 1616 and issued the Order of Discipline, setting out the rules and regulations by which their Church was constituted.

Within a year, however, Ferdinand II had become King of Bohemia and once again the Protestants came under suspicion at the Imperial Court. Ferdinand issued a decree forbidding Catholics to marry Protestants—in direct violation of the terms of the Charter. When Protestant Church lands were confiscated in 1618, the nobles assembled at Prague Castle, demanding that the terms of the Charter be enforced. Following the 'Defenestration of Prague'—a euphemistic term for the casting of two councillors from the windows of the Castle—the noblemen declared King Ferdinand deposed and nominated Frederick, the Elector Palatine, to replace him. In the ensuing struggle the Protestants were routed at the Battle of the White Mountain, near Prague, in 1620. Following the defeat, their churches were destroyed, villages were sacked and plundered and thousands of innocent people were killed. The leaders of the Protestant cause were executed publicly in front of the Thein Chapel in the Old Town Square in Prague on June 21, 1621. Half of those executed were members of the Unitas Fratrum; the others were Lutherans, Calvinists and Utraquists. Effectively, this marked the end of the Bohemian branch of the Unity Church. Its members fled the country, seeking exile in Poland and Germany. A savage persecution of the remaining Protestants continued for several years, during which over 36,000 families fled from the country. The Protestant movement that had come into existence under Hus more than two centuries previously was virtually at an end.

It survived in exile, however, and amongst those who were foremost in promoting the future of the Unity Church abroad was the community led by Comenius at Leszno in Poland. The fortunes of the Church in Poland have been described in an earlier chapter. It survived for several decades under the leadership of Comenius, inspired in large measure by his writings and by his personal exemplification of its teachings. Following the events in Leszno of 1655,[11] however, and the subsequent dispersal of the Polish Brethren throughout the rest of Europe, the Church entered a period of virtual oblivion and remained so for several decades to come. When the revival came in 1722, with the founding of Herrnhut, it was largely through the inspiration of Comenius's writings that it did so. The Constitution adopted by Count Zinzendorf, the founder of Herrnhut, was the *Ratio Disciplinae*, Comenius's commentary on the Order of Discipline that had been issued at Žeravice in 1616. (Zinzendorf in fact had been ordained a pastor of the Church by Daniel Jablonsky, the grandson of Comenius.) And Comenius's writings, together with those of Chelčický, Gregory the Patriarch, John Augusta and Von Budowa, formed the basis of the teachings propagated at Herrnhut.

Though the Herrnhut renewal of Moravian Christianity occurred several decades after the death of Comenius, it is worth describing it briefly, firstly, because it embodied so much of the essential spirit of the whole tradition that had been initiated by Chelčický in the 1450s, and secondly, because it so vividly exemplified the values that inspired the life and work of Comenius himself. The renewal occurred in Lusatia, a state immediately across the border from Bohemia, under the leadership of Zinzendorf, a native of Dresden who had devoted himself since childhood to the propagation of his Christian beliefs. As a student at Wittenberg in the early 1700s he was active in promoting intersectarian harmony, like Comenius before him, and continued this work as a lay preacher and Councillor of the City of Dresden for some years. Eventually he established a Christian community on his estate at Berthelsdorf, where he was joined by an expatriate group of Moravian Brethren who had recently left Bohemia under their leader, Christian David. The latter, a native of Fulneck, a former soldier and a Catholic, had converted to Protestantism after he left the armed forces and had subsequently travelled the countryside of Moravia, preaching to the people in accordance with the teachings of the Unity Church. As a result, the Church enjoyed a temporary revival in Bohemia after a a period of oblivion that had lasted almost a century since the exodus that followed the defeat at the White Mountain in 1620. Largely as a result of renewed persecution, however, David and his followers left Moravia in June 1722 and joined Zinzendorf's community at Berthelsdorf. They settled on a hillside near Zinzendorf's estate which they renamed 'Herrnhut' or 'The Watch of the Lord.' Gradually, they were integrated with the Lusatian community and all of them eventually adopted the rules and practices of the Moravian Church. They were joined there by further groups of immigrants from Moravia, including a group from Kunwald who were descendants of the original community that had been formed there in 1457.

The 'Statutes, Injunctions and Prohibitions' of the Herrnhut Church were issued on May 12, 1727—an historic date in the history of Moravian Christianity. Rules were laid down for the life of the Church in accordance with the Order of Discipline drawn up by Comenius. Regular prayer-meetings were to be held and the conduct of all members was to be strictly regulated in accordance with the teachings of the leading figures in the movement from Chelčický to Comenius. Normally, the day began with early morning prayer, followed by Bible readings at noon and hymns and prayers in the evening. Work practices were arranged in such a way as to ensure that some of the Brethren were engaged in prayer at all times of the day and night. About sixteen hours of every day were devoted to work, which usually consisted of the cultivation of the soil and the provision of food for the needs of the community. Particular emphasis was given to the practice of religious tolerance, in accordance with the ideals laid down by Comenius in *The Bequest of the Unity of Brethren*. The members were urged to avoid theological dispute and to model their behaviour on the injunctions of the scriptures, particularly those of the Sermon on the Mount. A particularly distinctive feature of the movement was the democratic procedure that was adopted for the organisation of all Church activities. Elders elected by the members were given responsibility for the implementation of all Church rules. They drew up laws on marriage, supervised arrangements for the education of children, made provision for the care of the poor and the sick, and administered courts for the trial and punishment of offenders. Members were expected to share their resources in a spirit of cooperation and equality.

What was initiated at Herrnhut became the inspiration of a world wide movement that led to the spread of Moravian Christianity through various countries across the globe in the first half of the eighteenth century. Initially, Church members went to a number of European countries—they included Sweden, Denmark, Silesia, Hungary, Austria, England and Ireland—in each of which they established small Moravian communities that in some instances grew into major national movements. Following a meeting between Zinzendorf and a West Indian trader at the Danish court in 1732, the first non-European mission was launched and a Moravian Community was established by Brethren from Herrnhut at St. Thomas in the Danish West Indies in December of that year. Missions were sent out to the Eskimos in Greenland in 1733 and shortly afterwards to Labrador, Surinam, Antigua and Jamaica. Communities were established later amongst the Dutch settlers in Cape Colony, following which further missions were sent to the Gold Coast, Persia, India and Ceylon.[12]

Generally, Moravian missionaries travelled in small groups or choirs (their favoured term), preaching the gospel, ministering to the poor and the sick, founding schools, working side by side with their newly found converts in the fields. They found particularly strong support amongst the slaves in the cotton and coffee plantations of America, North and South. A community was founded in Georgia in 1740, in Pennsylvania shortly afterwards (the latter under the personal supervision of Zinzendorf himself), and in Maryland and North Carolina in 1748. A few years earlier the Moravians had made several converts also amongst the American Indians. By the end of the eighteenth century Moravian Christianity had become a world wide movement. A century after the first band of evangelists had gone out from Herrnhut, its missions had spread to Nicaragua, Alaska, East Central Africa, Northern Queensland, Western Australia, Palestine and Tibet. By and large, despite the great diversity of cultures it eventually embraced, the movement retained the distinctive Christian identity it had been given by its early pioneering teachers, the most notable of whom were Chelčický, Comenius and Zinzendorf.

The degree to which the values and ideals that informed Comenius's educational writings were influenced by their origins in Moravian Christianity will be demonstrated in detail in later chapters. It will be shown that the aims and ideals he defined for the educational process were primarily the religious and moral teachings enshrined in the traditions of that movement. It will be shown also that the radically concrete methodology of his educational thought was significantly influenced by the simple, non-rationalist style of the writers in the Moravian tradition from Chelčický onwards. But Moravian Christianity, for all the intensity of its impact, was not the exclusive determinant of the shape and content of Comenius's educational writings. Its influence was profoundly reinforced by developments that had been occurring in liberal educational thought throughout the sixteenth century, largely through the inspiration of major religious reformers such as Luther, Calvin and the Puritans. While differing in many respects from the later reformers, the Moravians shared the general thrust of their opposition to the dominance of Roman Catholic dogmatism and had much in common with them on matters such as the authority of scripture, the doctrine of justification by faith and the ethics of personal responsibility.

The nature of Comenius's attitudes to the Protestant reformers can be identified most clearly from the words he addressed to them in *The Bequest of the Unity of Brethren*—his definitive statement of the future policies to be followed by his own Church and of the way in which he envisaged its relations with the other Protestant Churches. His comments indicate a deep affection for Luther himself and for the whole movement that he had founded. He addresses the Lutheran Church as 'my dearest sister' and affirms his affection for the German Protestants and for the beliefs that they all held in common. His words are qualified, however, by some criticism of the corruption of the original ideals of Luther by some of the later reformers. 'The beginnings of him whom the Lord gave you for your teacher out of darkness were good,' he writes, 'but those who later took his place have ill served his good cause.' He appealed to the Lutherans to give up their theological disputes and to strive to live their lives in accordance with the spirit of Christian love:

> Thou, O Church of Germany, hast been my dearest sister whom the Lord had given to my comfort when I was still alone; I have loved thee sincerely, although thy love for me has soon cooled off, because of my simplicity. I have freely offered thee from the beginning that which, as my most precious jewel, the Lord had entrusted to me, for I have desired to share it with thee. Now in the hour of my death I still wish to be of benefit to thee. That which I desire

most for thy welfare, I bequeath thee as my inheritance: namely, more order than thou hast, a better order and discipline, and a better understanding of the article of justification, without its shameful abuse now prevailing among thy sons . . . O my friends! I, suffering the discipline of the mighty God, teach and exhort you to apprehend, that knowledge of Christ without the following of Christ, and rejoicing in the gospel without the keeping of the law of love in which the gospel is founded, is nothing less than an abuse of the gospel, a sure deception and an error.[13]

These words were written in 1650, more than a century after Luther's death. In the intervening years Europe had been torn apart by religious conflict, culminating in the devastation of the Thirty Years' War. In all this Comenius saw tragic confirmation of the failure of the reformers to live up to the ideals that had originally inspired the Protestant cause. In one sphere, however, he felt they had been generally faithful to those ideals. While the teachings of the early reformers may have been compromised by the sectarian conflicts that swept through Europe in the middle of the sixteenth century, they were universally honoured in the educational reform movements in which all of them were involved. Luther's emphasis on private judgement and the authority of scripture necessitated the provision of universal access to education if all men were to be guided in matters of faith by their own interpretations of the Biblical text. This was recognised by all the Reform Churches of the sixteenth century, as it had been a century before by the leaders of the Moravian movement, who had given practical expression to it in the schools that they founded wherever they established Christian communities. The ideals of religious reform and of universal access to education were inextricably intertwined in the teachings of the Moravians, as they were in the writings that Luther devoted specifically to education in the early years of the sixteenth century.

The most significant of these writings were his *Letter to the Mayors and Aldermen on Behalf of Church Schools*, which was issued in 1524, and in his *Sermon on the Duty of Sending Children to School*, which was written in 1530.[14] In both works he called on the state authorities to discharge their responsibility to provide education for all children and suggested that it should be compulsory, at least in the years of elementary schooling. Like Comenius in later years, he argued passionately that schools should be open to children of all classes and backgrounds so that all might have the benefit of a sound Christian education. Like Comenius also, he saw the need to reform the harsh and inhuman practices occurring in the schools of the time. Schools, he argued, should be cheerful places where children could enjoy learning. He suggested that periods of study be followed always by periods of recreation and that a careful balance be maintained between work and play in the life of the school.[15]

To those who objected that the poor could not afford to send their children to school, since they needed them to work in the fields, Luther responded: 'Let them go to school for one or two hours daily, and spend the rest of their time in learning a trade.'[16] He spoke of the pedagogic advances that would facilitate the extension of education to the masses who had historically been denied its benefits. 'Is it not evident,' he wrote in the Letter of 1524, 'that it is now possible to educate a boy in three years so that when he is fifteen or eighteen years old he shall know more than the whole sum of knowledge of the high schools and monasteries up to this time? Hitherto, in the high schools and monasteries, men have only learned to be asses, blocks and stones. They have studied for twenty and forty years and have learned neither Latin nor German.' Seeing the importance of giving all children access to a wide range of subject-matter, he favoured a broadening of the traditional classical curriculum. 'Had I had children,' he said, 'I should make them learn not only languages and history, but also singing, music and mathematics.'[17]

Philip Melanchton, Luther's close associate, wrote extensively on the subject of educational reform and urged the further extension of the curriculum to include the newly emerging sciences. Arguing for a careful balancing of the humanities and sciences, he spoke of the distinctive contribution that each could make to the formation of the individual student. He wrote eloquently on the importance of grammar study as essential for the effective reading of the scriptures and—almost a century before Bacon and Comenius were to write in almost identical fashion on the subject— he wrote of the value of scientific study in the fostering of a spirit of piety and reverence for God's creation. 'Although,' Melanchton wrote, 'the nature of things cannot be absolutely known, nor the marvellous works of God traced to their original, until, in the future life, we shall listen to the eternal counsel of the Father, nevertheless even amidst this our present darkness, every hint of harmony of this fair creation forms a step toward the knowledge of God and toward virtue, whereby we ourselves shall also learn to love and maintain order and moderation in all our acts.' 'Since,' he added, 'it is evident that men are endowed by their Creator with faculties fitted for the contemplation of nature, they must, of necessity, take delight in investigating the elements, the laws, the qualities, and the forces of the various bodies by which they are surrounded.'[18]

All of this, as will be shown presently, found powerful echoes a century later in Comenius's pedagogic writings. Sharing Luther's radically democratic vision of education, Comenius developed the pedagogic methodology that was essential to make this vision a realisable and practicable goal. Between Luther and Comenius, however, some significant advances in educational theory and practice had been made by other thinkers who shared many of their beliefs and aspirations. These were writers falling broadly within the reform movement initiated by Jean Calvin in Geneva in the 1530s, though differing profoundly from Calvin himself on some of its ideals. There were, as Nicholas Hans has written, two traditions of Puritanism, the one profoundly liberal, the other characterised by tendencies virtually contradicting the ideals which brought the Reformation into being. 'We have to distinguish two currents in Calvinist thought,' he writes, 'the one orthodox, intolerant and domineering, and the other liberal and conciliating.'[19] In the first category he places the Genevan Calvinists, the Precisians in Holland, the followers of John Knox in Scotland, the English Presbyterians and the American Congregationalists. The more liberal tradition emphasised individual responsibility, tolerance and freedom of conscience. Its chief exponents were Mathurin Cordier and Sebastian Chateillon (Castellio) in Switzerland, the Huguenots in France, Grotius and his followers in Holland, Priestly and the Dissenters in England. In *The Bequest of the Unity of Brethren* Comenius denounced the former group for their intolerance and bigotry while clearly identifying himself with the latter, whom he commended for their 'love of order and discipline', and whom he urged to remain steadfast in their constancy, their piety and simplicity. In a passage addressed to all his fellow Puritans he singled out the English Presbyterians for debasing the original ideals of the Puritan movement:

> To thee, thou Swiss Church, who hast been granted me as a comforter by reason of thy love of order and discipline, what shall I leave? I bequeath thee a determination to constancy and to an increase in all worthy things, according to Christ's command that the righteous should increase in his righteousness, and the holy grow in his holiness, and His promise that whosoever hath, to him shall be given, and he shall have greater abundance.
>
> If then, my dear sister, thou art of the number of those who are to increase in God's gifts and grace, allow me to add something to your store: at least the desire that thou mayest really possess the precious realities which thou imaginest to enjoy. Lest, deceiving thyself, thou mayest be constant with the husks instead of penetrating to the kernel. I admonish thee, therefore, first of all that thou mayest hold to piety and to the disciplining order pertaining thereto, with sincere single-mindedness, and that not only in appearance but in reality. Then in method I admonish thee to more simplicity and less speculation; also to a more discreet discussion concerning God and His most profound mysteries than some of your sons were wont to indulge. For thereby was caused a sorry disruption among themselves and thee. . . . Especially is this evident in England, where thy sons, after the terror of wars has subsided, are making a sad and derogatory exhibition of themselves and have defamed thy name among their fellows by their practice of ever searching for novelties and never attaining to stable convictions.[20]

Though Calvin himself provided the main inspiration for the harsh and repressive regime that was created in Geneva by the City Council—the burning of the Unitarian dissenter, Michael Servetus, being a particularly horrific manifestation of its intolerance and bigotry—he nonetheless initiated reforms in education that were to provide inspiration for a liberal movement that was led by other Puritan thinkers a good deal more liberal than himself. The school he established in Geneva was a model of its kind and it was there that some of the most enlightened and influential of Puritan educators, such as Cordier and Castellio, directly encountered the process of educational reform in the actual conditions of the school classroom. The Geneva School had seven classes and, like the schools later organised by Comenius at Přerau and Leszno, followed a classical humanist curriculum which blended easily with the new reformist teachings in matters of morality and faith. The work of the school was strictly regulated—each session began with a prayer and a strong emphasis was laid on disciplined behaviour in all spheres of the school's activity. Calvin, however, insisted that the teachers be humane and sensitive in their treatment of the pupils. The Order of Discipline, for example, defined the role of the Principal in the following terms: 'Que le principal, estant de moyen scavoir pour le moins, soit surtout d'un esprit debonnaire et non point de complexion rude ni apre; afin qu'il donne bon exemple aux enfants en toute sa vie, et aussi qu'il puisse porter tant plus doucement le travail de sa charge.'[21]

In common with Luther, Calvin believed strongly in the ideal of universal education and particularly emphasised the importance of fostering basic literacy in the elementary school as the means to its achievement. Two of his followers, Cordier and Castellio, who shared his basic religious beliefs, did much to liberalise his educational policies. Originally a Catholic priest and a professor at the University of Paris, Cordier became interested in Calvinism while teaching at the Collège de Guyenne in Bordeaux—an institution where Catholic and Huguenot children were educated together—and eventually went to teach under Calvin at the Collège de la Rive in Geneva, where he remained from 1536 until his death in 1564. Though he converted to Puritanism, he disapproved of Calvin's intolerance and fanaticism and sought to promote the same spirit of religious tolerance in Geneva as he had earlier advocated in Bordeaux. He saw the fostering of individual responsibility as the hallmark of Puritan education. The integration of religious and academic activities was central to his educational philosophy, the simultaneous fostering of learning and piety being its primary objective. He was responsible for some significant innovations in the teaching of Latin, particularly in the sphere of Latin conversation. The method he advocated in the *Colloquia*, a collection of model conversations between pupils on a variety of different topics, was later praised by Comenius, who recommended that it be used as a foundation for the formal study of Latin texts in the upper grades of the secondary school. G.W. Keatinge, who found them more practical than similar collections by Erasmus and Vives, gives this assessment of Cordier's *Colloquia*: 'The choice of words and phrases speaks of a long life spent in intelligent teaching, while the vivid descriptions of the life and conversation of the typical school-boy show that Cordier, kindly and observant, did not confine his interest in his pupils to the hours of class-instruction.'[22]

The reforms initiated by Cordier were further developed by Castellio, his colleague at the Collège de la Rive A friend of Calvin during his years in Paris, and the author of a French translation of the Bible, Castellio came to Geneva following the proscription of the Huguenots by Francis I in 1535. He too strongly advocated religious tolerance and urged that reconciliation be promoted between the different Protestant sects. Having challenged Calvin on the issue of the execution of Servetus, he left Geneva and worked thenceforth as a professor at the University of Basle. There his teachings on religious tolerance attracted large numbers of moderate Calvinists and Zwinglians. Together with Cordier, Castellio did much to reform the teachings of Calvin and, in the process, ensured the growth of a democratic system of education in Switzerland, inspired by the most enlightened principles of the Puritan heritage. In a section of the *Pampaedia* where he dealt with religious and moral education, Comenius acknowledged his debt to the *Sacred Dialogues* of Castellio and modelled his exercises in scripture reading on the methods advocated by the latter in this work.[23]

Meanwhile, similarly liberal policies on education had been emerging in France under the Huguenots. Despite the hostility that was shown them during the reign of Francis I, the Huguenots continued to pursue their goal of founding schools in every parish in the country. At the States-General of Orleans in 1560 they sent the following petition to the King: 'May it please the King to levy a contribution on the Church revenues for the reasonable support of teachers and men of learning in every city and village, for the instruction of the needy youth of the country; and let all parents be required, under penalty of fine, to send their children to school, and let them be constrained to observe this law by the lords and the ordinary magistrates.'[24] Their request was denied at the time but, following the Edict of Nantes of 1598, Huguenots were allowed to establish their own schools once again, and some of the most enlightened academies emerged in these years. They included those at Nice, Nimes, Montauban and Saumur, in each of which vigorous efforts were made to promote interdenominational harmony and to lessen the evils of social inequality. Following the Revocation of the Edict of Nantes by Louis XIV, and the renewed persecution of Huguenots which followed it, many of the schools were closed again and the whole process of democratising education came to an end for the time being. It was to be more than a century before the goal of universal education was to be taken seriously again in France, though the seeds sown by the Huguenots of the sixteenth century were eventually to bear fruit in the spread of elementary schools there in the late eighteenth and early nineteenth centuries.

Contemporaneously with the Huguenot movement in France, Arminian Protestantism took root in Holland in the late sixteenth century. Led by Jacob Harmensz (Arminius), the Professor of Theology at Leyden, the Arminians offered a more liberal and benign brand of Calvinism than the Precisians, whose dogmatism and intolerance they vehemently condemned. In later years Comenius established close links with the Arminian movement through friends at the University of Leyden. From the outset they advocated the creation of a Republic in Holland, organised on the basis of local democratic structures. Their most influential thinker, Hugo Grotius, was a passionate advocate of religious tolerance and wrote extensively on the subject of law reform and its importance for the creation of a humane and just society. Largely under the influence of the Arminians, William the Silent enacted laws that led to the establishment of a liberal democratic system of education in Holland. The Synod of Dort in 1618 decreed that 'schools must be instituted in country places, towns and cities. Religious instruction must be given. . . . The children of the poor should be instructed free. . . . The duty of the ministers with an elder is to visit all schools, private as well as public.'[25] A university had been founded at Leyden in 1579, largely under Arminian influence; others followed in Franeker (1584), Groningen (1614), Amsterdam (1632), Utrecht (1636) and Harderwijk (1646). Amongst the scholars attracted to these institutions were Descartes, a Catholic, and Spinoza, a Jew—both drawn by the liberal ethos they projected. Puritan students, excluded from Oxford and Cambridge after the Restoration, went to Leyden in large numbers in the 1660s and continued to do so well into the eighteenth century.

In England and Scotland the Puritan movement manifested the extremes of liberalism and intolerance described by Hans as characterising its history since its origins in the 1530s. Those who dominated the Long Parliament of the 1650s fully deserved Comenius's criticism that they had 'made a sad and derogatory exhibition of themselves' and had 'defamed the name of their founders'.[26] But there were many enlightened and moderate English Puritans who did much to further the cause of universal education. These were the people of whom Comenius wrote to his friends in Leszno in 1640: 'They are eagerly debating on the reform of schools in the whole kingdom, namely that all young people should be instructed, none neglected.'[27] Despite the outbreak of civil war, a number of schools—about 40 elementary schools and over 30 grammar schools—were.founded by Puritans between 1651 and 1660. The Quakers, who originated in England at this time also, founded about fifteen schools in the years immediately following the Restoration.

One of the most influential of the Puritan educators in England was John Brinsley, in whose writings there are significant pointers to the pedagogic reforms later advocated by Comenius. In his *Ludus Literarius*, published two decades before *The Great Didactic*, Brinsley discussed the whole process of education from the elementary to the upper secondary school. Presented in the form of a dialogue between two schoolmasters, the work strongly emphasised the principle of learning through play and stressed the need for a broadened curriculum in the grammar school, involving the teaching of the vernacular side by side with Latin, Greek and Hebrew. An early advocate of reforms in teacher training, Brinsley spoke of the 'manifold evils which grow from ignorance of the right order of teaching.'[28] In a work called *A Consolation for Our Grammar Schools* he urged that teachers be trained in methods that would ensure they did not 'subject their pupils to extreme labour and terror . . . with enduring far overmuch and long severity'[29] He anticipated Comenius in his recommendation that colleges be founded specifically for the function of training teachers in accordance with the principles of enlightened pedagogic theory. Brinsley suffered the fate of many liberal Puritans in Cromwellian England, being eventually dismissed from his teaching post because of his unorthodox religious views.

John Dury, the Scottish theologian and educationalist, was largely responsible for introducing Comenius to the traditions of liberal English Protestantism. A passionate advocate of religious tolerance, he had been educated at Leyden in the early 1600s and ministered to a colony of English Protestants at Elbing for some years. There he worked vigorously to promote reconciliation between the Lutheran and Calvinist Churches. Returning to England in 1632, he wrote *The Reformed School*, a work in which he set out his philosophy of Christian education, arguing that learning should always be enjoyable, that nothing should be 'tedious or grievous' in the work of the school.[30] He urged that the natural capacities of children should be studied by the teacher as a basis for the planning of good pedagogic practice and advocated a broadening of the curriculum to include the study of the sciences. Like Comenius and the Moravians, he saw the ultimate aim of education as the fostering of the community spirit in accordance with the principles of scriptural Christianity.

All the movements that have been described were inspired by one common purpose: the provision of *all* children with the educational foundation that would ensure their growth and formation were guided by the teachings of the Christian scriptures. It was this championing of the rights of the masses to a good basic education that was their most significant contribution to the whole process of educational reform. Comparing the educators of the Reform movement with the Renaissance humanists, S.S. Laurie wrote: 'The Church Reformers . . . had an interest in the progress of culture scarcely less sincere than that of the Humanists, but to this they added compassion for the dense ignorance of the masses of the people. The human soul, wherever found, was to them an object of infinite concern, and, unlike the pure humanists, they aimed at universal instruction. The new form of the old faith could sustain itself only on the basis of popular education. The Reformers were educational philanthropists in the truest sense, and hence the people's school is rightly called the child of the Reformation.'[31] It was significant, however, that the kind of education the Reformers proposed for the masses was still conceived—particularly in matters of curricular content—in accordance with the traditional humanist model that had spread throughout Europe in the middle of the fifteenth century. This they sought to make available to all children but, significantly, their primary concern was to ensure it was informed in all respects by the spirit of the Christian scriptures. What they taught in their schools was a reformed, thoroughly Christianised humanism, in which classical culture was permeated by the all-embracing ideals of the Christian faith. In the work of Comenius the convergence of these two streams—the humanist and the religious—is especially exemplified. The process by which this came about, and the manner in which it influenced the shape and content of Comenius' pedagogical writings, will be the concern of the forthcoming section.

3. HUMANIST PRECURSORS: ERASMUS TO VIVES

Two of the movements which influenced the evolution of Comenius's educational thought have been identified. The first was the simple, non-dogmatic, scripture-based heritage of morality and faith which he encountered through the traditions of Moravian Christianity. Its values and ideals provided the moral and religious foundation of the whole vision of educational reform that was projected in his writings. This was greatly reinforced by the democratising tendencies that had been introduced into education by the liberal thinkers of the Reformation. Their concern that education be provided for the masses of the deprived and the down-trodden—who had historically been denied access to its benefits—gave powerful expression to an ideal that had already been promoted in the teachings and practices of the Moravian Church. This was the second source from which he derived much of the inspiration for his proposed reforms. The third was the humanist tradition of classical learning to which he was indebted for much of his thinking on the more specific matters of pedagogic and curricular reform. Little more than a century before Comenius was born, the Turks had taken Constantinople, thus precipitating the flight of large numbers of classical scholars to the West, which, in turn, heralded the great flowering of classical learning associated with the Renaissance. A great liberation followed in the schools and academies of Western Europe, as a result of which the sterile methods of teaching practised in the mediaeval schools gave way both to a revitalised pedagogy and to a curriculum renewed through its assimilation of the newly discovered literary-classical heritage.

The humanist tradition on which Comenius drew so extensively was one therefore that was already undergoing a major transformation at the time he encountered it. A few decades before his birth, the French priest-writer, François Rabelais, had satirised the activities of the scholastic institutions in his prose burlesque, *Gargantua and Pantagruel*. Attacking the 'grammar grind' which turned Gargantua into 'a fool, a sot, a dolt and a blockhead,'[32] he described how the latter's tutor, Tubal Holfernes, spent five and a quarter years teaching him to say his ABCs backward, thirteen years teaching him to master the rules of Latin grammar and composition, and a further thirty-four years giving him instruction in Latin eloquence. Through the medium of his satire Rabelais identified some of the major deficiencies of the scholastic tradition which subsequent thinkers, such as Erasmus, Montaigne and Comenius, were to seek to rectify through their proposed reforms.

The primary deficiencies of the mediaeval schools lay in the methods adopted for the teaching of Latin. Latin was effectively the lingua franca of all Europe at the time, being the chief means of communication between all educated citizens, the gateway to all forms of academic advancement, and an essential prerequisite for entry to the learned professions. In the schools all instruction was conducted through the medium of Latin. The greater part of a student's work in the elementary school consisted of the mastery of a vast number of rules and constructions, most of which had to be learned by heart. Generally, the study of Latin authors did not begin until the secondary school years when it was then combined with studies in history and logic. The study of these authors was usually conducted with a view, not to developing a love for the literature, but to enhancing eloquence in the spoken language and encouraging the mastery of a style appropriate for the writing of learned treatises and disputations. The authors taught most frequently were Horace, Virgil and Cicero, their ornate style of writing generally facilitating the lessons in eloquence to which most of the teaching was directed. The use of the vernacular was generally forbidden in the mediaeval schools—the Jesuit *Ratio*, for example, prohibited its use except during holidays, and even an enlightened educator such as John Sturm forbade his pupils from using French in his school at Strasbourg.

Many of the old mediaeval Grammars were still in use by the beginning of the sixteenth century. The *Graecism* of Ebrard, with its systematised classification of the parts of speech and various grammatical constructions, had first been issued in 1212 and was still widely used. (Erasmus had learned Latin from this text in the 1470s). Like all texts of its kind, its treatment of the language was formal and abstract, and largely unrelated to the conditions of everyday life. Another widely used work was John De Garlande's *Compendium Grammaticae*, which adopted a similarly archaic approach to the teaching of the language. Significant improvements came, however, with the appearance of various Colloquies, or Dialogues, early in the sixteenth century. These were model conversations on topics of common interest which were intended to provide students with expressions and phrases suitable for everyday discourse. Mathurin Cordier's Colloquies have already been mentioned; these appeared in 1564. Yet another collection, the Colloquies of Schottenius, a schoolmaster from Cologne, had appeared in 1535; their detailed treatment of eating customs provides some valuable insights into the social conventions of the time. John Sturm, the founder of the Strasbourg school, similarly emphasised the importance of conversation and published his *Neanisci* in 1570. Also popular were the Dialogues of Barland, published in Louvain in 1530, Juan Luis Vives's *Linguae Latinae Exercitatio*, published in 1539, and the work that Comenius recommended for his pansophic school, the *Colloquia* of Erasmus which appeared around 1530.

The most significant change in the teaching of Latin came, however, with the adoption of the vernacular as the medium through which the second language was to be acquired. Largely through the influence of the Reformation, the status of Latin as the exclusive language of learning was now being challenged. Many of the Reformers had condemned the manner in which the language was being taught in the mediaeval schools, as was shown in the last section. Luther wrote disparagingly of the classical texts he had studied in school. 'Instead of sound books,' he cried, 'the insane, useless, harmful, monkish books, like the *Catholicon*, the *Florista*, the *Graecista*, the *Labyrinth*, the *Dormi Secure*, and such-like stable refuse, have been introduced by the Devil, so that the Latin tongue has decayed, and in no place is any good school or instruction or method of study left.'[33] Melanchton's Grammar, which appeared in 1525, greatly simplified the rules and conventions of the language, and gradually from this time onward grammarians began to encourage the use of the vernacular as the medium of instruction. The first texts to encourage the study of Latin through the medium of the vernacular appeared in England shortly before the Reformation. As early as 1510 Holt's *Lac Puerorum* had offered explanations of the rules of Latin in English. This was followed by Linacre's *Grammar* of 1523, Vaus's of 1528 and Wolsey's of 1529—in each of which English was the medium of instruction. The English texts were followed by several in other European languages, of which Comenius's *Janua*, published in 1631, was to be the most influential, being still in print almost three centuries after it first appeared.

The changing practices in the teaching of Latin were accompanied by a general broadening of the mediaeval curriculum, a process which derived powerful stimulus from the Reformers. The narrowness of the scholastic curriculum was one of the criticisms of education put forward by Rabelais in *Gargantua and Pantagruel*. In his letter to his son, Pantagruel, Gargantua outlines his vision of a well-rounded curriculum. He advises him to study Greek, Latin, Hebrew, Scripture, literature, music, art and athletics, and tells him that learning must follow the 'laws of nature.'[34] Wide concern was expressed by educators at the low status of mathematics and science. In the mediaeval period arithmetic was generally seen as a subject serving certain practical functions in the years of elementary and secondary education, and was rarely seen as a discipline deserving the kind of attention that was given to Latin and the humanities. The first indication of a changed appreciation of its importance came with Cuthbert Tonstall's *De Arte Supputandi* in 1522. This work advocated the study of arithmetic as an academic subject comparable in importance to the classical languages. Tonstall's work was reprinted by John Sturm for use in his school at Strasbourg in 1544. In his preface to the work Sturm recommended it to all schools wishing to undertake a deeper study of mathematics. The views of Tonstall and Sturm were endorsed by Philip Melanchton who recommended the extension of the humanist curriculum to include mathematics, physics and astronomy.

A further advance in the status of mathematics came with the publication of Robert Recorde's *The Grounde of Artes* in 1561. Recorde argued that the 'capacity for numbering' is what distinguishes man from the 'brute beasts': 'Whoso setteth small price by the witty device and knowledge of numbering, he little considereth to be the chief point (in manner) whereby men differ from all brute beasts; for as in all other things (almost) beasts are partakers with us, so in numbering we differ cleane from them and in manner peculiarly, sith that in many things they excell us againe.'[35] As well as offering a philosophical justification of the place of mathematics in a properly balanced curriculum, Recorde's work offered practical pedagogic guidance that was to lead to significant advances in the teaching of the subject in many European schools. Parallel works on the subject appeared in France and Germany in the 1560s—Peter Ramus's *Arithmetic* was published in France in 1565 and a similar work by Christopher Clavius appeared in Germany shortly afterwards. Comenius's teacher at Herborn, Johann Heinrich Alsted, was also the author of an Arithmetic. By the time Comenius wrote *The Great Didactic* the subject was firmly established as an essential component in a well rounded curriculum. A similar process had occurred in respect of science—due largely to the influence of Bacon and the realists—as will be demonstrated in detail in the forthcoming section.

All these changes in pedagogic and curricular practice took place, however, within a cultural framework that remained firmly within the classical-humanist tradition. This can be exemplified from a brief consideration of the writings of three of the most influential educators in the humanist tradition, each of whom can be shown to have anticipated the reforms of Comenius in several respects. From an educational standpoint, the most significant of the humanists was the Dutch priest and scholar, Desiderius Erasmus. There are numerous references to his work in Comenius's writings and Erasmus clearly foreshadowed many of the educational innovations that the latter developed and refined. The affinities between the two men are quite striking. Like Comenius, Erasmus lost his parents in early childhood and his education was subsequently entrusted to guardians. He too experienced great cruelty in his early schooling. The following passage from *The Liberal Education of Children*, in which he gives his impressions of contemporary teachers, finds many echoes in the passages from the *Labyrinth* and *The Great Didactic* where Comenius denounced the brutality of the schools he had attended: 'The school is, in effect, a torture chamber; blows and shouts, sobs and howls, fill the air. Then it is wondered that the growing boy hates learning; and that in riper years he hates it still.'[36]

Like Comenius, Erasmus became a priest and, though he never formally left the Roman Catholic Church, was nonetheless deeply committed to the cause of religious reform. Both men shared a profound reverence for the scriptures and were deeply committed to asserting their authority in matters of morals and faith. Erasmus's edition of the New Testament, first published in 1516, was read all over Europe and was the text used for vernacular translations of the Bible by Luther in 1519, Lefévre in 1520 and Tyndall in 1525. Like Comenius, Erasmus condemned violence and war as incompatible with the teachings of Christ and set out his arguments for the promotion of peace in his *Complaint of Peace*. In his Prefaces to his translations of the Biblical text he denounced the corruptions of the institutional Church with the same spirit of Christian concern as Comenius exemplified a century later in his own religious writings.

The essential characteristic of Erasmus's Christian-humanist vision of education was its synthesis of three complementary objectives: the fostering of piety, morality and learning. 'The first and principal function of education,' he wrote, 'is that the tender spirit may drink in the seeds of piety, the next that he may love and learn thoroughly the liberal studies, the third is that he may be informed concerning the duties of life, the fourth is that from earliest childhood he may be habituated in courteous manners.'[37] The Platonist ideal of a liberal education (the term 'liberal' is used in its original classical connotation as the freeing or releasing of individual potentiality) is here absorbed in a vision which is primarily religious and conceived specifically within the traditions of scriptural Christianity. This, as will be shown presently, was also the defining characteristic of the Comenian vision of a liberal education. In both cases what was projected was a vision which fully respected the priorities of the humanist tradition—particularly its emphasis on the fostering of intelligence, reason and imagination—within the all-encompassing framework of religious faith. Identifying the distinctive character of Erasmus's brand of humanism, one historian has written: 'Erasmus treasured not only the classical heritage but that of the Gospel as well. Between the two he saw no deep gulf but believed that they could be joined together and that their union would produce the fruits of sound learning, peace, moral conduct, and the good life.'[38] In *The Order of Learning* Erasmus fully endorsed the merits of the humanist curriculum—stressing the value of the great classical texts in the formation of the young person—while advocating its integration with the spiritual traditions of the Christian faith. Like Comenius he believed in the universality of all culture and saw the Latin language and the traditions of classical learning as the common heritage that would give all men access to its riches.

Erasmus further anticipated Comenius in the specific reforms he advocated in the sphere of school pedagogy. Both men were deeply impressed by the conditions they had seen in English schools and their educational writings were profoundly influenced by what they had witnessed there. Like his successor, Erasmus passionately denounced the inhuman methods of enforcing discipline practised in European schools at the time. In *The Liberal Education of Children* (*De Pueris Statim Ac Liberaliter Instituendis*) he wrote: 'Teaching by beating is not a liberal education. . . . Let us watch, let us encourage, let us press and yet again press, that by learning, by repeating, by diligent listening, the boy may feel himself carried onward towards his goal. . . . These are your instruments of discipline, my Christian teacher, worthy of your calling and of your flock.'[39] In the same work he put forward a view of elementary education that was based on the graded, or developmental conception of individual maturation, similar to that which Comenius later elaborated in *The Great Didactic*. Learning, Erasmus wrote, was to be guided through its natural stages, the material being graded according to difficulty and matched to the needs of individual pupils. He emphasised the importance of allowing learning to occur spontaneously, though it was to be promoted actively under the formative guidance of the teacher.

'He [the teacher] will follow in his first instruction the methods of the mother in the earliest training of her nurseling,' he wrote. 'As she prattles baby language, stirs and softens baby food, stoops and guides the tottering steps—so will the master act in things of the mind.'[40] He suggested formal education should begin as early as seven years of age so that good study habits could be cultivated as soon as possible. Again, like Comenius, he stressed the value of play as a mode of learning appropriate to early childhood. The section of *The Liberal Education of Children* which is entitled 'Pleasurable Methods Must Be Devised In The First Stages of Teaching' describes various playful activities that can be encouraged by the teacher for the development of verbal and visual perception in young children.[41] Erasmus strongly condemned the excessive use of rote memorisation in the teaching of grammar, urging that the learning of rules and definitions be subordinated always to the practical usage of the language itself. 'For it is not by learning rules that we acquire the power of speaking a language, but by daily intercourse with those accustomed to express themselves with exactness and refinement and by the copious reading of the best authors,' he writes in a passage from *The Order of Learning*[42] which closely anticipates the methods advocated by Comenius in the *Orbis Pictus*. A passionate advocate of a curriculum based on well chosen texts, Erasmus prepared his own anthology of readings from the great authors, providing detailed commentaries to assist interpretation. This work, the *Adages* or *Familiar Quotations from the Classics*, became enormously popular in European schools in the sixteenth century. In his editions of the scriptures he also provided extensive exegetic commentaries— drawing in particular on the writings of the Early Fathers—and sought thereby to establish scripture study as a discipline requiring the same degree of intellectual rigour as the study of classical texts.

This broadly conceived Christian-humanist view of education profoundly influenced the writings of Comenius a century later, as will be shown in later chapters of this work. Comenius was further influenced by the holistic conception of the whole process put forward by the French essayist, Michel de Montaigne in his essays, 'Of Pedantry' and 'Of the Upbringing of Children'. Montaigne's interest in education, like that of Erasmus and Comenius, was stimulated in the first instance by his horror at the brutality occurring in contemporary schools. 'Instead of inviting children to learning, we really accustom them to horror and cruelty,' he wrote. 'Let me have no more violence and driving: in my opinion there is nothing else which so brutalises and dulls a high-mettled nature.' 'Our schools,' he cried, 'are houses of correction for imprisoned youths, and children are made incorrigible by punishment. Visit them when the children are getting their lessons, and you will hear nothing but the outcries of boys under execution and the thundering noises of their teachers, drunk with fury.'[43]

Side by side with this, Montaigne recalled his own youthful enthusiasm for the Latin authors—he was reading Ovid's *Metamorphosis* at the age of seven and shortly afterwards was studying Virgil, Terence and Plautus, 'lured ever onwards by the attractiveness of the contents.'[44] While reaffirming the value of classical studies as the cornerstone of an enlightened curriculum, he proclaimed his belief that education should ultimately be concerned with the whole man, with all his needs and potentialities. 'It is not a mind, it is not a body that we are educating, it is a man.' he wrote. 'We must not cut him in half, and, as Plato says, we must not cultivate the one without the other, we must develop them equally, like a pair of horses harnessed to the same pole.'[45] He urged teachers to strive 'to really educate our understandings' and believed pupils should be encouraged to think independently. True wisdom, he declared, comes with self-knowledge. 'We take other men's knowledge and opinions under our protection and that is all, whereas we ought to make them our very own, part of ourselves,' he writes in his essay, 'Of Pedantry.'[46]

Montaigne's emphasis on learning through experience was further developed by another of the Christian humanists to whom Comenius was also heavily indebted, the Spanish philosopher, Juan Luis Vives. At once a traditionalist and an innovator, Vives closely anticipates Comenius in his integration of Christian and classical-humanist ideals, his passionate commitment to social reform and his innovative approaches to school pedagogy. Spanish by birth, he left the country following his condemnation by the Inquisition, and lived the greater part of his life in Louvain and Bruges. Deeply influenced by Erasmus, who was one of his professors in Louvain, he too decided to devote himself to academic learning, initially taking up an appointment at Corpus Christi College in Oxford. In *De Institutione Feminae Christianae*, written during his years at Oxford, he strongly advocated the education of women—the work was immensely popular and eventually went into over forty editions. In a further work, *De Ratione Studii Puerilis*, he put forward a radically new vision of education, advocating a broadening of the curriculum to include the study of the vernacular and the study of geography and suggesting even that instruction in the vernacular begin in the elementary school. He continued, however, to extol the virtues of classical learning and produced a highly popular manual for teachers, *Exercitatio Linguae Latinae*, to ensure the subject was more effectively taught. Ostracised at Oxford after he championed the cause of Catherine of Aragon against Henry VIII, he returned to Flanders where he devoted himself to organising schemes for the relief of poverty. He advocated increased taxes on churches and monasteries to finance these schemes—they included the founding of asylums for the mentally ill, together with schools for orphans and foundlings. In *De Communione Rerum*, a major treatise on social reform, he questioned traditional moral teaching on private property and advocated various measures for a more equitable sharing of wealth.

From an educational standpoint, the most significant of Vives's reforms was his reconception of humanist ideals to accommodate the newly emerging insights from the natural sciences. Drawing his epistemological theories mainly from Aristotle—especially on the functions of sense-experience—he put forward an inductive theory of knowledge in *De Anima et Vita*, in which he foreshadowed many of the realist principles developed by Descartes and Bacon. His synthesis of classical-humanist and realist principles was strongly in evidence in *De Disciplinis*, the work in which he set out the main principles of his pedagogic philosophy. He stressed the importance of nature study, emphasising the need for the learner to encounter all material reality through the immediate experience of the senses. 'It is at once school and schoolmaster,' he wrote of the world of nature, 'for it presents something a man can look at with admiration and at the same time his culture is advanced by it.'[47] 'The senses are the sources of all cognition,' he declared. Urging teachers to promote learning through the child's innate powers of discovery, he spoke out against the evils of rote memorisation and the mechanistic styles of teaching practised in contemporary schools. The child, he said, should be encouraged to discover the wonders of natural phenomena for himself. 'The senses open up the way to all knowledge; whatever is in the arts was in Nature first, just as pearls are in shells or gems in the sand,' he wrote.[48]

4. REALIST PRECURSORS: BACON TO ALSTED

What was most significant about the classical-humanist ideals given expression by Erasmus, Montaigne and Vives was their capacity to accommodate the Christian traditions, to which all of them wholeheartedly subscribed, together with the newly emerging spirit of scientific realism which they saw as enriching those traditions, by virtue of the new insights it provided into the mysteries and complexities of the world of created being. The new spirit of scientific enquiry was given practical expression in the founding of new academies devoted to the study of science at various centres throughout Europe at the end of the fifteenth century. The founding of the Accademia Platonica in Florence by Gemistos Pletho in 1470 was followed by the founding of the Accademia Romana by Bishop Bessarion in 1498. Both Pletho and Bessarion had emphasised the value of scientific enquiry as a means of attaining a deepened understanding of the natural universe, the order and harmony of which they saw as a manifestation of the divine presence in creation. In this way they incorporated the insights of science into the general pattern of religious truth. That same principle was given eloquent expression by Comenius in his *Via Lucis* more than a century after the first scientific institutes were established. Faced with the suspicion, and frequently the hostility, manifested by the Roman Catholic Church towards the new academies, their members were generally obliged to conduct their work in secrecy, but the movement spread rapidly in the sixteenth century as new institutions, all of them founded specifically for the promotion of scientific research, sprang up at various locations throughout Europe. Most notable were the Accademia dei Lincei founded by della Porto in Rome in 1603, the Akademie des Palm Baumes founded in Weimar in 1616, the Accademia del Cimento founded by pupils of Galileo at Florence in 1657, the Royal Society established, largely through the inspiration of Comenius, in London in 1662, the French Academy of Sciences, founded in 1666, and the Royal Academy of Berlin, established by Leibnitz in 1700.

This great fostering of scientific scholarship and enquiry required a number of corresponding reforms in education. It required not only a broadening of the traditional school curriculum to accommodate the study of natural phenomena, but it also necessitated more fundamental reforms in the way that learning was to be fostered in schools. The traditional classical pedagogy had been overwhelmingly didactic—despite the ancient traditions of heuristic learning that had been advocated by Socrates and his successors—and the work of the schools consisted predominantly of the concentrated study of texts under the close, and usually authoritarian, direction of the teacher. With the emergence of science came a new emphasis on self-initiated learning, a process that was given powerful impetus by the writings of Bacon, which in turn greatly influenced the work of Comenius. Bacon, it will be recalled, was identified by Comenius himself as one of his foremost mentors and was singled out in the *Via Lucis* as the person 'to whom we owe the first suggestion and opportunity for common counsel with regard to the universal reform of the sciences.'[49] 'It was Bacon's *Instauratio Magna* that opened his eyes to the possibilities of our knowledge of nature and its place in the educational scheme,' wrote one of Comenius's editors in 1892.[50]

Bacon had condemned mediaeval scholars for allowing their minds to 'be shut up in the cells of a few authors, chiefly Aristotle, their dictator, as their persons were shut up in the cells of monasteries and colleges.'[51] They knew little, he wrote, 'either of nature or time, did out of no great quantity of matter, and infinite agitation of wit, spin cobwebs of learning, admirable for the fineness of the thread and work, but of no substance or profit.'[52] Attacking the mediaeval institutions for their almost exclusive concentration on Latin, grammar and logic, he called on the new schools to devote their energies to the study of nature and the wonders of God's creation. 'Let them with a teachable spirit approach the great volume of creation, patiently decipher its secret characters, and converse with its lofty truths,' he wrote; 'so shall they leave behind the delusive echoes of prejudice, and dwell within the perpetual outgoings of divine wisdom. This is that speech and language whose lines have gone out into all the earth, and no confusion of tongues has ever befallen it,' he declared. 'This language we should all strive to understand, first condescending, like little children, to master its alphabet.'[53]

He called on teachers, therefore, to direct their pupils to the immediate realities of nature as well as to the more elevated sources of wisdom available in the traditional classical texts. In language strongly resonant of the tones of the scriptures, he urged them to facilitate a childlike openness towards nature amongst their pupils. 'We must,' he said, 'come as new born children, with open and fresh minds, to the observation of nature. For it is no less true in this human kingdom of knowledge than in God's kingdom of heaven, that no man shall enter into it except as he becomes first as a little child.'[54] Direct experience of nature, precise observation of its laws and phenomena, should be the hallmarks of the new learning, he said. The method of scientific induction became his model for all learning; this led him, in turn, to a recognition of the importance of individual differences and of the need to allow each pupil to learn at his own natural pace—proceeding step by step from the known realities of present experience to the newly discovered realities of the previously unknown. In the *Novum Organum* he had represented the entire process' of knowing as a radically inductive activity. 'Man who is the servant and interpreter of Nature,' he wrote, 'can act and understand no further than he has, either in operation or contemplation, observed the method or order of Nature.'[55] In *De Augmentis* he describes the teacher as someone who 'transplants knowledge into the scholar's mind as it grew in his own.'[56] Using the famous gardener metaphor—a favourite image with Comenius also—he wrote: 'A gardener takes more pains with the young than with the full-grown plant, and men commonly find it needful in any undertaking to begin well.'[57]

Both Bacon and Comenius recognised the necessity of nurturing the *method* of learning in all children in accordance with the spontaneous modes of knowing which are innate in their nature. 'The secret of education lies in method,'[58] Comenius declared. Previously Bacon had said: 'A good method will solve all problems. A cripple on the right path will beat a racer on the wrong path.'[59] Both men were strong advocates of the study of science side by side with the traditional classical disciplines. Both saw the study of nature as ultimately the study of God's creation and both saw the laws of nature as reflecting the presence of God in the conditions of the material universe. Comenius, however, much more emphatically than Bacon, represented all knowledge and wisdom as emanating ultimately from religious faith. This is evident in his discussion of the interrelation of physical, metaphysical and hyperphysical truths in the opening pages of the *Via Lucis*. In the Dedication to the work he spoke of faith as the repository of all wisdom; a similar conviction is affirmed in the opening pages of *The Great Didactic*. To a far greater degree than Bacon, he insisted that the study of finite reality must be conducted from the ultimate perspective of the infinite, i.e. from the standpoint of the inexplicable, mysterious reality that is knowable only through faith.

Comenius was further indebted to Bacon for his ideas on curricular issues, though with the same qualifications as applied in the sphere of classroom pedagogy. In several passages from *The Advancement of Learning* Bacon clearly foreshadowed the Comenian concept of pansophic knowledge. 'For it is necessary to the progression of sciences,' he wrote, 'that readers be of the most able and sufficient men; as those which are ordained for generating and propagating of sciences, and not for transitory use.'[60] He warned against the dangers of over-specialisation, using the ancient metaphor of the interdependence of all physical functions for the healthy functioning of bodily processes: 'First therefore, amongst so many great foundations of colleges in Europe, I find it strange that they are all dedicated to professions, and none left free to arts and sciences at large. For if men judge that learning should be referred to action, they judge well; but in this they fall into the error described in the ancient fable, in which the other parts of the body did suppose the stomach had been idle, because it neither performed the office of motion, as the limbs do, nor of sense, as the head doth: but yet notwithstanding it is the stomach that digesteth and distributeth to all the rest.'[61] In *New Atlantis* he put forward the ideal of encyclopaedic knowledge as the goal of all learning. This is the vision which is conveyed to the traveller by the Father of Solomon's House:

> God bless thee, my son; I will give thee the greatest jewel I have. For I will impart unto thee, for the love of God and men, a relation of the true state of Solomon's House. Son, to make you know the true state of Solomon's House, I will keep this order. First, I will set forth unto you the end of our foundation. Secondly, the preparations and instruments we have for our works. Thirdly, the several employments and functions whereto our fellows are assigned. And fourthly, the ordinances and rites which we observe.
>
> The End of our Foundation is the knowledge of the Causes, and secret motions of things; and the enlarging of the bounds of human Empire, to the effecting of all things possible.[62]

This, as will be shown in more detail presently, clearly points forward to the pansophic ideal that is the foundation of all Comenius's educational thought. It will also become apparent that the Baconian concept of universal knowledge was greatly expanded by Comenius and was much more explicitly informed by the integrating potencies of faith. Before this is discussed, however, it is necessary to demonstrate the subsequent influence of Bacon's pedagogic ideas on the work of some later educators whose writings further anticipate the work of Comenius. The methodological principles developed by Bacon were greatly refined in the work of the German educator, Wolfgang Ratke—one of the figures whom Comenius specifically includes amongst his pedagogic mentors in the Dedicatory Letter preceding *The Great Didactic*.[63] (Comenius probably encountered Ratke's ideas while a student at Herborn.) Following the completion of his education at the Universities of Hamburg and Rostok,

Ratke spent some time in England where he became interested in Bacon's writings and was profoundly influenced by the new realist pedagogy. A Lutheran evangelist, committed both to the Reformation ideal of universal education and to the fostering of self-initiated learning in the manner advocated by Bacon, Ratke effected a sophisticated synthesis of both ideals in a series of pedagogic treatises designed to bring about fundamental reforms in the conditions existing in German schools.

In his Memorial to the Imperial Diet that assembled at Frankfurt in May, 1612, Ratke asked the members to consider how 'there might be conveniently introduced and peacefully established throughout the whole Empire a uniform speech, a uniform government and a uniform religion.'[64] He proposed the idea of a school in which all subjects should be taught through the medium of the vernacular and in which the Bible should be the basic text for linguistic as well as religious instruction. Like Comenius, he tested out his ideas in the practical conditions of the school classroom. There are striking similarities in the two men's careers in this respect. Initially, Ratke took responsibility for the reform of schools in Augsburg, following which he was invited by Prince Anhalt-Gotha to organise schools in the Gotha region along similar lines. At Gotha he trained teachers in the new pedagogic methodology, established a printing press for the production of new textbooks, and supervised the implementation of his reforms in the school classrooms of the region. Special fonts were imported from Holland and skilled compositors were recruited in Rostok and Jena for the production of the new texts. All instruction in the elementary school was conducted through the medium of the mother-tongue. Arithmetic, singing and religion, together with the German vernacular, were taught in the early years; Latin was introduced in the fourth year and Greek in the sixth. The school was visited by teachers from all over Europe. However, much controversy surrounded these experiments—centring mainly on the use of the mother-tongue— and Ratke was imprisoned for eighteen months on charges of professional negligence. Following some short-lived reforms that he introduced in the schools of Magdeburg and Rudolfstadt following his release, he was invited by Chancellor Oxenstierna to introduce similar measures in Swedish schools, but was unable to take up the offer and lived in virtual obscurity at Rudolfstadt for the remainder of his life.

It is in his elaboration of a pedagogic methodology for the elementary school that the importance of Ratke's writings primarily consists. Whereas Bacon's pedagogic reforms were directed largely towards the education of adolescents and young adults, Ratke's were focussed predominantly on the years of early childhood. The fundamental principle of his method was the imitation of nature in all modes of learning. 'Everything according to the order or course of nature' was the guiding principle of his pedagogic thought. 'Since nature uses a specific order proper to herself, by which the understanding of man comprehends everything, regard must be had to this, in the art of teaching; for all non-natural and violent or forcible teaching and learning is harmful and weakens nature,' he wrote.[65] There should be a spontaneous progression, he said, from each stage of learning to the next, in keeping with the processes of nature itself. 'Nothing is a greater hindrance to the understanding than to undertake to learn many things together and at once. It is as if one should undertake to cook pap, fruit, meat, milk and fish in the same kettle. But things should be taken up orderly one after another and one thoroughly dealt with before proceeding to the next.' 'One should undertake nothing new until that which precedes it has been comprehended thoroughly and sufficiently for all purposes,' he wrote.[66] Most importantly, he declared, it is essential that all learning begin with instruction in the mother-tongue:

> Everything first in the mother tongue. For there is this advantage in the mother tongue that the scholar has to think only about the thing he has to learn; and need not trouble himself about the language of it. Besides, if knowledge useful and necessary in common life were put into German and learned in it, everyone, whatever his business, could acquire a much better knowledge of it, so that he could better guide himself in all sorts of things, and better judge of them. How important this would be in religion and government, and in human life generally, will easily be imagined if we reflect what a miserable condition of ignorance and inexperience now prevails. Out of the mother tongue into other languages.[67]

Consistently with this, he opposed compulsion in the classroom in all its forms. 'By compulsion and blows youths are disgusted with their studies, so that study becomes hateful to them. Moreover, it is contrary to nature,' he wrote.[68] He condemned methods of enforcing discipline that relied on fear and coercion: 'The pupil should not be afraid of the teacher but should hold him in love and reverence. . . . For if the teacher rightly exercises his office it will not fail but that the boy shall take up a love for him and for his studies.'[69] He especially opposed the widely encouraged practice of learning by rote: 'Nothing must be learned by heart (i.e. by rote). It is a compulsion of nature; violence is done to the understanding; and accordingly experience shows us that any one who applies himself much to learning by heart loses much in understanding and intellectual keenness.'[70] All learning, he declared, should be based on individual experience and on the innate powers of intellectual discovery present in the nature of every child. Adopting the Baconian motto, *Per inductionem et experimentum omnia*, he urged educators to insist that all truths be verified through empirical investigation: 'No rule or system is admissible which is not thoroughly investigated anew and rightly founded on proof, whether or not many or all have written about it or held so and so. . . . No authority is admissible simply as such, unless cause and ground are given. Nor has established prescription any validity, for it gives no certainty.'[71]

All of this signified a sea-change from the methods of teaching that had been practised for centuries in the scholastic institutions. The ideas developed by Ratke were to find expression in a fully developed pedagogic system in the writings of Comenius. Both shared a passionate belief that learning should follow the laws and order of nature; both shared a profound belief in the importance of vernacular instruction, in the value of sense experience, and in the need for non-coercive discipline. Most of all, they were both motivated ultimately by their faith in the power of education to effect moral and religious reform. This became the ruling and all-encompassing aim of all their initiatives in education.

Similar affinities can be seen between Comenius and another of the realists whom he also acknowledges in *The Great Didactic* as one of the educators whose work inspired his projected innovations in school pedagogy. In the Introduction to the work he speaks of John Valentine Andreae as one who 'in his golden writings has laid bare the diseases not only of the Church and the state but also of the schools, and has pointed out the remedies.'[72] He generously acknowledges a letter which he had received from Andreae approving of his writings and urging him to 'proceed with my efforts.' 'Stimulated by this, my spirit began to take more daring flights,' he writes, 'till at last my unbounded solicitude for the public good led me to take the matter thoroughly in hand.' Encouraged by Andreae, he resolved, he said, to 'investigate the matter thoughtfully and seek out the causes, principles, the methods and the objects of the art of teaching.'[73] He was impressed by the attention given to mathematics and science by Andreae and was especially enthusiastic for the moral regeneration of society that he put forward in the Christianopolis, his vision of a utopian Christian society.[74] There are significant affinities between the treatment of elementary education in this work and the proposals developed by Comenius for the School of Infancy both in The Great Didactic and the Pampaedia.

It was John Henry Alsted, Comenius's friend and teacher at Herborn, however, who represented his most direct link with the realist movement. Though a mere four years older than his most famous pupil, Alsted already had a well-established reputation as a scholar when Comenius arrived in Herborn in 1610. By that time Alsted had already made important contributions to philosophy and theology. The major work of his life, his *Encyclopaedia Scientiarum Omnium*, which was completed some years later, foreshadowed Comenius's ideal of pansophic knowledge. Significantly indebted to Ratke for its pedagogic insights, the work defined an approach to classroom methodology that closely followed the realist ideal of fostering the natural processes of learning in the child. The following series of pedagogic axioms from the work includes familiar Baconian (and Comenian) principles, such as the grading of subject-content, the encouraging of a spirit of natural discipline, and the provision of instruction in the mother-tongue:

1. Not more than one thing should be taught at a time.
2. Not more than one book should be used on one subject, and not more than one subject should be taught on one day.
3. Everything should be taught through the medium of what is more familiar.
4. All superfluity should be avoided.
5. All study should be mapped out in fixed periods.
6. All rules should be as short as possible.
7. Everything should be taught without severity, though discipline must be maintained.
8. Corporal punishment should be reserved for moral offences, and never inflicted for lack of industry.
9. Authority should not be allowed to prejudice the mind against the facts gleaned from experience; nor should custom or preconceived opinion prevail.
10. The constructions of a new language should first be explained in the vernacular.
11. No language should be taught by means of grammar.
12. Grammatical terms should be the same in all languages.[75]

Alsted put forward elaborate proposals for the founding of vernacular schools, though what he envisaged was significantly more restricted than what Comenius put forward in *The Great Didactic*. He saw the vernacular school as being appropriate only for those who were unsuited to the more erudite standards of the Latin school. Thus, he suggested the vernacular schools provide for two categories of pupil, i.e. for girls and for boys who were destined to work as manual labourers. Latin schools, he said, should be founded for boys 'whose parents are in such a station that they may hope for a more fruitful intellectual culture.'[76] Even in the Latin schools, however, he conceded that some pupils might have to be instructed in the vernacular, if they found studying through the medium of a second language was too difficult. Underlying his views on this issue was a keen concern to provide adequately for individual differences. 'The teacher,' he wrote, 'should be a skilled reader of character, that he may be able to classify the dispositions of his pupils. . . . Unless he pays great attention to differences of disposition, he will but waste all the effort that he expends in teaching.'[77] Like Comenius, Alsted saw the

fostering of piety side by side with the fostering of learning as the twin
objectives of all elementary and secondary education. 'O ye schools,
inscribe the characters of piety and humanity,' he cried.[78]

From the realists, therefore, Comenius derived some of the most
fundamental and most liberal principles of his pedagogic philosophy. Just
as the Moravian Church had provided him with his all-embracing religious ideals, and the Reformation with his vision of education as a universal activity accessible to the whole of mankind, just as the Renaissance
heritage of classical humanism provided him with much of his thinking
on the character and content of school learning, so the realist movement
provided him with some of the most innovative principles of his pedagogic methodology. Its influence was manifested in his conviction that
the fostering of learning should be modelled on the spontaneous, self-
initiated and enquiry-based tendencies of nature itself; it was further
manifested in his insistence on the need for elementary instruction to be
conducted always through the medium of the mother tongue, in his
emphasis on the importance of sense-experience, in his recognition of the
need to accommodate individual differences, in his advocacy of consensual,
non-coercive modes of discipline. It was manifested yet again in his
affirmation of the essentially integrated character of all knowledge, in his
sense of the need for a curriculum sufficiently broad to include the
whole world of science and the study of natural phenomena, and in his
insistence that the content of the curriculum be graded systematically to
take account of the sequential stages of each children's formation and
development.

His pedagogic insights reflected the character of their realist origins,
not only in their emphasis on the grounding of all learning in individual
experience but in their inductive derivation of pedagogic method from
direct observation of classroom practice. In this they revolutionised the
character of educational theory, replacing the *a priori* determined abstrac-
tions of classical philosophy with the empirically based insights of a
pedagogy that was based on direct observation of how children learn. In
all these areas, however, his guiding principles remained those of the
Christian vision that informed every facet of his educational thought.
The reforms he advocated in the method and content of learning were
simply part of a more general process of spiritual and moral betterment
to which all his life's activities were directed. The ideal of universal
education was ultimately an ethico-religious ideal; it derived its full
justification from his belief in the educability of all men and in their
right to have access to the processes of education and learning that
would ensure their full personal formation. The reforms he advocated in
matters of school pedagogy were simply the means he considered
necessary for the full realisation of this vision.

I V

THE COMENIAN VISION OF UNIVERSAL EDUCATION

I. THE AIMS OF UNIVERSAL EDUCATION

The ideal of universal education, as conceived by Comenius, was concerned with the cultivation of an integrated concept of wisdom that comprehended three main elements: learning, morality and faith. It aimed to do so in a manner that would emphasise the essential and indivisible unity of the ideal of wisdom and that would ensure its accessibility to all, regardless of social background, intellectual ability or religious creed. The manner in which this ideal was formulated and developed in his writings will be the concern of the opening section of this chapter. A further section will explore the institutional implications of this ideal and will look particularly at the concept of the school that was developed by Comenius to ensure the fulfilment of the goal of universal education. A third section will examine his theories of learning, giving particular attention to the ideal of 'learning through experience' which was his most radical and innovative contribution to an understanding of the nature of the educational process. A fourth will examine the role of the teacher and the principles of effective pedagogic practice that are developed in his writings. A final section will identify the principles of curriculum content and practice that he considered necessary for the realisation of the ideal of universal education.

But firstly it is necessary to dwell briefly on the method and style of his work so that an appropriate conceptual framework can be defined for the elucidation of the basic principles of his educational thought. The previous chapter described the new style of empirically-oriented educational thought that emerged in Europe under the influence of the realist movement in the early decades of the seventeenth century. This was a style characterised by concretion and simplicity and by a particularised clarity of statement that differed radically from the abstract, rationalistic formulations of classical thought. In the case of Comenius this method of thought formulation blended easily with the non-rationalistic, mythic style of the Moravian tradition of Christian thought in which he had been immersed since his childhood. His assimilation of these two traditions was manifested in a highly personalistic, narrative-evocative style of writing that proved to be entirely appropriate for the authentic expression of the integrated ideal of faith, learning and moral truth that he sought to convey in his educational writings.

The justification of this method may be found in two of his major treatises: the *Labyrinth* and the *Via Lucis*. In the first of these his distaste for rationalistic abstraction is conveyed vividly in the Pilgrim's ironic caricature of the world of classical scholarship. In the tenth chapter of the work he describes the 'strange warfare' that passed for learned debate amongst the scholars: 'Then we again enter the market-place of the learned, and behold, there were quarrels, strife, scuffles, tumult among them. Rarely was there one who had not a squabble with another; for not only the young ones (with whom it could be imputed to the insolence of undeveloped youth) but even the old men plundered one another. . . . For no sooner had one given out an opinion than another straightly contradicted it; they disputed even as to whether snow was white or black, fire hot or cold.'[1] In the sequence where the Pilgrim finds himself amongst the logicians, natural philosophers and metaphysicians, he bitingly satirises their rationalistic methods of discourse. The logicians are shown purchasing eye-glasses called 'notiones secundae' which they believe will enable them 'to perceive everything, not superficially only, but also to the innermost core.'[2] Finding the glasses inadequate for this purpose, they join forces with the natural philosophers whom they expect, by virtue of *their* greater rationalistic resources, to be able to penetrate the essence of reality more successfully. Again they are unsuccessful. 'I saw clearly,' the Pilgrim says, 'that they had indeed broken and crushed the outward rind and shell in which the kernel lay embedded was intact. Then seeing here also vain ostentation and idle striving (for some indeed, stared till their eyes pained them, and gnawed till they broke their teeth), I proposed that we should go elsewhere.'[3] Thereafter he joins the metaphysicians:

> Then we enter another hall, and behold here, these philosophical gentlemen—having before them cows, donkeys, wolves, serpents, and various wild animals, birds and reptiles, as well as wood, stone, water, fire, clouds, stars and planets, and even angels—disputed as to how each creature could be deprived of that which distinguished it from the others, so that all should become similar; and they took from them first the shape, then the material, at last all accessories, so that at last the mere ens remained. And then they disputed as to whether all things were one and the same, whether all things are verily that which they are; and they asked each other more questions such as these. Noticing this, some began to wonder, and to tell how

high human wit had risen, so that it was able to surpass all creatures, and to divest all corporeal things of their corporeality. At last I also began to delight in these subtleties. But then, one rising up declared that such things were mere phantasies, and they should desist from them. And he drew some away with him; but others, again, arose and condemned him as a heretic, saying that he separated men from philosophy, which is the highest knowledge, and, as it were, the head 'atrium'. And after listening sufficiently to these disputes, I went away from this spot.[4]

A key passage for an understanding of the precise method of Comenius's thought, its subtle mockery points to the absurdity of thought that is founded exclusively on rationalistic sources. The theme is sustained in the sequence from Chapter 16 where the Pilgrim reflects on the essential ignorance of the academic masters and doctors. In this instance his target is the distortion of truth that occurs in the name of specialisation and abstraction. 'But none the less, I, who ever wished to see what would happen to these men, watched one of these masters of arts; then they asked him to count something together, but he knew not how to do so; then they told him to measure something, he knew not how to do so. They asked him to name the stars, he knew not how to do it; they asked him how to expound syllogisms, he knew not how to do it; they asked him to talk in strange tongues, he knew not how to do it . . . '[5] In the *Via Lucis*, as he ponders further on the inadequacies of rationalist thought—in this instance attributing them specifically to the influence of the post-Socratic Greek philosophers—he calls for a new holistic philosophy to replace the sterility of classical abstraction:

> Finally, for this end a new philosophy must be set up in a new light, so that there may be no reason for the continuance of that old philosophy of the Greeks which has been convicted in so many ways of being inferior and insufficient, confused and ill-ordered and yet noisy and impetuous, and has inflicted so many injuries upon the Christian spirit. A new philosophy must be set up so that the children of Israel need no more be forced to turn to the Philistines to get their ploughs and hoes and axes and trowels sharpened, but may possess at home their own swords and all other necessary equipment, and not be found wanting in the day of battle.[6]

The passage provides the key to the integrated concept of thought that pervades all of Comenius's writings. Wisdom, not mere knowledge, is the means to truth; wisdom comprehends reason and faith, embracing both their harmony and conflict. Though he saw reason as being ultimately subordinate to faith—in the *Via Lucis* he spoke of 'bringing the

whole intellect to accept the sovereignty of faith'[7]—he equally emphasised
its potentiality, particularly in the sphere of scientific enquiry, to disclose
the mysteries of the infinite in the finite reality of the material world. 'It
was not without reason,' he writes, 'that Augustine uttered the warning
that no man ignorant of numbers and science should presume to investigate the mysteries of God.'[8] The ultimate meaningfulness of reality
would be disclosed only, he said, by way of this radical integration of
reason and faith. Correspondingly, he saw the mythic-narrative method of
thought as alone being sufficiently comprehensive to embrace its depth
and complexity.

The fundamental justification of this insistence on a necessary fusion
of reason and faith is to be found in his beliefs about the ultimate
destiny of man—beliefs that were profoundly and intrinsically religious
within the traditions of the Moravian interpretations of Christian truth.
In the opening pages of *The Great Didactic* he wrote: 'Reason itself
dictates that such a perfect creature [as man] is destined to a higher end
than all other creatures, that of being united with God, the culmination
of all perfection, glory and happiness, and of enjoying with Him absolute
glory and happiness for ever.'[9] In the same pages he stressed the complexity of man's nature: its comprehension of the material and the
spiritual, the finite and the infinite. Because of the peculiar complexity
of his nature, he says, man must necessarily reach towards the infinite by
way of the finite; he must reach towards the spiritual by way of the
materiality of the temporal universe. For this he must draw from the
resources both of reason and faith—from their tensions and contradictions,
and ultimately, from their intrinsic harmony.

The 'way of light', therefore—to adopt the metaphorical language of
the *Via Lucis*—is the way of reason and faith, of the unified wisdom that
leads finally to God. This is the central theme of that work. Significantly,
the title comes both from the Book of Job—the great Biblical treatise on
man's triumph over despair—and the Book of Jeremiah, the treatise on
justice and the rights of all men to the spiritual and material benefits
conferred on them by God. Both principles are central to the Comenian
vision of education: the first pointing to the primary function of
education as the fostering of wisdom and the quest for truth, the second
pointing to the necessity of ensuring its accessibility to the whole of
humankind. Underlying both is the fundamental axiom that wisdom—
both the light of reason and of faith—is to be attained in the conditions
of the material world. Though the ultimate concern of man is union
with his Creator, that prospect, he suggests, must be fulfilled in the
conditions of everyday life. The process, he says, is endlessly empowered
by the innate potentiality for its fulfilment which is universally present
in the nature of humankind:

For we human beings love what is good for us so far as we perceive it; for our will, the mistress and queen of our actions, always and everywhere follows reason, the servant of her purposes, and whatever at the dictate of reason she sees or believes to be good and useful commands our strength to pursue and attain it. The human will cannot but act in this way, for it is made in the image of God and cannot divest itself of the love of what is good—whether good in reality or only in seeming.

If, then, there be granted this Universal Light of the mind, in which men can truly see all things which are truly good and recognise that all things which are below the sky have been placed and are intended to remain below it (unless, indeed, they are to pass away and perish), the fervent desire to seek after those good things and to avoid the evils which are contrary to them, will be indeed kindled.[10]

If wisdom is the light which illuminates existence, ignorance, he says, is the darkness of man's unfulfilled potentiality for wisdom and truth. This is the darkness of unawareness, the darkness of a mind unillumined by its own innate resources: 'He who knows not that he is ill cannot heal himself; he who feels not his pain utters no sigh; he who sees not his danger does not start back, even though he be on the edge of the abyss.'[11] The ignorant man is one who lacks awareness of his own destiny: 'Instead of the circumspection with which those who are destined for eternity ought to prepare themselves for it, there reigns such forgetfulness, not only of eternity but also of mortality, that most men give themselves up to what is earthly and transient, yea, even to the death that stands before them.'[12] Ignorance, he further suggests, holds a certain attraction for man, since it facilitates an evasion of his *responsibility* for the attainment of wisdom and truth: 'Persons who are ignorant and astray, because of their unsteadiness and inconstancy, generally flee from or refuse the light of truth.'[13] Ignorance, like wisdom, is a condition deeply rooted in man's nature, being indicative of its radical fallenness. Man, he suggests, lives in perpetual tension between the darkness of ignorance and unbelief and the light of wisdom and truth. 'As the light retreats, the darkness comes on; when the light advances the darkness withdraws. . . .

Every opaque body, the interior of which is shut up, is a spectacle of darkness (as a stone at its heart). So a man, deprived of his senses, or unwilling to direct them to the contemplation of things, or not knowing how to do so, or neglecting to do it, must be full of darkness within himself. . . . An opaque body when placed in the light is illuminated on one side, but remains in darkness on the other. . . . So man, established in the world and surrounded by his

own body and by corporeal things, is illuminated so far as he turns
himself to gather the light of wisdom; but in so far as he is beset
and affected and influenced by earthly things, so far he is plunged
in darkness. Anything which turns itself away from the light, by
that very act covers itself with darkness. . . . So the intellect, if it
turns inward upon itself and away from facts, produces for itself
the darkness of hallucination in preference to true knowledge. So
the will of man if it turns from God and from his true light,
whatever other pleasures it may get for its delight, is responsible
for having darkness instead of facts.[14]

Deliverance from darkness comes with man's perception of light: the
light that dispels ignorance and confusion. The fostering of the innate
potentiality for light that is present in all men is one of the chief goals of
education. 'And if any human aid were needed for this,' he writes in the
Via Lucis, 'I thought that it would only come from the better instruction
of the young in all matters from the most elementary to the most
fundamental if they are to be delivered from the mazes of the world.'[15]
The wisdom that illuminates the mind and that education seeks to foster
is the harmony of all knowing potencies—of reason, will and faith. Its
growth is not automatic or spontaneous: it requires the formative attention
of the educator. 'For men must be taught eternal things, because being
destined for eternity they cannot be ignorant of their end without risk of
eternal loss.'[16] Again he emphasises the need to reach towards the
infinite and the spiritual by way of the material and the finite. 'And they
must also be taught temporal things, because the path to the eternal is
through the temporal.'[17] All modes of knowing must necessarily be
unified in facilitating the perception of this finite-infinite panharmony
which is the ultimate source of all meaning in life. A truly universal
education, therefore, must accommodate the perspectives of reason and
faith, the material and the spiritual, the secular and the sacred:

> I have said also that theological and philosophical matters are to be
> taught: I mean those which belong on the one hand to the domain
> of faith and on the other to the domain of reason and of the senses.
> Those that belong to the domain of faith must on all accounts be
> taught, because the just man shall live by his faith; this is the one
> and only way of eternal life. Those matters which belong to the
> domain of reason we must also know; because by these we are
> distinguished from the brutes, and are protected from being easily
> persuaded by impostors to accept in a false belief things which are
> contrary to reason. But we must not be ignorant of the things of
> the senses; because they smooth the way for reason and safeguard it
> against deception. The senses minister to reason, and reason ministers

to Faith, and therefore none of these things can be absent from the perfect Light, or else we shall certainly be deprived of the instruments for illuminating the mind.[18]

What emerges from all this is a holistic vision of education, the focus of which is the simultaneous and integrated development of all the fundamental potentialities of nature. In *The Great Didactic* Comenius identifies three elements as constituting the ideal of holistic development. They are: learning, virtue and piety. The first he defines as 'knowledge of all things, arts and tongues'; the second as 'the whole disposition of our movements, internal and external'; and the third as 'the inner veneration by which the mind of man attaches and binds itself to the supreme Godhead.'[19] The fostering of these three is the primary goal of a genuinely universal education. 'To know oneself (and with oneself all things), to rule oneself, and to direct oneself to God'—these, he declares are the three primary objectives governing the entire educational process. 'In these three things is situated the whole excellence of man, for they alone are the foundation of the present and of the future life.'[20] These aims are further elaborated in the *Pampaedia* where he insists again that 'not only some part of man but the WHOLE MAN must be fully developed in all the qualities that help to make human nature perfect.'[21] Advocating the education of all men in the fundamentals of knowledge, morality and faith, he draws on the authority of classical and Judaeo-Christian sources to underline the historical continuity of the universal ideal:

If Cicero was right in declaring that the function of wisdom is to promote the culture of mankind; if it was the holy wish of Moses, the man of God, that God would put his spirit upon all the people; if there is comfort in the promise of our most holy God that one day He will pour out His spirit upon all flesh; if in time we must absolutely obey Christ's command that all nations shall be taught all things whatsoever he hath commanded; if we are to emulate the zeal of the holy apostles in teaching every man in all wisdom to present every man perfect in Christ; it is my desire that we should come closer to that function, that prayer, that hope, that commandment and that zeal during the present age, and find a way of applying men's minds to the task of putting the world in order, just as things have already been put in order by the spreading of light, so that as all things are co-ordinated and connected by the eternal laws of truth (as we have already seen in my *Pansophia*) men also may be able to share in the light, the truth and the order of our world, every individual and every community achieving true harmony.[22]

In the *Via Lucis* the same theme is expressed in terms of the three main types of knowledge that Comenius suggests education must foster. They are: knowledge of external reality (physical knowledge), knowledge of internal reality (metaphysical knowledge) and the knowledge that reaches beyond the realm of nature (hyperphysical knowledge). Each of these serves as a means by which the other can be attained, he says. Man must proceed from sense experience (physical knowledge) to the knowledge disclosed through reason, and must further proceed from the world of reason to the world of faith. The first is nurtured by nature itself, the second by the inner resources of the mind, the third by the revealed word of the scriptures. Taking the central metaphor of wisdom as light, he sees the growth of knowledge as a cumulative process—a cumulative illumination of sense, mind and spirit: 'Every light-giving thing sends forth rays . . . so everything that is true has an idea or form which it sends forth from itself and by which it may be known. . . . Every light-giving thing sends forth rays *always* . . . sends forth rays in all directions . . . the more anything has the quality of light-giving, the more it sends forth rays.'[23] Truth manifests itself in all things, endlessly radiating its own light on all which the mind sees and contemplates. The profoundest illumination comes when all rays converge on a single unifying focus:

> When several lights unite their rays cause a greater illumination. (This is evident: a room is much more brightly illuminated by several candles than by a single candle). So with the mind; the greater the number of things which can be known or are known it possesses, the greater is its light of knowledge. . . .
>
> Rays of light can be gathered, united and condensed in such a way as that they come together in a point. This result is produced by the gathering and forcing together of the rays of light, by a transparent concave instrument. By a similar procedure the powers of the mind can be concentrated through the recollection of sensations and images, and by their fastening upon some single subject.
>
> Light condensed in this way shines and burns with its highest potency. . . . So the rays of the intellect, if collected upon a single point, can be bent and brought to bear most powerfully upon the spirit, so that, not only do they set the intellect vehemently ablaze, but also kindle and inflame the will; and this is true even when they are collected and turned upon matters—earthly, impure and unwholesome matters—quite unworthy of that ardent concentration.
>
> Light is to be found principally in light-giving things, and next and secondarily in things illuminated. So truth is to be found principally in things and next and secondarily in the minds of persons who shrewdly perceive and understand things.[24]

If, as Comenius repeatedly affirms, the common human need for personal self-fulfilment is attained through the three-fold process of moral, spiritual and intellectual illumination just described, it must follow that all men, without exception, should be given access to this. Emphasising the general applicability of this truth, he affirms the accompanying principle of universal educability: all men, he declares, innately possess the potency to learn. In the Dedication to the *Via Lucis* he writes: 'For all men alike have innate principles of three kinds, matching the necessities of all kinds of action, knowing, willing and achieving. In every man there are innate Norms of knowledge, which are called common Notions, and the stimuli of Desire, which we name Common Instincts; and the organs for doing everything, which it may be permissible to call Common Faculties.'[25] He further insists on the common basic character of these potentialities. 'We believe,' he writes, 'that knowing, willing and doing are present in the same manner throughout the order of human nature in all nations, ages and conditions.'[26] In one of the most eloquent passages in the work he describes the universal presence in all mankind of the 'inborn desire to know':

> Go into the shops of the workmen, the cottages of country folk, the houses of high civil and military officers, the palaces of Kings, the assemblies of Empires, the dwellings in which parents live with their children, and wherever men are to be found, you will find them—nay, you will find even the solitary man in the wilderness—occupied in teaching and learning. And that men do not fall into these occupations (of teaching and learning) by chance, but that they are born to them, is evident from this fact: that every man has inborn in him the desire to know, and to inquire into things which may be known, and then to communicate to others what he has learnt, and even to draw other men by winning persuasion, or if that should not suffice, to compel them by force if they show any unwillingness to accept what he knows or believes or thinks.[27]

These positions are reiterated both in *The Great Didactic* and in the *Pampaedia*. In Chapters 5, 6 and 7 of the former he emphasises the innate tendencies towards learning, virtue and piety that are present in all, though he equally stresses the counter-tendencies to ignorance, sloth and corruption with which they must contend. 'It is evident,' he writes, 'that man is naturally capable of acquiring a knowledge of all things since, in the first place, he is the image of God.' 'So unlimited is the capacity of the mind,' he writes, 'that, in the process of perception, it resembles an abyss . . . for the mind, neither in heaven nor anywhere outside heaven, can a boundary be fixed.'[28] In the *Pampaedia* he declares 'the means to wisdom are granted to all men' and he reaffirms the

common character of learning potentiality in all of mankind. 'For the
inner structure of all men is as uniform as their outward bodily structure,'
he writes. 'What one human being is or has or wishes or knows or is
capable of doing, all others are or have or wish or know or are capable
likewise.'[29] The inborn desire to know is accompanied by innate tendencies towards virtue and piety. In *The Great Didactic* he writes: 'The
truth of the statement that the seeds of virtue are born with man is
bound up with a twofold argument: 1) every man delights in harmony,
2) man himself, externally and internally, is nothing but a harmony.'[30]
The potency of will, he suggests, is the key to the pursuit of this harmony
inherent in the nature of man and in the universe he inhabits.

Given his belief in the universal need for education to achieve the
goals of moral, spiritual and intellectual illumination, and given his belief
in a corresponding presence in mankind of a universal potentiality for
knowledge, virtue and piety, it was entirely logical for Comenius to proclaim a vision of education that identified the goal of *universal provision
of education* as his primary and all-embracing objective. The title page of
The Great Didactic has the following inscription: 'The Great Didactic:
Setting Forth the Whole Art of Teaching All Things to All Men or A
Certain Inducement to Found Such Schools in all the Parishes, Towns
and Villages of every Christian Kingdom that the entire Youth of both
sexes, none being excepted, shall Quickly, Pleasantly and Thoroughly
Become learned in the Sciences, pure in Morals, trained to Piety and in
this manner instructed in all things necessary for the present and the
future life.'[31] 'Not the children of the rich and the powerful only, but of
all alike, boys and girls, both noble and ignoble, rich and poor, in all
cities and towns, villages and hamlets, should be sent to school'—he
declares emphatically in the tenth chapter of this work.[32] All men, he
writes, in the *Via Lucis*, deserve to enter on the Way of Light. Those
privileged to possess the light of wisdom must see to it, he says 'that
schools are set up in every nation, town and village and upon this matter
they will give advice to the magistrates and other persons who are in
power and authority.'[33] 'The expressed wish,' he writes in the *Pampaedia*,
'is for full power of development into full humanity not of one particular
person or a few or even many, but of *every single individual*, young and
old, rich and poor, noble and ignoble, men and women—in a word, of
every human being born on earth, with the ultimate aim of providing
education to the entire human race regardless of age, class, sex and
nationality.'[34]

The moral health of any society depends, he says, on its capacity to
provide a good education for all its citizens. 'For every man will understand,' he declares in the *Via Lucis*, 'that the welfare of each individual
(including his own) depends upon the general welfare of all.'[35] To the
charge that the indiscriminate promotion of learning must result inevitably

in a general deterioration of its quality and status he responds: 'The condition must be wretched, whether of state or religion, the stability of which depends upon the ignorance and slavery of its subjects.'[36] On the further charge that some will be unable to benefit from a full education— he specifically mentions the physically and mentally handicapped, the backward and the stupid—he argues that, in these instances, the need for education is all the greater, in view of the extent of individual need and inadequacy. 'There is no exemption from human education except for non-humans,' he declares in the *Pampaedia*.[37] In *The Great Didactic* he pleads for a sensitive response by educators to the special needs of those less gifted by nature than themselves:

> Nor is it any obstacle that some seem to be naturally dull and stupid, for this renders more imperative the universal culture of such intellects. The slower and the weaker the disposition of any man, the more he needs assistance, that he may throw off his brutish dullness and stupidity as much as possible. Nor can any man be found whose intellect is so weak that it cannot be improved by culture. A sieve, if you continually pour water through it, grows cleaner and cleaner, although it cannot retain the liquid; and, in the same way, the dull and the weak-minded, though they may make no advance in letters, become softer in disposition and learn to obey the civil magistrates and the ministers of the Church. There have, besides, been many instances in which those who are naturally stupid have gained such a grasp of the sciences as to excel those who were more gifted. As the poet truly says: 'Industry overcomes all obstacles.' Again, just as some men are strong as children, but afterwards grow sick and ailing, while others, whose bodies are sickly and undersized in youth, develop into robust and tall men; so it is with intellects. Some develop early, but soon wear out and grow dull, while others, originally stupid, become sharp and penetrating. In our orchards we like to have not only trees that bring forth early fruit, but also those that are late-bearing; for each thing, as says the son of Sirach, finds praise in its season, and at length, though late, shows that it has not existed in vain. Why, therefore, should we wish that in the garden of letters only one class of intellects, the forward and active, should be tolerated? Let none be excluded unless God has denied him sense and intelligence.[38]

Not alone did Comenius argue for the provision of education for all, without exception, but, as will be shown presently, he further insisted that a well-balanced education, embracing the classical range of disciplines, be made available to all, whether in the years of childhood or in adult life. 'Our wish is that every human being should be rightly developed and perfectly educated not in any limited sense but in every respect that makes for the perfection of human nature,' he writes in the *Pampaedia*.[39] All should be developed 'towards full humanity'; all should have the chance to become 'wholly civilised.' All this was subject, however, to one important qualification. The vision of universal education put forward by Comenius was wholly dependent on his belief in the educability of all mankind. But while asserting the educability of all men, and while affirming the innate potency towards learning, virtue and piety that is present in all, he qualified this with the further assertion that 'the actual knowledge, virtue and piety are not so given.' They must be acquired, he said, by 'prayer, by education and by action.'[40] The tendencies of nature itself must be carefully cultivated and trained:

> Let none believe, therefore, that any can really be a man, unless he have learned to act like one, that is, have been trained in those elements which constitute a man. This is evident from the example of all things created. which, although destined for man, do not suit his uses until fitted for them by his hands. For example, stones have been given to us as material with which to build houses, towers, walls, pillars etc.; but they are of no use until they are cut and laid in their place by us. Pearls and precious stones destined to adorn man must be cut, ground, and polished. The metals, which are of vital use in daily life, have to be dug out, melted, refined, and variously cast and hammered. Till this is done they are of less use to us than common earth.[41]

Comenius believed that major reforms in education would have to be undertaken if this wholly admirable ideal of universal education was to become a realisable goal. He envisaged reforms occurring in four main areas: a) in the institutions of learning, b) in a deepened understanding of the nature of learning and the needs of the individual learner, c) in the methodology of teaching, and d) in the construction and selection of school curricula. Each will be examined individually in the four remaining sections of this chapter.

2. THE UNIVERSAL SCHOOL

Comenius's writings provide a strong defence of the concept of formal schooling, albeit with some severe criticisms of contemporary educational institutions. He saw the conventional school as the most appropriate agency for the realisation of the goals of universal education. What he envisaged— both in terms of its uniform character, its ethos, its organisational structures, its curriculum and range of activities—strongly resembles the modern comprehensive school, though he saw both elementary and secondary schooling as merely phases in the process of lifelong education, for the later periods of which he envisaged a variety of alternative institutions. His conception of the elementary and secondary stages of schooling will be examined in this present section; a later chapter will deal specifically with his treatment of adult and higher education.

His defence of the conventional school rests on three main considerations. In common with all the major educational innovators of the Reformation period, Comenius believed firmly in the role of parents as the primary educators, and consistently emphasised this in his writings. In *The Great Didactic* he spoke of the duty of parents to ensure that 'the lives for which they are responsible shall be rational, virtuous and pious.'[42] Equally, he recognised their limitations in fulfilling this task satisfactorily—'it is rare to find men who have either sufficient knowledge or sufficient leisure to instruct their children', he writes.[43] He conceded the need, therefore, to employ persons professionally equipped with the skills of teaching to fulfil this task satisfactorily in the best interests of the child. The persons chosen, he said, should be 'conspicuous for their knowledge of affairs and their soberness of morals.'[44] Secondly, he defended schools on the basis of the need for uniformity of provision, seeing them as the means by which the goal of common and equitable educational practice could be ensured. In the *Pampaedia* he extols the virtues of 'group teaching' from this particular standpoint:

> Group teaching enables us to offer them more branches of learning and to implant better morals, and in the course of time to eliminate more errors, and finally to effect a great saving of labour and expense as the services of the best teachers are available not only for individuals but for all, to instil all the essentials into all pupils at the same time; and this has the effect of making every public school (1) *a health centre* to teach men how to live and grow strong, (2) *a wrestling-ring* for them to become accustomed to training in agility and strength to their life-long benefit, (3) *a place of enlightenment* where the minds of all may shine in the light of the sciences, (4) *a school of oratory* where all are given practice in the skilful use of language and speech, (5) *a laboratory*, where people are not allowed to live like crickets in the meadows, wasting time in idle chirping, but are all constantly at work like ants in their nest, (6) *workshops for the virtues*, all serving to refine every member of the school, (7) *a model of the political state*, where all are taught to serve and in turn be leaders as in a miniature republic, and to acquire even in boyhood the habit of exerting control over things, over themselves, and over others (where fate happens to have imposed on some the responsibility of leadership), (8) *lastly, a visible church* where a shep-

herd of their souls and guardian of their consciences will be appointed to inspire everyone through knowledge of God to true worship of divinity.[45]

The range of activities envisaged here—moral, religious, academic, social, physical and political—is extraordinarily comprehensive for its time, and the whole statement could serve as a general definition of objectives for the role of the school even in the enormously more complex conditions of the present age. Comenius further defended his belief in formal schooling on the basis of the historical evidence of its efficacy. The precedents which he cites—the Hebrew schools described by Josephus, the Chaldean schools in the age of Nebuchadnezzar, the synagogues where the Levites taught the Judaic Law, the Greek and Roman academies, the scholastic centres of learning—all, he said, provided historical confirmation of the virtues of group teaching. What they especially attested to was a process of moral exemplification through which desired habits of learning, virtue and piety were fostered, not only directly by individual teachers but indirectly through the collectivist ethos of the institution itself:

> And although there might be parents with leisure to educate their own children, it is nevertheless better that the young should be taught together and in large classes, since better results and more pleasure are to be obtained when one pupil serves as an example and a stimulus for another. For to do what we see others do, to go where others go, to follow those who are ahead of us, and to keep in front of those who are behind us, is the course of action to which we are all most naturally inclined. . . .
>
> Young children, especially, are always more easily led by example than by precept. If you give them a precept, it makes but little impression; if you point out that others are doing something, they imitate without being told to do so.
>
> Again, nature is always showing us by examples that whatever is to be produced in abundance must be produced in some one place. Thus, for instance, wood is produced in quantities in forests, grass in fields, fish in lakes, and metals in the bowels of the earth.[46]

'Schools,' he continues, must 'produce, purify and multiply the light of wisdom and distribute it to *the whole body* of the human community.'[47] Major reforms would have to be effected in conventional schools, he said, if such an ideal were to become a realisable aim. Those passages from the *Labyrinth* in which he describes the conditions in conventional schools—the mechanistic modes of didactic teaching, the grinding drill of repetitive learning, the harsh and brutal methods of enforcing discipline—will be recalled from an earlier chapter. The tenth chapter of *The*

Great Didactic, 'Is It Possible to Reform Schools', provides a general outline of the reforms he believed should be undertaken. Conceding that the 'perfect school has never yet existed,' he argues that the aspiration towards creating it must nonetheless be pursued. His specification of aims gives particular emphasis to the creation of a healthy, consensual, non-coercive school ethos, the provision of a broad traditionalist curriculum: and above all, the adoption of pedagogic practices that would foster 'natural' processes of learning:

> We promise, then, such a system of education that
> (1) All the young shall be educated (except those to whom God has denied understanding).
> (2) And in all those subjects which are able to make a man wise, virtuous and pious.
> (3) That the process of education, being a preparation for life, shall be completed before maturity is reached.
> (4) That this education shall be conducted without blows, rigour, or compulsion, as gently and pleasantly as possible, and in the most natural manner (just as a living body increases in size without any straining or forcible extension of the limbs; since if food, care and exercise are properly supplied, the body grows and becomes strong, gradually, imperceptibly, and of its own accord. In the same way I maintain that nutriment, care, and exercise, prudently supplied to the mind, lead it naturally to wisdom, virtue and piety.)
> (5) That the education given shall not be false but real, not superficial but thorough; that is to say, that the rational animal, man, shall be guided, not by the intellects of other men, but by his own; shall not merely read the opinions of others and grasp their meaning or commit them to memory and repeat them, but shall himself penetrate to the root of things and acquire the habit of genuinely understanding and making use of what he learns.
> (6) That this education shall not be laborious but very easy. The class instruction shall last only four hours each day, and shall be conducted in such a manner that one master may teach hundreds of pupils at the same time, with ten times as little trouble as is now expended on the teaching of one.[48]

Similar reforms are outlined in Chapter XXII of the *Panorthosia* (the sixth volume of the *Consultatio*), the theme of which is 'Universal Reform'. Schools, he says, must be 'fortresses of light', illuminating the young in the ways of learning, virtue and piety, their ultimate objective being to prepare them for eternal salvation through faith. 'Every school,' he says, 'should be a miniature republic, abiding by definite laws and executing them strictly.'[49] The use of corporal punishment is condemned, though there is a strong insistence nonetheless on the importance of maintaining order and discipline in the school. This is substantially the same vision as is projected in the *Via Lucis*, though in this instance the emphasis lies mainly on the fostering of educability and of enlightened habits of learning so as to ensure that education is sustained as a lifelong process. 'The schools which we desire must necessarily be preparatory to the greater School of Life itself,' he writes, 'and their one purpose must be to bring it about that every man who is in the world shall be nothing but a pupil in school, and make as much progress as he can in it.'[50] He stresses the importance of orderly instruction, calling on schools 'to seize and subdue them [the young] by a wise discipline and prepare them in advance for taking strong draughts of wisdom as a field is made ready for the proper reception of seed.'[51] The latter emphasis on the fostering of educability is seen specifically as the development of the basic powers of literacy, side by side with the promotion of virtue and piety, in the early years of schooling:

> Thus the end of the Universal Schools will be to provide opportunities, not only for all nations and tongues and orders of men, but for every single individual to rise out of the darkness of ignorance and barbarism. Now this must be done, first, by preparing their minds in good time, so that they may be made apt to receive those lessons which later and, indeed, throughout their lives, will be instilled into them: that is to say, they must be made tractable and dutiful towards God and their masters, and filled as they should be with reverence for the Deity and a sense of the future life. In the second place, this effect will be wrought by teaching them letters, as the necessary instruments for reading and understanding the Universal books: and thirdly, by giving them an intimate acquaintance with those elements of knowledge out of which they will afterwards recognise that the Universal books, and in particular the book of Pansophia, have been composed; and these are the sensible things in the whole world, all the historical parts of Holy Scripture, and the common notions of the mind, as the bases of human reasoning.[52]

As has been intimated earlier, Comenius repeatedly emphasised the notion of education as a lifelong process and his conception of the stages of schooling was designed primarily to accommodate this. 'As the whole world is a school for the human race from the beginning to the end of time, so every individual's lifetime is a school from the cradle to the grave,' he declared in the fifth chapter of the *Pampaedia*. 'Seneca's saying "No age is too late for learning" does not go far enough,' he writes, 'and we should say "Every age is destined for learning, and men are given the same period of time for studying as for living."'[53] He therefore envisaged successive stages in institutional schooling appropriate to the different stages of life, with the content and modes of educating being fashioned to suit the needs of the particular age-group for which it was intended. 'If each age is allotted the task that is suitable for it, then the whole life-time will have something to learn, something to do, some improvement to make, and some source of the fruit of life to find,' he wrote.[54] Essentially, what he conceived was a ladder system, a step by step progression from one stage of schooling to the next. In *The Great Didactic* this was set out as a four stage process, consisting of the infant school, the vernacular school, the Latin school or gymnasium, and the university. This is extended into a seven stage process in the *Pampaedia*, consisting of the school of birth and the infant school, the schools of boyhood, adolescenceœ, early manhood, mature manhood, and old age.

Comenius saw the 'school of birth' as the place where the conditions are created for the upbringing of the child in a spirit of love. The careful and loving nurturing of the unborn child is the responsibility of parents in the months between conception and birth, he says. The duties of parents in this period of the child's life are described in Chapter 8 of the *Pampaedia*. He urges them to love one another and to ensure the healthy development of their unborn child. He saw formal education as beginning with the infant school. Moral and religious formation, together with carefully designed programmes for the cultivation of literacy and numeracy, are seen as its main concern. Comenius fully recognised the importance of pre-primary education, seeing it as the key to equality of opportunity, long before Froebel, Pestalozzi and others were to call for the focussing of initiatives in educational reform on the years of infancy and early childhood. 'It is when it first comes into being that a tree puts forth the shoots that are later on to be its principal branches, and it is in this first school that we must plant in a man the seeds of all the knowledge with which we wish him to be equipped in his journey through life,' he writes in *The Great Didactic*.[55]

In the *Pampaedia* he traced all the ills of society to the neglect of the education of the child in the years of infancy. 'The universal corruption of the world begins in its roots,' he writes. 'Therefore its universal refor-mation must begin there also. . . . The hope of universal reform of the world depends entirely on the first stage of education,' he says.[56] He recognised the crucial importance of rendering the child educable in the pre-school years, if subsequent education was to have a real chance of success. 'Our nature (in body, mind, morals, pursuits, conversation and gestures) is conditioned by our earliest education,' he declares. 'A whole lifetime's happiness depends on this, since moral and spiritual things no less than the natural and the artificial are conditioned by their origin.'[57] In this passage from the *Pampaedia* he uses his favourite metaphor of the cultivation of the seed to illustrate the importance of the pre-school years in the whole process of child formation and development:

Infancy is the springtime of life, when we must not neglect the opportunity to prepare the field of the intellect. At this stage it is essential that he who desires a full harvest should sow the entire field in his possession, leaving nothing uncultivated. Just as the seeds of the year's harvest are sown at the beginning of spring, if not in the preceding autumn, so the seeds of a good life must be sown at its very beginning. As a plant that is diseased in the early stages finds it difficult and even impossible to recover once it has grown and hardened for lack of treatment, so a human being will retain the habits of his childhood as he grows old. The faults of our early education go with us all our lives. Therefore the most important nurture of the human race occurs in our cradles, and if this is administered with due care it is of wonderful benefit in later life; if it is neglected we live under handicap. It is important to pursue the right course towards our goal from the beginning.[58]

The emphasis here on character formation, side by side with the fostering of educability, lends a distinctly modern appeal to Comenius's views on the role of the pre-primary school. At a time when so much research has traced the incidence of teenage delinquency and criminality to the neglect of education in early childhood, his words seem extraordinarily far-seeing and prophetic. In another passage from the *Pampaedia* he specifically points to the cause-effect relationship that exists between the provision of pre-primary education and the prevention of social corruption, crime and depravity. Given its relevance to the conditions of the present time—a relevance made more acute by the widespread failure by governments even now to recognise the importance of the pre-primary years—it is worth quoting the passage at some length:

We complain of the depravity of our era and the growing confusion in every rank, sex and age-group. We even try to reform one another everywhere through our homes, our schools, our churches, and our states in various ways involving the use of force. We see parents reforming grown-up children by thrashing them, and tyrants reforming their underlings with imprisonment, the sword, the noose and the wheel. Kings inflict the Machiavellian treatment of fraud and trickery on their subjects. The latter in their turn take vengeance on their kings by acts of rebellion: hence the whole atmosphere is one of war, violence and disaster. How much better to have men restrained by the curb of reason than by legal compulsion and executions! They say that the brutish intellects of most mortals do not follow the path of reason, and that leniency is futile in face of such widespread wickedness and deep-rooted rebellion. But we have to inquire why a rational creature cannot be controlled by the curb of reason. Surely the very nature of the control as it is applied would introduce an irrational element. Doctors will tell us that the faults of the first digestion are not corrected in a second or a third. It is in the early stages of experience that we go astray. We do not train the mind for its rightful function of providing a guiding light to the will; and we do not control the will to such good purpose that conscience is eliminated. Therefore we need far-seeing care in dealing with our infants.[59]

Here again he stresses the crucial role of the parent in the process of character formation. While acknowledging the need to entrust infant education to professionally trained teachers (for the reasons outlined above), he nonetheless insists on the complementary responsibility of parents to reinforce the whole process of moral formation occurring in the school. 'Parents who fail to give their children profitable instruction right from the beginning must realise,' he says, 'that they are losing an opportunity that will not occur again. . . . It is clear from examples in every sphere that the lesson learned in early childhood is the only firm and lasting one. . . . It is a common saying that infants know every language but speak only the one that they actually learn.'[60]

Comenius proposed that at least two years of kindergarten education be provided for all children, following which he envisaged a six-year perioød of primary education to cater for those between the ages of six and twelve. The system of primary education that he envisaged anticipates the model that developed all over Europe two centuries after he described it. Its basis was the uniform primary school which aimed to provide a sound moral and religious education side by side with the basic skills of literacy and numeracy so as to ensure that children could progress satisfactorily to secondary and higher education subsequently. In *The Great Didactic* he took issue with his predecessors—particularly with J.H. Alsted—on the question of selective entry to primary education.[61] Alsted, amongst others, had recommended two types of primary education: a common basic form that would cater for all girls and for boys destined for manual labour; and an elitist, preparatory model designed for those likely to proceed to the gymnasium. Comenius argued passionately that a uniform system of primary education be provided for all children, regardless of social background, sex difference or religious creed. The kind of primary education historically considered appropriate only for those who could avail of it by virtue of their privileged status in society should be made available to all, he argued—on grounds of basic justice and morality. He particularly objected to selection on grounds of social background or the expected vocational destiny of the child:

The education that I propose includes all that is proper for a man, and is one in which all men who are born into this world would share. All therefore, as far as is possible, should be educated together, that they may stimulate and urge on one another.

We wish all men to be trained in all the virtues, especially in modesty, sociability, and politeness, and it is therefore undesirable to create class distinctions at such an early age, or to give some children the opportunity of considering their own lot with satisfaction and that of others with scorn.

When boys are only six years old, it is too early to determine their vocation in life, or whether they are more suited for learning or for manual labour. At this age, neither the mind nor the inclinations are sufficiently developed, while, later on, it will be easy to form a sound opinion on both. In the same way, while plants are quite small, a gardener cannot tell which to hoe up and which to leave, but has to wait until they are more advanced. Nor should admission to the Latin-School be reserved for the sons of rich men, nobles and magistrates, as if these were the only boys who would ever be able to fill similar positions. The wind blows where it will, and does not always begin to blow at a fixed time.[62]

The passage stands out as one of the most eloquent and compelling formulations of the ideal of equality of educational opportunity in the entire history of educational thought. In accordance with his belief in the right of all to get access to a good primary education, Comenius insisted— against the overwhelming burden of tradition and contemporary school practice—that instruction in the primary school be given through the medium of the vernacular. Correspondingly, he stressed the special responsibility of teachers at this level to develop learning potentiality in their pupils and to ensure they had the cognitional and moral training necessary to enable all who wished to do so to proceed successfully to further levels of education. On this he cited the words of Erasmus: 'In the quest for learning a single year in childhood is more valuable than ten when the mind has become preoccupied with other cares and has hardened against teaching.'[63] Believing that a higher level of teaching competence is required at this than at any other stage in the educational process, he argued that primary teachers deserved greater incentives—financial and otherwise—than their colleagues in the Latin schools and universities.[64]

Though he conceded the principle of selective entry to the Latin school (variously termed the 'gymnasium' and 'School of Adolescence), Comenius insisted that all who aspired towards education at this level should have the opportunity to have it, regardless of social circumstances. He insisted that education at this level should be guided by genuinely liberal ideals: in particular he insisted that the curriculum should not be dominated by vocational considerations—an emphasis that finds powerful echoes in contemporary thinking on secondary education.[65] What he envisaged for the Latin School was the realisation of the pansophic ideal of an education that would provide access to the universals of human knowledge. The curriculum that he proposed, as will be shown in detail presently, embraced a breath-taking range of subject-content. Its main objective, he said, was to provide the greatest possible degree of intellectual formation within the general framework of moral and spiritual development. 'The aim of this school, he writes, 'will be to present in orderly form the subject-matter of learning as perceived by the senses with a view to the fuller and clearer use of reasoning since "the superior status of man over beast depends on reason." Therefore reason must be assiduously cultivated, so that we may leave the beasts as far behind as possible, and come as near as possible to the angels.'[66] A different mode of teaching methodology would be required at this level, he says, to meet the changed nature of curriculum content. 'We must go through the world, the mind, and holy scripture synthetically to reach an understanding of the reasons for the existence of things. Therefore at this stage reasons for everything must be given, but in popular language,' he writes in the *Pampaedia*.[67]

Comenius envisaged six years of education being provided in the Latin school for pupils between the ages of twelve and eighteen. This was to be followed by a university education for an elite, chosen primarily on meritocratic criteria, and by various forms of adult education for others. His treatment of higher education and adult education will be discussed in detail in a later chapter. Meanwhile, it is necessary to consider the theories of learning and teaching he put forward for the realisation of the aims of the primary and post-primary schools and to consider the proposals he made for the selection and structuring of curriculum content in both.

3. LEARNING THROUGH EXPERIENCE: FROM THE FINITE TO THE INFINITE

The innateness of the desire to know and the universal potentiality for learning are amongst the strongest assertions of Comenius's educational writings. 'Every man has inborn in him the desire to know and to inquire into things which may be known,' he declared in the opening pages of the *Via Lucis*. 'The impulse towards knowledge,' he wrote, 'is common to human nature, although it may not reveal itself in so lively a fashion in all men or direct itself only to the better things as it ought.'[68] In the fifth chapter of *The Great Didactic*, 'The Seeds of Learning, Virtue and Piety Are Naturally Implanted in Us', he affirms his conviction that 'man is naturally capable of acquiring a knowledge of all things'—that

man is naturally a 'learning being.' 'So unlimited is the capacity of the
mind that in the process of perception it resembles an abyss,' he writes.
He continues: 'The body is enclosed by small boundaries; the voice roams
within wider limits; the sight is bounded only by the vault of heaven;
but for the mind, neither in heaven nor anywhere outside heaven, can a
boundary be fixed.'[69] He uses the familiar image of the seed to intimate
the potential for growth from its own internal resources that is present
in the mind, though adding the qualifying caveat that major obstacles
may lie in the way of its progress:

> Philosophers have called man a Microcosm or Epitome of the
> Universe, since he inwardly comprehends all the elements that are
> spread far and wide through the Macrocosm, or world at large; a
> statement the truth of which is shown elsewhere. The mind,
> therefore, of a man who enters this world is very justly compared
> to a seed or a kernel in which the plant or tree really does exist,
> although its image cannot actually be seen. This is evident; since
> the seed, if placed in the ground, puts forth roots beneath it and
> shoots above it, and these, later on, by their innate force, spread
> into branches and leaves, are covered with foliage, and adorned
> with flowers and fruit. It is not necessary, therefore, that anything
> be brought to a man from without, but only that that which he
> possesses rolled up within himself be unfolded and disclosed, and
> that stress be laid on each separate element. Thus Pythagoras used
> to say that it was so natural for a man to be possessed of all knowl-
> edge, that a boy of seven years old, if prudently questioned on all the
> problems of philosophy, ought to be able to give a correct answer
> to each interrogation; since the light of Reason is a sufficient
> standard and measure of all things. Still it is true that, since the
> Fall, Reason has become obscure and involved, and does not know
> how to set itself free; while those who ought to have done so have
> rather entangled it the more.[70]

Further to all this, Comenius affirms the presence in all men of the
active powers of intelligence that ensure the growth of learning
potentialities. 'In addition to the desire for knowledge that is implanted
in him, man is imbued,' he writes, 'not merely with a tolerance of, but
with an actual appetite for toil. This is evident in earliest childhood, and
accompanies us throughout life.' Referring to examples of men who have
taken responsibility for their own education, he asks: 'Does not this teach
us that, in very truth, all things exist in man; that the lamp, the oil, the
tinder, and all the appliances are there, and that if only he be sufficiently
skilled to strike sparks, or catch them, and to kindle the lamp, he can
forthwith see and can reap the fullest enjoyment of the marvellous trea-

sures of God's wisdom, both in himself and in the larger world; that is to say, can appreciate the numerical and proportional arrangement of the whole creation.'[71]

In the *Via Lucis* he adopts a more elaborate style of expression to convey the same principle of the universality of intellectual potential: 'Those Universal Notions, original and innate, not yet perverted by monstrous conceptions, the divinely laid foundations of our reason, remain the same for man and woman, for the child and the old man, for the Greek and the Arab, for the Christian and the Mohammedan, for the religious and the irreligious; and from these from day to day ever richer treasures are derived.'[72] In the plainer, more clinical language of the *Pampaedia* he reaffirms the same point, again insisting vigorously on the commonality of all mental structures: 'For the inner structure of all men is as uniform as their outward bodily structure. What one human being is or has or wishes or knows or is capable of doing, all others are or have or wish or know or are capable likewise.'[73] These words were re-echoed three centuries later by an American educator, writing also in the liberal Christian tradition. In *The Learning Society* R.M. Hutchins declared: 'The evidence is that every child who has not sustained some damage to his brain can learn the basic subjects and that it can no longer be said that any member of the human race is ineducable. . . . The conviction of former ages that only the few could be educated must be attributed to social, political and economic conditions and not to the incapacity of men of any colour, race, nationality, social status or background.'[74]

In asserting the universality of learning potentiality, Comenius did not ignore differences in individual ability, nor did he underestimate the difficulties that lie in the way of fostering it in backward or under-motivated pupils. His treatment of these difficulties will be examined in detail later. For the moment it is necessary to inquire further into his conception of the nature of the learning process itself. It is represented primarily in his writings as the perception of the underlying order of the universe—an order reflecting its integration of three main spheres of reality: the physical, the metaphysical and the hyperphysical. All three, he said in the *Via Lucis*, are complementary facets of a single harmonious whole. The perception of the reality of each is the means to the perception of the reality of the other. The process is described as follows in the *Via Lucis*:

Our subject, then, is presented to us in three aspects; first the whole of this world which surrounds us on all sides, full of various creatures of various forms: it is, as it were, God's great book full of various letters. Now for the learning of these we have been provided with Organs, our five senses, as we all know. The world itself, then, which we inhabit is man's first school, and everyone who is

born enters it. It is to be called the School of Nature, or the
Physical School. . . .

This Physical school is followed by another, the Metaphysical,
higher and in its whole nature, quite different from the former. In
it our objects, our Books and our Masters, are not outside us, as in
the Physical School, but within us—our own mind, in fact, or the
image of God impressed upon our mind, and marked by countless
characters of innate Notions, instincts and faculties. . . .

Then comes the third school, which we must call the Hyperphysical: the school in which no creature and no man can teach
anyone anything, but God alone, who is above all things. For the
subjects which are taught and learned in this school are such as the
eye of no man has seen, nor ear heard, nor do they come into the
heart of man, but God alone reveals them through his Spirit. . . .
Accordingly, the books of this school are first the inspirations
which have been granted to Patriarchs, Prophets, Apostles; and,
then, books divinely inspired and written by command of God for
the use of the Church.[75]

The ultimate objective of all learning, as the passage suggests, is to grasp
the wholeness of reality comprehended in the interrelated spheres of the
physical, the metaphysical and the hyperphysical. To see things in their
disorder and fragmentation is to have a defective understanding of their
true reality, he says. In the *Prodromus* Comenius spoke of the laws of
nature as 'being so interconnected that not even the smallest part is super-
fluous' and he compared their functioning to that of a musical composition, in which there is both 'the sweet consonance of diverse tones' and
'the perfect agreement of opposites.'[76] In the *Diatyposis* he spoke again of
the underlying coherence of the entire natural order: 'Perpetual Coherence
is in this that all things, the greatest and the least, from the first even to
the last, shall be chained together; one thing shall so depend upon another,
that nothing of all those things which are anywhere, may either escape or
chance to be seen in any other than its own place.'[77] True understanding,
he suggests, therefore, consists in the perception of the principles of order
underlying an apparently chaotic and fragmented reality. This is the
opening affirmation in Chapter XIII of *The Great Didactic*:

We find on investigation that the principle that really holds together
the fabric of this world of ours, down to its smallest detail, is none
other than order; that is to say, the proper division of what comes
before and what comes after, of the superior and the subordinate,
of the large and the small, of the similar and dissimilar, according
to place, time, number, size, and weight, so that each may fulfil its
function well. Order, therefore, has been called the soul of affairs.

For everything that is well ordered preserves its position and its strength as long as it maintains its order; it is when it ceases to do so that it grows weak, totters, and falls. This may be seen clearly in instances taken from nature and from art.

Through what agency, I ask, does the world maintain its present condition? What is it that gives it its great stability? It is this, that each creature, obeying the commands of nature, restrains its action within the proper limits; and thus, by careful observation of order in small details, the order of the universe is maintained.[78]

There have been some misguided attempts—emanating mainly from Marxist and pragmatist sources—to explain Comenius's concept of learning in terms of a scientific process of logical deduction, by virtue of which the principles of order underlying reality may be determined through the agencies of reason alone. Comenius undoubtedly drew heavily on the methods of the newly emerging sciences for his understanding of the functioning of the natural order but, as both the *Via Lucis* and the *Pampaedia* make abundantly clear, his sense of the ultimate coherence of the natural order was based on his perception of the unity of the finite and the infinite which it comprehends. It is in the context of this integration of the worlds of the material and the spiritual, of the finite and the infinite, that his theories of experience and his empirically based concept of learning must be understood.

Initially, it would appear that he drew his concept of experience predominantly from the principles of Baconian realism. Bacon's influence was undoubtedly a potent factor in its evolution, as Comenius himself acknowledged in the *Via Lucis*. From Bacon he discovered how the methods and techniques of scientific experimentation, observation and analysis could unravel the complexities of the phenomenal universe. He described *The Advancement of Learning* as 'an admirable work which I look upon as a most bright beam of a new age of philosophers.'[79] Much of his learning theory, and the pedagogic principles he devised for its implementation, were based on the experimental methods described in this work, particularly the principles of unfolding the realities of nature through direct discovery and observation. And from all this followed one of the most radical of his educational insights: the principle that all knowledge begins with the perceptions of sense experience. In a much quoted passage from *The Great Didactic* he wrote: 'And since nothing exists in the mind that has not previously existed in the senses, the intellect takes the material of all its thought from the senses, and performs the operations of thought in a manner that may be termed "inner sensation", that is to say, by acting on the images of things that are brought before it.'[80] This principle is further developed in the chapter entitled 'The Principles of Facility in Teaching and Learning.' He gives concrete

illustrations of the methods he advocated for the fostering of learning—
especially in the sphere of linguistic development—through the medium
of multi-sensory experience, and spells out the pedagogic strategies he
considered necessary to promote it:

> As far as possible, instruction should be given through the senses,
> that it may be retained in the memory with less effort. For example,
> the sense of hearing should always be conjoined with that of sight,
> and the tongue should be trained in combination with the hand.
> The subjects that are taught should not merely be taught orally,
> and thus appeal to the ear alone, but should be pictorially illustrated,
> and thus develop the imagination by the help of the eye. Again, the
> pupils should learn to speak with their mouths and at the same time
> to express what they say with their hands, that no study may be
> proceeded with before what has already been learned is thoroughly
> impressed on the eyes, the ears, the understanding and the memory.
> With this object, it is desirable to represent pictorially, on the walls
> of the classroom, everything that is treated of in the class, by putting
> up either precepts and rules or pictures and diagrams illustrative of
> the subjects taught. If this be done, it is incredible how much it
> assists a teacher to impress his instruction on the pupils' minds. It
> is also useful if the scholars learn to write down in their note-books
> or among their collections of idioms everything that they hear or
> read, since in this way the imagination is assisted and it is easier to
> remember them later on.[81]

The full significance of all this becomes apparent from Comenius's elaboration of the concept of learning through experience in the *Pampaedia*
and the *Via Lucis*. In the former he points to the threefold process by
which truth becomes known: 'Everything can be known that has been set
out in God's three-fold book, and we have been given the organs, namely,
sense, reason, and faith, to acquire it all from that source. For it is through
our external senses that the whole external world penetrates to us, through
reason that things largely hidden are investigated, and through faith that
one comprehends what is hidden but God has been pleased to reveal.'[82]
But while in the *Pampaedia* he stresses the complementary roles of sense,
reason and faith in disclosing all truth, in the *Via Lucis* each is shown as
leading progressively to the other in the process of discovering truth.
While each is shown to have its own distinct function—there is a meaning,
he says, which is knowable only to sense, or to reason or to faith—each
is shown as leading inexorably to the sphere where the ultimate significance of all truth is made known: the sphere of the spiritual and the
infinite. Thus he speaks of the processes of learning and knowing as
essentially a progression from the finite to the infinite, from the material

to the spiritual, from nature to God. In this passage he points to the ultimacy of the truths disclosed by the spheres of materiality and sense, stressing their immanent disclosure of truths finally illuminated in the revealed word of the scriptures. He begins with three major propositions:

> (1) that the material world is a beginning of the works of God, the first specimen or example of the uncreated Wisdom which fashions all things to numbers, measurements and weights:
> (2) that a greater theatre of this wisdom has been set up in created man, on whom as upon its own image, while it imprints those numbers, measurements and weights in accordance with which all things have been made, it has also imprinted the characters of infinity, for thinking, seeking and attempting infinite things:
> (3) that the greatest mysteries of wisdom are presented to our contemplation in man, fallen, corrupt and lost and then to be restored; in whom, in a word, all the depths of wisdom and of folly, of righteousness and of sin, of life and of death, of salvation and perdition, are disclosed for the angels themselves to marvel at.
>
> Let us then, assume, that you, indefatigable investigators of Nature, have conquered her whole domain, so that with Solomon you understand the constitution of the world; the power of the elements; the beginning, the end, the intervening spaces of time; the changes of the solstices, the succession of the seasons; the circuit of the year, the positions of the stars; the natures of living things, the tempers of beasts, and the powers of spirits, and the thoughts of men, the various kinds of plants and the properties of roots; everything in effect that is either plain or obscure—let us assume all this, and then you must know that you have at last mastered but the alphabet of divine wisdom, but reached the threshold in the temple of God; and that his courts and his secret places are only now upon your horizon![83]

The passage clearly establishes Comenius's concept of empirical knowledge as ultimately a disclosure of spiritual truths. He sees experience as unequivocally the gateway to the spheres of the metaphysical, the spiritual and the religious by virtue of his belief in the immanent presence of the infinite in all material being. Though he placed experience at the heart of the learning process, he insisted on its radical interrelation with the spheres of the non-empirical—with the realms of meaning and truth disclosable only to reason and faith. With the passage of the centuries this all-embracing concept of experience has regrettably been reduced to a narrow and purely naturalistic formula by many of Comenius's interpreters, particularly those approaching his work from pragmatist and Marxist standpoints.

The primacy accorded by Comenius to sense-experience leads to a second closely related principle in his theories of learning and knowing: the intrinsic individuality of the learner and the unique nature of the process by which he or she discovers truth. Since experience, of its nature, is individualised and unique, it follows, he argues, that learning must necessarily be an individualised process as well. While he stressed the commonality of basic intellectual structures and functions, he also emphasised the great variety of individual abilities, interests and aptitudes through which these structures and functions are manifested. In *The Great Didactic* he gives some instances of this:

> In the first division must be placed those who are sharp-witted, anxious to learn and easily influenced. These, more than all others, are suitable for instruction. . . .
>
> Others are sharp-witted, but inclined to be slow and lazy. These must be urged on.
>
> In the third place we have those who are sharp-witted and anxious to learn, but who at the same time are perverse and refractory. These are usually a great source of difficulty in schools, and for the most part are given up in despair. If treated in the right way, however, they frequently develop into the greatest men . . .
>
> In the fourth place we have those who are flexible and anxious to learn, but who at the same time are slow and heavy. These can follow in the footsteps of the last-mentioned. But to render this possible the teacher must meet their weak natures half-way, must lay no heavy burden on them, must not demand anything excessive, but rather have patience, help them, strengthen them, and set them right, that they may not be disheartened. . . .
>
> The fifth type are those who are weak-minded and at the same time lazy and idle. With these also a great improvement can be made, provided they are not obstinate. But great skill and patience are necessary.
>
> Finally, we have those whose intellects are weak and whose dispositions are perverse and wicked as well. These seldom come to any good. But, as it is certain that nature always provides some antidote for pernicious things, and that barren trees can be rendered fruitful if properly transplanted, we ought not to give up all hope, but should see if the perverseness, at least, cannot be combated and got rid of.[84]

Comenius's treatment of the subject of individual differences includes some especially enlightened views on the needs of weak, backward and under-motivated pupils. Before this is discussed, however, it is necessary to emphasise two further aspects of his concept of the process of learning through experience. While emphasising the spontaneous character of this whole process, he simultaneously stresses the need to nurture and cultivate the ways of nature and he saw a decisive and highly formative role for the teacher in bringing this about. In *The Great Didactic* he writes: 'The seeds of knowledge, of virtue, and of piety are, as we have seen, naturally implanted in us; but the actual knowledge, virtue and piety are not so given. These must be acquired by prayer, by education, and by action. He gave no bad definition who said that a man was a "teachable animal." And indeed it is only by a proper education that he can become a man.'[85] The whole process is elaborated in the following passage from the work:

> From plants we derive food, drink, and medicines; but first the herbs and grains have to be sown, hoed, gathered, winnowed, and ground; trees have to be planted, pruned and manured, while their fruits must be plucked off and dried; and if any of these things are required for medicine, or for building purposes, much more preparation is needed. Animals, whose essential characteristics are life and motion, seem to be self-sufficing, but if you wish to use them for the purposes for which they are suitable, some training is necessary. For example, the horse is naturally suited for use in war, the ox for drawing, the ass for carrying burdens, the dog for guarding and hunting, the falcon and hawk for fowling; but they are all of little use until we accustom them to their work by training.
>
> Man, as far as his body is concerned, is born to labour; and yet we see that nothing but the bare aptitude is born in him. He needs instruction before he can sit, stand, walk, or use his hands. Why, therefore should it be claimed for our mind that, of itself, it can exist in its full development, and without any previous preparation; since it is the law of all things created that they take their origin from nothing and develop themselves gradually, in respect both of their material and of the process of development?[86]

The same image is used in the *Pampaedia* as he reiterates the need for the process of growth to be assisted and given direction by the teacher. In this instance the image of the gardener is complemented by that of the skilled craftsman fashioning crude timber into a finished piece of art. 'Children,' he says, 'do not train themselves spontaneously but are shaped only by tireless labour. A young sapling, planned for a tree, must be planted, watered, hedged around for protection, and propped up. A tree of wood designed for a special purpose must be split, planed, carved, polished and stained.'[87] He insists, however, that the intervention of the teacher must in no way hinder the natural character of the learning process. In this instance he uses the age-old Biblical image of the teacher as midwife bringing new life into being. 'We must comply with nature,' he says, 'and permit students, whatever their level of maturity, to do that in which they find pleasure at the time . . . in this way we shall not struggle against nature but rather act as midwives in her travail.'[88]

This delicate balance that Comenius maintained between the goals of formative development and natural growth is particularly in evidence in his treatment of the principle of graded learning. The principle is set forth in Chapters 16 and 17 of *The Great Didactic*. 'Nature,' he declares, 'makes no leaps but proceeds step by step.' 'It is easy,' he says, 'to see how necessary it is that each of these processes should take place at the right time; that not only the time should be suitable but that the processes should be graduated; and that there should be not graduation merely, but an immutable graduation.'[89] What he envisaged bears a strong similarity to the developmental processes of learning described in later years by his fellow Slavic educator, Lev Vygotsky.[90] In common with Vygotsky, Comenius insisted that subject-matter be systematically ordered and classified to promote ease of learning. 'All studies,' he declared, 'should be carefully graduated throughout the various classes, in such a way that those that come first may prepare the way for and throw light on those that come after.'[91] The highly logical and systematised character of the process he envisaged becomes evident from the following passage in *The Great Didactic*:

> In schools therefore
> (i) All the studies should be so arranged that those which come later may depend on those that have gone before, and that those which come first may be fixed in the mind by those that follow.
> (ii) Each subject taught, when it has been thoroughly grasped by the understanding, must be impressed on the memory as well.
> For since, in this natural method of ours, all that precedes should be the foundation of all that comes after, it is absolutely essential that this foundation be thoroughly laid. For that only which has been thoroughly understood, and committed to memory as well, can be called the property of the mind.[92]

Facility, ease, rapidity and thoroughness of learning are the goals Comenius defines for the teacher in the chapters of *The Great Didactic* where he identifies the principles of good pedagogy. All are united by a single dynamic factor that pervades his thinking on the entire learning process. Learning, he repeatedly insists, is most effective when it is stimulating, interesting and enjoyable. As if to give moral sanction to this, he cites the authority of Luther on the value of the 'pleasure principle.' In the nineteenth chapter he speaks of 'fulfilling Luther's wish that the studies of the young at school could be so organised that the scholars might take as much pleasure in them as in playing at ball all day, and thus for the first time would schools be a real prelude to practical life.'[93] He called therefore for the creation of the conditions in school that would render learning enjoyable in the highest possible degree. A carefully planned pedagogy is the key to this, he says. In the *Pampaedia* he writes: The most important factor in pleasant study will be a method that is thoroughly practical and agreeable and such as to make the school really a form of play, that is, a pleasant prelude to the whole of life. This will be achieved if all the tasks of life are presented in a way that appeals to children and combines understanding with enjoyment.'[94]

One of his key guidelines for the teacher, therefore, is that he must 'ensure that men learn everything with pleasure.' 'You must make sure that the pupil knows that it is natural for him to wish as you advise, and soon he will rejoice to wish for it; and to have power to attain his wish, and soon he will rejoice to have the power; and to know what he thinks he does not know, and he will come to rejoice that he knows it.'[95] Above all, this means that learning must be conducted in conditions of freedom. The aim, he says, is 'to ensure that everything flows onward without compulsion.'[96] He sees individual interest, in turn, as the source of the pleasure to be derived from learning. This applies particularly to the education of the undermotivated, weak or backward pupil, as will be shown in the next section. 'It will be found that nothing is difficult for the willing pupil because, as St. Augustine says, anything that we like is either no work or likeable work,' he writes in the *Pampaedia*.[97] To a great degree, he saw this as a matter of how subject-matter is presented by the teacher. A vivid passage in *The Analytical Didactic* expresses it like this: 'The teacher should know how to guard against aversion, how to excite interest, and how to foster enthusiasm; he must learn this from the character of nature itself, which spontaneously reveals what pleases it and what offends it.'[98] Repeatedly, he insists, the challenge for the teacher is to release the motivational potential that is present in the nature of the child. In the chapter of the *Pampaedia* which is entitled 'Universal Teaching' he writes:

> For human nature is so designed that sense, intellect, will and faculties constantly require their own form of sustenance. Deny them this and they decline, languish, wither and perish. Take care to provide it and they rejoice, grow, wax strong, and fulfil all their functions. But if you give them an overdose, you dull, corrupt and stifle them. Therefore only prudence is required, to present light to the eye in the right way, and then the light will contain everything that you wish, the truth of things for your intellect, goodness for your will, material and instruments for your bodily powers; you will then see how everything is received by the eye and the rest of

the internal and external senses and grasped by the will, and all the bodily organs apply themselves to their proper tasks. Moreover it has been proved elsewhere in my work that God's three theatres, the world, the mind, and scripture, are full of light. Therefore since the light of God shines over all men, and His word enlightens them, why should it not be possible for everything to be clearly presented to all human minds in a popular way devoid of philosophic rigidity? But what is philosophic rigidity? To present teaching matter in the form of rigid decrees. And the meaning of 'In a popular way'? To use appeal, persuasion and encouragement; in a word to address our audience rather than soliloquise and to use exhortation rather than a dogmatic style. For the latter either insults or threatens intelligent minds and thereby intimidates them. The former inspires the inborn light to burst into flame.[99]

It remains now to clarify the pedagogic and curricular principles envisaged by Comenius to ensure that these ideals are brought to fruition in the conditions of the school classroom.

4. THE PAMPAEDIC TEACHER

As should be clear from an earlier discussion of the aims of universal education, Comenius saw the moral and spiritual formation of the child as the primary objective of the whole process. While he spoke in *The Great Didactic* and the *Pampaedia* of the need to foster knowledge, virtue and piety simultaneously, it is abundantly clear from both sources that ultimately he subordinated all facets of the educational process to its primary ethico-religious concerns. All knowledge, he said in the *Pampaedia*, must be harnessed to God's will, the ultimate aim being the moral and spiritual transformation of the learner. This is the primary focus of his ideal of holistic development. And this, in turn, becomes the focus of the teacher's responsibility towards his pupils.

Primarily, he saw the teacher as a moral exemplar. Children, he wrote, 'should be committed to the care of the most respected men and matrons, meaning that such a grave matter cannot be left to any man of the crowd, but only to the most select. . . . '[100] 'Teaching is leading,' he wrote in the *Pampaedia*. 'No real teaching is done by those who do not constantly set a good example, that is, who order pupils to do what they do not do themselves.'[101] In a notable passage from his *Outline of a Pansophic School* he characterises the kind of person who should perform this task. The essential requirements, he says, are moral integrity and wisdom. He suggests that men of high moral character be eagerly sought out and encouraged to undertake the responsibility of teaching the young. Significantly, he sees wisdom not as intellectual endowment but as the product of the love of learning. The *love* of learning, he suggests, is itself the chief factor in promoting its attainment. (Though the kind of teacher he describes here would have been working at the senior level of the pansophic school, the qualities he identifies are intended to apply to teachers at any level of schooling):

> It will be in the case of our pansophic schools a difficult undertaking to look for fit masters equal to such a task. As nothing can be done in anything that does not hold its essence, only a wise man can make others wise . . . in a word only a pansoph can make pansophs and therefore it will be necessary to seek men wise and eloquent and conversant with mathematics and metaphysics, i.e. pansophs.
>
> But where could we find such men? My view is apparent from what I have said above. We must look for them at home; we must find in our own nation these faithful future leaders who shall lead us to what is ours. Are there any grounds for hope for this to happen? There are three reasons indeed. The first is inborn in the pansophic method which has the quality to produce its own instruments and to form its own craftsmen through these instruments. . . . The second reason is based on the natural qualities of your intellects which are not afraid of hard toil which they can bear if they are well directed. Thus two kinds of men should be looked for as leaders towards this higher culture of the mind: either such who already possess a higher culture and encyclopaedic learning, or men who are eager to acquire this standard of refinement and who are therefore the bitterest enemies of indolence and barbarity. The third reason lies in preserving in the proper place in this fashion that the classes are entrusted to masters who will continually improve their own education by teaching others according to the set directions. Then they will keep learning from day to day and know today what they did not know yesterday. Thus teachers and learners will proceed together by stages.
>
> Men of this kind (who love wisdom, who do not mind toiling in its service, who obey good advice, who are of a gentle disposition) must be sought for this work of God like precious jewels and, whenever such men can be seen as though pointed out by the finger of God, they must be received, prevailed upon to come, and allured with any entreaties and rewards to their place. For these excellent men will learn everything by teaching everything to others.[102]

A more detailed profile of the ideal teacher is offered in the *Pampaedia*. Here Comenius takes Christ and the apostles as the primary models of

the exemplary teacher. 'What is a universal teacher?' he asks. 'He is a
Pampaedic teacher who knows how to instruct all men in all the subjects
that make human nature perfect to produce altogether perfect men. The
apostles ordained by Christ were teachers of this kind, and we must see
to it that those who undertake the instruction of men in modern post-
apostolic times are of the same quality, and we must make provision for
their training.'[103] He then gives a detailed characterisation of the good
teacher, his model probably being inspired by the example of the teachers
of the Unitas Fratrum. He emphasises moral integrity, enthusiasm,
diligence and pedagogic efficacy:

> This provision will ensure that the following three requirements are
> distinctly fulfilled in a universal teacher: (1) that each should be of
> the quality he ought to be developing in others, (2) that he should
> be master of the necessary techniques, (3) that he should be an
> enthusiast in his work. In a word, he must have the ability, the
> knowledge, and the desire to produce Pansophic men.
>
> Educators of men must therefore be the most select of all people,
> pious, honourable, serious, conscientious, industrious, and prudent,
> setting the same standards as we desire the whole population of the
> last of the ages to attain, when all shall be enlightened, peaceful,
> religious, and holy. In saying that they must be pious and utterly
> devoted to God I mean that they should have God as a partner;
> honourable, that they should be altogether blameless in the eyes of
> men; serious, that a kindly severity should mark all their actions;
> conscientious, that they should never be ashamed of their work, nor
> find it irksome, nor readily break down under pressure of work; and
> lastly, prudent, because human minds, especially the most excitable,
> are like Proteus, liable to change into a thousand monsters unless
> they are under control and firmly constrained in the bonds of
> order.[104]

The passage characterises the ideal teacher in general terms, the more
specific details of the teacher's pedagogic responsibilities being set out in
the chapter of the *Pampaedia* devoted to the theme of 'Universal
Teaching'. Initially, Comenius's emphasis falls on the importance of the
teacher awaiting the pupil's readiness for learning. 'We must wait for
opportunities to train our youth in all things and not anticipate them,' he
writes. 'We must begin in good time but not before it, as that would be
no help to nature but would corrupt it.'[105] In Chapter 16 of *The Great
Didactic* he employs one of his most colourful metaphors to illustrate the
pedagogic principle of enabling the processes of learning to take their
natural course:

Nature observes a suitable time. For example: a bird that wishes to multiply its species, does not set about it in winter, when everything is stiff with cold, nor in summer, when everything is parched and withered by the heat; nor yet in autumn, when the vital force of all creatures declines with the sun's declining rays, and a new winter with hostile mien is approaching; but in spring when the sun brings back life and strength to all. Again, the process consists of several steps. While it is yet cold the bird conceives the eggs and warms them inside its body, where they are protected from the cold; when the air grows warmer it lays them in its nest, but does not hatch them out until the warm season comes, that the tender chicks may grow accustomed to light and warmth by degrees.[106]

Readiness to learn, however, as liberal educators have consistently recognised, is a potentiality that can itself be fostered by the teacher. It is interesting therefore to see Comenius, in the same context as he emphasised the spontaneity and naturalness of learning, employing the image of the teacher as artist to intimate the manner in which he can assist the process of natural development in the child. 'We must therefore see if it be possible to place the art of intellectual discipline on such a firm basis that sure and certain progress may be made,' he writes. 'Since this basis can be properly laid only by assimilating the processes of art as much as possible to those of nature, we will follow the method of nature, taking as our example a bird hatching out its young; and if we see with what good results gardeners, painters, and builders follow in the track of nature, we shall have to recognise that the educator of the young should follow in the same path.'[107] He continues, however, to warn against any efforts to force or accelerate the pupil's natural pace of learning. Warning against excessive instruction (he recommended that not more than four hours per day be devoted to formal teaching), overburdening with homework—'until nausea and in some cases insanity is produced'— he advises the teacher simply to enable the natural rate of learning to take its course in each of his pupils. 'Nature compels nothing to advance that is not driven forward by its own mature strength,' he writes. In particular he advises against the contemporary practice of promoting learning through rote memorisation. 'Nothing should be learnt by heart that hasn't been thoroughly grasped by the understanding,' he declares.[108]

All of this suggests a role for the teacher that is highly formative while being deeply sensitive to the natural and individualised processes of learning occurring in every child. In *The Analytical Didactic* he writes: 'The student should work and the teacher should direct. In keeping with this rule, always put implements into the hands of a pupil, so that he will realise that he must get things done and so that he will not think of any subject as remote, arduous or difficult. In this way you will quickly make him enthusiastic, spirited, and eager.'[109] But assisting the course of nature would also mean ensuring that the process of learning could proceed on an orderly and effective course. He spoke of the need for the teacher to 'demonstrate the all-ruling force of order in nature.' Thus, he stressed the need for logical structure in teaching, emphasising the importance of ordered content and coherent and systematic explication. 'The basis of school reform must be exact order in all things,' he declares in *The Great Didactic*. 'The art of teaching,' he continues, 'demands nothing more than the skilful arrangement of time, of the subjects taught, and of the method.'[110] The following passage from *The Analytical Didactic* indicates how systematically he wished the whole process to be conducted:

> It would be a wise policy to have the study of every science, art and language divided into definite grades; and, where the subject-matter is rather extensive, it should be arranged into several scales of such grades, through which pupils would be slowly guided from step to step. The major division into grades or scales would be threefold: for those who are beginning, those who are continuing, and those who are completing their studies. Beginners are taught that which gives a foundation to knowledge; more advanced pupils are taught that which builds up the structure; their studies add support, strength and some degree of ornament to the structure. But each of these grades again has its minor grades, just as a lofty tower has a series of ladders provided for climbers and each of these ladders again has its steps.[111]

This emphasis on orderly instruction is taken further still in the *Outline of a Pansophic School* where Comenius writes: 'I want to imitate the features of the most exact clockwork so that this arrangement may be endowed with the wisdom of God; in such a clockwork nothing is missing that is required for the purpose of spontaneous motion and nothing (not even the smallest pillar, wheel or tooth) is useless. Everything is really arranged in such a way that it moves by the winding and unwinding of the weights like living matter, thus providing the world by its well-regulated motion with the picture of heaven itself which divides the course of time.'[112] The planning and sequencing of subject-content was seen by Comenius as a crucial part of the whole process of ensuring effectiveness in teaching and learning. Carefully planned teaching, proceeding progressively, step by step, from simple and rudimentary to more complex and more challenging content, is essential for ease of learning, he writes in the *Pampaedia*. 'Begin always from fundamentals and proceed right up to the topmost heights,' he says, 'and similarly go from the easiest to the more difficult until even the greatest difficulties are overcome.'[113] In his guidance on lesson planning, he emphasises systematic presentation, the careful graduation of subject content, and the closest possible integration of all its parts:

> A boy can be taught other subjects just as easily as reading and writing, provided that all his lessons are (1) methodically linked together, (2) developed from small beginnings, (3) arranged in stages like a ladder so that the early lessons prepare the way for those that follow. The universal teacher will therefore be one who (1) presents the whole subject to his pupil, so that whatever he is ordered to learn is there before his eyes; (2) takes it to pieces like a machine so that the component parts are clearly seen; (3) asks him to do likewise, either by pointing to the same things and naming them in the case of theoretical lessons, or by demonstration if a practical lesson is to be taught . . . [114]

Further emphasising the goal of pedagogic effectiveness, he speaks of the need for the teacher to ensure that all knowledge is assimilated in the sphere of practical experience. 'Things should be taught thoroughly, i.e, not perfunctorily and formally' he writes in the *Via Lucis*, 'but in such a way that whatever is taught is really known, and that any pupil . . . may be able to say what the Samaritans said to the woman who first called them together, "Now we believe not because of thy saying, but because we ourselves have learnt and know.' 'Let us teach men to learn,' he continues, 'not for the sake of learning, but for the sake of knowing; and yet to know not for the sake of knowing but for the sake of exercising themselves in action.'[115] In the *Pampaedia* he further emphasises the need for concretion and practical exemplification in teaching. 'The aim of teaching thoroughly is achieved,' he writes, 'by the constant association of three things, i.e. the training of the mind, the tongue and the hand.' 'The instructed man,' he continues, 'is one who, like a living image of God, grasps everything with his understanding, expresses everything in speech and demonstrates everything in action as fully as his finite nature will allow.'[116] In *The Great Didactic* he speaks of the need for knowledge to be 'deeply rooted' and urges the teacher to ensure that opportunities occur at all times to give practical expression to what has been learned by the child:

> The development. of the branches above the earth is proportionate to that of the roots beneath. This could not be otherwise; for if the tree were only to grow upwards it would be unable to maintain its erect position, since it is the roots that help it to do so. If, on the other hand, it only grew downwards it would be useless, for it is the branches and not the roots that bear the fruit. With animals also

there is a close connection between the external and the internal organs, for if the internal organs are healthy the external ones are so also.

The same holds good of education. It must first be applied to the inner roots of knowledge, and thus develop and gain strength, while at the same time care must be taken that it afterwards spread out into branches and foliage. That is to say, whenever instruction is given the pupil should be taught to apply his knowledge practically, as in the case of a language by speaking, and not merely to assimilate it mentally. Therefore, with every subject of instruction the question of its practical use must be raised, that nothing useless may be learned.[117]

Continuing on the same theme in *The Analytical Didactic* he concludes that the principle of practical application is 'the highest law of teaching.' 'The highest law and guiding light, the centre and circumference, the foundation and summit of the art of teaching is this alone: Teach everything through examples, precepts, and use or imitation. That is, always place the material of instruction before the student's eyes and explain what you have put before him; as for the student, when he has had the material explained and understands it, let him try to express it in a variety of forms until he can reproduce it perfectly.'[118]

Effective teaching, he suggests, both in *The Great Didactic* and the *Pampaedia*, involves two further principles concerned with the methodical presentation of subject content. In the chapter entitled 'The Principles of Conciseness and Rapidity in Teaching' in *The Great Didactic* he speaks of the need to ensure the comprehension of the greatest possible amount of subject-content in the shortest possible period of time, so that a truly substantial curriculum can be mastered by all pupils in the years of conventional schooling. He advises the careful selection and ordering of subject-matter, condensation of the lesson material and conciseness in its presentation. In the *Pampaedia* he gives the following advice to teachers on how they can achieve the objective of 'learning everything quickly': 'Without elaborating every point separately, I mention three rules: (1) secure a correct grasp of essentials, (2) eliminate useless matter, (3) condense what remains, if it is complicated. If you follow the procedure consistently, you will be astonished how much can be mastered by the senses, mind and hand in a short space of time.'[119] These principles, he suggests, hold particularly important implications for the design of school textbooks. 'It is therefore necessary,' he writes in *The Great Didactic*, 'to select or write handbooks of the sciences and languages which are small in compass and practically arranged—cover the whole subject and contain a great deal of matter in a short space—that is to say, which place before the scholar the whole of the subject-matter by means of a small number of rules and definitions expressed in the simplest and clearest language, and sufficient in themselves to lead to more profound study.'[120] In pursuit of this objective he further advises the logical linking and integration of the content of the curriculum, wherever this is feasible. Addressing the question, 'How is it possible to do two or three things by a single operation?' he responds:

> The example of nature shows that several things can be done at one time and by means of the same operation. It is an undoubted fact that a tree grows above the ground and beneath it at the same time, and that its wood, its bark, its leaves and its fruit, all develop simultaneously. The same observation applies to animals, whose limbs all develop and grow stronger at the same time. Further, each limb performs several operations. The feet, for instance, not only support a man but also move him forwards and backwards in various ways. The mouth is not only the entrance to the body, but also serves as a masticator and as a trumpet that sounds whenever called upon to do so. With a single inspiration the lungs cool the heart, purify the brain, and assist in voice-production. . . .
>
> The instruction of the young should be similarly organised, so that every activity may produce several results. It may be laid down as a general rule that each subject should be taught in combination with those which are correlative to it; that is to say, words should be studied in combination with the things to which they refer; while reading and writing, exercises in style and in logical thought, teaching and learning, amusement and serious study, should be continually joined together.[121]

Side by side with all this is a consistent emphasis on the crucial importance of pupil motivation. This, he suggests, is achieved mainly by appealing to the personal interests of the pupil and to the pleasure he can derive from the act of learning. His own aim, he said, was to 'convert to playrooms all schools that are at present treadmills or workshops.' He urges the teacher to 'stimulate greater enthusiasm, so that everything is done with pleasure.' 'It will be found,' he says, 'that nothing is difficult for the willing pupil because, as St. Augustine says, anything that we like is either no work or likeable work.'[122] He sees the stimulation of enthusiasm as being facilitated in turn by the individualisation of the learning process. 'How then,' he asks, 'is enthusiasm to be stimulated?' 'Both by commending the subject concerned and by presenting it attractively in four ways (1) *autopsia*, i.e. personal observation; (2) *autolexia*, personal reading, (3) *autopraxia*, personal handling and *autochresia*, personal application.'[123] An entire section of *The Analytical Didactic* is devoted to the question of ensuring 'agreeableness in instruction.'

Encouragement, kindness, individual attention, openness to the learner, a non-coercive atmosphere, variety and practicality in the presentation of subject-matter, are identified as the essential elements in this:

> In the first place human nature is free, loves spontaneity, and abhors compulsion. Consequently, it wishes to be guided on its course; it does not wish to be pulled, pushed or driven. That is why teachers who are morose, domineering, and given to flogging are the enemies of human nature, born with the gift to discourage and ruin native abilities rather than to encourage and develop them. Here also belongs the dry and sterile dogmatist who teaches only from barren precepts and does not even divert his students enough to stimulate them but fills them with aversion and repugnance or makes them like himself, stiff and unbending. . . .
> Whatever is taught should be tempered with pleasing variety. Human nature . . . takes particular delight in games and recreations, as is shown by the way we are devoted to games during our youth and find pleasure in jests and similar relaxations of the mind throughout our lives.[124]

Underlying all this is a deep concern for the accommodation of individual differences and for maintaining sensitivity to the needs of pupils of varying interests and abilities. Given his commitment to the education of all children, this was necessarily a major objective of Comenius's whole pedagogic philosophy. In the *Pampaedia* he writes: 'The question arises, are the blind, the deaf, and the stupid, whose defect prevents any impression being made upon them, to be provided with education? My answer is: There is no exemption from human education except for non-humans. Therefore their share in education should correspond to their share of human nature, increasing, if necessary, owing to the greater need for external help when nature through an internal fault is hardly able to help itself.'[125] In *The Great Didactic* he gives particular attention to the problems of slow learners. 'It will be urged,' he writes, 'that some men have such weak intellects that it is not possible for them to acquire knowledge. I answer, it is scarcely possible to find a mirror so dulled that it will not reflect images of some kind, or for a tablet to have such a rough surface that nothing can be inscribed on it.'[126] His faith in the innate educability of all—apart from the severely brain damaged—is consistently affirmed in his writings, as is his conviction that educators have a profound responsibility to cater for all kinds of learning needs. Essentially, he saw the problem as one of creating the motivation to learn amongst those disinclined, either by limited ability, low self-confidence, physical incapacity or the vagaries of social conditions, to engage in the activity of learning. He saw a crucial role for the elementary teacher in fostering the readiness to learn—itself a potent motivating factor—amongst all such children. Self-confidence, he suggests, comes from the pupil's sense of being able to master what the teacher expects of him—a principle which, in turn, dictates the need to match pedagogic practice to individual learning styles. The passage from the *Pampaedia* in which this principle is explained is one of the most eloquent in Comenius's pedagogic writings:

> What are we to do if we encounter an obstinate and refractory pupil who utterly resists the light and refuses even to listen to good advice and warning? My answer is: They say that one can find horses so wild and intractable that although they allow a man to take and lead or even to ride them, they still refuse to be put into any stable. In spite of this they are in fact stabled, if men resort to the trick of blindfolding them, for then they follow their leader without knowing where they are going. In that case, if in fact men also are found too refractory and wild to accept better teaching, surely it should be appropriate to use the same trick? But here three questions arise:
> 1. How could we get to grips with the man who is intractable and averse to learning?
> 2. How can we blindfold him to prevent his escape?
> 3. How can we lead him to the point that we wish him to reach?
>   My answers are as follows:
> 1. Man can only be taught by the halter that comes from his own heart, which means his innate desire for any good thing and we must grant him the right to acquire, possess, and enjoy it, if he wishes to follow the example of Paul (Acts XVII, 23)
> 3. We must deprive him of all external authorities, which means references to examples, what others say or do not say, do or refuse to do, hope for or despair of; and instead we must ensure that every man chooses to rely for guidance on himself and the light of his own innate personal knowledge, instincts and faculties. For then it will be easier for him to reject other leaders, no longer fearing to be led astray by himself since he will be capable of using his own judgement on everything.

If you make sure of this, it will be easy to lead him the rest of the way if you always proceed gradually, slowly, and calmly, so that he does not suffer any gap in his knowledge to alarm him and make him come to a stop or even retreat. This will mean speaking to him at every stage only according to the common light that is innate in all men, so that when he sees that he is making progress at every point with no external adviser or leader he may continue ever forward along the path that his own eyes appoint for him and witness as safe, until you have steered him to the stable of the Highest Good now truly seen and tested, that is, to the enjoyment of full wisdom.[127]

In this, as in all other aspects of his pedagogic philosophy, Comenius achieved a delicate balance between the formative role of the teacher and the particular needs of the individual learner. That balance is further exemplified in his views on school discipline—itself, he suggests, an important factor in strengthening pupil motivation. In *The Great Didactic* he writes: 'There is a proverb in Bohemia, "A school without discipline is like a mill without water," and this is very true. For, if you withdraw the water from a mill, it stops, and, in the same way, if you deprive a school of discipline, you take away from it its motive power. . . .'[128] The kind of discipline he envisaged was voluntary and consensual, rational, non-coercive, but nevertheless insistent, orderly and firm. He strongly urged teachers to ensure that pupils were fully aware of the reasons for its existence. He advised the assignment of some responsibility for discipline to the pupils themselves. 'Every pupil should acquire the habit of acting also as a teacher,' he writes in *The Analytical Didactic*.[129] The Decurion system whereby one pupil in every ten assumed such responsibility was standard practice in the schools at Přerov, Leszno and Sáros Pátak. Ultimately, he suggests, discipline is most effectively achieved through example, advice, encouragement and exhortation. Corporal punishment he abhorred; he recommended that punishment of any kind should be administered only for serious misbehaviour—never for failure at lessons. He gives some instances of the kind of misbehaviour he felt would merit punishment: they include impiety, obscenity, stubbornness, disobedience and persistent idleness. His position on the whole matter of discipline is aptly summarised in the following guidelines for teachers that are set out in *The Analytical Didactic*:

> In Latin the word discipline has several meanings. Sometimes it signifies that which is taught and learned . . . sometimes it denotes the act of teaching and learning (as when we are said to be brought up under someone's discipline); but the word is used most properly, as here, to denote a means of enforcing instruction. . . .
>
> Without discipline one learns nothing or at least nothing correctly. It is desirable, however, to provide a discipline that is adjusted (1) to the end in view; that is, discipline should be efficient in compelling a student to accomplish a task at hand; (2) to human nature; that is, discipline should develop human nature, not destroy it; and three, to levels of need; that is, just as there are various kinds of talent, so there are various sources and levels of error and the correction of error. . . .

There are about ten levels of discipline:

1. A teacher whose learning merits esteem should possess such authority and command such respect that a pupil would think it sinful to offend him.

2. A teacher should watch his pupils intently, so that they will realise that they are being watched.

3. A teacher should always lead the way, so that his pupils may see that they have someone to follow.

4. A teacher should always look about him to see whether he is being followed and how well.

5. A teacher should constantly lead pupils by the hand, to make sure that the pupil follows him properly and does not deviate into error.

6. A teacher should incite his pupils to rivalry (based on friendly competition), so that they may sharpen one another's wits.

7. A teacher should give frequent tests (sometimes at set intervals, sometimes unexpectedly, especially to the least trustworthy pupils, in order to make sure that they are not missing any part of the instruction.)

8. To make sure that no error becomes a habit, a teacher should always admonish a pupil as soon as the pupil commits a fault.

9. A teacher should rebuke those who are guilty of wilful error or conspicuous negligence; he should reprimand them and hold them up as a warning example to others, lest impunity become license.

10. If, however, any pupil should refuse such guidance (although this does not seem possible except in one extremely evil), let him be expelled, lest he prove a hindrance and a stumbling block to others.[130]

5. A CURRICULUM FOR THE UNIVERSAL SCHOOL

Order, depth, range and coherence are the characteristic features of the Comenian curriculum. 'What men learn and are taught should be (1) not partial or piecemeal but complete and total, (2) not superficial and deceptive but solid and real, (3) not harsh and forced but smooth and peaceful and therefore enduring,' he declared in the fourth chapter of the *Pampaedia*.[131] And in *The Great Didactic* he further declared: 'It is the principles, the causes and the uses of all the most important things in existence that we wish all men to learn. . . . For we must take strong and vigorous measures that no man, in his journey through life, may encounter anything so unknown to him that he cannot pass sound judgement upon it and turn it to its proper use without serious error.' He qualified this with the assertion that 'we do not demand for all men a knowledge, that is to say, an exact or deep knowledge of all the arts and sciences,' but a range of subject-matter sufficient to ensure that all have

the opportunity to fulfil the pansophic ideal.[132] The curriculum he envisaged was one which would have sufficient range and depth to provide
every student, not with an encyclopaedic body of knowledge, but with a
sense of the *unity and order* of all truth. In the *Via Lucis* he wrote: 'And
this we name Pansophia, a scheme which can state all things of this or
any future age, hidden or revealed, in an order inviolable and in fact
never broken, with such clearness that no man who surveys them with
attentive mind can fail to understand all things, or give them his genuine
assent.'[133] A pansophic, as distinct from an encyclopaedic, curriculum
should give access to what he considered the three main sources of
wisdom: knowledge of nature, intellectual knowledge and knowledge of
God. These are the essential elements in the philosophy of curriculum
defined in the *Via Lucis*:

> The first and greatest book of God is the visible world inscribed
> and illustrated with as many characters as there are creatures of
> God to be seen in it. The second book is man himself, made in the
> likeness of God. . . . Man wishes to be wise and to know as many
> things as possible: he therefore presumes that God, his archetype is
> most wise. Further man longs for power under the sway of which
> other things may be brought. . . . Finally, man longs to be good or
> at least to be thought good and better than his neighbour: so he is
> led unhesitatingly to the belief that God is good in the highest
> degree. And so it comes about that man is able to learn more about
> his Creator from himself than from all other created things. So, then,
> in truth, man is the book of God—presented, not like the great
> world to his eyes, but to his own heart. But God has given into
> man's hands a third book, to serve, as it were, as a commentary
> upon the book of the external world, and as a guide to that inner
> book, his own conscience—namely, the Holy Scriptures, in which
> he throws light from one quarter and another upon certain some-
> what obscure things, and teaches us the true purposes and uses of
> all things.[134]

Elaborating further on the implications of all this, he insists the curriculum must have *substantive* content: that is, content sufficiently profound
to guarantee depth and thoroughness in the pupil's comprehension of all
varieties of essential knowledge and truth. 'The category of substance
advises us that books ought to be written about substantial things likely
to bring substantial knowledge,' he writes in the *Pampaedia*. 'Quality
bids us that they should be incontrovertible, spreading the clear light of
truth and not a smoke-screen of opinions.'[135] The requirements for
'substantiveness' are set out explicitly both in the *Via Lucis* and the
Pampaedia. 'We wish that our universal books shall be true and perfectly

arranged summaries of all things that can be known,' he writes in the *Via Lucis*. 'They will therefore have a threefold virtue—fullness, order and truth.' The first term requires that they 'contain everything which touches our condition in time and eternity'; the second that they 'shall flow on from their beginnings, through their successive developments, to their end without any break'; the third that 'all things shall be set forth exactly as they are, or as they have become, or are becoming, without any mixture of what is false or idle.'[136] These three conditions are varied slightly in the *Pampaedia*. Here he insists the 'books of wisdom', i.e. the curriculum, must 'relate *directly, fully and clearly* to their own true end of true human education. . . .

> *Directly*: so that no one under this kind of guidance could possibly be diverted from his own true end or fail to reach it. It will be achieved if God, our everlasting highest good, is for ever established as the transcendent life and soul, as it were, constantly animating our human life and soul until we reach heaven.
>
> *Fully*: so that no one under this kind of guidance can possibly fail to obtain any part of what is good for him in this life or the life to come. This will be achieved if everything that God has displayed in His own theatre is set forth in print to produce men who are fully educated, that is, wise in mind, saintly in will, and mighty in God through their works.
>
> *Clearly*: so that nothing should seem inaccessible to anyone on this course. This will be achieved (1) if these school books are few and brief instead of numerous and bulky, and are neither deficient in the essentials nor padded with the superfluous; (2) if they are presented methodically with the combination of fresh pleasure and constant enlightenment, and avoid any boredom from repetition or tedious obscurity; (3) if they present everything with such clear and genuine truth that readers are forced to acknowledge them as the true keys to the books of God and the understanding of all their contents.[137]

He stresses the need for the classification and simplification of all knowledge to ensure 'ease and rapidity in learning.' He advises a conscious and systematic sequencing of subject content to assist understanding in the fullest possible degree. Taking as his axiom the principle that 'nature prepares the material before she begins to give it form,' he draws analogies between the teacher and the builder laying a sound foundation for his building, the artist carefully preparing his canvas, and the gardener systematically planting his shoots. A careful preparation (i.e. sequencing and classification of subject-content) is, he suggests, just as essential for effective teaching as the selection of the content itself:

When a builder lays foundations he does not build the walls at the same time, much less does he put on the roof, but does each of these things in the proper time and in the proper place.

In the same way a painter does not work at twenty or thirty pictures at once, but occupies himself with one only. For, though he may from time to time put a few touches to some others or give his attention to something else, it is on one picture and one only that he concentrates his energies.

In the same way the gardener does not plant several shoots at once, but plants them one after the other, that he may neither confuse himself nor spoil the operation of nature. . . .

Confusion has arisen in the schools through the endeavour to teach the scholars many things at one time. . . . Let us imitate these people and take care not to confuse scholars who are learning grammar by teaching them dialectic, or by introducing rhetoric into their studies. . . . Schools, therefore, should be organised in such a manner that the scholar shall be occupied with only one object of study at any given time.[138]

Given his emphasis on the unity and order of all truth, it was logical for Comenius to emphasise the need for structural integration in the curriculum. This, together with the emphasis on pansophic order and substantiveness in content, constitutes the third of his main curricular principles. He saw all learning as a quest for the order or panharmony present in the universe and believed therefore that the curriculum must facilitate this in the highest possible degree. 'In the education of the young,' he writes in *The Great Didactic*, 'care should be taken that everything that is taught be carefully defined and kept in its place.' In a section entitled 'Nature Knits Everything in Continuous Combination' he compares the integration of the curriculum to the organic unity of the bodily limbs, the branches and buds in a tree, the foundations, walls and ceilings of a house.[139] 'The studies of a lifeztime should be so arranged that they form an encyclopaedic whole in which all the parts spring from a common source and each is in its right place,' he writes.[140]

What he insisted most vehemently, however, was that the unity of the curriculum is, in essence, a moral unity, deriving from the all-informing presence of the spiritual in the sphere of material and finite being. The final purpose of education, he declared in the *Pampaedia*, is to demonstrate to all men 'how all things are co-ordinated and connected by the eternal laws of truth.'[141] The curricular implications of this are worked out in the *Via Lucis*. It will be recalled that he spoke of the act of learning as a reaching towards the infinite by means of the finite, a reaching towards the supraphysical by means of the metaphysical and the physical. It is the presence of the infinite in the finite, of the spiritual immanently informing the materiality of the natural world, which is the source of its ultimate order and harmony, he wrote.[142] It is this principle, he argued, that renders all life intelligible and meaningful. Thus, he insisted, the curriculum would have to be designed so as to ensure that the interdependence of the material and the spiritual, of the sacred and secular, was visibly exemplified. The interrelatedness of all knowledge—the arts, the sciences, the revealed word of the scriptures—should be apparent, he says, from the selection and ordering of all the elements constituting the curriculum. The latter should ensure that all knowledge is pointed to the sources which render it meaningful in the ultimate order of truth—an order that is finally accessible only through faith. The mind's insatiable longing for knowledge, he declares, is fundamentally a longing for the infinity where the ultimate meaningfulness of all truth can be disclosed:

> The world then asks, and by asking shows that it lacks, some fuller way of fuller light. And if this longing is planted in our heart with no hope whatever of satisfying it, then it is high time such longing was destroyed. God and our own nature make nothing for no purpose. If, then, this longing is ineradicable, it is capable of satisfaction and has not been given to us for no purpose.
>
> I know the answer which can be offered at this point: it is that God our Creator has implanted in the minds of men longings for ever greater and better things, in order that mortals, seeing that here their eyes can never be satisfied with vision or their ears with hearing or their desires with the objects of desire, may be spurred on, as it were, by themselves, to direct their desires to eternity itself (where all things are brought together, and therefore the fulfilment and end of all things are to be found.) But even in this life—for anything else would be incredible—ever richer food is supplied to our longings, while we are here, until we reach the supreme goal which can be granted to us in this world, after which there can remain nothing but the crowning height of eternity. For the perfect wisdom of our God demands such a complete series of stages or grades. For, as the fact that there can be no vacuum in nature has made possible the discovery of the most delicate arts, so we may not unwarrantably believe that this flight of men from the emptiness of the human spirit and the unceasing desire to fill it may be the occasion for God to grant and for us to seek and find still nobler arts. And if this be so, why should we not extend our desires as far as a kind of omniscience? I mean a knowledge which in the highest sense is full of all those things which are offered for our learning here on earth, and set forth in that threefold book which has been given to us.[143]

The principle of curricular integrity is represented metaphorically in the *Via Lucis* through the central image of an all-informing light that penetrates and illuminates all modes of knowledge and truth. The light of empirical truth, he says, is contained in nature itself, in the phenomenal reality that is accessible to the senses. The light of reason is fuelled by the heritage of knowledge passed down through the ages and made accessible through the disciplines of the traditional curriculum. The light of conscience and faith is nurtured by the body of received truth contained in the scriptures. All modes of light are wholly complementary; all must be allowed to illuminate the mind and spirit through their interdependent harmony. All must be informed ultimately by the spirit of love—the key to the mysteries of the infinite. Religion and science, the secular and the sacred, must combine together in the disclosure of the light of wisdom which is the final objective of all learning and knowing:

> We have said further that a true knowledge of the world of Nature will be a key to the mysteries of the Scriptures, and here we rest upon a solid foundation. For as every man is the best interpreter of his own words, so, since the all-wise God is the author of Nature and of Scripture too, the truth which is imprinted upon things cannot possibly fail to harmonise at all points with the truth expressed in his words, or to explain and interpret itself, though here or there it should have seemed somewhat difficult to understand. For Nature and Scripture serve each the other, as commentator and interpreter, Scripture speaking in more general terms, and Nature in particular instances. For scripture teaches us in general what is the origin of created things, and by what power they are sustained, and what end they are at last to have.[144]

Because of his insistence on the moral unity of all knowledge, Comenius opposed the principle of specialisation at all stages of the schooling process. This can be illustrated particularly from his treatment of science. Largely through the influence of Bacon, the study of science had become prominent in the new educational institutions that had been founded, specifically to promote scientific experiment and enquiry, throughout various parts of Europe in the seventeenth century. Comenius shared the view of the new innovators that the study of science and mathematics should have much more prominence at all levels of education. But he insisted that all scientific enquiry be pointed towards its ultimate objective: the disclosure of the presence of the infinite in the phenomena of the natural world. Science, as the systematic study of the nature of the created universe, could disclose—more visibly and more penetratingly even than the scriptures themselves—the reality of the infinite, i.e. its impinging presence in the materiality of the natural world. He insisted, therefore, on its necessary interrelation with all other modes of access to the ultimacy of spiritual truth. 'I humbly pray to God to strengthen the desire which is planted in your hearts to search out the truth of natural objects,' he wrote in the Dedication to the *Via Lucis*, addressing the members of the Royal Society and urging them to dedicate themselves wholeheartedly to their work. 'It is manifest,' he said, 'that men who renew their efforts to rescue the truth in all its forms both in the school of sensible and in that of intellectual things are engaged in the most sacred labour. And since the first school makes ready the way for the second and the second for the third, so Truth in the domain of Nature will certainly prepare for moral and spiritual truths.'[145] He strongly urges the study of science in every school with this same objective in view:

> I said moreover, that in natural things the forms and meanings of our activities are foretold: and that for this reason the processes of nature must be accurately known, so that our own processes may be carried through without uncertainty or error. This has been seen by men who have called art the imitator and even the child of Nature, and have also declared that Nature is the best guide, since he who follows her cannot go astray, and have made many more statements in the same sense. But it has never been so clear as soon, by God's help, it will be, when the torches of the universal harmony have been kindled, that all the shortcomings and errors of former ages in the realms of Art, Morals, Politics and Ecclesiastical affairs, have sprung from ignorance of natural things; and that the restoration of the world for which we look will come from a better observation of the way of God's wisdom concerning his creatures. Not less than this is the difference in effect between knowledge and ignorance of the things which God has given to us as norms or standards. Let the claim, then, which we have made stand unchallenged, that everything which is embraced in the realm of Nature must be included in the list of things to be learnt.[146]

Having stressed the importance of pointing scientific enquiry towards its ultimate objectives in the total process of discovering knowable truths, Comenius provided detailed guidance on the ways in which all this can be fostered in the school classroom. Writing several centuries before advances in modern science necessitated radically new developments in classroom practice, his pedagogic principles seem remarkably far-seeing and eminently practical for the teaching of school science. His advice was focussed mainly on the development of perceptual abilities and the training of the young pupil in the methods of systematic observation and experiment. The whole process was focussed on knowledge gained through direct sensory experience. 'The truth and certainty of science depend more on the witness of the senses than anything else,' he declares in *The Great Didactic*. He stressed the need to verify all theoretical knowledge from the evidence of sensory experience. 'It follows,' he writes, 'that if we wish to implant a true and certain knowledge of things in our pupils, we must take especial care that everything be learned by means of actual observation and sensuous perception.'[147] He saw an important role for the training of good habits of memorisation to ensure the retention of scientific knowledge. Here again he maintained a delicate balance between the need for the teacher to encourage individual enquiry on the part of the pupil, and the pupil's need, in turn, for sound guidance to ensure it was conducted effectively and purposefully. He saw a particularly significant role for the teacher in guiding the pupil towards a realisation of the ultimate significance of all scientific truth. In the chapter from *The Great Didactic* entitled 'The Method of the Sciences, Specifically' he gives this advice to the teacher:

> If any be uncertain if all things can be placed before the senses in this way, even things spiritual and things absent (things in heaven, or in hell, or beyond the sea), let him remember that all things have been harmoniously arranged by God in such a manner that the higher in the scale of existence can be represented by the lower, the absent by the present, and the invisible by the visible.[148]

Side by side with his provision for the fostering of scientific enquiry was a strong emphasis on the development of the imagination through an extensive programme in the arts. Long before drawing and painting were introduced into European schools (they were not introduced, for example, until 1872 in the schools of the Austro-Hungarian Empire), Comenius recognised the importance of an education in the visual arts. In the *Informatorium* he urges that 'children be encouraged to try painting and calligraphy . . . as early as the third and fourth year' and suggests they be given 'chalk (or charcoal) with which they can make dots and draw lines, hooks, zig-zags, crosses and circles at will.'[149] He gives detailed instruction on the development of visual awareness and perception. 'In optics,' he writes, 'it is useful to teach children what light is, and what darkness, as well as the names of some colours.' He continues: 'In the second and third year in optics, it is an exercise for children when they are shown something painted and colourful, as well as the beauty of the sky, trees, flowers and flowing water.'[150] In the same work he advocates detailed lessons in music appreciation, similarly stressing the importance of auditory creativity for the all-round development of the young student. Jaromir Uždil has described the place of music in Comenius's work. He indicates the extent of his debt to the hymn-singing traditions of the *Unitas Fratrum:*

Music has a special place in Comenius's aesthetic and educational considerations. It is a cement which very strongly links people of the same convictions and faith. Of course, most important are vocal expressions, songs, which address listeners not only by their religious content but also by the emotional ardour of the melody. . . . Care for the purity of the musical treasure of the Unity was an unwritten obligation of its leading representatives. After 1501 when the 'Kancionalnik' (hymn-book) of the Unity was published as the first printed book of its kind in Europe, the repertory of songs of the Unity of Czech Brethren underwent considerable purification, especially due to the work of Jan Blahoslav, the learned bishop, who did his task, well equipped with all accessible musicological knowledge of the period.

Comenius, guided by his sense of practice, was impelled to publish a small, Dhandy hymnal, and recognising the need to explain such a daring undertaking, he wrote a foreword which attests to his pedagogical views in this sphere. It contains words which prove not only his sense of democracy (all people should sing), but also his awareness of the limited validity of this requirement if prerequisites do not exist for it in the culture of the senses and spirit (non est harmoniae factus, qui harmonia non delectantur—'not made for music is he who is incapable of being enchanted by it.')

For Comenius vocal music is a higher (i.e. truly artistic) level of speech, of language. Prophets composed songs and psalms in the languages of their peoples. Therefore 'also to-day nations should use their own languages in songs' . . . . Comenius himself composed hymns full of ardent piety, and there is no doubt that his talent as a poet was greater than that of other members of the Unity of Brethren who sought self-expression. His literary talent is evident after all, in his entire work, both Czech and Latin, in the colourful and full-bodied metaphors he uses abundantly in his writings, in the wonderful conciseness of his autobiography.[151]

Another commentator, Olga Settari, has emphasised the manner in which moral and aesthetic education were linked by Comenius: 'When reading Comenius's observations concerning music and art, as formulated in a number of his books, we find out that his views on music and art, and their role in society, were influenced not only by ideals of the period, but also by ancient philosophical and aesthetic opinions concerning the mission of music and art. Comenius emphasises especially the ideational and ethical content of art, and according to him, only art imbued with wisdom and ethics is real art, and as such should pervade man's entire life.'[152] It was precisely because of his belief in the ethical potential of the arts that, like Tolstoy two centuries later, he insisted all children have access to their benefits. 'Comenius,' Settari writes, 'took over democratic and humanistic components of the educational system of the Unity of Brethren. He formulated the well-known requirement that art should be accessible to all people, regardless of age, state, or occupation.' She continues: 'In Comenius's pedagogical work, ethical considerations are always interwoven with aesthetic considerations: music is not mere amusement for him but a need. The function of art in general is to help shape moral conduct, educate to wisdom and prepare for life.'[153]

Comenius provided detailed demonstration of the practical application of all these principles in *The Great Didactic* and the *Pampaedia*. In both works he sets out the details of the content he envisaged as being appropriate for the kindergarten, the primary school and the secondary school. For the kindergarten he envisaged an integrated programme of activities comprehending the spheres of language, number, art, music, nature study, moral and religious education. He urged teachers to give rudimentary instruction in the alphabet, the construction of simple sentences, the mastery of basic word-attack skills (detailed guidance is given in his writings on the decoding of vowel and consonant formations), side by side with provision for pre-reading and pre-writing activities, painting and drawing, singing, and story-telling.[154] In the *Informatorium* he provides guidance on elementary voice training and the playing of simple musical instruments. He recommends that children under three be trained to listen to songs as well as singing them themselves; four year-olds, he suggests, should begin to learn an instrument (e.g. the pipe or tambourine.)[155] For religious education he recommended the use of a Bible manual specially designed for the age-group and containing vivid narratives of all the main stories from the scriptures.[156] Beyond specifying the range of content and the kinds of activities he considered appropriate for the age-group, he left decisions on its implementation largely to the discretion of the individual teacher.

The curriculum he envisaged for the primary school shows some extraordinarily far seeing thinking on a number of issues.[157] Firstly, there is his sense of the importance of the mother-tongue. Comenius saw this as the key to fostering educability and, therefore, to the realisation of the ideal of universal education. He insisted that maximum attention be given to the development of vernacular proficiency, through a carefully graded programme of studies in the spheres of oracy-auracy, reading and writing. To ensure the highest possible level of vernacular competence he insisted that a second language should not be introduced before the age of 10—a very radical proposal in an age when Latin ('that nymph on whom such unbounded admiration is generally wasted') was the chief medium of instruction in most schools. 'To attempt to teach a foreign language before the mother-tongue has been learned is as irrational as to teach a boy to ride before he can walk,' he declares.[158] The prominence given to vernacular studies in an otherwise broad and well-balanced curriculum will be seen from the following listing of objectives for the work of the primary school:

> The aim and object of the Vernacular-School should be to teach to all the young, between the ages of six and twelve, such things as will be of use to them throughout their whole lives. That is to say:
> 1. To read with ease both print and writing in their mother-tongue.
> 2. To write, first with accuracy, then with speed, and finally with confidence, in accordance with the grammatical rules of the mother-tongue. These rules should be written in a popular form, and the boys should be exercised in them.
> 3. To count, with ciphers and with counters, as far as is necessary for practical purposes.
> 4. To measure spaces, such as length, breadth and distance with skill.
> 5. To sing well-known melodies, and in the case of those who display especial aptitude, to learn the elements of advanced music.
> 6. To learn by heart the greater number of the psalms and hymns that are used in the country.
> 7. Besides the Catechism they should know the most important stories and verses in the Bible, and should be able to read them word for word.
> 8. They should learn the principles of morality, which should be drawn up in the shape of rules and accompanied by illustrations suitable to the age and understanding of the pupils. They should also begin to put these principles into practice.
> 9. They should also learn as much economics and politics as is necessary to enable them to understand what they see daily at home and in the state.
> 10. They should also learn the general history of the world; its creation, its fall, its redemption, and its preservation by God up to the present day.
> 11. In addition, they should learn the most important facts of cosmography, such as the spherical shape of the heavens . . . the tides of the ocean, the courses of rivers . . . but in particular, the cities, mountains, rivers, and other remarkable features of their own country.
> 12. Finally, they should learn the most important principles of the mechanical arts . . .[159]

Comenius recommended the use of a comprehensive textbook for each of the six years of the primary school. Long before the development of sophisticated printing technology, he recognised the need for attractively designed textbooks. He also stressed the importance of combining seriousness of treatment with humour and playfulness. 'Care must be taken to suit all these books to the children for whom they are intended,' he wrote, 'for children like whimsicality and humour, and detest pedantry and severity. Instruction, therefore, should ever be combined with amusement, that they may take pleasure in learning serious things which will be of genuine use to them later on. . . . '[160] He suggested a careful balancing of work and recreation in the organisation of the school day. He recommended no more than four periods of class teaching which were to be followed by an equivalent allocation of time for recreation and 'domestic activities.'[161] He placed a strong emphasis on the teaching of mathematics—a subject for long either neglected or crudely taught in schools until Reformist educators, such as Philip Melanchton, recognised its importance. This passage from the chapter of the *Pampaedia* dealing with the primary school indicates the prominence given to the subject by Comenius:

> As the foundation of all this is mathematics, and the basis of all our ability to calculate consists of counting, weighing or measuring . . . we must certainly ensure that arithmetic, geometry and statics are treated in our national schools as universal subjects. My reasons for saying this are (1) that these three are simply essential to the reasoning life. Just as the art of reading books cannot be acquired without a knowledge of the alphabet, so without a knowledge of numbers, weights and measures, it is impossible to investigate the mysteries of the world, where in fact everything has been made by divine skill with numbers, weights and measures. And there is no better way to observe the integration of nature. (2) These three are the whetstone of intellect, the keys to wisdom, and a commendable course of study. (3) They appeal to this youthful age group which we do well to humour by our choice of subject. (4) They are useful for a whole lifetime.[162]

He also recognised the value of a good musical education at this level, seeing it both as a means to the cultivation of imaginative sensibilities and a source of personal pleasure and relaxation. As with all other subjects of the curriculum, he stressed its place in the 'eternal order of truth'. 'Pupils,' he writes in the *Pampaedia*, 'should all have an introduction to music because (1) everything ought to be in harmony, and this is obviously the most harmonious of subjects, (2) it is a means of honest relaxation, (3) it contributes to God's praises so that they all emulate David.'[163] He particularly stressed the benefits of choral singing. The sophistication of his knowledge of this subject is intimated in this passage from Olga Settari 's study, 'J.A. Comenius: Musicologist, Pedagogue and Hymnographer':

In accordance with the aesthetic ideals of the period, and the then prevalent pedagogic concepts, Comenius regarded singing as the most important component of music education. It was to singing that he devoted a large part of his relatively extensive preface to the Amsterdam Hymnal. From the viewpoint of music education the preface is valuable in that Comenius presents his definition of singing, deals with questions of reproduction, the relationship between content and form in songs etc. He stresses the priority of the musical component of songs by demanding that singers maintain melody. The aesthetic impact of songs is determined by their rendition which depends on the lyrics. Comenius aims at unity of lyrics and melody in songs also by paying attention to questions of musical declamation and quantitative meter.

Comenius's main aesthetic criteria for songs and singing can be summed up as follows: above all, he formulates the requirement of intelligibility of the lyrics, by which he continues the efforts of Jan Blahoslav, and which logically constitutes his links with the main aesthetic principle of Florentine madrigalists of the early Baroque period. Another criterion is organised unity of content and form in songs, understood by Comenius as respect for harmony between lyrics and melody, in his view achievable on the basis of organised quantitative meter. Finally, it is the postulate of suitability and intelligibility of songs according to age groups; Comenius recommends a smaller number of songs to be practised, but with concrete and comprehensible content. In the spirit of his aesthetic norms, Comenius arranged a number of songs in the Amsterdam Hymnal, and wrote new lyrics for several; songs, which are examples of his endeavour in creative music.[164]

The programme envisaged by Comenius for the secondary school is essentially a development of the traditional classical curriculum, its main features having evolved from the mediaeval *trivium* and *quadrivium*. It was clearly designed to meet the three main objectives that he envisaged as the goals of the educational process: the fostering of learning, virtue and piety. The main innovations lie in the spheres of science and mathematics. Here Comenius made significant advances on the mediaeval curriculum where both subjects were catered for only minimally through the disciplines of arithmetic and astronomy. He insisted that language studies should remain the dominant discipline in the early years of the second-level school, with the full range of subjects being offered only in the final years. He outlines the objectives of this truly comprehensive curriculum, designed to cater for the needs of all children, in the following passage from *The Great Didactic*:

In this school the pupils should learn four languages and acquire an encyclopaedic knowledge of the arts. Those youth who have completed its whole curriculum should have training as:

1. Grammarians who are well-versed in Latin and in the mother-tongue, and have a sufficient acquaintance with Greek and Hebrew.

2. Dialecticians, who are well skilled in making definitions, in drawing distinctions, in arguing a point, and in solving hard questions.

3. Rhetoricians or orators who can talk well on any given subject.

4. Arithmeticians, and

5. Geometricians; both on account of the use of these sciences in daily life, and because they sharpen the intellect more than anything else.

6. Musicians, both practical and theoretical.

7. Astronomers, who have, at any rate, mastered the rudiments, such as the knowledge of the heavenly bodies, and the calculation of their movements, since without this science it is impossible to understand not only physics but also geography and a great part of history. . . .

8. Physicists, who know the composition of the earth, the force of the elements, the different species of animals . . . and the structure of the human body. Under this head is thus comprised a part of medicine, of agriculture and of other mechanical arts.

9. Geographers.

10. Historians.

11. Moralists, who can draw fine distinctions between the various kinds of virtue and vice and who can follow the one and avoid the other.

12. Theologians who, besides understanding the principles of their faith, can also prove them from the Scriptures.[165]

Extensive detail is provided by Comenius on the subject-matter to be covered in order to realise each of these objectives. A particularly innovative feature of the programme is the attention given to health education—an area not generally covered in mediaeval schools. The pupils themselves were allowed a good deal of flexibility at this level of schooling; considerable provision was to be made for independent study; pupils were encouraged to make their own choice of textbooks for this purpose, in addition to those prescribed for the general work of the school.[166] A detailed examination of curricular provision in the spheres of language, moral and religious education will be made in later chapters of this book.

The Comenian curriculum commands attention principally for its synthesis of the traditions of the Judaeo-Christian and classical heritage of knowledge, wisdom and learning with the egalitarian ideals articulated by Reformist educators—a synthesis that was not to find complete realisation until the emergence of comprehensive education in the modern age. Crucially, he recognised the importance of fostering educability, and he sought, through his insistence that all children be given a sound foundation in the basics of language and number, to achieve this effectively in the early years of schooling. His meticulous attention to the selection, grading and sequencing of subject content ensured that teaching and learning were conducted at the highest degree of efficacy at all levels of schooling—a vital factor in the achievement of his radically democratic ideals of providing all children with access to the riches of their cultural heritage. What he envisaged can truly be designated a liberal curriculum, by virtue of its cultivation of the full range of human potentialities— spiritual, religious, moral, emotional, aesthetic, intellectual, social and physical. In this context he recognised the importance of providing a broad, balanced, substantive and largely undifferentiated curriculum for the entire populace, regardless of intellectual ability, socio-cultural background or religious creed. Most importantly of all, he identified the principles of order and unity which would render this whole process truly self-fulfilling and meaningful through his compelling demonstration of the convergence and harmonisation of all modes of knowledge, learning and wisdom in the spheres of metaphysical, moral, spiritual and religious truth. The full implications of this latter principle will be examined in a later chapter dealing exclusively with moral and religious education.

CHRISTIANITY, FREEDOM AND EDUCATION

As the world is ever perverse, and catches at the shadow rather than at the truth, so doth it here also; it founds its liberty on this, that he who is free should grant nothing to others, and should give himself over to sloth, pride, or passion. But the conduct of the Christian is far different. Only guarding his heart well that he may in freedom preserve it for God alone, he employs everything else for the wants of his fellowmen.

> Comenius, *The Labyrinth of the World and the Paradise of the Heart*.[1]

Thou wouldst go into the world, and art going with empty hands, with some promise of freedom which men in their simplicity and their natural unruliness cannot even understand, which they fear and dread—for nothing has ever been more insupportable for a man and human society than freedom. . . . Instead of taking men's freedom from them, Thou didst make it greater than ever.

> Dostoevsky, *The Brothers Karamazov*[2]

Love can exist only with freedom.

> Tolstoy, 'Progress and Education'[3]

History as we know it began with Christ, it was founded by him on the Gospels. Now what is history? Its beginning is that of the centuries of systematic work devoted to the solution of the enigma of death, so that death itself may eventually be overcome. That is why people write symphonies, and why they discover mathematical infinity and electromagnetic waves. You can't make such discoveries without spiritual equipment, and for this, everything necessary has been given us in the Gospels. What is it? Firstly, love of one's neighbour—the supreme form of living energy. Once it fills the heart of man it has to overflow and spend itself. And secondly, the two concepts which are the main part of the make-up of modern

man—without them he is inconceivable—the ideas of free personality
and of life regarded as sacrifice

Pasternak, *Doctor Zhivago*[4]

1. TOWARDS A LIBERATING FAITH

It is through his conception of education as primarily an ethico-religious
process that Comenius most fully reveals the liberal character of his educational thought. The degree to which his commitment to the promotion of
egalitarian ideals was inspired by his deeply radical Christian convictions
will be recalled from an earlier chapter. It was shown that his commitment to the ideal of universal education derived principally from his belief
that education is the means to the spiritual and religious illumination that
is necessary for the full realisation of individual personhood. It is something, therefore, he said, which should be made accessible to all men,
regardless of social background, individual ability, vocational expectation
or denominational creed. The present chapter will attempt to define a
more specific sense in which those same convictions influenced his educational thought. It will explore his ideas on the cultivation of moral responsibility and on the fostering of religious faith through those areas of the
school curriculum specifically designated for that purpose. It will further
explore the kind of pedagogic method he considered appropriate for the
realisation of these objectives.

It may be useful, in the first instance, briefly to reiterate his assertion
of the primacy of ethico-religious goals in education so that the place of
moral and religious programmes in the whole process can be precisely
defined. 'The ultimate concern of man is the eternal,' he wrote in the *Via
Lucis*. 'For men must be taught eternal things,' he said, 'because being
destined for eternity they cannot be ignorant of their end without risk of
eternal loss.'[5] It will be recalled that in *The Great Didactic* he saw education as the key to the regeneration of mankind, by virtue of its potential
for fostering moral responsibility amongst the young. 'The most useful
thing that the Holy Scriptures teach us in this connection is that there is
no more certain way under the sun for the raising of sunken humanity
than the proper education of the young,' he wrote.[6] The *Pampaedia* opens
with quotations from Cicero, Moses, Christ and St. Paul to emphasise
the integration of Judaeo-Christian and classical aims in Comenius's
conception of the goals of education. But he stresses the primacy of its
ethico-religious objectives. 'If we are to emulate the zeal of the holy
apostles in teaching every man in all wisdom, to present every man
perfect in Christ, it is my desire,' he said, 'that we should come closer to
that function, that prayer, that hope, that commandment and that zeal
during the present age . . . so that as all things are coordinated and

connected by the eternal laws of truth, men also may be able to share in the light, the truth and the order of our world, every individual and every community achieving true harmony.'[7]

These were the general principles on which Comenius's entire approach to education was based, as has been shown in an earlier chapter. They were also the principles which guided his thinking on the moral and religious formation of every child through the programmes he specifically designed to achieve that end. To identify the true nature of these programmes, and to appreciate their extraordinarily radical and innovative character, it is necessary firstly to define the kinds of religious convictions on which they were based. Some attention was given earlier to the emergence and growth of the Moravian movement and to the teachings of its leaders from Chelčický onwards. It was shown that the Moravians saw education as crucially necessary for the promotion of the way of life to which they were committed by their beliefs, and that they saw the foundation of schools as essential for the full realisation of this. Education was seen by them as a communal responsibility, requiring a commitment by all believers to the propagation of the ideals by which they sought to conduct their lives. Those ideals were born of their rejection of religious dogmatism, authoritarianism and intolerance; they were grounded in a profound belief that the essential message of Christ was the freedom of individual conscience, as manifested in a personal interpretation of the word of the scriptures and the assumption of individual responsibility for its implementation in the affairs of everyday life. Comenius, like his forebears in the Moravian movement—and like the later Slavic writers whose words were cited at the beginning of this chapter—was a Christian in this radical sense of the term. He saw Christianity as primarily an affirmation of the freedom of the individual person—a freedom he believed was manifested and ultimately fulfilled in the all-encompassing law of love, as enjoined by Christ in the scriptures. It is this conviction that his writings on religious and moral education primarily seek to convey.

Like his confrères in the Moravian movement he saw the scriptures as the sole authority in matters of faith and the sole guarantor of the freedom of individual conscience in which they all believed that faith was rooted. Distrusting rationalist theorising, the Moravians had never attempted to create a body of theological doctrine, but sought in their daily lives to exemplify a way of life which was modelled on a close and authentic interpretation of the scripture text. Their teachings were handed down through agreements reached by their communities at successive periods throughout their history. These agreements set forth the disciplines and rules they decided should be followed by their communities; they provided regulations for prayer services, marriage laws, the organisation of schools and the conduct of economic and material affairs. One Moravian Handbook describes the life of a typical community in the following terms: 'It is a fellowship of witness where Christian love may be seen in action, and where the seeker may find the way to God. It is a fellowship of service, following our master who came not to be served but to serve.' 'It is the call of God rather than any particular ritual that makes a ministry valid,' the manual says. 'Moravians believe that there is nothing that need separate all those who truly love Christ.' 'Their congregations,' it says, 'provide a focal point for the commitment of the individual to Christ and a place of spiritual growth and mutual encouragement in the faith.'[8]

The movement particularly emphasised simplicity of religious practice, its services consisting largely of the recitation of the Creed, readings from the scriptures, the chanting of psalms and hymns, and the commemorative ritual of the Eucharist. The simplicity—and radicalism—of the movement derived from its affirmation of the all-embracing principle of love as the essential message of Christ and the heart of the Christian faith. Freedom, they believed, is manifested and fulfilled in a truly selfless devotion to others, as enjoined by Christ in the Gospels. 'No one in the world is more ready to serve than a man who is devoted to God. . . . If he but sees what can benefit a fellowman he does not hesitate, does not delay, spares no trouble,' Comenius writes in the *Labyrinth*.[9] In his characterisation of the 'true Christian' the Pilgrim reflects on the paradox that freedom is manifested in the denial of self for the welfare of others: 'Only guarding his heart well that he in freedom preserve it for God alone, he employs everything else for the wants of his fellowman.'[10] The greatest wealth that men possess, he says, is the spiritual reward that comes from the free exercise of brotherly love. In this passage he further reflects on the good fortune of those whose lives are empowered by a loving trust in God and the love of their fellowman:

Now I beheld here a wondrous thing. There were some among these holy men who had an ample supply of riches, silver, gold crowns and sceptres (for there are such men also among God's chosen); others had scarcely anything beyond a half-naked body, that was dried up by hunger and thirst. Yet the former said they had nothing, and the latter said they had everything, and both were of good cheer. And then I understood that he is truly rich and in want of nothing who knows how to be content with that which he has. To have a large, a small, or no house, costly, poor, or no clothing, many friends or one, or none, high rank, low rank, or no rank, to have or not to have rank or office or glory, generally to be something or to be nothing, is to them one and the same thing; for as man must believe that to go, to stand, to sit wherever God leads, or places, or seats him is the only truly good thing, better even than man can imagine.[11]

The Pilgrim insists that Christians do not require either elaborate rituals
or complex thought-systems to make them aware of their primary responsibility towards love of their fellowman. He suggests that this responsibility may in fact be confused by excessive concentration on abstract
principles and rules. The externalisation of religion through elaborate
ceremonial, side by side with legalism and formalised religious and ethical
doctrines, can ultimately, he suggests, lead to a stifling of the promptings
of individual conscience. In this passage he affirms the primacy of the
latter in all matters of morality and faith:

> To him who verily loves God with his whole heart, it is not neces-
> sary to give many commandments as to when, where, how, and
> how often he should serve God, worship and honour Him; for his
> hearty union with God, and his readiness to obey Him is the fashion
> in which he honours God best, and it leads a man to ever and
> everywhere praise God in his mind, and to strive for His glory in
> all his deeds. He also who loves his fellowmen as himself requires
> not copious commandments as to where, when and wherein he
> should serve them, how he should avoid to injure them, and return
> to them what is due to them. This love for his fellowmen will in
> itself tell him fully, and show him how he should bear himself
> towards them. It is the sign of the evil man that he always demands
> rules, and wishes to know only from the books of law what he
> should do; yet at home in our heart God's finger shows us that it is
> our duty to do unto our neighbours that which we wish that they
> should do unto us. But as the world cares not for this inward testi-
> mony of our own conscience, but heeds external laws only, therefore
> is there no true order in the world; there is but suspicion, distrust,
> misunderstanding, ill-will, discord, envy, theft, murder, and so forth.
> Those who are truly subject to God heed but their own conscience;
> what it forbids them they do not, but they do that which it tells them
> they may do; of gain, favour, and such things they take no care.[12]

Comenius, again following the traditions of Moravian Christianity, emphasised three principles as particularly manifesting the Christian responsibility towards love. He saw each as representing a particular challenge
for the educator, as will be shown in some detail presently. The first is
the principle of religious tolerance—one particularly needing to be emphasised in the conditions of seventeenth century Europe. The second is the
more fundamental responsibility towards the promotion of peace—that
is, towards an active quest for peace through reconciliation and brotherhood. The third is the commitment towards equity and justice in all
things, a principle implicit in the ideal of service of one's fellowmen and
the assumption by every individual of his responsibility towards the

whole of mankind. In each case he fully substantiated his teachings from the words of the scripture text.

The Moravians saw religious intolerance as one of the most widely manifested corruptions of the Christian doctrine of love. As one historian has written: 'The characteristic fellowship of the Moravian Church was never to be thought of as the indulgence of the few but as the nature of the whole Church of Christ, and of the true nature of the world. Thus the ecumenical spirit has been in the Moravian Church from the beginning. . . . This aim was so deeply held to, that it was affirmed that Moravian existence as a separate body must disappear in the interests of the wider unity of the people of God.'[13] It will be recalled that Comenius, in *The Bequest of the Unity of Brethren*, held out the hand of friendship to all other Christian communions, even to the Roman Catholic Church which had persistently harassed and persecuted the Moravian Brethren throughout the first two centuries of their existence. He profoundly condemned the Churches for failing to reconcile their differences. Some of his sharpest satire in the *Labyrinth* is directed at the petty squabbles conducted by the Churches over trivial matters of theological doctrine. This example occurs in the chapter entitled 'The Pilgrim Beholds the Christian Religion':

> Then going outside of this railing, lo! I see that this church had many little chapels, to which those went who had not been able to agree when before this touchstone, and behind each of them followed a number of men. They gave the people rules as to how they should differ from the others; some said that one should be marked by water or fire; others, that one should always have the sign ready at hand and in the pocket; others said that beside the principal image, at which all should gaze, men should, for greater perfection, carry with them also as many small ones as was possible; others said that when praying one should not kneel, for that was a thing of the Pharisees; others, again, said that they would not endure music among them, as it was a wanton thing; others again, said that one should accept the teaching of no man, and be content with the innermost revelation of the spirit.[14]

He contrasts the theological squabbling of the Churches with the spirit of tolerance and fellowship that exists between genuine Christian communities. Using the analogy of musical harmony, the Pilgrim describes the spirit of unity in diversity that is the mark of genuine Christian fellowship: 'Though there was a great variety in their gifts, just as on a musical instrument the sound of the strings or pipes differs, and is now weaker, now stronger, yet a delightful harmony resounded among them. This is the purpose of the Christian unity, and the foretoken of eternity, when everything will be done in one spirit.'[15] In the section from the *Labyrinth* that is entitled 'There is Intimacy among True Christians' Comenius further writes: 'Therefore there is great intimacy among them, openness, and holy companionship; therefore all, however different their gifts and their callings may be, consider and hold themselves as brethren; for they say they have all sprung from the same blood, have been redeemed and cleansed by the same blood, that we are children of one Father, approach the same table, await the same inheritance in heaven, and so forth.'[16] One of the most moving passages in the *Unum Necessarium*—Comenius's last great testament to his faith—conveys his sense of the relative unimportance of formal doctrine when compared with the overruling Christian commitment to love. He stresses the essential simplicity of the Christian faith when seen from this radical and wholly authentic standpoint:

> If someone should ask me about my theology, I would (with the dying Acquinas, for I myself am also about to die) seize the Bible, and would say with all my heart and in a plain language: 'I believe all that is written in this book!' If someone should inquire more closely about my confession of faith, I would show him the Apostolic, for I know nothing shorter, simpler, or pithier, nothing that could sooner bring me to a decision in all controversies, and to save me the endless labyrinths of disputation. If someone should ask me for a book of prayers, I would point him to the Lord's Prayer. For I am persuaded that no one can show a key that opens the Father's heart easier than the only begotten Son who proceeded from the Father. . . . I have said that all the endeavours of my life hitherto were similar to the care of Martha for the Lord and his disciples; motivated by love, indeed, for I am not conscious of anything to the contrary. For cursed be every hour and every moment of whatever labour spent on anything else![17]

The realisation of the spirit of ecumenicity and the practice of a non-sectarian Christianity was seen by Comenius as an essential witness to all this. Throughout his life he sought to promote the practice of a faith that could transcend sectarian boundaries. He reached out not only to other Christian communions but also to the worlds of Judaism and Islam, and he called on all believers to suppress their differences and come together in a spirit of fellowship and brotherhood. Christian institutions, he felt, had failed the first and most basic test of their faith: their responsibility to respond to one another in a spirit of tolerance and love. 'Now everyone considers his own Babylon beautiful and believes that his is the true Jerusalem which surpasses all things and everything gives way to it,' he declared ruefully in the *Unum Necessarium*.[18] Blaming much of this on the excessive rationalisation—and in many cases the distortion—of the truths of the scriptures, he called for a more balanced synthesis of reason and faith that would reflect the true spirit of the Gospels. Such a synthesis, he suggested, could be achieved by his ideal of pansophic wisdom. In this passage from the *Via Lucis* he describes how it might facilitate greater unity in matters of religious faith:

> Moreover, there is no reason for us to despair of the support of men. For our work is directed to the injury of none, and the good of all. We are not by human schemes devising some monarchy beneath which kings and peoples will be forced to bow their necks; nor establishing some school in philosophy or religion from which the other schools will have anything to fear, nor vaunting any new doctrines or mysteries from which long-cherished convention may look for any damage or disrespect. Our aim is only that all men may know what things are good for them, and bringing these things into a common store may use and enjoy them with common delight: that all men, abandoning every device against the liberty of their neighbours, may begin to reign under Christ the supreme monarch in his Kingdom of freedom—that they may no longer be divided into rival parties and indulge hatreds, but rather bring their mind to have, as a common possession, all the arts and sciences and the mysteries and treasures of wisdom—our aim is to persuade them to labour for this consummation.[19]

Comenius, however, saw the problem of religious disunity and intolerance as merely a manifestation of a deeper tendency towards interpersonal and intercommunal conflict which he believed is endemic in the nature of mankind. This, he felt, could only be addressed ultimately through measures that would seek to improve relations between peoples in every sphere of their lives. He considered the rejection of violence as an essential condition for this, once again citing support for his position from the Christian scriptures. 'Do not resist one who is evil,' Christ had proclaimed in the Sermon on the Mount. 'But if any one strikes you on the right cheek, turn to him the other also.'[20] Moravian Christianity was fundamentally pacifist, being opposed to violence in all its forms. One of its historians writes: 'In the first period of Moravian Church life Pacifism was enjoined, as wars of religion swept over them and great affliction abounded as a result of them. The teaching of Peter of Chelcitz, and of the Moravian educator, John Amos Comenius, was to non-violence and non-resistance, as the true Christian vocation. When the Church was renewed the same principle of pacifism was enjoined on all its members as a strict principle of their conduct.'[21] Some of the most forceful passages in the *Labyrinth* give expression to Comenius's abhorrence of violence and war. He bitterly denounced the clergy of the other Christian Churches for their ambivalence on the matter. The Pilgrim declares it is 'monstrous to wear a coat of mail over a surplice, a helmet over a barret, to hold the Word of God in one hand, a sword in the other.'[22] In the chapter entitled 'The Estate of Soldiery' he exposes the horror of military combat, giving full vent to his disgust at the savagery of all warfare, at the subhuman barbarity of soldiery. The spectacle that confronts him as he enters the armoury prompts one of the most impassioned condemnations of violence in the whole of Christian literature:

> And now becoming desirous to see what was in this vault, I immediately enter it. And behold, there lay there on the ground an endless mass of cruel weapons that thousands of carts could not have transported. There were weapons for stabbing, chopping, cutting, pricking, hacking, stinging, cutting down, tearing, burning; there were altogether so many instruments destined to destroy life, fashioned out of iron, lead, wood and stone, that terror befell me, and I exclaimed: 'Against what wild beasts are they preparing all these things?' 'Against men,' the interpreter answered. 'Against men!' quoth I. 'Alas! I had thought it was against some mad animal, or wild furious beasts. But, in the name of God, what cruelty this is that men should devise such terrible things against other men!' 'Thou art too fastidious,' he said, laughing.
>
> And going onward, we come to a market-place, where I see herds of these men who were clothed in iron, and had horns and claws, and were fettered together in troops. They were crouching before what seemed troughs and jugs, into which that which they were to eat and drink was strewn and poured out for them; and they, one after the other, gobbled and lapped it up. And I said: 'Are hogs, then, being here fattened for butchery? I see, indeed, the appearances of men, but swinish deeds.' 'That is no inconvenience for men of that estate,' said the interpreter. Meanwhile, they rise from these troughs, giving themselves to frolics and dancing, skipping and shouting. . . .
>
> Then suddenly the drums beat, the trumpet resounds; then behold, all rise up, seize daggers, cutlasses, bayonets, or whatever they have, and strike mercilessly at one another, till blood spurts out. They hack and hew at one another more savagely than the most savage animals. Then the cries increase in every direction; one could hear the tramping of horses, the clashing of armour, the clattering of swords, the growl of the artillery, the whistle of shots and bullets round our ears, the sound of trumpets, the crash of drums, the cries of those who urged on the soldiers, the shouting of the victors, the shrieking of the wounded and dying. An awful leaden hail-storm could be seen; dreadful fiery thunder and lightning

could be heard; now this, now that man's arm, head, leg flew away; here one fell over the other, while everything swam in blood. 'Almighty God,' quoth I, 'what is happening? Must the whole world perish?'[23]

For Comenius humility and total trust in God's grace represented the only answer to the problem of interhuman conflict. Christ, meekly surrendering to his torturers, forgiving them in his dying moments on the Cross, exemplified for him the spirit of humble submission to God's grace which is the true mark of the pacifist: 'And he having made reconciliation through his blood sent his grace to all nations and caused it to be proclaimed to every creature.'[24] Only through the miracle of God's grace could such an apparently impossible ideal be fulfilled, the Pilgrim concludes, as he vows to follow the example of Christ, seeing the doctrine of non-resistance as providing the only true hope for peace. As he listens to the voice of Christ, this is what he hears: 'But this shall be thy knowledge of law: not to envy any man either the property of others or his own; to leave everyone what he has; not to refuse to any man that which he requires; to give to each one that which thou owest, and even beyond that, as much as thou canst; to be conciliant in all for the sake of peace. If one takes away thy coat, give him thy cloak also; if one strikes thee on one cheek, put forth the other also. These are my laws, and if thou heedest them, thou wilt secure peace.'[25] Not by human resources, therefore, is peace attainable, but by the grace that comes from total trust in God. With this, the Pilgrim suggests, comes a sublime indifference to the affairs of the world and the conflicts that divide mankind:

Nay, this also did I understand, that these true Christians would not even hear of the distinctions between what the world calls happiness or unhappiness, riches or poverty, honour or dishonour; for everything, they said, that proceeds from the hand of God is good, happy, and salutary. Nothing, therefore, grieves them; they are never irresolute or reluctant. To command or to obey, to teach others or to be taught by them, to have plenty or to suffer want, is one and the same thing to the true Christian; he proceeds on his way with a calm countenance, striving only to please God. They say that the world is not so heavy that it may not be endured, nor so valuable that its loss need be regretted. Therefore neither the desire for anything nor the loss of anything causes the true Christian suffering. If someone smites him on the right cheek, he cheerfully turns to him the other one also. And if one disputes with him about his cloak, he lets him have his coat also. He leaves everything to God, his witness and judge, and feels assured that all these things will, in the course of time, be revised, amended, and at last justly decided.[26]

There follows a vision of infinite peace—the 'peace that passeth under-standing'—the basis of which, the Pilgrim declares, is total trust in the power of God's love. 'The godly have not only simple peace within them, but also joy and pleasure which flow to their hearts from the presence and feeling of God's love,' he says. That peace is the source of true freedom, i.e. freedom from desire, greed, selfishness, from the soul's enslavement to materiality and worldliness. Its roots are in the total conquest of self that is made possible by the altruistic power of love:

> For how can anything be otherwise than sweet and joyful to a man who possesses this divine light within him through the Spirit of God, such freedom from the world and its slavery, such certain and ample divine protection, such safety from enemies and accidents; lastly, as has been shown, that feeling of continuous peace? This is that sweetness that the world understandeth not; this that sweetness that he who once tasted it strives for at any risk; this that sweetness from which no other sweetness can separate us, no bitterness drive us away, no other charm entice us away, and from which no bitterness, not even death, can turn us away.
>
> And then I understood what sometimes impels many of God's saints to throw from them so willingly honours, favour of the people, their worldly estates. They would be equally ready to cast from them the whole world, if it were theirs. I understood also how others, again, cheerfully gave over their bodies to prison, whip, or death, ready to suffer a thousand deaths, could the world repeat the penalty. Should they perish by means of water or fire, or under the sword of the executioner, they were yet prepared cheerfully to sing hymns. Oh, Lord Jesus, how sweet art Thou to the souls that have tasted of Thee! Blessed is he who comprehends this delight![27]

The emphasis on freedom from material selfishness and greed in this passage points to the third of the principles of Christian living affirmed in the Moravian creed. Alone amongst the Reformation movements, the Moravians advocated a radical social vision, the basis of which was the promotion of justice and equity at all levels of society. (By contrast, some other Reform movements were credited with giving birth to European capitalism through their emphasis on thrift, productivity and industri-ousness!) Seeing the ideal of justice as a practical implementation of the Christian injunction to 'love thy neighbour,' the Moravians preached the virtues of austerity in all material affairs, they stressed the virtues of a simple, frugal lifestyle and advocated an equitable sharing of material goods in accordance with the spirit of the Gospels. Taking as their axiom the words of the Acts of the Apostles, 'And they had all things in common,' they sought to promote the spirit of brotherly cooperation and a sharing of all material resources amongst their own communities, hoping thereby to provide an example of Christian responsibility to others. That spirit is vividly expressed in a passage from the *Labyrinth* where the Pilgrim, observing the lifestyle of the Christians, describes the spirit of communality which characterised their attitude to all worldly goods:

> As regards possessions, I saw that, though most of them were poor, had but little of the things that the world calls treasures, and cared but little for them, yet almost everyone had something that was his own. But he did not hide this, nor conceal it from the others (as is the world's way); he held it as in common, readily and gladly granting and lending it to him who might require it. Thus they all dealt with their possessions not otherwise than those who sit together at one table deal with their utensils of the table, which all use with equal right. Seeing this, I thought with shame that with us everything befalls in contrary fashion. Some fill and overfill their houses with utensils, clothing, food, gold and silver, as much as they can; meanwhile others, who are equally servants of God, have hardly wherewith to clothe and feed themselves. But, I must say, I understood that this was by no means the will of God; rather is it the way of the world, the perverse world, that some should go forth in festive attire, others naked; that some should belch from overfilling, while others yawn from hunger; some should laboriously earn silver, some vainly squander it; some make merry, others wail. Thence there sprung up among the one, pride and contempt of the others; and among these again, fury, hatred and misdeeds. But here there was nothing such. All were in community with all; indeed, their souls also.[28]

'For every man will understand that the welfare of each individual (including his own) depends upon the welfare of all,' Comenius writes in the *Via Lucis*.[29] (His words were echoed two centuries later in Dostoevsky's 'each one of us is undoubtedly responsible for all men and everything on earth.'[30]) As a practical expression of this, he urges the rich to take responsibility for the education of the poor and, failing this, urges the state to assume its responsibility to ensure that all children have the means to the attainment of wisdom and personal fulfilment through education. 'The end of universal schools will be to provide opportunities, not only for all nations and tongues and orders of men, but for every single individual to rise out of the darkness of ignorance and barbarism.' he writes.[31] He advocated the application of the principle of Christian responsibility to all spheres of life, seeing the realisation of a just society as an idea that would have to be espoused by all Christian believers, seriously committed to the implementation of the message of the Gospels.

   Unlike the socialists of later years, however, Comenius saw this being achieved, not through a process of radical political change, but by a process of individual self-reform initiated by every person in the privacy of his own conscience and, by extension, in the conduct of all aspects of his daily life. Social reform, he suggests, is rooted in self-reform; it is achieved not through radical political action but as a natural outcome of the genuine practice of Christian love. The fallenness and corruptibility of mankind, he suggests, requires that social reform begin with the spiritual transformation of the individual person—a process that can be achieved only through penitence, faith and the soul's humble submission to God. (That same principle was reasserted by Dostoevsky in the parable of the doctor who loved mankind but hated his neighbour and again by Tolstoy in his ironic characterisation of the fanatical socialists in *Anna Karenina* and *Resurrection* who devoted themselves tirelessly to an abstract, generalised ideal while being harsh and insensitive in their relations with their immediate circle of family, friends and acquaintances.)[32] The fallenness of man and the priority of individual reform in the regeneration of society is one of the foremost themes of the *Labyrinth*, *The Great Didactic* and the *Pampaedia*. In the *Labyrinth* the theme of man's corruptibility is evoked through images of physical disease and decay which abound in the opening chapters of the work. *The Great Didactic* opens with similar images of the diseased condition of mankind. It is essential, Comenius insists in the Dedication to the work, that the nature of man's illness be diagnosed and identified before the process of healing can be set in train:

> He who knows not that he is ill cannot heal himself; he who feels not his pain utters no sigh; he who sees not his danger does not start back, even though he be on the brink of an abyss; and so it is not to be wondered at that he who perceives not the wave of disorder which is sweeping over the human race and over the Church, does not lament the fact. But he who sees himself and others covered with countless wounds; he who remarks that the wounds and boils, both his own and other men's, fester ever more and more; and who knows that he, with others, stands in the midst of gulfs and precipices and wanders among snares, in which he sees one man after another being caught, it is hard for him not to be terrified, not to marvel, not to perish with grief.[33]

This theme is reinvoked in the fifth chapter of the work where the innate tendencies in man towards learning, virtue and piety are seen to be constantly frustrated by the counter-tendencies towards evil present in his nature. Here, as in the *Via Lucis*, Comenius sees the fallenness of man as being compounded by his ignorance and unawareness of the means to redemption that are available to him through the infinity of

God's love. 'There are not wanting men,' he declares, 'who . . . throw away all things, thinking that all are alike uncertain, even God Himself, and seek light in the deepest darkness and peace of mind in mental stupefaction.'[34] Man, he writes in the *Pampaedia*, 'is a most complex creature who requires as much anxious care as all other creatures put together, if he is to be preserved from corruption.' The tendency towards evil, he writes, 'is the innate character of all the descendants of Adam, the monstrous fault transmitted from one to another by right of inheritance.'[35] Man's hope lies not in his own potentiality but in his faith in the power of God's grace. This is Christ's message to the Pilgrim: 'Thou hast seen in other conditions how the men who seek gain busy themselves with endless labours, what artifices they employ, what perils they risk. They must now consider all this striving as vanity, knowing that one thing alone is necessary, the grace of God. Therefore, limiting thyself to the one calling which I have entrusted to thee, conduct thy labours faithfully, conscientiously, quietly, entrusting to me the end and aim of all things.'[36] Not worldly labour, nor praxis, but faith and trust in God's grace, is the way to the reform of humankind. This is the message conveyed in the following passage from the *Pampaedia*:

> Man's perplexities have been increased by the unfortunate lapse into sin of our first ancestors, which has caused us all to be caught up in a kind of dizziness, blinding us and leaving us deaf to the very voices that warned us to move towards better things, deluding ourselves about obvious things, and faltering and stumbling even on level ground, counting good things evil and evil things good, regarding light as darkness and darkness as light, and thereby walking in the ways of death instead of the paths of life. We have always been more inclined to follow ourselves rather than God or His ministers, and to follow our senses rather than reason, even when the former are demented and misled by material temptations. This is the innate character of all the descendants of Adam, the monstrous fault transmitted from one to another by right of inheritance. God's wisdom would lead us back to the standard of righteousness, having clothed itself in human flesh and shown the example of Christ denying his own will and following the will of God. But it is hard to persuade men to do likewise even on their entry into the world as small boys, because they lapse into animal behaviour and prefer to be guided by their senses like animals rather than follow the rational guidance of men. This explains why even the wisest men go astray, and the most pious commit sin, and too many degenerate even with the best education. The spirit of Christ . . . truly helps us in our infirmities (and without it none of mankind could be reformed.) Yet as this grace seeks not to reject nature but to reform

it, and nature in fact preserves its inborn character as long as possible, there arises the struggle between the spirit and the flesh which Scripture describes and every man born again of God experiences within him; when the spirit prevails, the flesh is mortified; or again the flesh prevails and the spirit is cast down.[37]

Comenius, therefore, in common with all the religious reformers of his age, emphasised the primacy of faith in the relation between man and God—a faith, he declared repeatedly, which is nurtured by love, prayer, humility, selflessness, altruistic service and, above all, trust in God's grace. 'For the salvation of man dependeth not on deeds but on faith, the Pilgrim says; 'if this, then, is true, they cannot fail to achieve salvation; if but their faith is certain, it is enough.'[38] He stresses the importance of virtuous behaviour, but sees it as subordinate to faith, i.e., man's affirmation of his ultimate dependence on the grace and mercy of God. In Chapter 37 of the *Labyrinth* he speaks of the 'first conversion' as being effected through God's grace; the second, he writes, 'requires our own endeavours also.' He speaks of the need for faith to be illumined by reason, but insists that 'corrupt nature cannot be mended by wisdom alone.'[39] Ultimately, salvation depends on the soul's trust in God and total submission to His will:

> The world ever demands proof; the Christian thinks the Word of God alone sufficient. The world seeks bonds, pledges, pawns, seals; the Christian sets up faith alone as a security for all things. The world examines things for her own purpose in divers fashions, distrusts, tests, suspects. The Christian relies fully on the trustfulness of God. And whereas the world will ever cavil, doubt, question, feel uncertain, the Christian hath ever Him in whom he can place his entire confidence, whom he can obey, and before whom he can humble himself; therefore the light of faith gleams on him, and he can see and know what things are unchangeable, and must be so, even though he cannot grasp them by the light of reason.[40]

In the humble followers of the Moravian movement—driven from their homes and forced to roam throughout Europe seeking refuge from their persecutors—Comenius found his most obvious exemplars for his ideal of the man of faith. Their behaviour, he says, was marked by humility, tolerance and charity. These are the people he almost certainly has in mind in the passage from the *Labyrinth* where he extols religious tolerance and condemns sectarian bigotry: 'Among these men there were some who said they had no concern with this strife; they walked on silently, quietly, as in thought, looking heavenward, and bearing themselves affably towards all, and they were insignificant and ragged, exhausted by fasting and thirst; but the others but laughed at them, cried shame on them, hissed them, scratched and toused them, pointed at them with their fingers, tripped them up and mocked them. But they, enduring everything, went their way, as if they had been blind, deaf, dumb.'[41] Comenius stressed the essential simplicity of the ideal of faith, insisting that ultimately it is nurtured by prayer—not the ostentatious, ritualistic prayer of the denominational churches, with its pomp and splendour and lavish ceremonial, but the humble engagement of the soul with God which Christ himself advocated in the Sermon on the Mount. He took his inspiration particularly from the following words in St Matthew's Gospel: 'When you pray you must not be like the hypocrites, for they love to stand and pray in the synagogues and at the street corners that they may be seen by men. Truly I say to you they have received their reward. But when you pray go into your room and shut the door and pray to your Father who is in secret; and our Father who sees in secret will reward you.'[42] This is the spirit of Christ's words to the Pilgrim in Chapter XXXIX of the *Labyrinth*:

> Thou hast seen in the world how men imagine vain ceremonies and strife while performing their religious duties. Thy religion shall be to serve me in quiet, and not to bind thyself by any ceremonies, for I do not bind thee by them. If thou wilt—according to my teaching—serve me in the spirit and in the truth, then wrangle no further on these matters, with any man, even if men call thee a hypocrite, heretic, or I know not what. Cling quietly to me only and to my service.[43]

While emphasising the essential simplicity of faith and while pointing to its roots in penitence and prayer, Comenius nonetheless stressed the enriching role of reason in its advancement and growth. In the *Via Lucis* he speaks of faith as the supreme wisdom which penetrates beyond phenomenal reality to give access to the truth of the transcendental and the hyperphysical. But just as he spoke of the need to approach the sphere of reason through the mediating powers of sense, he similarly spoke of reason as having the potential to deepen and enrich faith. He cites St. Cyril who declared philosophy was given to man as a 'catechism for faith', Clement of Alexandria who declared that just as the law was the 'pedagogue that led the Jews to God', philosophy was the 'pedagogue that led the Gentiles to Christ'.[44] He also cites St Augustine who declared that science can unravel 'the mysteries of God.' Science, he says, by its disclosure of the full reality of the natural world, prepares the mind for the apprehension of the infinite: 'For the divine wisdom does not scorn to move step by step upon its way, and to build its works upon foundations which it has laid beforehand, and so to crown lesser gifts which have been well appropriated by greater gifts added to them.'[45] In this passage from the *Via Lucis* he provides vital clarification of the whole relationship of reason, science and faith:

> I have said also that theological and philosophical matters are to be taught: I mean those which belong on the one hand to the domain of faith and on the other to the domain of reason and of the senses. Those that belong to the domain of faith must on all accounts be taught, because the just man shall live by his faith; this is the one and only way of eternal life. Those matters which belong to the domain of reason we must also know; because by these we are distinguished from the brutes, and are protected from being easily persuaded by impostors to accept in a false belief things which are contrary to reason. But we must not be ignorant of the things of the senses; because they smooth the way for reason and safeguard it against deception. The senses minister to reason and reason ministers to faith, and therefore none of these things can be absent from the perfect Light, or else we shall certainly be deprived of the instruments for illuminating the mind. For I cannot speak to unbelievers about our faith except by using rational words and showing that there is nothing that is not true and wholesome in any part of our faith. For no man can believe what he thinks unbelievable; nor can he be forced by any power except that of reasoning to conclude that a thing is believable.[46]

Reason 'ministers to faith'; science enables us to 'investigate the mysteries of God.' These words have profound implications for the educator, as will be shown in some detail presently. Before considering this, however, it is essential to reiterate Comenius's insistence on the primacy of scripture as the ultimate authority in all matters of faith, side by side with his acknowledgement of the role of reason as a means to its growth and enrichment. All the distinctive features of Comenian Christianity—its radical pacifism and ecumenism, its concern for equity and justice, its strictly non-dogmatic character, its emphasis on individual judgement, faith, personal responsibility and salvation through grace—all were authenticated scrupulously from the words of the scripture text. In the *Labyrinth* the Pilgrim speaks of scripture as 'the touchstone of faith'; the 'true fountain of knowledge is Holy Writ,' he declares.[47] The revealed word of God, appealing simultaneously to 'the simplest and the wisest,' is the ultimate source of all wisdom and truth, he concludes. This is the message conveyed to him by Christ as he reaches the final stage of his quest for the truth:

> 'Thou hast seen, when among the scholars, how they strive to fathom all things. Let it be the summit of thy learning to seek me

in my works, and to see how wondrously I rule thee and every-thing. Here wilt thou find more matter for reflection than those yonder, and it will be with unspeakable delight. Instead of all libraries, to read which is endless labour, with little use and often with harm, while there is always weariness and anxiety, I will give thee this little book in which thou wilt find all arts. Here thy grammar will be to consider my words, thy dialectics faith in them, thy rhetoric prayers and sighs, thy physic meditation of my works, thy metaphysics delight in me and in the eternal things; thy mathe-matics will consist in the weighing and measuring of my benefac-tions, and, on the other hand, of the ingratitude of the world; thy ethics will be love of me, which will give thee all instructions concerning thy conduct both towards me and towards thy fellow-creatures. But thou must seek all this learning, not that thou mayest please others, but that thou mayest come nearer to me. And in all these things, the simpler thou art, the more learned shalt thou be; for my light inflames simple hearts.[48]

All this is reiterated in the *Via Lucis*, the absolute authority of the scriptures being even more explicitly confirmed there than in the metaphoric language of the *Labyrinth*. 'If you wish to cause the mind of man to be powerfully illuminated, bring to it,' he writes, 'the most efful-gent of all light-giving things, namely the Word of God.'[49] At another point in the work he speaks of the irreducible authority, yet the universal accessibility, of the scripture text: 'The written word of God,' he writes, 'is kept pure against all the devices of this world and of hell, and is for ever unveiling more mysteries to those who reverently scan it for the common advantage of all men, appealing to all nations and peoples.'[50] He speaks of its compatibility with all other modes of knowledge, particularly with the newly emerging disciplines of natural science. 'For Nature and Scripture serve each other as commentator and interpreter, Scripture speaking in more general terms, and Nature in particular instances.'[51] Scripture, he concludes, is the focus around which all other modes of knowledge naturally converge:

But the time is come for us to rise from the rudiments to com-pleteness of knowledge, no longer to be like children tossed hither and thither by the waves, or permit ourselves to be blown about by every wind of doctrine, but to have such knowledge as befits grown men, so that no one can justly charge our knowledge with emptiness or obscurity or any other harmful defect. And this condition will be attained when we have turned our backs upon all human authorities and follow God alone as the unique, supreme and only sufficient teacher of the Truth; when we refuse to draw our knowledge and our faith from any other source, and derive it directly from his own genuine sources (the tables of Nature, of Scripture and of Conscience) and take it in our own vessels (our own senses, our own reason, our own faith). God forbid, then, that henceforth we should deceive the world by leading it through the mazes of human evidences and authorities upon all sorts of subjects. God forbid that we should offer ourselves as guides to the blind (blind as we ourselves should soon be proved by this argument) and ourselves read and present to other people this or that copy of the books of God instead of the originals written by his own hand.[52]

These, therefore, are the fundamental principles which characterise the Comenian vision of Christian truth. It remains now to consider the ways in which Comenius considered these ideals could be fostered through the medium of the educational process. The principles that have been outlined might be said to constitute a basic curriculum for moral and religious education. The two forthcoming sections will examine his ideas on the pedagogic methods that might be adopted for the presentation of this curriculum in the years of pre-primary, primary and post-primary education.

2. MORAL EDUCATION: NATURE, SCRIPTURE AND CONSCIENCE

'What then is our true work?' Comenius asks in the chapter from *The Great Didactic* which is entitled 'The Method of Morals.' 'It is that study of wisdom which elevates us and makes us steadfast and noble-minded,' he writes, 'the study to which we have given the name of morality and of piety, and by means of which we are exalted above all other creatures, and draw nigh to God Himself.'[53] Rationality, self-control, conscience illumination and the assumption of personal responsibility are the consistent themes of his writings on this issue. 'The principle which underlies this [the method of morals] is that we should accustom boys to do everything by reason, and nothing under the guidance of impulse,' he writes, again in *The Great Didactic*.[54] 'The foundation of morals is either full self-control or submission to others,' he declares in the *Pampaedia*. 'The former means that man should be accustomed to do nothing by impulse, everything by reason, as in the saying of Claudian—"Only when you are able to master yourself will you have the right to be monarch of the world."'[55]

Two principles are central to his treatment of the process of moral education. The first is his insistence on the need to integrate all aspects of school activity around moral and religious objectives. The second is his view that the process itself should be conducted by way of experiential learning rather than depend on didactic advocacy or the regulation of behaviour in accordance with pre-defined axioms and norms. The first principle is asserted at various points throughout the *Via Lucis*. All our knowledge, he writes, is drawn from three main sources—the 'tables of Nature, Scripture and Conscience.' All three are interdependent and complementary, the study of nature being guided at all times by the dictates of conscience, these in turn being illuminated by the authority of scripture. He speaks of conscience as the internal light or brightness that penetrates all man's activities, 'shedding its beams on his intellect, his will, his affections', 'illuminating them in every part and directing them upon their ways.'[56] In the *Pampaedia* he condemns the pursuit of knowledge for its own sake, taking as an example the Cynics of ancient Greece 'who made unscrupulous use of philosophising to the point of neglecting morals.'[57] All modes of knowing, he affirms, must be guided ultimately by the promptings of conscience, which together with rationality and will, constitutes a three-fold process of inner illumination, guiding man towards the pursuit of the Good in all his decisions and actions:

> The light which shines in the intellect is the rational knowledge of things; by it, if a man follows after the truth of things and contemplates their inner reasons and principles, he gets a gentle happiness of spirit. And this light is called wisdom because it is a glowing light: for it is a true knowledge of all that is and a wise and wholesome use of it. . . .
>
> The second development of the inner light is found in the Will. By it, if a man seeks the goodness of things and tastes its sweetness, he has for his pleasure things which are holy and pure. And the darkness which is opposed to this light is impurity of mind: men who are defiled by this are in the Scripture called sons of darkness, because they take their pleasure in the works of darkness.
>
> The third development of the inner light is found in the conscience or in the affections; it consists in a serenity and happiness of heart which comes from the sense of knowing the truth and partaking in holiness. . . . The darkness which is opposed to this light is the anguish of the mind which convicts itself of falsity and illwill, and this anguish is a foretaste of the eternal darkness of hell.[58]

It will be shown presently how Comenius sought to implement the principle of moral integration in the curricula he proposed for the infant school, the school of boyhood and the Latin school. But, first, the pedagogic method he advocated for all moral education needs to be explained. Here the emphasis lies entirely on moral formation through a direct experiencing of the principles of ethical behaviour. 'The virtues are learned by constantly doing what is right,' he declares in *The Great Didactic*.[59] 'In

an eloquent passage from the *Labyrinth* he points to the inefficacy of
sermons, lampooning the feeble efforts of preachers to promote virtue
amongst their congregations. In the section entitled 'On the Barrenness
of Preachers' he writes:

> And my guide then led me to those who stood on the steps; and
> these, indeed, exhorted the people to love the image, but, as it
> seemed to me, but feebly. For if one listened and obeyed, well and
> good; if he did not do so it was well also. Some clanked keys, saying
> they had the power to close on those who did not obey them the
> gate by which man reaches God; but meanwhile they closed it on
> no man, or, at least, when they did so, did it as it were in jest.
> Indeed, I saw that they dared not do this very daringly; for if one
> attempted to speak somewhat sharply, they reviled him, saying that
> he preached against persons. Therefore some, daring not to do so
> by word of mouth, in writing raged against sin; but they screamed
> against these also, saying that they spread lampoons. Therefore,
> they either turned away from these men or threw them down the
> steps, replacing them by other more moderate men. Seeing this, I
> said: 'This is folly that, as their leaders and councillors, they wish
> to have followers and flatterers.' 'That is the way of the world,'
> said the interpreter, 'and it harms not. If these criers were given
> entire freedom, who knows what they would not dare to do. A line
> must be drawn for them beyond which they cannot go.'[60]

'Virtue,' he declares in *The Great Didactic*, 'is practised by deed and not
by words.' Moral behaviour, he says, is fostered through direct experience
on the part of the pupil, not through advocacy by the teacher: 'As boys
easily learn to walk by walking, to talk by talking, and to write by writing,
in the same way they will learn obedience by obeying, abstinence by
abstaining, truth by speaking the truth, and constancy by being constant.'[61]
Experience of moral behaviour, he suggests, develops and enriches the
innate desire for the Good that is present in us all. He particularly
emphasises the need to cultivate the spirit of altruism by giving children
direct experience of their responsibilities towards others: 'The young
should learn to practise justice by hurting no man, by giving each his due,
by avoiding falsehood and deceit, and by being obliging and agreeable.'
He continues:

> The abominable vice of selfishness is inherent in our corrupt nature,
> and through it each man thinks of nothing but his own welfare,
> and troubles his head about no one else. This is a great source of
> confusion in life, since all are occupied with their own affairs and
> neglect the common good. The true object of life must therefore be

diligently instilled into the youth, and they must be taught that we are born not for ourselves alone, but for God and for our neighbour, that is to say, for the human race.

Thus they will become seriously persuaded of this truth and will learn from their boyhood to imitate God, the angels, the sun, and the more noble of things created, that is to say, by desiring and striving to be of good service to as many as possible. Thus will the good fortune of private and public life be assured, since all men will be ready to work together for the common good, and to help one another. And they actually will do so if they have been properly taught.[62]

The same emphasis on experiential awareness is evident in his treatment of the theme of discipline. While he recognises the need for codes of good conduct, he nonetheless stresses the importance of a consensual acceptance of their purposes by the pupils. The need for discipline, he insists, must be apparent to the pupils and be fully agreed by them. 'The principle which underlies this is that we should accustom boys to do everything by reason, and nothing under the guidance of impulse. For man is a rational animal, and should therefore be led by reason, and, before action, ought to deliberate how each operation should be performed, so that he really may be master of his own actions.'[63] In this context also Comenius stresses the importance of exemplary behaviour on the part of the teacher:

Examples of well-ordered lives, in the persons of their parents, nurses, tutors, and school-fellows, must continually be set before children. For boys are like apes, and love to imitate whatever they see, whether good or bad, even though not bidden to do so; and on this account they learn to imitate before they learn to use their minds. By 'examples' I mean living ones as well as those taken from books; in fact living ones are the more important, because they make a stronger impression. And therefore, if parents are worthy and careful guardians of domestic discipline, and if tutors are chosen with the greatest possible care, and are men of exceptional virtue, a great advance will have been made towards the proper training of the young in morals.[64]

He also stressed the potential of purposeful work activities in fostering good habits of self-discipline amongst the young. Quoting Seneca's words, 'It is toil that nourishes noble minds,' he writes of the need to avoid sloth and idleness at all costs and to ensure that pupils are engaged constantly in meaningful and worthwhile activities: 'It is by working, therefore, that we must learn how to work, just as we must learn how to act by acting;

and in this way the combined occupations of mind and body, in which, at the same time, all over-pressure must be avoided, will produce an industrious disposition, and make a man so active that sluggish ease will be intolerable to him.'[65] This principle is stated even more emphatically in the *Pampaedia*:

> Second place after piety should be given to good morals, so useful to human intercourse throughout our whole lifetime. There is a common saying: 'The man who is expert in literature but deficient in morals finds that his deficiencies outweigh his expertise.' Hence we must take the greatest pains to ensure that all our pupils are habituated not to idleness but to hard and diligent work from a tender age. Schools will earn the title of factories of true humanity only if they habituate our young people to hard work and not to idleness, not making them idle speculators about life or empty chatterers about any subject, however ill-understood, or facile debaters of pros and cons, but rather vital doers of deeds and thoughtful administrators, by training them to constant activity and skill in performing their duties correctly. Schools should all be public laboratories, arenas for exercises that are most useful to human life, affording an efficient cure for the indifference commonly contracted in schools and continued for life by most mortals. This is a good illustration of Seneca's well-known criticism, 'Most of life is spent in doing ill, most of it in doing nothing, and the whole in doing what is not to the purpose.'[66]

Education in the pre-primary years was seen by Comenius as being concerned predominantly with moral formation. *The Great Didactic* lists the virtues that need to be fostered in young children. A formidable listing, it includes obedience, truthfulness, industriousness, patience, politeness and temperance, as well as reticence—a virtue unlikely to be so enthusiastically endorsed by modern educators as it was by Comenius. 'They [i.e. infants] should be taught to speak but little and to refrain from saying all that rises to their lips, nay even to maintain absolute silence when the occasion demands it,' he writes.[67] Given his emphasis on the all-embracing virtue of love, it is not surprising to find Comenius insisting that the primary responsibility of the teacher is to foster charitable behaviour amongst these young pupils. 'It is of greater importance that they learn to practise charity, so that they may be ready to give alms to those whom need compels to ask for them,' he declares. 'For love is the especial virtue of Christians. Christ bids us practise it; and, now that the world is growing aged and cold, it is greatly to the interest of the Church to kindle in men's hearts the flame of love.'[68] He suggested these virtues should be promoted through three main methods: example, discipline and instruction. He saw leadership by the teacher as crucial to the success of the whole process:

> Teaching is leading. But the man who leads sets an example. No real teaching is done by those who do not constantly set a good example, that is, who order pupils to do what they do not do themselves. Therefore we must not allow the child an opportunity of learning evil, either through looking for it or by accident. It is not enough to avoid setting bad examples; good ones must take their place. In the words of the apostle Paul, 'Provide things honest in the sight of all men.' Therefore it is of the utmost importance to do so in the sight of those still in the age of innocence. Woe to the man who tempts any of them to evil! If there is only an absence of bad examples, and good examples are not set, children will remain in a state of uncertainty, ready to go either way. When they are sent out into the world they soon find wicked examples bringing them to corruption. To prevent this they must be carefully trained to respect the good so that their character is formed by the time that they go out into the world.[69]

In his treatment of discipline Comenius emphasises the need for a full understanding of its purposes by the pupils. Sanctions, he suggests, should be imposed only for gross misbehaviour and he insists that harsh and draconian methods of discipline must be avoided, no matter how serious the offence. In this context again he stressed the need to interrelate moral and religious objectives, pointing to the ultimate justification of all morality in the sphere of religious truth. It is this principle which underlies his conception of moral formation as ultimately the fostering of humility and submissiveness to God's will. That principle is clearly intimated in this passage from the *Pampaedia*:

> Instruction should be openly expressed in clear language, and it will be more effective if comparisons are made with natural things. For example, the need for obedience may be shown by comparing the new tree with the old. At the infant stage the first general rule to observe is that whenever any tendency occurs in the course of nature, we should begin at once to direct and train it so that nothing is left to go grievously wrong. But the first act of direction should be persuasive and, above all, wise. Man's chief end must be set before their eyes even at this stage so often and so emphatically that they cannot possibly strive for it without attaining it. I mean that everyone born into the human race (1) should exercise wise dominion over other creatures, (2) should control himself wisely, (3) being fashioned in the image of God as his original should be

able from Him, through Him, and in Him to enjoy blessedness
here and to all eternity. Therefore, submissiveness must be taught
in the infant school so that pupils consider it safer to accept the
advice of others and form the habit of obedience.[70]

The emphasis on obedience may be thought inappropriate in a modern
context, with educators nowadays generally extolling the value of fostering
individual autonomy and independence amongst the young. The term is
used by Comenius, however, to signify the pupil's *voluntary* submission to
the teacher's guidance and authority. Generally, it has connotations of
acceptance and trust, a conception supported by his repeated emphasis on
encouragement and kindness and on the merits of a non-coercive pedagogy.

Moral formation remains a primary objective again of his conception
of the functions of the primary school. Here some of the most innovative
and imaginative of his pedagogic principles are disclosed. Instruction, he
insists, must be conducted in accordance with the experiential principles
described earlier. In *The Great Didactic* he writes: 'They should learn the
principles of morality, which should be drawn up in the shape of rules
and accompanied by illustrations suitable to the age and understanding
of the pupils. They should also begin to put these principles into
practice.'[71] He insists further that textbook content be light-hearted and
free of pedantry: 'Care must be taken to suit all these books to the
children for whom they are intended; for children like whimsicality and
humour, and detest pedantry and severity. Instruction, therefore, should
ever be combined with amusement, that they may take pleasure in
learning serious things which will be of general use to them later on, and
that their dispositions may be, as it were, perpetually enticed to develop
in the manner desired.'[72] This principle is further developed in the
Pampaedia in a section where he provides instances of the kinds of rules
and axioms to be taught at this level. While his list includes all the main
precepts of traditionalist morality, they are presented in a form likely to
be attractive and immediately meaningful to young pupils.

Short list of principles of moral wisdom

1. Do not covet everything you see and you will be wise.
2. Do not believe everything you hear and you will be wise.
3. Do not say everything you know and you will be wise.
4. Do not do everything that you can and you will be wise.
Likewise:
5. Do not befriend everyone you happen to know.
6. See that you trust the right people.
7. Have no regrets over what you have lost.
8. Do not let your past troubles disturb or torment you.

9. Look to your front and not behind.
10. Concern yourself not with what is done but with what remains to be done.

Above all else boys should be taught to understand, ponder and keep in view the purpose of their life, the reason for their birth, and the goal for which they strive. Living without knowing the reason for existence is like the life of a fly or a nettle, which also have been granted life and nourishment.[73]

Some particularly innovative pedagogic approaches are evident in the section of the *Pampaedia* where he advises teachers on how to utilise sensory experience for purposes of moral development. Applying the principle that what reason comprehends must first be assimilated through the senses, he shows how moral principles can be extrapolated from the study of natural phenomena. Taking as an example the nature study lesson, he demonstrates how analogies may be drawn between the processes of natural growth and the moral formation of the human person. The following is a shortened version of a section dealing with the instruction of nine year old pupils:

The boy's introduction to morals through sensory experience

1. The surface of water, unless ruffled by the wind, is level in all directions, and no part of it seeks to rise above any other. Men should emulate it, so that insofar as they are all of the same nature, they should not strive for preferment one above another.
2. Water dampens whatever it touches, i.e. infects it with its quality of wetness. Man should make every possible impression by his quality of humanity.
3. A river conveys its waters freely this way and that to supply cities and villages. In so doing it maintains its own freshness and performs a service for others, whereas swamps stagnate and lose their purity. So the man who is ready to do a service earns affection, whereas the lazy man incurs hatred, and in time becomes useless to himself and others.

Similarly of the sun. The sun pursues a constant course to supply everyone with light. The conscientious man would wish to do likewise for everyone, if possible.

Similarly of the tree. A tree is not the growth of a single year but of many: so it is with man, both in body and mind. Every year the tree increases in size; in fact in summer it grows every day without fail (frost prevents it from growing in winter), and men ought to do likewise.

The barren tree is cut down and cast into the fire: the same should apply to the man who does not bear good fruit. The tree first produces blossoms and then fruit. So man should first learn before teaching others or performing other services for human society. . . .

The rose has a lovely perfume but nature sets it among thorns: so learning and virtue are lovely things, but the exercises that produce them, namely, work and discipline, appear beset with thorns. When the sun is not shining and we need light, we content ourselves with the moon or stars or even light a small lamp. So when deprived of great blessings man should be content with small ones and praise God.[74]

At the level of post-primary education Comenius continues to emphasise the need for moral education to penetrate all facets of the work of the school. The approach is still based on the integration of all knowledge and learning around the process of ethico-religious formation. At this stage, however, he advocates the formal study of ethics along the same lines as the other disciplines constituting the curriculum. The objective, he says, should be to train 'moralists, who can draw fine distinctions between the various kinds of virtue and vice, and who can follow the one and avoid the other. This knowledge they should possess both in its general form and in its special application to the life of the family, of the state, and of the Church.'[75] He insists, however, that the study of ethics be based on a sound foundation in a number of secular disciplines—e.g. grammar, natural philosophy, mathematics and metaphysics.

Since, he argues, grammar is the 'key to all knowledge', it is logical that it should take precedence over the study of all other subjects, including theology and ethics. Similarly, he says, natural philosophy, being the study of the objective phenomena of nature, should also come logically before the study of moral principles. He cites the authority of Lipsius who declared in his *Physiology* that 'its study is productive of great pleasure, stimulates and retains the attention and forms a suitable introduction to ethics.' The same holds for mathematics, he says: the sciences that 'deal with number and quantity make a special appeal to the senses and are therefore easy to grasp.' Besides, he argues, they 'make a powerful impression on the imagination, and thus prepare the mind for studies of a more abstract nature.' He advocates further study in the field of metaphysics before formal instruction begins in ethics: 'For this science embraces the primary and most important principles of existence, dealing with the essential hypotheses on which all things depend, their attributes and logical differences; and includes the most general definitions, axioms, and laws of nature.'[76] With this formidable array of subjects serving as an appropriate foundation, the formal study of ethics can begin, he says, in the fourth year of the Latin school, i.e., at about the age of sixteen. The following is the rationale for the teaching of the subject that is provided in Chapter XXX of *The Great Didactic*:

> The pupils must next investigate man himself, viewed as a free agent and as the lord of creation. They must learn to notice what things are in our power, what are not, and how everything must submit to the inflexible laws of the universe.
>
> This they will learn in the fourth year, in the Ethics class. But this must not consist of an historical course or of a mere statement of facts, as in the Vernacular-School. The reasons which underlie each fact must be given, that the pupils may acquire the habit of concentrating their attention on cause and effect. All controversial matter, however, must be carefully excluded from these first four classes, since we wish this to be reserved for the fifth class that follows.[77]

Further details are given in the *Pampaedia* on the content and present-ation of ethical studies in the Latin school. Comenius's comments here are focused on the *prevention* of immorality amongst adolescent students. He sees immorality as springing from three main sources: 'external objects,' 'humours within the body', and 'natural instincts or fantasies acquired from an outside source.'[78] In all three cases he advocates the merits of prevention, particularly stressing the benefits of temperate living. This, he suggests, applies especially to matters of sexual morality: 'The humours of the flesh produce in us the strongest inner stimulus to evil. Therefore such humours must either be counteracted in our way of living by temperance and fasting, or the mind must resolutely remain master of the body.'[79] He emphasises the need to isolate wrongdoers from the company of their peers so that their potential influence will be minimised. He applies his comments particularly to the problem of per-sistent drunkenness: 'The patient afflicted with vices must be debarred from the company of evil people and denied any opportunity for evil-doing. Just as it is impossible . . . to clean out a tank without stopping the pipes, and to cure dropsy in one who over-indulges in drinking water, or gout in one addicted to love and wine, so the confirmed drunkard cannot be won back to sobriety so long as he is left in the company of drunkards.'[80] Though his advice might be thought puritanical—at least in the benign sense in which that term has to be applied to Moravian Christianity—it may be found to hold considerable relevance at a time when countless young lives are blighted by sex- and alcohol-related diseases. In this, as in all other instances in which he discusses the process of moral education, Comenius's final emphasis lies on the expe-riential assimilation of all abstract principles. These are his concluding words of advice to the teacher in Chapter XI of the *Pampaedia*:

Virtues are implanted as follows:

1. Through the enlightenment of the intellect to know the difference in things, what is truly honourable, useful, pleasant, or the opposite, and this is achieved through teaching.

2. By pointing our desires in the best direction to embrace things that bring joy and no regrets. This is done by regular admonition and examples and by the following rule: when proposing to take any action, consider your position at the end of it, or the situation likely to arise if it turns out as you intend or otherwise.

3. By practice, which comes with experience. In this respect it is easy for a man to be trained to virtue when his will is by nature inclined towards the good. Therefore confront him with good and convince him of its goodness and invite him to put it to the test, and keep him in its path until he is accustomed to righteousness. In the end he will form the desired habit of virtue.[81]

3. RELIGIOUS EDUCATION: KINDLING THE FLAME OF LOVE

Education, as Comenius repeatedly declared throughout his writings, is ultimately concerned with the fostering of faith—that alone which makes life meaningful and provides the final key to its mysteries. In *The Great Didactic* he stresses the need to subordinate all other modes of educational formation to this all-embracing goal: 'Whatever is taught to the young in addition to the Scriptures (sciences, art, languages etc.) should be taught as purely subordinate subjects. In this way it will be made evident to the pupils that all that does not relate to God and to the future life is nothing but vanity.'[82] Explaining what he means by the 'spirit of piety', he writes: 'Our hearts should learn to seek God everywhere (since He has concealed Himself with His works as with a curtain, and, invisibly present in all visible things, directs all, though unseen), and when we have found Him we should follow Him, and when we have attained Him should enjoy Him.'[83] In words closely anticipating Zossima's counsel to the monks in *The Brothers Karamazov*, he identifies the practice of active love, extended to the whole of creation, as the way by which the soul finds faith and thereby attains communion with God: 'We seek God by noticing signs of His divinity in all things created. We follow God by giving ourselves up completely to His will, both to do and to suffer whatever shall have seemed good to Him.'[84] It is this spirit of humility and love that he urges the teacher to foster in his pupils as the means to the attainment of an active, living faith. Again he advocates a pedagogic method based on the principle of learning through experience, i.e., through the practical application of belief in the conditions of everyday life:

Faith, charity and hope will be taught in a practical manner, if boys and all men are taught to believe implicitly in all that God reveals, to do all that He commands, and to expect all that He promises. . . . Boys should be carefully habituated to the outward works which are commanded by God, that they may know that it is true Christianity to express faith by works. Such works are the exercise of temperance, justice, pity and patience, which should continually occupy our attention. 'For unless our faith brings forth such fruit it is manifestly dead.' (James II). But it must be living if it is to bring us salvation.'[85]

His words, with their emphasis on a practically manifested, living faith, powerfully echo those of Father Zossima to Madame Hohlakhov, the lady who comes to ask him how she can recover her lost faith. 'Strive,' he says, 'to love your neighbour actively and indefatigably. In as far as you advance in love you will grow surer of the reality of God and of the immortality of your soul. If you strive to self-forgetfulness in the love of your neighbour, then you will believe without doubt, and no doubt can possibly enter your soul.'[86] Comenius stresses the need to foster the propensity towards faith actively through effective and enlightened teaching. Though the tendency towards piety is innate, he says, it needs to be strengthened, formed and given direction by the teacher: 'It is clear from Scripture,' he writes in the *Pampaedia*, 'that piety itself is teachable, i.e., not immediately or miraculously infused by God, but transmitted in the ordinary course of instruction. Otherwise God would not have praised Abraham for training his household in piety, nor would he have instructed parents so consistently to bring up their children in the nurture and admonition of the Lord.'[87] The process, he says, must occur from earliest infancy: 'The purpose of this life is preparation for eternity, and if that is neglected, life is wasted. As it is through death that men come to eternity, they must be prepared to meet death correctly. As it is only by means of a good life that they come to a good death, their preparation for a good life must start at its very beginning.'[88]

Three basic methods are identified by Comenius as being appropriate for the fostering of religious faith. They are: meditation, self-examination and prayer. The first he describes as 'the constant, attentive and devoted consideration of the works, the words and the goodness of God; the thoughtful acknowledgement that it is from the good-will of God alone (either active or permissive) that all things come, and that all the counsels of the divine will attain their end in the most marvellous ways.'[89] The idea of self-examination is conceived similarly to that of conscience illumination, as described in the previous section. 'For men,' he says, 'should examine themselves to see if they are faithful, and do the will of God; and it is necessary that we should be tested by other men, by our

friends, and by our enemies.'⁹⁰ Prayer is defined as 'the frequent, or
rather the continual yearning after God and the supplication that He
may sustain us in His mercy and guide us with His Spirit.'⁹¹ Each must
be fostered, he says, in the practical manner described above, the teacher
continually promoting all three modes of communing with God in his
pupils through direct, practical experience. Details are given both in *The
Great Didactic* and the *Pampaedia* on how this is to occur at the levels of
pre-primary, primary and post-primary education.⁹²

Before all this is considered, however, it is necessary firstly to identify
the place of the scriptures in the whole process. Moravian Christianity, as
has been shown earlier in this chapter, was a radically scripture-based faith,
and Comenius, in common with his co-religionists, saw the Bible as the
one authoritative and irrefutable source of truth. It occupies a central place,
therefore, in the curriculum he envisaged for religious education. 'The
Holy Scriptures must be the Alpha and the Omega of Christian schools,'
he declares in *The Great Didactic*. Emphasising its universal accessibility,
together with its narrative vividness and simplicity—'it can be comprehended by the lowest intelligences, it is none the less an object of wonder
to the highest'—he cites the authority of Erasmus in support of his
conviction that it should be the foundation of all the work of the school
and the key to the realisation of the goal of a truly universal education:

> In Christian schools, therefore, God's Book should rank before all
> other books; that, like Timothy, all the Christian youth may, from
> boyhood, know the sacred writings which are able to make them wise
> unto salvation and may be nourished in the words of the faith. On
> this subject Erasmus has written well in his *Paraclesis, or Exhortation
> to the Study of Christian Philosophy*. 'The Holy Scripture is equally
> suitable to all, is within the capacity of little ones, nourishes them
> with milk, cherishes them, sustains them, and does all for them until
> they grow up in Christ. But, while it can be comprehended by the
> lowest intelligences, it is none the less an object of wonder to the
> highest. There is no age, no sex, no rank of life to which it is unsuit-
> able. The sun is not more the common property of mankind than is
> the teaching of Christ. It rejects none save those who hold themselves
> at a distance.' He continues: 'Would that the ploughman might sing it
> at his plough, that the weaver might repeat it at his loom, that the
> traveller might beguile the tedium of the journey by its sacred story,
> and that the conversations of Christians were taken from its pages; for
> our daily conversation represents our true character. Let each one
> get and read as much of Holy Writ as he can. Let him who is
> behind not envy him who is in front. Let him who is in front
> beckon forward him who is behind, and despise him not. Why do
> we confine to a few the book that contains the faith of all?'⁹³

These sentiments were re-echoed two centuries later by another Slavic educator who also recognised the potential of the scriptures for the attainment of this same goal. 'There is no book like the Bible to open up a new world to the pupil,' Tolstoy wrote in his report on the work of his school at Yasnaya Polyana. 'I discovered,' he recalled, 'that of all oral information which I had tried in the period of three years nothing so fitted the comprehension of the boys' minds as the Bible. The Old Testament left such an impression on the children that two months after it had been told to them, they wrote down sacred history from memory in their notebooks with but few omissions.'[94] Like Tolstoy, Comenius saw the particular appeal of scripture as lying in its narrative excitement and linguistic simplicity. He recommended it as a suitable text even for the teaching of the rudiments of literacy to pupils in the early stages of the primary school. 'Methods should be devised,' he said, 'by which the Bible may be given to children . . . as a means of learning their ABC . . . For as language is made up of sounds and the symbols of letters, thus is the whole structure of religion and piety formed out of the elements of Holy Scripture.'[95] Like yet another Slavic educator, the Jewish philosopher, Martin Buber, he wrote of the need for authentic dialogue between reader and text, suggesting to the student that he approach the scriptures with prayerful humility, being willing to 'listen to the word' and to respond to its meaning in a spirit of sincere reciprocation:

> It should be carefully impressed on the young that, if they wish the word of God to supply them with divine strength, they should bring to it a humble and devoted heart, prepared to submit itself to God on all occasions, and actually doing so at the time. The sunlight reveals nothing to him who refuses to open his eyes, nor can a banquet satisfy him who refuses to eat; and in the same way the divine light supplied to our minds, the rules given for our actions, and the happiness promised to those who fear God, are all in vain unless they are received with prompt faith, earnest charity, and firm hope.[96]

Applying these principles—the primacy of the scripture text, the fostering of piety through meditation, self-examination and prayer—to the work of the mother-school, the primary school and the Latin school, Comenius provides detailed pedagogic guidance, both in *The Great Didactic* and the *Pampaedia*, on the methods to be adopted by the teacher for their effective realisation. In the former he expressed his belief that by six years of age all pupils should have 'learned the heads of the Catechism and the principles of Christianity and should understand these and live up to them as far as their age permits.' From the outset, he writes, all religious education should be conducted in a spirit of Christian love: 'It is of great importance that they learn to practise charity,' he writes. 'For love is the especial virtue of Christians.'[97] In the *Pampaedia* he lays particular emphasis on the role of parents in the infant years. He stresses their responsibility to ensure that religious formation begins from earliest infancy: 'Temples built in God's honour are consecrated to Him as soon as the building is completed, and not left until they become ancient ruins. Men who are destined for God's temples must be dedicated to God before they begin to run their own lives, so that they bear in mind that heaven is their destiny and know what must be done to attain it. And the means to this are prayer, baptism and good training from their earliest infancy.'[98] He urges parents to create an atmosphere conducive to pious living in their homes, recommending that they engage in prayer with their children in the morning, at meal times and at bedtime. In the *Pampaedia* he gives examples of the kinds of prayer that might be appropriate for each of these occasions. His advice both to parents and teachers on the kind of instruction that is appropriate for infants has the same practical quality as his advice on moral education. He suggests they relate the practice of faith to the events of everyday life:

> 1. Whenever opportunity arises, we must speak to them personally about God, e.g. when there is thunder, lightning or hail. On the occasion of a funeral, or if a criminal is being taken to a place of execution, they should be made to form their own early impression of the other life, good or evil, that follows this earthly one.
> 2. They must have stories read to them about God's judgements, how God has punished the wicked as an example, and still does.
> 3. They should be made to say prayers, but these should be brief and expressed not in figurative language but in their own.
> 4. In the act of prayer they should be taught to fold their hands, raise their eyes to heaven, and stand respectfully or kneel without looking round, and they should learn this both by word and by example.
> 5. They should not be especially praised for their respectful conduct. For they will at once despise all this, as if it was only done to please adults and they were free to comply or to refuse, or as if they thought that the desire to please God did not enter into it.
> 6. The elements of the Christian religion, Faith, Hope and Charity, should be specially instilled into them early.[99]

In his treatment of religious education in the primary school Comenius strongly urges the teacher to begin systematic instruction in the scriptures from the outset. 'Besides the Catechism,' he writes, 'they should know the most important stories and verses in the Bible and should be able to repeat them word for word.'[100] Scripture lies at the centre of the curriculum he puts forward for the years of primary education. A particularly imaginative feature of the pedagogy he proposes is his suggestion that scripture readings be dramatised, along the lines suggested by Castellio in his Sacred Dialogues. This is an example from his own *Vestibulum Sacrae Scripturae* which was inspired by Castellio:

Class IV—Fourth Year
The Rose Garden

This is the time for an outline of the third principle, that of divine revelation. Exercises should be in dramatic form as constructed by Castellio in his Sacred Dialogues but with a fuller and more popular presentation.

Here is an example from my *Vestibulum Sacrae Scripturae* (Porchway to Holy Scripture):—

God is the everlasting power that has established and sustained everything, and the wisdom which rules everything, and the goodness which directs everything to good ends.

Man is the image of God, endowed with similar power, intelligence and will.

The world is man's home, his nursery, his school. Scripture is God's book, written by prophets and apostles, so that mankind may find in it words of admonition to turn from their preoccupation with external things to those that are internal and everlasting.

Prophets whose writings have come down to us include Moses, Joshua, David, Samuel, Nathan, Solomon, Isaiah etc. Likewise the apostles were Matthew, John, Paul, James etc.[101]

His advice for scripture instruction in the fifth grade (i.e. for 11 year-old pupils) proceeds along similar lines. Again he strongly urges the practical application of the message of the scriptures to the realities of everyday living. He emphasises the pre-eminence of charity and active love in the practice of the Christian faith. His whole approach is marked by the non-dogmatic style of teaching typified by the traditions of the Moravian Church:

Class V
The Shrubbery

This is the stage for a 'Medulla Biblica' or collection of Biblical sayings which can be based on the work of Hopf on *Flores Biblici* or Seleacted Biblical Sayings, arranged by him in alphabetical order. Now will be the time to concentrate on piety; especially when pupils are still open-minded, as their nature is not ill-disposed they must be taught to commit it to God or His direction and to resign themselves wholly to His good pleasure. Otherwise the boy or the youth whose heart becomes a nesting-place for impiety is like the ricinus plant of Jonah that is dried up by a worm harboured in its root. They will be particularly warned that they and their actions always have God's eye upon them. . . . Likewise, God exists in and among all God's creatures. Being everywhere, He must inevitably fill heaven and earth. As the soul fills the whole body and all its smallest and most insignificant parts, so God fills this bodily world which He has built as a theatre for His wisdom and a seat for His glory. No one therefore should ask the question, 'Where is God?' For He is within you, before and behind you, above and below you. He surrounds you on every side, holding you in His grasp with the hand of mercy if your life is humble, pious and pure, and with the hand of righteousness if you turn to sin. As our Creator alone knows our inmost being, and has sole power to form and reform us, we also need blessing and grace from Him alone to ensure that success goes with us. As soil cultivation is of no avail without the climate of rain and sunshine, so the cultivation of character does not succeed without God.[102]

Comenius's approach to catechetical instruction is based on the same experiential principles as he advocates in relation to scripture study. The practical application of the Christian message to the routine events of life is once again the determining factor in his approach. He drew extensively in this respect on the *Handbook for Christian Living* of Nathan Chytraeus, one of his professors at Herborn. He cities the words of Chytraeus on the profoundly humanistic principles that are embodied in Christian morality, seeing this as the basis of much of its appeal. 'If you perform only the actions of cattle, eating, drinking sleeping, etc.,' the latter wrote, 'you are living on a level with cattle. If you do things specific to mankind, human tasks and arts and wisdom, that is human life.'[103] The same kind of non-dogmatic simplicity permeates Comenius's own guidelines on the presentation of catechetical teaching. The following is an example of his approach to the teaching of the doctrine of justification by faith:

> 1. Clear indication should be quoted from the scriptures that all men are sinners, and have come short of the glory of God, for thus it is written etc. (Romans III)
> 2. The question should be asked, 'How then, do you expect to be supported in God's court of justice?' The answer is: By the intercession and advocacy of Jesus Christ our Lord who is with the Father.
> 3. Where is your proof of this? In the First Epistle of John, 1.2. 'My little children, do not sin. And if any man sin, we have an advocate with the Father.'

4. Is his advocacy effective? Yes, firstly because he did not thrust his way into this office but was appointed by the Father (Hebrews V, 5); secondly, because he himself is just, who has observed God's precepts in all things and has not transgressed them (Hebrews VII, 25–6); thirdly, because he also offered himself as a living sacrifice to make reconciliation for sinners (Hebrews II, 14) in propitiation of the sins of the whole world. (I John II, 2)

5. For whom does Christ intercede? For those who turn to repentance and believe. For he combined in those two words the whole of the Gospel. (Mark I, 15)

6. What is the meaning of 'turn to repentance'?

7. What is the meaning of 'believe'?

8. What then is justification? The declaration that we are righteous and free from guilt and the punishment of everlasting death. This comes from the remission of our sins (Romans IV, 5–8).

9. What does Christ require of the justified? The answer is: that they commit no further sin, but keep themselves safe in the grace of God and holy and undefiled lest any worse fate befall them.

10. But what if a man falls from grace? My answer is: If this is due to his weakness, God does not extinguish the glowing ember. If due to some wantonness, He chides him to make him mend his ways. If he does not mend them, He rejects him.[104]

Scripture study is once again the focus of religious education in the Latin school, though in this instance it is strongly reinforced by formal studies in metaphysics and theology. 'We wish them to be theologians who, besides understanding the principles of their faith, can also prove them from the scriptures,' he writes in the chapter from *The Great Didactic* devoted to the work of the Latin School.[105] He urges a close relationship between the study of all other disciplines of the curriculum and the study of 'the science of first principles called metaphysics.' Together with scripture study, metaphysics provides the basis of a sound and lasting faith, he said.[106] The two are seen as entirely complementary. Most of all, he urges the importance of prayer, seeing this as the means by which the individual finds union with God and fellowship with the whole of mankind:

To acquire confidence in his approach to God, the pupil should do the same as any holy man and meditate upon the object of our prayer, God the Father, Son and Holy Spirit.

1. Who is the object of your prayer? I pray to the father, the brother, and the intercessor.

2. At whose instance do you pray? The father bids me, the brother instructs me, the intercessor impels me.

3. Wherein lies your trust? In the father's promise, the brother's
help, the intercessor's testimony.
4. What do you seek? The inheritance which the brother obtained,
the father granted, and the intercessor confirmed. For I am one of
God's heirs and co-heir of Christ. I see therefore that all godliness
is not only open but clearly reserved for me, whenever I approach
it. How wicked am I, therefore, when I fail to approach, or make
my approach without due preparation.[107]

To conclude, therefore, Comenius's approach to ethico-religious education
might be said to embody two central principles, each of which marked a
radical departure from traditional practice in this field. The first is his
insistence on Christianity as essentially a way of life, modelled on the
simplicity of the teachings of Christ, and deriving its authority solely
from the authentic message of the scripture text. From this he deduced
its central teachings: its emphasis on tolerance towards others, its radical
pacifism, its concern with justice and peace: these he emphasised side by
side with the doctrines he shared with his fellow reformers—private
judgement, justification by faith, freedom of conscience and the assumption of individual responsibility. All of this might be said to represent his
thinking on the *content* of ethico-religious education. Its *method* was that
of the liberal pedagogy he developed for all aspects of the educational
process. The new methodology of teaching was to be directed towards
the application of the truths of faith to all the circumstances of daily life.
It was a behaviour oriented approach, aimed at promoting the practical
implementation of the principles of Christian truth—i.e. the primary
virtues of tolerance, fellowship and active love—in the ordinary, routine
conditions of life itself. Freed from the complexities—and, in many
instances, the contradictions—of didactic rationalism, it aimed to ensure
the authentic expression of the message of the scriptures in every facet
of the lives of those to whom it was taught.

The essential radicalism of his approach to ethico-religious education
consisted in his application of the primary Christian message of love to
every facet of the educational process. Seeing that this was the heart of
Christ's teaching, he sought to define its implications in terms of ethical
and religious responsibility as fully as he could and identified the ways
in which it could be fostered through education. Seeing that all men
have the potentiality for love, while also recognising that it would have
to be actively promoted by the teacher, he saw the achievement of this
ideal as the primary and all-embracing goal of the work of the school.
Underlying his belief in its primacy was his insistence on a crucial conjuncture: that between the twin goals of self-fulfilment through freedom
and self-fulfilment through love. Seeing the two as complementary and
interdependent forces in the realisation of all human potentiality—freedom

being the ultimate source of love and love representing the final fulfilment of individual freedom—he devised an approach to moral and religious education that ensured the primacy of both principles at every stage and in every facet of the whole process.

All those forces Comenius saw as being inimical to the Christian traditions of love and freedom—religious intolerance, sectarian conflict, the doctrine of the 'just war', the law of property, the widespread prevalence of social injustice and inequity—all of these he sought to undermine through the medium of enlightened schooling. Three centuries before the modern ecumenical movement came into being, he recognised the evils of sectarianism, and advocated religious tolerance, extending it not only to the various Christian denominations but to all other creeds as well. Additionally, he saw the contradictions of traditional Church teaching on violence and war and reaffirmed the hugely challenging, but nonetheless clear and compelling, message of Christ on non-resistance to evil. He furthermore recognised the ever present threat to peace and freedom that comes from social injustice and inequity, seeing much of this as deriving a spurious moral justification from traditional theological teaching on property and wealth. In this again he anticipated modern thinking, though, unlike his socialist compatriots of later years, he saw the key to all this as lying not in political revolution but in the enlightenment of personal conscience, in individual self-reform and in the assumption of personal responsibility in accordance with the dictates of faith. That whole vision, he believed, could be achieved through education: through its active fostering of conscience awareness and its promotion of the spirit of faith, not as a set of abstract rules and principles but quite simply as a way of life focussed on the practical expression of the law of love.

In three senses, therefore, Comenius can be described as a truly liberal educator, i.e. 'liberal' in its classical signification as indicating a fundamental concern with the advancement of individual freedom. He can be described as liberal by virtue both of the radicalism of the message he sought to promote and of the radical methods by which he endeavoured to promote it. In common with his successors in the Slavic tradition—particularly with Dostoevsky, Tolstoy and Pasternak—he saw the conjuncture of love and freedom as the distinctive mark of New Testament Christianity. Secondly, his development of a pedagogy that promoted learning as fundamentally an individualised process places him as the seminal figure in the modern liberal movement in education that found fulfilment centuries later in the work of writers such as Tolstoy and Buber. And finally, because of his belief in its intrinsic importance for all men, he further conceived the right to an education, fashioned in accordance with the freedom-affirming traditions of Christianity, as one that would have to be extended universally to the whole of humankind. This is the third sense in which the term 'liberal' is to be applied to his educational thought.

LANGUAGE EDUCATION: TOWARDS UNIVERSAL LITERACY

1. PRINCIPLES OF LANGUAGE PEDAGOGY

Comenius, like most liberal educators, saw the attainment of literacy as the key to the realisation of the goal of universal education. As the basic medium by which children (or adults) learn, its mastery, he believed, was crucial to progress in school and to the effective advancement of the learning process. Like his egalitarian successors of later years, he equated literacy with educability, seeing it as providing access to learning and therefore as an indispensable requirement for educational progress and growth. It occupied a prominent place in his educational writings and guided his various initiatives on educational reform from the outset. He published numerous volumes on the subject, including some of the most innovative and imaginative school texts that have ever been produced for the teaching of both vernacular and non-vernacular languages.

His approaches to language education marked a radical departure, both in terms of curricular content and pedagogic method, from those that had been followed in the mediaeval schools. In the first place, he recognised the absurdity of focussing teaching on the acquisition of a second language (usually Latin) from the earliest stages of schooling and emphasised the crucial importance of vernacular proficiency, both as a foundation for all learning and specifically for the acquisition of other languages. Additionally, he recognised the need for a radical shift in language pedagogy from the mechanistic and sterile approaches of the mediaevalists to the learner centred methods he believed would ensure that language acquisition was both an efficient and enjoyable process. These issues will be the main concern of this chapter. Following the present introductory section, which will deal with the general principles of Comenian language pedagogy, a second section will focus on the teaching of the mother-tongue and a third on the teaching of non-vernacular languages. A final section will examine Comenius's vision of a new universal order, the attainment of which he believed could be facilitated through literacy. That vision has not yet been fulfilled but it remains remarkably relevant to contemporary world-wide initiatives on educational reform, conceived as something intimately bound up with the pursuit of international harmony and peace.

Basically, Comenius envisaged the whole process of language education in terms of a multilingual progression, beginning with the mastery of the mother-tongue and proceeding therefrom to the acquisition of non-vernacular languages. The principle of sequential multilingualism is clearly stated in these words from Chapter XXII of *The Great Didactic*: 'One language should always be learned after, and not at the same time as another; since otherwise both will be learned confusedly.'[1] This same principle is explicitly affirmed in the *Methodus Linguarum Novissima*, a major treatise on language education which Comenius published in 1649.[2] The work outlines his philosophy of language education in the opening section and in subsequent sections defines the pedagogical principles on which instruction was to be based. The seventh section shows how these methods are to be implemented in the case of first and second language acquisition, clearly seeing the two as proceeding consecutively. In both cases he insisted on radical changes in the methods of instruction that were to be used. The translator of the *Orbis Pictus* succinctly conveys the extent of the changes that Comenius proposed. In his Preface to the English edition of the work Charles Hoole wrote:

> He hath therefore in some of his later works seemed to move retrograde, and striven to come nearer to the reach of tender wits; and in this present Book, he hath (according to my judgement), descended to the very bottom of what is to be taught, and proceedeth (as Nature itself doth) in an orderly way; first to exercise the senses well, by presenting their objects to them, and then to fasten upon the intellect by impressing the first notions of things upon it, and linking them one to another by rational discourse. Whereas indeed, We generally missing this way, do teach children, as we do Parrots, to speak they know not what, nay, which is worse, we, taking the Way of teaching little ones by Grammar only at the first, do puzzle their imaginations with abstractive terms and secondary intentions, which, till they be somewhat acquainted with things, and the words belonging to them, in the language which they learn, they cannot apprehend what they mean. And this I guess to be the reason why many greater persons do resolve sometimes not to put a child to school, till he be at least eleven or twelve years of age, presuming that he having then taken notice of most things, will sooner get the knowledge of the words which are applied to them in any language. But the gross misdemeanour of such children for the most part, have taught many parents to be hasty enough to send their own to school, if not that they may learn, yet (at least) that they may be

> kept out of harm's way; and yet if they do not profit, for the time
> they have been at school (no respect at all being had of their years)
> the Master shall be sure enough to bear the blame.[3]

The passage identifies all the major principles of Comenius's language
pedagogy. The central and all-embracing principle is one which was
discussed in detail in an earlier chapter, i.e. that learning must follow the
methods of nature. In *The Great Didactic* he spoke of 'placing the art of
intellectual discipline on such a firm basis that sure and certain progress
may be made.' He continued: 'Since this basis can be properly laid only by
assimilating the processes of art as much as possible to those of nature,
we will follow the method of nature.'[4] Applied to the specific requirements of language teaching, this issues in five main principles. They are:
one, 'nature observes a suitable time'[5] (the principle of readiness); two, 'in
all the operations of nature development is from within'[6] (the principle of
learning through experience); three, 'nature makes no leaps but proceeds
step by step, advancing from what is easy to what is more difficult'[7] (the
principle of graded, sequential progression); four, 'the teacher ensures
that learning is thoroughly agreeable, and such as to make the school a
form of play,'[8] (the pleasure principle); and five, 'nature prepares the
material before giving it form'[9] (the principle of curriculum structuring).
    Turning firstly to the principle of readiness, it is crucial to recognise
the delicate balance that Comenius maintained between the spontaneity
of the learning process and the formative role of the teacher in facilitating
its purposeful development. As we have seen, he believed passionately in
the educability of all—the 'seeds of knowledge exist in all men', he
declared in *The Great Didactic*. 'Each individual creature,' he wrote, 'not
only suffers itself to be easily led in the direction which its nature finds
congenial, but is actually impelled towards the desired goal, and suffers
pain if any obstacle be imposed.'[10] Equally, he recognised that the initial
motivation to learn, the basic source of the pupil's readiness, needs to be
fostered and guided by the teacher—an insistence we shall see presently
which is crucial for the development of basic literacy. These are the
words of *The Great Didactic*:

> With many not the capacity to learn but the inclination is lacking,
> and to compel these against their will is as unpleasant as it is useless.
> I answer: there is a story told of a philosopher who had two pupils,
> of whom one was idle and the other industrious. Both were sent away
> by their master; for one would not learn, though able to do so, while
> the other could not, though anxious to acquire knowledge. But how
> does the matter stand if it be shown that the teacher himself is the
> reason of the pupil's aversion to learning? Truly did Aristotle say
> that all men are born anxious to acquire knowledge. . . . In practice,

however, the tender indulgence of parents hinders the natural tendency of children, and later on frivolous society leads them into idle ways. . . . Thus it comes to pass that they show no desire to investigate what is unknown, and cannot concentrate their thoughts with ease. . . . In these cases the external distraction must first be removed; nature will then assert itself with its original vigour, and the desire for knowledge will once more be apparent. But how many of those who undertake to educate the young appreciate the necessity of first teaching them how to acquire knowledge? The turner shapes a block of wood with his axe before he turns it; the blacksmith heats iron before he hammers it; the cloth-weaver, before he spins his wool, first cleans, washes, cards and fulls it; the shoemaker, before he sews the shoe, prepares, shapes, and smooths the leather; but who, I ask, ever thinks it necessary that the teacher, in the same way, should make his pupils anxious for information, capable of receiving instruction, and therefore ready for a many-sided education, before he begins to place knowledge before them?[11]

Much controversy has been focussed on these issues in contemporary theories of language learning, with progressive thinkers, influenced in the main by the theories of Jean Piaget, making excessive claims for the spontaneity of the whole proceoss, and others, influenced mainly by developments in applied linguistics, excessively emphasising the need for highly systematised and structured teaching. Before this is discussed in the context both of the teaching of the mother tongue and of non-vernacular languages, however, the remaining principles must first be clarified. Closely linked with the principle of spontaneous, but guided, language growth is the doctrine of 'learning through experience', with its implication that language learning must be rooted in sense experience. 'It is only when a thing has been grasped by the senses that language can fulfil its function of explaining it further,' Comenius writes in *The Great Didactic.*[12] 'The senses are the primary and constant guides of knowl-edge,' he wrote in *The Analytical Didactic.*[13] Crucially, he insisted that sense experience be guided and given direction by the teacher. This is demonstrated clearly by the editor of the facsimile edition of the *Orbis Pictus*, published by Oxford University Press in 1968:

Comenius was of the opinion that sense experience needs to be guided. Even at the infant stage children 'see, hear, taste and touch, but are ignorant of the exact nature of their sensations', and there-fore things must be presented and explained to them and this implies the use of language so that they will always associate words with objects. Mothers must 'name whatever is seen' and the child must respond verbally and through action. Even in the first and second year a baby can understand 'what a wrinkled and what an unwrinkled brow means.' As the child grows older suitable objects must be 'rightly presented' to him and the objects chosen must be 'determinate, real and useful things that can make an impression on the senses and on the imagination.' In this we see the intimate connection which Comenius found between reality and language. 'Words should not be learnt apart from objects . . . but objects cannot be apprehended without words' and the correct order of learning is that a suitable object should be clearly shown to as many of the senses as possible until the mind has duly received its image. Then the child should learn the name of the object and the names of its particular parts.[14]

It is essential to recognise the fact that Comenius saw experience as the gateway to the perception of realities beyond the sphere of the sensual and the empirical. Piaget, despite the inadequacies of his interpretations of Comenius in many respects, recognised the importance of this. 'Comenius was not a sensualist,' he writes; 'his metaphysics lies between scholasticism as inspired by Aristotle and the mechanicalism of the seventeenth century. Everyone can see the kinship between his philosophy and Bacon's but, in respect of empiricism, this direct connection should not be overstressed.'[15] The term 'metaphysical,' while it conveys the transcendence of the empirical which is the essential point about Comenius's view of the ultimate nature of reality, does not, however, adequately describe the nature of the finite-infinite tension that lies at the heart of it. For Piaget's notion of a 'dynamism linking together the formative order of the material world'—which he sees as the central principle of Comenian metaphysics—must be substituted the hierarchical order of finite and infinite, material and spiritual which ultimately Comenius based not on metaphysics but on faith. It is to this transcendent order he was referring when he spoke of enabling the learner to penetrate 'the inner constitution of things'[16] through language, i.e., penetrating the realm of infinity in being where reality becomes ultimately meaningful. The immediate sphere of meaning to which language gives access is that of the material, the sensual and the empirical; ultimately, he suggests, it discloses the higher reality of the spiritual—but crucially, it does this *by way of* the material, the sensual and the empirical.

This whole process was seen by Comenius as requiring careful guidance and direction from the teacher, particularly in the complex matter of enabling the learner to perceive the full meaningfulness of the truths disclosed by sense. For this Comenius advised systematic teaching, involving a step by step progression from one stage of learning to the next. The progression he describes has been compared by Piaget to the genetic stages in learning conceived by developmental psychologists, such as

Vygotsky and himself, several centuries later. 'Comenius,' he writes, 'may undoubtedly be considered as one of the precursors of the genetic idea in developmental psychology, and as the founder of a system of progressive instruction adjusted to the stages of development the pupil has reached.' He continues: 'With really remarkable intuition he grasps the fact that the same forms of knowledge are necessary at each of the different levels, because they correspond to permanent needs. . . . This is a very accurate anticipation of the successive reconstructions of the same kind of knowledge from stage to stage . . . which modern genetic psychology has enabled us to analyse.'[17] In general terms at least, this analysis seems quite sound. Its identification of the concept of developmental stages, together with the emphasis on the graduated presentation of the universals of knowledge, as the basic principles of Comenian learning theory, can be fully substantiated from his writings. Comenius's prescription of programme content for a number of distinct stages—infancy, childhood, adolescence, youth, manhood etc.—together with the step by step sequencing of subject-matter, corresponds closely to the process described by Piaget himself, as will be illustrated in the forthcoming section. But there were profound differences between Comenius and Piaget on the nature of the teacher's intervention in this whole process, as will also be demonstrated shortly.

The importance of the pleasure principle as providing the basic motivation for all language learning is repeatedly stressed by Comenius in *The Great Didactic*, *The Analytical Didactic*, the *Pampaedia* and the language texts. An earlier chapter has shown the importance of imagination and creativity in Comenian learning theory and the extent to which drawing and painting, music and drama were represented in the curricula he recommended for the infant, primary and senior schools. The provision for drama has a particular bearing on his treatment of language education. Comenius was himself a prolific dramatist; he is known to have written at least ten plays, all of which were intended for production in schools. The *Labyrinth* has strong elements of dramatic monologue and dialogue and has been adapted for theatrical presentation on several occasions, most recently at theatres in Brno and Copenhagen.[18]

It is not surprising therefore that he should emphasise the use of drama and various forms of dramatic play so strongly in his pedagogic writings. He speaks in the *Pampaedia* of 'treating everything as a form of game or competition according to the pupils' ages, in the school for boyhood, adolescence, early manhood etc.'[19] He gives examples in the *Janua* of the kind of dramatic dialogues that could be used to ensure that language learning becomes a playful activity. 'Textbooks will be specially effective if they are mainly written in dialogue form,'[20] he says, as he urges teachers to incorporate the principle of play as fully as possible into the whole process. The texts, he says, 'must combine understanding with enjoyment,' thereby extending the principle of playful learning into all the work of the school. It is crucial, he argues, that this be organised in a manner appropriate to the stage of development that the learner has reached. Two principles—the genetic and motivational—are combined in this passage from the *Pampaedia*:

> The most important factor in pleasant study will be a method that is thoroughly practical and agreeable and such as to make the school really a form of play, that is, a pleasant prelude to the whole of life. This will be achieved if all the tasks of life are presented in a way that appeals to children and combines understanding with enjoyment. The tasks will be applied, of course, to objects which cannot fail to delight that age-group, so that on leaving school and engaging in the business of life they should appear to face nothing so very new, but only novel and pleasant applications of what they have already learned. To this end it will be good to have things so arranged that every school is like (1) a small household, full of exercises in daily living, (2) a small state, divided into decuries (tenths) like a tribe of citizens, having its consuls, praetors, senate, and system of justice, all in thoroughly good order, (3) a small church, full of holy practices and the praises of God. . . . If this is done, the well known maxim will apply—'True school, pure play.'
>
> Every school can become a universal playroom if we insist on the right and proper development of natural instincts the moment they appear. For since human nature itself invites us to meet every human situation, surely it would be easier simply to direct it rather than to frustrate it altogether. Do we not find that some boys enjoy riding hobby-horses, building huts, calling up soldiers, deploying troops, practising fighting, choosing kings, allocating duties, holding their own law-courts, and so representing a model state? Others are eager to make public speeches, conduct funerals etc. There we see a perfect example of the trend of their individual nature, and it is perfectly clear that they should not be simply left to themselves but need to be well-informed.[21]

The instrument through which all these objectives were to be achieved was the class textbook, the requirements for which are given extensive attention by Comenius in his pedagogic writings. He envisaged the work of the school, and indeed the provision of pansophic education throughout the whole of life, as being guided to a large degree by the content of well-designed texts. 'There is one factor which by its absence or presence can render the whole organisation of a school of no avail or can aid it in the highest degree and that is a proper supply of comprehensive and methodical textbooks,' he writes in *The Great Didactic*.[22] He insists that the task of producing good texts be entrusted to those with the necessary authority to undertake this work:

> It is evident, therefore, that the success of my scheme depends entirely upon the supply of encyclopaedic classbooks, and these can be provided only by the collaboration of several original-minded, energetic and learned men. For such a task transcends the strength of one man, and especially of one who is unable to devote his whole time to it, or who may be imperfectly acquainted with some of the subjects that must be included in the comprehensive scheme.[23]

Comenius saw the textbook as ensuring that all pupils would be guaranteed a sound education, regardless of the pedagogic competence of the teacher. He insisted that it satisfy a number of basic criteria: a) that its content be profound and substantial, b) that it embrace and demonstrate the encyclopaedic character of all knowledge, c) that its content by presented in a orderly and systematic fashion, d) that it consistently facilitate enjoyment and pleasure in the activity of learning. Texts, he insists, should be few in number, a single volume generally being considered sufficient for each stage in the student's education. He placed strong emphasis on brevity, clarity and simplicity, insisting that these qualities be in evidence at every stage of schooling from the elementary years to the highest levels of the Latin school. The following passage from the *Pampaedia* summarises the qualities he expected in a good textbook— qualities we shall see which were superlatively exemplified in his own language texts, especially the *Orbis Pictus*:

> To sum up: every book in the new age, especially for use in school, will conform completely to Pansophia, Pampaedia, Panglottia and Panorthosia, i.e. it must be Pansophic in imparting the core of full and total wisdom, each book at its own stage progressing at a faster or slower rate, Pampaedic in serving all men's minds in every subject, again each at its own stage, Panglottic in allowing translation into every language in the world by virtue of the simple style, and Panorthotic in serving the important purpose of preventing or reforming corruptions, against each in its own place and in its own way.
>
> But, you may ask, how is this to be done? My answer is: by composing public books aimed at the reformation of the world, and embracing Pansophia, Pampaedia, Panglottia, and Panorthosia; the Pansophic to differentiate the true from the false, the Pampaedic the advantageous from the disadvantageous, the Panglottic the clear from the obscure, the Panorthotic the helpful from the harmful, all designed to maintain the first alternative and utterly reject the second.[24]

It remains now to show how all these principles were applied by
Comenius to the process of language teaching. The next section will
examine them in the context of vernacular instruction, the following
section in relation to the teaching of non-vernacular languages.

2. TEACHING THE MOTHER TONGUE

In the fifth place, I bequeath thee and thy sons an eagerness for the
enrichment, purification and development of our beloved, melodious,
mother tongue. In this endeavour the zeal of my sons was known
of old, when it was said by competent judges that no purer Czech
existed than that in use among the Brethren in their books. And
even now some of my sons, although exiles, have produced useful
and most excellently written books for the enrichment of our
knowledge and language, our store of wisdom and eloquence. For
thereby might perhaps be righted the present ruinous condition, as
soon as the Lord will grant a time of revival. Therefore, as many
books, both old and new, as thou findest, accept from my sons and
use them to thy best advantage.[25]

Thus wrote Comenius in a passage from *The Bequest of the Unity of
Brethren* where he was extolling the linguistic purity and vitality of his
native language. To the Moravian Brethren the Czech language was the
hallmark of their cultural identity. Comenius urged them to preserve it
as such for generations to come, seeing this as an especial responsibility
for all of them, following their expulsion from Bohemia during the Thirty
Years' War. Throughout his life he himself had ardently promoted the
language, in the face of the prejudiced policies of the Hapsburg establishment which had sought for two centuries to discourage its usage
amongst the people of Bohemia and Moravia. One of his earliest works,
the *Theatrum Universitatis Rerum*, begun while he was still a student at
Herborn, had a preface in the Czech language. At about the same time
he also began work on his *Treasury of the Bohemian Language*, a collection
of idioms and proverbs in popular usage, following which he produced a
study of Czech poetry in which he argued for the superiority of the
Czech language over Germanic and Romance languages as a medium for
poetic composition.[26] In *The Bequest of the Unity of Brethren*, as indicated
in the words quoted above, he saw the language as a potent and authentic
expression of the people's faith and urged the Brethren to 'purify, enrich
and develop' it for that purpose.[27]

This association of national consciousness and identity with the use of
the vernacular language found expression in his commitment to the
teaching of the mother-tongue, in the face of long standing traditions of

according primacy to the teaching of Latin from the earliest years of schooling. In the words of Jiřina Popelova, Comenius 'proceeded from the conviction that raising the level of the national language means, at the same time, raising the level of the common people.' 'His love of the Czech language as the language of the common people,' she writes, 'makes him formulate a demand, which he then proclaims as valid for all nations. It is the demand for education in the national language both in and out of school, which he formulates as a natural right of general validity.'[28]

As was indicated in an earlier chapter, Latin still dominated the schools of Europe in the middle of the seventeenth century and the use of the vernacular was discouraged as a medium not only for school learning but even for popular conversation as well. Comenius was one of a small group of educators who recognised the importance of the mother-tongue, not only as something of intrinsic value in itself, culturally and educationally, but as the natural foundation for the teaching of all other languages also. Others who recognised this principle included the English educators, Richard Mulcaster and Hezekiah Woodward. Mulcaster had advocated the teaching of the vernacular in schools as early as 1582[29] and Woodward, a contemporary of Comenius, spoke of it as 'the foundation of all'—'the child goes on with ease and delight when the understanding and the tongue are drawn along parallel lines,' he wrote.[30] In France the vernacular was taught in the Little Schools of Port Royal, its use being strongly advocated by Pierre Coustel who described it in his *Rules for the Education of Children* as the basis of all true learning, a view that brought him into conflict with leading Jesuit educators.[31] Wolfgang Ratke, as previously mentioned, was another near contemporary of Comenius who similarly argued for vernacular instruction in the primary school. 'Now the right practice and course of nature is that the dear youth should first learn to read, write, and speak their inherited mother-tongue', he declared in his *Memorial* in 1612.[32]

All this was strongly echoed by Comenius in his pedagogic writings. Two principles were central to his approach to the teaching of the mother-tongue, each of which remains crucially important in contemporary first language pedagogy. The first is the centrality of oral-aural development in the whole process of language growth; the second is the continuity of language and thought, language and meaning, language and experience. Comenius saw the speech behaviour of the young child as holding the key to his entire linguistic formation; he saw it as the foundation on which the subsequent development of reading and writing competence is to be based. He advised parents and infant teachers to give careful attention to the babbling speech of the young child—to its rhythms, sounds and seminal grammatical structures—urging them to develop effective rapport with the child, stimulating responses which would lead to the mastery of more sophisticated speech usage later. The priority given to this whole process is evident from his statement of objectives for the work of the mother-school in *The Great Didactic*:

> The elements of the process of reasoning, namely dialectic, are learned when the child observes that conversations are carried on by means of question and answer, and himself acquires the habit of asking and answering questions. He should, however, be taught to ask sensible questions and to give direct answers, and also not to wander from the point at issue.
>
> The grammar of childhood consists in learning to speak the mother-tongue correctly, that is to say, in pronouncing with distinctness the letters, syllables and words.
>
> The beginnings of rhetoric consist in imitating the figures of speech that occur in family conversation, but more especially in the appropriate use of gesture, and in inflecting the voice so as to suit the words; that is to say, the voice should be raised in the last syllables of words, in asking questions, and lowered in answering them. This and similar points are acquired naturally, but a little instruction is of great assistance if any mistakes are made.[33]

In giving priority to speech development in the early years Comenius anticipated by several centuries some of the most important developments that have occurred in the principles and methods of first language pedagogy. From the time the vernacular was first taught in schools— sometime in the late sixteenth century—up to the middle of the twentieth century, language teaching was focussed almost entirely on the development of reading and writing competence and little attention was given to the fostering of oral-aural fluency. It was not until the 1960s—largely through the influence of linguisticians such as Halliday and Wilkinson[34]— that the importance of oral-aural development was generally recognised and that it was seen as the foundation of all linguistic growth. Not alone did Comenius anticipate all this, but the pedagogic methods he advised are remarkably close to those now universally practised in infant schools.

Basically, he advised that oral-aural formation follow the natural modes of language growth, i.e. that it be facilitated through three main processes: listening, imitation and practice. Within this general context of experiential language growth he identified a process of development that closely resembles the linguistic reconstruction of reality described by developmental learning theorists such as Vygotsky and Piaget. Though his thinking differs significantly from that of the latter in a number of important respects, it is quite close to the former in some of its most fundamental principles. Given the importance of this issue for an understanding of Comenius's ideas on language teaching, it is worth considering it at some length, particularly in the light of some recently published work by Piaget himself on Comenian learning theory.

The initial stage of language growth is represented by Comenius as a process of naming, seen as essentially an association of words with concepts or the 'things' they represent. In *The Great Didactic* he stresses the interdependence of words and the objectified realities they name or describe. 'Words,' he writes, 'should not be learned apart from the objects to which they refer; since the objects do not exist separately and cannot be apprehended without words but both exist and perform their functions together.' Children he says, 'see, hear, taste and touch, but are ignorant of the exact object of their sensations.'[35] Learning, he insists, must be guided towards the precise identification of the word and the object or concept to which it refers. He stresses the obligation on the teacher, therefore, to ensure the simultaneous development of cognitional and linguistic processes:

> The study of languages, especially in youth, should be joined to that of objects, that our acquaintance with the objective world and with language, that is to say, our knowledge of facts and our power to express them, may progress side by side. For it is men we are forming and not parrots. . . .
>
> If you are not thinking of loquacity (which is due more to nature than to training) but of the ability to express thoughts suitably in speech, then this can be promised to any man who has learned to distinguish one thing from another correctly with his mind and give the right name to each of them, and to connect words together aptly. For then you are able to talk sense and not nonsense, to use words and not monstrosities of words, to put together a coherent speech, not sand without lime. Thus in the end, even the simplest of men, little gifted for speaking, can become eloquent.[36]

'Analysis, synthesis and syncrisis' are the terms used by Comenius in the *Pampaedia* to signify the nature of the conceptualising and naming processes involved in all this.[37] These three processes, he writes, are based on an initial act of disassociation by virtue of which a concept is broken into its constituent parts so that it may be more easily comprehended before being reconceived again in its complex totality. He compares the process to that involved in understanding the workings of a mechanical object such as a clock. 'If anyone wishes to make a close study of the mechanical structure of anything, for example a clock, the only possible way will be to take it in his hands and dismantle it carefully, then to reassemble it after observing what components, large or small, have gone into its construction and how many they are and what purposes they serve. . . . Similarly in coming to understand the composition of things in nature it is necessary to apply the processes of analysis, synthesis and syncrisis.'[38] Piaget saw close parallels between this and his own theory of the child's verbal deconstruction and subsequent restructuring of reality. In place of the Comenian emphasis on the interdependence of word and concept, however, he suggests that cognition *precedes* language, a reformulation that has significant implications for the whole process of language learning:

> This functional character of the activity or spontaneity in which Comenius believes naturally leads him to take a clear stand with regard to the relationship between practical and formal methods. The question is discussed in an interesting way in connection with the seconcd principle of the 'Necessary Conditions for Teaching and Learning', which is expressed as follows: 'Nature prepares matter before giving it a form.' After a few reflections upon the need for school equipment (books, pictures, specimens, models, etc.) before lessons begin, Comenius takes up the central question of the relation between speech and the knowledge of things. As a former teacher of Latin and other languages he pronounces this decisive verdict: 'Schools teach how to prepare a speech before teaching the knowledge with which the speech should deal; for years, pupils are obliged to learn the rules of rhetoric; then, at some time, they are at last allowed to study the positive sciences, mathematics, physics etc. And since things are substance and words accidents, the thing the grain and the word the straw, the thing the almond and the word the skin and shell, they ought to be presented to the human mind at the same time; but (and the underlining is mine) *care must be taken to start with things*, for they are the subject dealt with by the intellect as well as by discourse.'[39]

Piaget has used these words from *The Great Didactic* to imply support by Comenius for a concept of readiness which his work as a whole quite clearly rejects. Repeatedly in his writings, Comenius stressed the *simultaneity* of cognitional and linguistic development. 'How is it possible to do two or three things by a single operation?' he asks at one point in *The Great Didactic*. 'The example of nature,' he writes, 'shows that several things can be done at one time and by means of the same operation.' 'It may be laid down as a general rule,' he continues, 'that each subject should be taught in combination with those that are correlative to it; that is to say, *words should be studied in combination with the things to which they refer.*'[40] The passage cited by Piaget points to the need for a pedagogic sequencing of two closely related kinds of comprehension within a single lesson, and cannot cannot be taken to indicate the substantial time-lag between conceptual and linguistic comprehension that he himself sees as characterising the process of intellectual maturation in early childhood. This is made clear by the editor of the *Orbis Pictus* who quotes Comenius's

'Words should not be learnt apart from objects . . . but objects cannot be apprehended without words,' and adds this interpretation of its pedagogic implications: 'The correct order of learning is that a suitable object should be clearly shown to as many of the senses as possible until the mind has duly received its image. Then the child should learn the name of the object and the names of its particular parts.'[41] What the editor advises is that objects be first perceived through the senses and named immediately their material character has been grasped—a matter purely of orderly pedagogic presentation and not the gradual process of experiential conceptualisation which Piaget insists must occur before linguistic instruction is attempted. This principle is repeatedly illustrated in the *Orbis Pictus* as will be shown later in this chapter.

Piaget gives much attention to the Comenian principle that 'nature awaits a favourable moment,' seeing this as further implying the need for the teacher to *await* the spontaneous growth and development of the learning processes in the child. He is deeply critical of the dominance of the curriculum in contemporary approaches to infant education and sees external intervention as a barrier to the normal development of the learning process: 'How many schools,' he asks, 'invoke the ideas of development, interest, spontaneous activity etc., although in real fact, the only development is that laid down in the curriculum, the only interests are imposed, and the only activities suggested by adult authority!'[42] He goes on to stress the emphasis given by Comenius to self-initiated learning, seeing this as the only truly authentic mode of intellectual development for the young child: 'There is no authentic activity so long as the pupil accepts the truth of an assertion merely because it is conveyed from an adult to a child, with all the aura of explicit or implicit authority attached to the teacher's words or those of the textbooks; but there is an activity when the pupil rediscovers or reconstructs truth by means of external, or internal mental, action consisting in experiment and independent reasoning. This all-important fact appears to me to have been clearly grasped by Comenius.'[43]

This analysis needs to be challenged for its imputation to Comenius of a view of the learning process that modern research has shown to be seriously flawed, especially in respect of its implications for language learning. It would be wrong, as Piaget himself has acknowledged, to draw very close parallels between Comenius and modern learning theorists. Writing, as he was, centuries before the emergence of modern psychological theory, it is inevitable that there would have been certain shortcomings in Comenius's thinking on these issues, but there are matters of general pedagogic principle on which he can be shown to have anticipated modern developments nonetheless, even to the extent of avoiding the pitfalls into which Piaget himself has been led, by virtue of his extravagant claims for the child's capacity to initiate and sustain the activity of learning.

Research by theorists such as Donaldson, Brown, Desforges, Bryant, Ausubel and Bruner[44]—all of them drawing substantially on Vygotsky— has demonstrated the flaws in the Piagetian concepts of readiness and spontaneous learning development, and has reaffirmed the vital role of the teacher both in providing the initial motivation for learning and purpose- fully fostering and directing its growth. Donaldson, Brown and Desforges have shown that higher levels of cognitive and linguistic development occur in young children as a result of direct verbal instruction than those which occur from independent, self-initiated discovery. Bryant has further emphasised the need for pedagogic intervention to develop cognitive and linguistic potential and rejects the case by Piaget that cognitive advance- ment precedes the linguistic. Ausubel, again drawing heavily on Vygotsky, has severely criticised Piaget for underestimating the role of verbal instruc- tion in effecting the transition from one stage of development to the next and rejects his claim that children must progress unhindered from one to the other. Bruner, the most distinguished of contemporary Vygotskeyans, has shown the importance not only of pedagogic intervention but of structured subject-content in the development of the learning process. Rejecting the Piagetian concept of readiness, he wrote: 'The idea of readiness is a mischievous half-truth. It is a half-truth largely because it turns out that one teaches readiness or provides opportunities for its nurture, one does not simply wait for it.'[45] These are the four character- istics he identifies for an effective process of instruction:

> 1. *Predisposition to Learn*: A theory of instruction must be con- cerned with the experiences and contexts that will tend to make the child willing and able to learn when he enters school.
> 2. *Structure of Knowledge*: A theory of instruction must specify ways in which a body of knowledge should be structured so that it can be most readily grasped by the learner.
> 3. *Sequence*: A theory of instruction should specify the most effective sequences in which to present the materials.
> 4. *Reinforcement*: A theory of instruction should specify the nature and pacing of rewards, moving from extrinsic rewards to intrinsic ones.[46]

While exemplifying little of the theoretical sophistication of these writers, Comenius is much closer to them than he is to Piaget in his conception of the principles of teaching and learning. While recognising the importance of individual rates of learning, he shared their sense of the need for formative pedagogy and structured subject-content as vital factors in its development. The passage just quoted from Bruner bears more than an incidental resemblance to much of the content of Chapters XVIII to XIX of *The Great Didactic*, in which Comenius details the principles of 'facility, thoroughness, conciseness and rapidity in teaching and learning'. His understanding of the nature and development of mental processes might be considered crude and inadequate by modern standards. Based largely on a faculty view of the mind, and a theory of perception that oversimplifies the relationship of sensation and cognition, his conception of the whole process of learning leads nonetheless to the affirmation of principles that are themselves intrinsically sound. His assertion of the parallelism of word and concept, emphasised repeatedly for example in the *Methodus*,[47] runs counter to the Piagetian prioritisation of cognitive processes and provides a theoretical foundation for a pedagogy of language growth that is entirely consistent with the interactive method advocated by Vygotsky, Bruner and others, which has now generally replaced the Piagetian model for language pedagogy. Similarly, the earlier mentioned theory of syncritistic reconstruction—the key elements of which are disassociation, reconstruction and synthesis—remains a highly plausible, if somewhat loosely formulated, foundation for the development of crucial forms of basic learning competence, such as the mastery of reading comprehension. This is the relevant passage from the *Pampaedia* where this whole process is explained:

> *Analysis* is the breaking-down of a whole into its parts, the first and lowest foundation of all true learning. For things that are not subdivided and differentiated are confusing and disturbing to the sense, the mind, and themselves. Enlightenment lies in differentiating things, and it has three aspects: 1) differentiation or discrimination between the whole and other wholes, 2) subdivision of the whole into its parts, 3) distribution of the whole into species. Analysis must not be haphazard but accurate; otherwise the contemplation of things will suffer, and learning will become vague, uncertain and faulty. . . .
>
> *Synthesis* consists of reassembling parts into their whole and it is therefore invaluable in confirming the learning of things, if it is true. There is indeed no advantage in considering the parts by themselves, and it is not easy to understand their purpose, but when they are reassembled in proper order and connected to one another they soon reveal their use and resume their function as can be seen in the case of the clock that is taken to pieces and put together again.
>
> *Syncrisis* consists of the comparison of one part with others and one whole with others, and it therefore sheds some light on the learning process and improves it immensely. In fact, to understand things in isolation, as men generally do, is a minor part of it, but to understand the harmony of things and the proportions of all the related parts is the vital factor which brings pure and all-pervading light to men's minds.[48]

It is significant that this passage is headed by the objective 'To teach thoroughly,' and that in the chapter from the *Pampaedia* from which it is taken Comenius represented the whole process of learning as requiring regular and systematic guidance from the teacher. Regarding the development of vernacular competence, for instance, he saw the parent or teacher playing a crucial rule in guiding the 'naming' process, i.e., the identification of word and concept. This excerpt from the *Pampaedia* will indicate the formative and systematic nature of the guidance he expected parents and teachers to provide:

> Even infants should be taught words with the aid of things, that is, to speak and gather wisdom at the same time. . . . This will be done if every object is shown to the infant before being referred to by name.
>
> Nurses should teach language as it was done in the Garden of Eden.
>
> 1. When they see infants looking round at different things with all the intentness of their age, they should point to the same and name them.
>
> 2. They should begin with larger units, for example, they should name the dog before the head, eye, tail etc.
>
> 3. They should begin by using simpler names rather than compounds or diminutives, e.g. dog rather than puppy-dog. There is no need yet for terms of endearment to be learned; speaking and pronunciation are enough.
>
> 4. They should insist on a two-way method, that is to say, on pointing to a thing one should say: 'What is this?' and on supplying the name again, they should ask to have it pointed to, saying, 'Where is the dog?' 'Where is the table?' 'Where is your head?'[49]

At the heart of Comenius's pedagogic strategies for teaching the mother tongue lies the principle of language growth through the medium of sense experience. He saw the language of sense as providing the crucial bridgehead between word and concept, between language and experience, language and thought. In the chapter of the *Pampaedia* dealing with the work of the Infant School he writes: 'At this age they are as novices coming to live in the world with no preformed concepts either good or bad. They must be introduced to these, and surely the only way is through the gates of the senses.'[50] He saw the whole process as one of ordering, classifying and distinguishing various modes of objective reality: 'But knowledge of subtle things is too much to expect of boys, who are still unaware of the broader distinctions between things. They should not be concerned with these, but their training should cover the rudiments of things, and gradually progress towards a wide range of more notable distinctions.'[51] In the case of the infant school all speech development should be reinforced, he says, by sense experience:

> Similarly speech should simply begin with baby-talk and pass through a lisping stage to conversation, always following personal experience by sight and touch. For we cannot speak of things in abstract terms to children who have not yet formed abstract concepts nor acquired mental impressions so clear that the sound of a word evokes its concept. It is difficult, therefore, to speak to infants; but it is easy to take real things and point to them and then name them. In other words, as we cannot yet speak to infants, let nature itself do the speaking by making its own impression on their eyes, ears, nostrils, taste and touch.
>
> It will be of lasting benefit to these novices to have their senses firmly associated with objects, because in this way they will form the habit of accepting the truth only when it has been tried and tested, and of relying on their own judgement in every situation. As this way of acquiring knowledge is perfectly reliable and is the only sound method, by introducing at this stage the process of measuring everything by our own senses we shall produce pupils who are no slaves to mere opinion, other people's or their own, but searchers after truth, aspirants to true wisdom with free judgement in their circumstances, rejecting all that is false, vain and unreasonable and treasuring for themselves only the solid sustenance of truth and wisdom.[52]

He placed particularly strong emphasis on the benefits of visual experience for the development of linguistic competence and advocated the consistent use of visual stimuli in school textbooks to reinforce the acquisition of basic reading and writing skills. Defining the act of sensory perception as the transmission of 'images of things' from the senses to the brain, he saw these images as being most effectively conveyed through visual representation. Thus he recommended the use of picture books in which all the objects of knowledge would be set out comprehensively—both visually and verbally—for all levels of schooling. He gives clear and specific guidance on how this is to be done for pupils in the mother-school in the following passage from *The Great Didactic*:

> The other aid to study in the Mother-School is a picture-book which should be put straight into the child's hands. At this stage instruction should mainly be carried out through the medium of sense-perception, and, as sight is the chiefest of the senses, our object will be attained if we give the children pictures of the most important objects in physics, optics, astronomy, geometry etc., and

these may be arranged in the order of the subjects of knowledge that we have just sketched. In this book should be depicted mountains, valleys, trees, birds, fishes, horses, oxen, sheep, and men of varied age and height. Light and darkness also should be presented, as well as the heavens with the sun, moon, stars, and clouds, while to these the principal colours should be added. Articles connected with the house and the workshop, such as pots, plates, hammers, pincers etc., should not be omitted. State functionaries should be represented; the king with his sceptre and crown, the soldier with his arms, the husbandman with his plough, the waggoner with his waggon, and the post-cart going at full speed; while over each picture should be written the name of the object that it represents, as 'house', 'ox', 'dog', 'tree' etc.

This picture-book will be of use in three ways: (1) It will assist objects to make an impression on the mind, as we have already pointed out. (2) It will accustom the little ones to the idea that pleasure is to be derived from books. (3) It will aid them in learning to read. For, since the name of each object is written above the picture that represents it, the first steps in reading may thus be made.[53]

The work envisaged here—a text devoted exclusively to the mother-tongue—was never in fact produced by Comenius. The *Orbis Pictus*, however, being essentially a bilingual text, could be used for this same purpose, and Comenius himself recommended that the English version of the work be used both for the teaching of English and of Latin. The work vividly illustrates the effectiveness of visual illustration for language learning, as will be demonstrated in detail in the forthcoming section. Significantly, in the passage from the Preface where he recommends the *Orbis* for use as a vernacular text, he insists that the study of grammatical rules and structures be subordinated to the mastery of grammar as a medium of everyday communication:

> The same Book being used in English in English schooles will serve for the perfect learning of the whole English tongue, and that from the bottome; because by the aforesaid descriptions of things, the words and phrases of the whole language are found set orderly in their own places. And a short English Grammar might be added at the end, clearly resolving the speech already understood into its parts, shewing the declining of the several words, and reducing those that are joined together under certain Rules.[54]

Comenius's thinking on this issue is entirely consistent with the modern emphasis on the mastery of grammatical rules and conventions primarily through communicative usage and secondarily through the practical application of 'knowledge about language' in that same context. His approach to the teaching of reading is similarly in line with the most widely favoured methods in modern first language pedagogy. While he did not develop a methodology for the teaching of reading that could be compared with the highly sophisticated approaches advocated in modern pedagogy, the balance he maintained between the teaching of basic decoding and word-attack skills and the promotion of independent reading, through what was essentially a whole language approach, compares quite favourably with the methods most widely in use in contemporary primary school classrooms. He expected basic reading competence to be attained by the end of the first year of the vernacular school, i.e. at age 6–7, thereafter advocating a graded, systematic approach to its further development. For all this he advised the use of carefully designed, well illustrated textbooks that would provide children with access to a wide variety of reading material—narrative, fictional, factual, expositional, historical, scientific etc.

Comenius's approach to the teaching of writing was less satisfactory, being confined to the development of a narrow range of technical skills, consisting mainly of penmanship, speed writing and spelling. He gives detailed advice in the *Pampaedia* on letter and word formation, stressing the importance of precision in outline, the formation of points, lines and letter shapes, before the pupil could proceed eventually to the mastery of cursive writing. Good handwriting, he said, should have three main qualities: letters should be 'pleasing to the eye and never out of shape'; they should be 'readily distinguishable from one another'; they should be 'well formed, well rounded and not square or broken.'[55] With regard to developing the skills of 'writing with speed', he suggested pupils be taught to copy material from their textbooks—initially in eraseable pencil and later in black ink—a rather mechanical exercise, designed simply to enable pupils to write fluently and with ease, having mastered basic skills of letter and word formation. All this was to be accompanied by systematic lessons in spelling, beginning with phonetically regular, monosyllabic words and proceeding to the more challenging task of encoding multisyllabic, irregular words. Again, this was a routine and largely mechanical exercise designed simply to equip pupils with basic spelling competence. These three steps were seen by Comenius as the essential prerequisites for the development of writing competence. Coming several centuries before the nurturing of creative and imaginative uses of language was seen as the key to the fostering of writing ability, his methods seem, in this instance at least, rather unimaginative and rudimentary. His methods compare quite poorly, for example, with those promoted by Lev Tolstoy two centuries later in the schools of Yasnaya Polyana.[56] On the teaching of reading, however, and particularly on the development of oral-aural competence, Comenius's methods compare very favourably with modern theory and practice. In the case of oral-aural development they exemplify

a remarkably enlightened balancing of sensitive teaching with the fostering of the spontaneous growth of innate linguistic potentialities.

3. TEACHING NON-VERNACULAR LANGUAGES

For the teaching of non-vernacular languages Comenius advocated a
methodology that closely foreshadows the communicative approach now
widely adopted in contemporary second language pedagogy. Though obviously lacking the theoretical foundation provided for the communicative
method in modern theoretical and applied linguistics, his methods are
extraordinarily close nonetheless to those now generally associated with
that approach. Indeed, a Russian scholar has recently published the
findings of a research project which demonstrates the suitability of the
methods exemplified in the *Orbis Pictus* for the challenging task of teaching
modern European languages in the changed conditions of post-communist
Eastern Europe—a remarkable tribute to the soundness of the Comenian
approach.[57] Comenius anticipated contemporary second language methodology by his insistence that the child's urge to communicate is the basic
motivation for all language learning and the means to its speedy and
competent acquisition. To this he subordinated the knowledge and mastery
of grammatical conventions, seeing these as being acquired most effectively
through the process of practical usage. Emphasising the importance of
acquiring language as primarily a medium for social communication, he
insisted that language growth be allowed to emerge from a context of
experiential meaning, teaching being directed towards the fostering of
purposeful uses of language through various forms of socio-communicative activity. The texts he prepared were designed to give all students
practice in the everyday uses of language in a variety of ever-expanding
social situations; all were carefully and systematically graded to meet the
learning needs and stage of maturity of the individual pupil. What he
advocated was essentially a learner-centred approach, allowing every child
to proceed at his own natural rate; but, crucially, he identified a clear
directional role for the teacher in guiding the whole process and designed
a highly structured and systematically ordered curriculum for its successful implementation.

Inevitably, given the circumstances of his time, the second language
on which Comenius focussed his thinking was Latin, though he was
insistent that what he sought was the promotion of Latin as a living
tongue rather than the literary language that had been promoted for
centuries in the scholastic institutions. Thus, from the outset he insisted
that Latin be taught through the medium of the vernacular, so as to
ensure that all learning was given a meaningful context in the familiar
experience of everyday life. Secondly, in pursuit of this same objective,

he sought to implement the complementary pansophic aim of providing children with all the knowledge necessary for a fully comprehensive education at all stages of the schooling process. It will be recalled that he believed students should be given the same range of knowledge at every stage of their education, the complexity of its content being matched to the different levels taught. Texts, he wrote in *The Great Didactic*, 'should differ not in their subject-matter but in their way of presenting it.'[58] 'In the school of adolescence the same things should be taught as in the vernacular school of boyhood, but . . . with plenty of new incentives to prevent the spread of boredom,' he wrote in the *Pampaedia*.[59] Thus the language texts provided a vast amount of detail—all illustrated graphically through visual representations—on various occupations, lifestyles, the world of nature, plant and animal life, the cosmos, the physical universe, the history of mankind, moral and religious truths, hobbies and games—to mention only a selection of the content they included. Seldom in the history of language teaching has it been so closely related to the personal and social environment of the learner as it was in these new texts, which probably explains their survival more than three centuries after their creation and their continued use in certain parts of Europe even at the present time.

Three methods were central to Comenius's proposals for the implementation of the socio-communicative, experience-based approach to language teaching. The first was based on the pleasure principle, seen as simultaneously ensuring both the highest possible degree of individual motivation in the learner and the assimilation of the content of learning in the personally meaningful context of individual experience. The second involved the employment of a broad curriculum, providing a wide range of reading material both to guarantee contact with language in a variety of contexts and modes and to accommodate individual interests in the fullest possible degree. The third involved the extensive use of visual illustration in the basic textbooks to ensure the effective reinforcement of learning through the maximum utilisation of sense experience.

With regard to the first of these methods, it will be recalled that a bitter controversy occurred in Comenius's years as adviser on educational reform at Saros Patak as a result of his plans to make extensive use of dramatic dialogue in the teaching of Latin to the pupils of the gymnasium there. Seeing the value of combining learning with play, he devised methods of developing the material in the *Janua Linguarum Reserata* into a series of dramatic dialogues for presentation by the pupils themselves, at first in the school hall and subsequently at open air performances throughout the region. The *Continuatio* records the words of the scholarchs to Comenius as they witnessed the impact his methods had made: 'We confess, Comenius, that hitherto we have not fathomed the many secrets which your book, *The Gate of Languages*, contains, and how much benefit it brings the pupils. Now we are eye-witnesses of it. We abjure you, Comenius, that you leave us not until the whole of the Gate be transformed into such pleasant play. We promise that these plays shall be held in our schools for the eternal memory of your name.'[60]

As a result of his experience at Saros Patak, Comenius was convinced of the value of dramatic play as a medium for language learning. Earlier, he had prepared a special text, the *Schola Ludus*, which was to be used entirely for this purpose.[61] Much of the material in all his later language texts was presented in the form of dialogue which could be used for dramatic performance by teacher and pupils. In addition to this, he urged the regular use of conversational dialogue for the furtherance of linguistic fluency. 'It is strange,' he writes in the *Pampaedia*, 'that schools have not hitherto taught the art of conversation, although it plays a large part in life. This art should be prescribed for them with set exercises and all their textbooks may well be in dialogue form, e.g. in the Porchway stage, dialogues; in the Gateway stage, practice in play-acting; in the Hall stage, similar exercises consisting of proverbial sayings and parables.'[62] As a complementary exercise he further advised teachers to encourage their students to keep diaries on their progress as learners. This is how he describes the method in the *Pampaedia*:

> *Pupils in the school of adolescence should begin to keep diaries.* (1) As more things happen at this stage and in greater variety, pupils are more liable to confusion. (2) Imagination and memory now charged with a surfeit of sensory experience have unusual difficulty in grasping or retaining everything: they therefore need support. (3) For the rest of their lifetime (not only in their course of studies) pupils need diaries: therefore they must be taught how to keep them and the sooner the better. There is no time like the present, when they have passed the stage of sensory learning and are beginning to make proper use of their imagination and power of reasoning. (They should be instructed as to method and scope.)
>
> *They must therefore be taught the use of diaries.* (1) Any extraordinary piece of learning should be kept for future reference and not lost but learned more thoroughly by the use of a diary. (2) If anything happens that pupils do not understand, they should not forget to make inquiry or question their fellow-pupils and then their teacher.[63]

In conjunction with all this, he advocated the provision of a wide range of reading material to ensure that individual interests and needs were adequately accommodated. 'Study should not be limited to the writers of any age or nationality,' he writes in the *Pampaedia*. 'It must include any memorable writing in any language that has ever been transmitted to us from our understanding.'[64] In the *Atrium* and the *Thesaurus* he sought to provide pupils with a selection of readings from a wide range of Latin authors of various periods. (Nowadays this would be called the 'authentic texts' approach.) As a means both of encouraging pupils to read widely and to gain the maximum benefits from the experience, he recommended an imaginative and (pedagogically speaking) a highly effective process of group reading in which pupils could share their reading experiences with their peers. He describes the process in some detail in the *Pampaedia*:

> *Group reading of authors should therefore be allowed.* (1) at the discretion of the teacher, (2) each student reading a different author privately, and recommending selections or reciting them in public. This will serve three useful purposes. (1) It will produce careful reading habits, since the test is conducted in public with a reputation to earn. (2) Observations made by several people will become common knowledge and the slower students will also benefit. (3) Students will adopt the procedure of the Gellian society which is a regular feature of the academy.
>
> *Each student will present extracts from his own author.* (1) In philology—words, phrases, sentences, similes, and examples. (2) In logic—unusual questions, clever answers, striking arguments. (3) Realities—things hitherto unknown, stories of noble events, skilful and profitable action in the field of economics in every kind of station or walk of life.[65]

It is generally agreed that the visual material provided by Comenius for his textbooks, especially the *Orbis* and *Janua*, was the main reason for their phenomenal popularity throughout Europe for more than three centuries after they were first produced. There had been a tradition of illustrated books in Bohemia before Comenius began his work, and this almost certainly influenced his beliefs about the value of the visual image in language teaching. By his own testimony in *The Great Didactic*, however, it was the work of a German scholar, Eilhard Lubinus, which most decisively influenced his thinking on this whole issue.[66] Lubinus, born in Oldenberg in 1565, was Professor of Theology in Rostok University but had interests also in mathematics, philology and literature. In 1617 he published a trilingual version of the New Testament, prefaced by an Epistolary Discourse in which he denounced contemporary methods of teaching Latin, calling for the replacement of the traditional grammar-based approach by one based on the practical usage of Latin as a living tongue. Additionally, he recommended that pictures be used side by side with the prose text to enable reading competence to develop more rapidly—a view which immediately commended him to Comenius.

In *The Great Didactic* Comenius argued that by linking words with pictures his texts would ensure the full assimilation of concepts by children at the same time as they encountered the language in which those concepts were expressed. He declared that sight is 'the chiefest of the senses' and visual perception is 'the surest way to understanding.'[67] The visual image, he said, would be particularly efficacious in the case of words and concepts that the pupil had not previously encountered. By reinforcing understanding through the medium of visual perception, it would ensure immediate comprehension of both. The whole process would also make learning a pleasing and enjoyable activity. In the years 1642–7 when Comenius was advising the Swedish government on education he strongly urged the authorities there to make maximum use of visual imagery in school textbooks. In the *Sketch for a Pansophic School* he proposed extensive use of illustrated charts for teaching and suggested the walls of school classrooms be covered with pictorial material illustrating all the work of the school. The whole rationale for this process is given in the Preface to the *Orbis Pictus*:

> Instruction is the means to expell rudeness; with which young Wits ought to be well-furbished in Schools: But so, as that the Teaching be 1. True, 2. Full, 3. Clear, and 4. Solid.
>
> It will be true, if nothing be taught but such as are beneficial to ones life; lest there be a cause of complaining afterwards. We know not necessary things, because we have not learned things necessary.
>
> It will be full, if the mind be polished for Wisdom, the Tongue for Eloquence, and the Hands for a neat way of Living. This will be that Grace of ones life, to be wise, to act, to speak.
>
> It will be clear, and by that firm and solid, that whatever is taught and learned, be not obscure, or confused, but apparent, distinct, and articulate, as the fingers on the hands.
>
> The ground of this business is that sensual objects be rightly presented to the senses, for fear they may not be received. I say, and say it again aloud, that this last is the foundation of all the rest: because we can neither act nor speak wisely, unlesse we first rightly understand all the things which are to be done, and whereof, we are to speak. Now there is nothing in the understanding which was not before in the sense. And therefore to exercise the senses well about the right perceiving the differences of things, will be to lay the grounds for all wisdom, and all wise discourse, and all discret actions in ones course of life. Which, because it is commonly neglected in Schooles, and the things that are to be learned are offered to Scholars, without being understood, or being rightly presented to the senses, it cometh to pass, that the work of teaching and learning goeth heavily onward, and affordeth little benefit.
>
> See here then a new help for Schooles, a Picture and Nomenclature of all the chief things in the World, and of men's actions in

their way of living! Which that you, good Masters, may not be loth to run over with your Scholars, I will tell you in short, what good you may expect from it. . . .

This same little Book will serve to stir up the Attention, which is to be fastened upon things, and ever to be sharpened more and more; which is also a great matter. For the senses (being the main guides of Child-hood, because therein the Mind doth not as yet raise up itself to an abstracted contemplation of things) evermore seek their own objects, and if they be away, they grow dull, and wry themselves hither and thither, out of a weariness of themselves: but when their objects are present, they grow merry, wax lively and willingly suffer themselves to be fastened upon them, till the thing be sufficiently discerned. This Book then will do a good piece of service in taking (especially flickering) Wits, and preparing them for deeper studies.[68]

The *Orbis* was the fruit of a lengthy period of trial and experimentation in language teaching that began at Leszno in 1624 when Comenius encountered the *Janua Linguarum* of the Irish Jesuits, William and John Bathe and their colleague, Stephen White, then living as expatriates at the University of Salamanca in Spain. Seeing this text as inadequate in various respects—though approving of its use of the vernacular as the basic medium of instruction—Comenius prepared a text of his own, the *Janua Linguarum Reserata*, in which he assembled a far greater body of information than was provided in the Spanish text. The new work contained over 8000 words and more than 1000 sentences. Shortly after its publication he prepared a preliminary text, the *Vestibulum*, intended for use as a foundation for the *Janua*, and two anthologies of Latin readings, the *Atrium* and *Thesaurus*. Eventually, however, he decided on a more basic text for beginners that would give equal attention both to Latin and the vernacular. From this emerged his plan for the *Orbis Pictus*.[69] Largely because of the great technical problems that had to be overcome if Comenius's plans for an extensive use of visual illustration were to be properly realised, the *Orbis* project was in preparation for several years and was not finally completed until 1658. Several printing presses capable of reproducing pictures from woodcuts existed through-out Europe at the time. The Unitas Fratrum had such a printing press to provide illustrations for its own publications and Comenius would have been familiar with the process as a leading member of the Church. What he envisaged for the *Orbis*, however, was a much more complex and elaborate process than most printers would have been able to undertake. A total of 150 reproductions, many of them requiring a very high level of visual detail, was planned for the work. The printer who agreed to undertake the project, George Endter of Nuremberg, took more than two years to produce the woodcuts, each of which had been prepared individually by a skilled craftsman, Paul Kreutzberger.

Shortly after its publication in 1658 an English translation was produced by Charles Hoole, with even better illustrations produced from metal engravings. An Oxford graduate and reforming schoolmaster—he was author of *A New Discovery of the Old Art of Teaching Schooles*[70]— Hoole decided to publish the *Orbis* principally because of its use of the vernacular as a medium of instruction, but also because of the attractiveness of its illustrations. 'Such a work as this,' he wrote, 'I observe to have been formerly much desired by some experienced Teachers, and I myself had some years since (whilst my own Child lived) begun the like, having found it most agreeable to the best witted Children, who are most taken up with pictures from their Infancy.'[71] Several other editions followed and the *Orbis* became not only a widely used text in English schools but a popular reader also for children to enjoy in their own homes. The work remained popular both in England and Germany up to the end of the nineteenth century. The first American edition was published in 1810, largely through the influence of the Moravian communities in Pennsylvania and North Carolina, and it remained in circulation for many years, the last known edition being published there as late as 1887.[72]

The *Orbis* particularly embodied Comenius's belief that a textbook, as well as enabling pupils to attain linguistic competence, should aim to provide them with the widest possible range of knowledge in the process. The book includes items on flowers, herbs, fruits, birds, insects, domestic animals, farm animals, wild animals, reptiles, vermin, various marine species, gardening, agriculture, cookery, domestic crafts, fishing, fowling, hunting, butchery, wine-making, weaving, carpentry, shoe-making, masonry, engineering, building, mining, pottery, painting, travel lore, shipping, sailing, printing, book-binding, music, philosophy, human anatomy, mathematics, geometry, astronomy, morality, comparative religion, medicine, drama, fencing, tennis, dice-playing, racing, athletics, politics, history—a truly comprehensive range of material, all of which was beautifully illustrated and presented in a manner immediately comprehensible to young pupils. The following three excerpts will give some indication of the way in which the content was presented. The first is an abbreviated excerpt from Lesson XXXVIII, 'The Outward Parts of a Man (*Membra Hominis Externa*).[73] (Numbers refer to illustrations):

Caput, 1. is above,	Caput, est supra,
the Feet, 20. below	infra, Pedes 20.
The forepart	Colli
of the Neck,	(quod definit)
(which ends, at the	in Axillas) 2.
Arm holes 2.)	pars anterior,

is the Throat, 3	est Jugulum, 3.
the hinder-part	posterior,
the Crag, 4.	Cervix. 4
The Breast, 5.	Pectus, 5
and is before,	est ante;
the back: 6.	retro, Dorsum: 6
behinde;	
Women have in it	in ilo sunt Foeminis,
two breasts 7	binae Mammae 7
with Nipples	cum Papillis.
under the breast	Sub pectore
is the Belly, 9	est Venter; 9.
in the middle of it,	in ejus medio,
the Navel, 10	Umbilicus, 10.
underneath the groyn, 11	subtus inguen, 11
and the privies.	& pudenda

The following excerpt will illustrate the ways in which Comenius sought to encourage dramatic play amongst the pupils.[74] The lesson describes the sounds made by different animals and birds, and provides the specific vowel sounds appropriate to each to encourage the pupils to imitate them playfully. (It was also a rudimentary exercise in phonics, the pupil being encouraged to associate vowel-consonant combinations with familiar sounds from nature).

Cornix cornicatur	á á
The Crow cryeth	
Agnus balat	bé é é
The Lamb blaiteth	
Cicáda stridet	cí cí
The Grasshopper chirpeth	
Anser gingrit	ga ga
The Goose gaggleth	
Mus mintrit	í í í
The Mouse chirpeth	
Anas retrinnit	kha kha
The duck quacketh	
Lupus úlulat	lu ulu
The Wolf howleth	
Urfus múrmurat	mum mum
The Bear grumbleth	
Serpens fibilat	si S
The Serpent hisseth	
Graculus clamat	tac tac

The jay cryeth
Rana coaxat   coax
The Frog croaketh

Lesson CXLVI[75] is one of a series on different world religions. The first
lesson in the series gives some basic features of four major religions,
Gentilism (Egyptian and Greek mythology), Christianity, Judaism and
Islam. The second gives the names of some of the Greek deities—Jupiter,
Neptune, Pluto, Mars etc. This is followed by lessons giving the basic
teachings of Judaism, Christianity and Mohammedanism. All the lessons
are remarkable for their simple but authentic presentation of the traditions
of each of these religions, clearly identifying the origins of each in the
Scriptures. Those on Judaism and Mohammedanism exemplify a spirit
of ecumenicity remarkable for a textbook produced in the seventeenth
century. The following is an excerpt from Lesson CXLVI, 'Judaism'
(*Judaismas*):

Yet the true Worship	Verus tamen Cultus
of the true God,	veri Dei, remansit
remained with the	apud Patriarchas
Patriarchs, who lived	qui vixerunt
before, after y flood	ante & post Diluvium.
Amongst these,	Inter hos
that seed of the woman,	Abrahamo, 1.
the Messias of y world	Judaeorum Conditori
was promised to	Patri Credentium
Abraham, 1. the Founder	promissus est,
of the Jewes	Semen illud Mulieris,
the Father of them	Mundi Messias;
that believe, and he	& ipse
(being called away	
from the Gentiles)	avocatus a Gentilibus
with his Posterity	cum Posteris,
being marked with the	Sacramento Circumcisionis
Sacrament of Circumcision	notatus
made a peculiar People	singularem Populum
and Church of God.	& Ecclesiam Dei constituit.

In each of these lessons the text is accompanied by detailed visual illustration—the lesson on the sounds of nature, for example, has no less
than twenty-four single images. In the Preface Comenius outlined the
steps the teacher should take to make the most effective use of the text.
The pupil was to begin by attempting a literal comprehension of the text
(this was to be achieved mainly through the association of words and

pictorial images under the guidance of the teacher), and then to memorise the content, following which he was to analyse the grammatical structures of the passage—identifying parts of speech, declining nouns, conjugating verbs etc. The latter was clearly subordinated to the primary act of individual comprehension of the text:

> Let him read the Description at large, first in English, and afterwards in Latine, till he can readily read, and distinctly pronounce the words in both Languages, ever minding how they are spelled. And withall, let him take notice of the Figures inserted, and to what part of the Picture they direct by their like, till he be well able to find out every particular thing of himself, and to name it on a suddain, either in English or Latine. Thus, he shall not only gain the most primitive words, but be understandingly grounded in Orthography, which is a thing too generally neglected by us; partly because our English-Schools think that Children should learn it at the Latine, and our Latine-Schools suppose they have already learn'd it at the English; partly because our Common-Grammar is much too defective in this Part, & Scholars so little exercised therein, that they pass from Schools to the Universities, and returne from thence (some of them) more unable to write true English, than either Latine, or Greek. Not to speak of our ordinary Trades-men, many of whom write such false English, that none but themselves can interpret what they scribble, in their Bills, and Shop-Books.
>
> Then let him get the Titles and Descriptions by heart, which he will more easily do by reason of those impressions which the viewing of the Pictures hath already made in his memory. And now let him also learn, 1. To construe, or give the words one by one, as they answer one another in Latine and English. 2. To parse, according to the Rules (which I presume by this time) he hath learn'd in the first part of the Accidence; where I would have him tell what Part of Speech any word is, and then what Accidents belong to it; but especially to decline the Nouns, and Conjugate the Verbs according to the examples in his Rudiments, and this doing will enable him to know the end and use of his Accidence.[76]

These methods were further developed by Comenius in the *Janua Linguarum Reserata*, in which the same range of content was presented in a more complex and more advanced form. The following example from the anatomy lesson will illustrate how the content presented in the above quoted excerpt from the *Orbis* was given in greater detail for an older age-group. The excerpt also illustrates the light-hearted manner in which the material was frequently presented. (The vernacular content only is being quoted to illustrate the nature of the textual presentation):

Of the Body (De Corpore)

The frame of the body is packt up of bones with marrow, gristles, tendons, sinews, flesh muscles, a threefold skin and divers thin films or coverings.

The parts of the body hold together by bonds close fastened all along in a most comely proportion. . . .

In the feature, or shape, of men's countenances [visages] it is wonderful strange what difference there is.

A narrow forehead is like a hog's, one bunching out like an ass's, a broad one is a sign of a towardly disposition, and of a good sort, a wrinkled forehead is a mark of a mind perplexed, a frowning one, of an angry man, a most high forehead sheweth a man to be brazen faced or cheerly.

The apple, or sight, of the eye, sitting on or cleaving to the white, is a looking-glass, receiving into itself the semblance of things set before it.

This the eyelids moisten by winking, or twinkling, but the eyebrows and the hair on the eyelids do sense it.

But the eye-corners sweat out tears. The whole set, or gang, of the teeth is fastened [mortized] into sockets that are digged into both jaws.[77]

A further instance from Lesson XXIV illustrates the homely and practical character of much of the material in the *Janua*. Again, the language is clear and simple and the descriptions lively and colourful. A greater use of complete sentences is evident here, the appeal clearly being to a more advanced and more highly literate pupil:

Of Making Bread (De Panificio)

The Baker, in a kneading trough with a treen slice kneadeth the lump [batch] of dough which, when it is mouldeth into loaves, and set in with a peel, the oven or baking pan baketh.

Leavened bread hath a double crust, and the crumb light and heaved [puffed] within; unleavened is soft manchet, is without all bran; household bread is of whole wheat; bisket is for lasting long.

The Sugar Baker makes ready sweet-meats and dainties of the finest flower. The kinds of cakes are: simnels, rolls, wafers, fritters, pan-cakes, spice-cakes, cracknels [buns], tarts, round cakes; as also fresh pasties, apple-pies, custards, cheese-cakes and the like.[78]

The method recommended by Comenius in the *Janua* was based on four main pedagogic strategies. The teacher first read the lesson himself, giving some rudimentary explanations of its content. The pupils next read the content aloud and discussed its meaning with the teacher. They then copied the material into their notebooks, and finally memorised it. Apart from the fourth stage, which would not now be widely recommended for language teaching, Comenius's approach embodied the basic elements of oral-aural, reading and written comprehension generally advocated for the effective development of communicative competence. All three were skilfully blended in a manner which ensured their full and effective interaction. He insisted that the vernacular be used at all times for the explanation of words, phrases and grammatical rules, all being comprehended in a rich variety of contextual meaning and practical communicative usage.

In its general and specific principles, therefore, the Comenian approach to non-vernacular language teaching conforms quite closely to modern pedagogic theory and practice. Though clearly lacking the sophistication of certain modern techniques—such as those made possible through the use of audio-visual technology—the whole approach commands attention nonetheless as an enlightened and highly effective methodology for the development of bilingual or multilingual competence in the years of second-level schooling. This fact is remarkably attested in a research project currently in progress at the Saratov Pedagogical Institute in Russia which aims to demonstrate the suitability of the *Orbis Pictus* as a text for language teaching in the new conditions existing in post-communist Eastern Europe. The project's director, Professor V.I. Strahov, in a report to a Conference of Directors of Educational Research at Nitra in Czechoslovakia in October 1992, declared that the 'artistic, psychological and pedagogic principles' exemplified in the *Orbis* are highly appropriate for the teaching of languages in the newly emerging democracies.[79] He praises the work for its creative approach to language teaching but, additionally, emphasises its social relevance for pupils in East European schools. The *Orbis*, he says, through its emphasis on individual freedom and morality, its positive work ethic, its reverence for the environment, together with its authentic and vivid presentation of the details and occupations of everyday life, embodies a profoundly egalitarian and democratic vision of society—one he feels is particularly appropriate for the education of young pupils in post-totalitarian states. These are the concluding comments in his report:

> Today in the time of de-politicisation of education, this book can be used in place of textbooks which are full of ideological dogma. Comenius's textbook is kind and we may admit that it is eternal. The admission is motivated by the fact that the book has already survived 330 years and is still relevant for discussion at present in the days of Comenius's anniversary. A slight adaptation will allow using this book at schools today. The main task is to keep its deep democratic spirit.[80]

Language, Comenius wrote in *The School of Infancy*, is the distinctive mark of humanness in man and the key to the ideal of universal harmony and brotherhood. 'Two things preeminently distinguish men from brutes—reason and speech,' he wrote. 'Man needs the former on his own account, the latter for the sake of his neighbour. Both, therefore, equally demand our care, so that man may have his mind and tongue equally trained, and exercised as well as possible.'[81] It was this conviction that underlay his belief in the power of education, by virtue of its capacity for the full development of linguistic and communicative potentialities, to serve as an agent for the civilisation of all mankind. That vision was re-echoed by the originators of the great literacy campaigns of the twentieth century, particularly those inspired by the writings of Paulo Freire, with his conception of the empowerment of man through cultural literacy. The words quoted above from *The School of Infancy* were re-echoed by Fernando Cardenal, the organiser of the Nicaraguan Literacy Campaign of 1980. 'It must be remembered,' he wrote, 'that literacy, the ability to read and write, is not simply a collection of academic skills. Literacy is what separates human beings from the beasts of the fields and empowers them not only to understand but also to change the world around them.'[82]

Though Comenius did not specifically use the term 'literacy', the ideal itself is implicit in his vision of a universal order achieved through effective communication between all men. It was a logical outcome of his commitment to educational equality and of his belief that this is a necessary pre-condition for the creation of truly democratic societies. Like Freire in later years, he saw linguistic communication as a source of social empowerment: as the means by which the individual can function as a fully active member of society. 'If this universal instruction of youth be brought about by the proper means,' he said, 'none will lack the material for thinking and doing good things. All will know how their efforts and actions must be governed, to what limits they must keep, and how each must find his right place. . . . The children of the rich and the nobles, or those holding public office, are not alone born to such positions, and should not alone have access to schools, others being excluded as if there were nothing to be hoped for them. The spirit bloweth when and where it will.'[83] What he envisaged was the full education of all men, irrespective of nationality, race, creed, social or economic conditions, seeing this as their inalienable right and the crucial guarantee of their freedom. He saw it as the essential pre-condition for civilised relations between men. It paralleled his ideal of universal order achieved through ecumenical understanding—intercultural communication and religious tolerance both being seen as essential conditions for the promotion of brotherhood and peace. It was an utopian vision in the same sense that

Freire's was, the term 'utopian' in both instances signifying a high-minded and profoundly radical, but nonetheless wholly realisable ideal.[84]

The promotion of linguistic communication was central to the vision of universal enlightenment put forward by Comenius in the *Via Lucis* and the *Pampaedia*. In the chapters from the *Via Lucius* where he unfolds his vision of a world transformed through 'universal light' he describes the evolution of linguistic communication from the rudimentary modes of speech of primitive man to the sophisticated modes of literacy of later periods. He begins by describing the emergence of dialogic speech as a necessary mode of communication between the first human beings to inhabit the earth:

> And now that there were two human beings, there began between them another method, different from the first, of increasing the knowledge of things—namely, speech between them, by which each, questioning the other and replying to questions, was able to effect a fuller advance towards wisdom. For the use of the ears is richer than that of the eyes for getting manifold knowledge of things; while in regard to those things which we have not the means to see, we are able to inform one another by speech and so mutually to increase our knowledge.[85]

Developing his thesis that literacy was a necessary stage in the full human-isation of mankind, i.e. its liberation from the enslavement of barbarism and ignorance, he describes the emergence of reading and writing as marking the evolution of man from the ignorance of the pre-literate state to the attainment of the more advanced wisdom afforded by the mastery of symbolic print. Characteristically, the process is described within the chronological framework of the Biblical narrative. This passage describes the emergence of writing:

> After the flood the span of human life was lessened, but the noise of their businesses and occupations increased, and hence distraction and confusion were caused for the human mind: accordingly to provide against the weakness of human memory and to supply the need of later generations, writing was invented by which persons who were separated from each other in time or in place could teach each other such matters as were necessary; and by the same invention even the dead could teach the living for ever (Isa. XXX 8) And as this art became known beyond the borders of Israel, a desire was conceived that it should become common, as we gather from Job XIX, 23, 24. For it is the only method of handing down to posterity things worth remembering: apart from it we should find that the record of the whole of antiquity entirely perished.

And we have evidence of this in the example of the barbarous peoples of the new world, who, lacking books, know nothing of the origin or development of things, nothing indeed that is worth knowing; and except in their physical form are more like brutes than men. And since the art of reading and writing appeared to be a profoundly difficult thing, as in fact in its nature it really is (for we ourselves should not be persuaded that writing and reading could be performed with so much precision unless we had learned from experience how much constant practice can achieve)—for these reasons, for the easier conquering of these difficulties public schools were opened in which a large number of persons (especially as they were young and not yet distracted by the cares of life) might yet learn things together.[86]

To a modern reader it is inevitable that this should appear inadequate as an historical description of the emergence of written language, since Comenius was writing before more scientifically sophisticated explanations of the whole process became available from social anthropology and comparative linguistics. Its sequential representation of the stages in the evolution of literacy is nonetheless quite sound in itself, even if one were to question the historical accuracy of the Biblical framework within which it is conveyed. Moreover, Comenius strongly anticipates modern thinking in his linking of literacy with the moral betterment of mankind—a theme deeply reflected in the writings of Freire, Habermas and others in recent years. Side by side with his identification of literacy with individual and social enlightenment is a strong emphasis on interpersonal and social communication as a means to moral growth and reform. 'The true religion and the true commonwealth are light-giving things, and derive their safety from light and not from darkness,' he writes in the *Via Lucis*. He continues: 'But our purpose is not that every man should become learned (for not every man's native ability nor his condition nor his place makes that possible, and there is no necessity for it) but that all men be made wise unto salvation.'[87] 'It is desirable that no man should be dumb and all should have the knowledge to explain their needs to God and man,' he declares in the *Pampaedia*. 'Man was not made to be a dumb statue,' he writes, 'for he has the gift of a tongue to proclaim the praises of his Creator and to win his neighbours to partake of the light by sharing information about all their needs.'[88] In words that powerfully anticipate the main motivating theme of the modern literacy campaigns he proclaims the responsibility of all nations to spread the light of wisdom to their less fortunate neighbours:

It is desirable that even the most backward nations should be enlightened and capable of release from their darkness because they are a part of the human race that must be assimilated into the whole, and because unity is incomplete if any part is missing, and also because to prefer the part to the whole, as in the ownership of any property, clearly indicates a lack of sound judgement or of good will. Therefore since you would not wish to show that you share any such folly or malice, you ought to prefer the welfare of all to that of yourself or a few friends or your nation alone. The whole body cannot be well, unless every single limb is well. For they are all so interconnected that if even the smallest is affected, the sense of weakness soon spreads to them all as a sound limb readily contracts infection from one that is diseased. The body of human society is the same, since man is infected by man, state by state, and nation by nation, whereas if all were healthy, they would enjoy a common share in the common good. It is therefore detrimental to human nature as a whole if anyone does not seriously desire the good of all. But men are their own worst enemies if in their individual lives the healthy are content to live beside the sick, the wise beside the foolish, the good beside the evil, the fortunate beside the unfortunate, which is bound to occur if they desire themselves but not their neighbours to be safe, wise, good and happy.[89]

The need for literacy as the means to the attainment of universal wisdom or enlightenment is the most fundamental implication to be drawn from Comenius's theories of linguistic communication. A closely related issue was the need for improved communication between peoples and nations to achieve the harmony and order he believed essential for a lasting world peace. In this context some brief mention might be made of his schemes for the creation of a universal language for the more effective promotion of the ideal of intercultural communication. Though the scheme was doomed to failure from the outset—just as later experiments such as Esperanto were similarly doomed—it serves nonetheless to exemplify the importance of intercultural communication in promoting international peace: a goal that has gained a vastly increased urgency in the three centuries that have passed since it was given expression by Comenius.

It was probably during his visit to England in 1640–41 that Comenius became aware of various initiatives that had been undertaken there to create a new global lingua franca that would enable peoples of various traditions and nationalities to communicate easily, regardless of cultural or geographical differences. In 1630 John Pell, a friend of Samuel Hartlib, published one such scheme which was based on the use of universally recognisable numerical signs and symbols.[90] Comenius probably learned of this initiative through his contacts with Hartlib. Later John Wilkins published a work called *Mercury or the Secret Messenger* in which he further discussed the possibility of developing a new language for international trading purposes. (In the *Via Lucis* Comenius speaks of 'a Mercury or Messenger who must make his way among all nations alike.')[91] In 1653 Thomas Urquhart in his Introduction to the Universal Language put forward a scheme based on alphabetic correspondence between letters and the objects they designated.[92] This was followed four years later by George Dalgarno's *Universal Character and a New Rational Language* (mentioned by Comenius in his correspondence with Hartlib) in which a number of 'primary words' were identified as providing a basis for an international language. That scheme was recommended to the King by the Royal Society as a means of 'spreading the Gospel,' promoting international trade, and 'civilising barbarous nations.'[93]

Comenius would almost certainly have been aware of these initiatives as he sought to devise a new language himself as a means of promoting his pansophic ideals. Recognising the inadequacies of Latin—its grammatical complexity, its elitist associations etc.—he argued for the creation of a new language that would be 'ten times easier than Latin . . . and a hundred times more perfect.' 'For it is full of variety in the case of nouns, in the moods and tenses of verbs, in its syntactical constructions; it overflows with innumerable instances of all these anomalies,' he complained in the section of the *Via Lucis* where he rejects Latin as being unsuitable for the purposes of his scheme and calls for an entirely new language—an 'Ariadne's thread to lead mankind out of the labyrinth.' In pursuit of his goal Comenius favoured a synthesis of the best features of existing languages—the short roots of Hebrew and German, the 'soft pronunciation' of Latin, the 'economy of inflexion' of English etc.—and provided elaborate technical details on how it would be achieved.[94] In the *Panglottia* he spoke of three essential requirements the new language would need to meet. 'It will firstly be an extension of the world in its totality, secondly, an equal richness of the mind whose concepts it communicates to others, and thirdly, a regularity like musical harmony, by which it will establish between things and concepts and between concepts and words a context in which it is possible to conceive things as they are and to express them as they are conceived.'[95] In the *Via Lucis* he provides further elaboration on these requirements:

> We may conclude, then, that for the manifold delays and confusions in human intercourse which spring from the number, the difficulty and the imperfection of languages, we can find no more potent remedy than the fashioning of a new language, which in comparison with all those that are now known will be (1) easier, so that it can be learnt without expense of time or substance; (2) pleasanter, so that it will be delightful in the process of learning and when it has been mastered; (3) and more perfect (as perfect, indeed, as may be in the nature of the case and considering our own imperfection in

this earthly school) so that to be skilled in it shall greatly help us towards the understanding of things themselves.

So, then, we conceive and pray for a language which shall be (1) Rational, having nothing which does not bear a meaning whether in its matter or in its form, and conforming to this rule in its finest and least points: (2) Analogical, containing no anomaly in any matter: (3) Harmonious, bringing no discrepancies between things and the concepts of things, in as much as by its very sounds it would express the essential qualities and characteristics of things—a language which for that very reason would be as it were a funnel through which wisdom would flow. If such a language could be accepted by the common consent of mankind, all men would delightedly recognise that it would be the most appropriate means for reconciling them to each other and their concepts of things to the truth. Then at last that age of illumination and of peace would have dawned and could be proclaimed, an age in which there would be light and quiet in things, in the concepts of things, and in words which are the vehicles of concepts.[96]

At best these proposals have been viewed as disingenuous and naive, being seen as excessively optimistic on the prospect of replacing existing languages with a single lingua franca. In most instances they have been dismissed as grossly oversimplifying linguistic realities and blithely ignoring the depth and complexity of the cultural traditions on which linguistic diversity is rooted. But what is most significant ultimately about Comenius's writings on the whole question of intercultural communication, as has been suggested earlier, is not so much his aspiration towards the technical or pragmatic processes of trans-national communication as his recognition of the place of language as a means to the *enlightenment* of all mankind through the universality of the vision it can ultimately afford. In the *Pampaedia* he spoke of his language project as not merely enabling men to communicate but to share 'the inward concepts of the spirit.'[97] Universal education and a universal language, he wrote in the *Via Lucis*, are 'the destined means for spreading the intellectual light throughout the whole realm of the human intellect.' 'As for the universal language, what will it be but the food of this light (i.e. the purest oil)' he declared.[98] By this he envisaged a spiritual awakening of mankind, facilitating intercultural harmony and brotherhood—a co-intentional process comparable to the ideal of conscientisation described by Paulo Freire three centuries later in *Cultural Action for Freedom* and *Pedagogy of the Oppressed*.[99]

Though there are fundamental philosophical differences between the two men, their common linking of literacy and linguistic communication with individual enlightenment—spiritual, moral, religious, aesthetic, cognitional—signifies a broadening of the whole notion of linguistic formation that holds immense implications for education at all levels, from school to adult life. By identifying literacy with enlightenment, they both ultimately identified it with freedom. That freedom they identified in turn with the traditions of apostolic Christianity, enunciating the universal right to freedom in terms of its primacy in that whole cultural inheritance. Both saw ignorance as dehumanising, the darkness and enslavement of the spirit described by Comenius being paralleled by the culture of silence, naive consciousness and semi-intransitive dependency described by Freire. Again, both men devised a radical, learner-centred, dialogic pedagogy for the achievement of their ultimate goal: the liberation of all mankind through education. In the final analysis both saw the attainment of this goal as the essential condition for the promotion of harmony and peace amongst mankind. It is significant that the words 'illumination' and 'peace' are directly linked by Comenius in the passage quoted above from the *Via Lucis*. He concludes his treatment of the ideal of universal communication with a vision of world order comparable to the utopian vision unfolded by Freire three centuries later in *Cultural Action for Freedom*: 'Then at last that age of illumination and of peace would have dawned and could be proclaimed, an age in which there would be light and quiet in things, in the concepts of things, and in words which are the vehicles of concepts.'[100] Some of the implications of this will be addressed in the forthcoming chapter on adult education. Particular attention will be given to the ideal of education for international brotherhood and peace.

VII

ADULT AND HIGHER EDUCATION

1. EDUCATION AS A LIFELONG PROCESS

Comenius's concept of education as a lifelong process was the logical outcome of the ideals that were described in Chapter 4. It will be recalled that he affirmed the right of all men to be given access to wisdom and truth, regardless of social circumstances, race, nationality or religious creed. All, he declared, should have access to the Way of Light, all should be saved from the darkness of mind and spirit to which ignorance would consign them. Additionally, he insisted that a full and balanced education should be made available to all, while making due allowance for differences in aptitude, interest and vocational inclination. 'Our wish,' he wrote, 'is that every human being should be rightly developed and perfectly educated, not in any limited sense, but in every respect that makes for the perfection of human nature. . . . Our wish is that not merely some but all men should be educated in the "encyclopaedic" style and that they should be instructed not only in all the facts which can be known, but also in all objects of action and subjects of discussion, so that they prove themselves far superior to the animal world through their three special endowments, namely, reason, speech and free and varied operation.'[1]

Repeatedly, Comenius emphasised the need to make such provision on a lifelong basis, seeing the process of universal education as necessarily embracing the whole of life's allotted span. The *Pampaedia* is explicitly addressed to people of all ages and emphasises the need for continuous education from infancy to old age, for the various stages of which it provides lengthy and detailed guidance. Its title page has the following inscription: 'In this part (i.e. of the seven-volume *Consultatio*) we consider the universal education of man throughout his lifetime, prescribing courses to occupy every individual human being pleasantly *at every age* and to make his mind a garden of delight.'[2] The aim of the work is set out as follows: 'The expressed wish is for full power of development into full humanity not of one particular person or a few or even many, but of every single individual, *young and old*, rich and poor, noble and ignoble, men and women—in a word, of every human being born on earth with the ultimate aim of providing education to the entire human race regardless of age, class, sex and nationality.'[3] (my italics.)

The aims, content and pedagogic methodology proposed by Comenius for the schools of infancy, boyhood and adolescence—the years of conventional schooling—have been described in earlier chapters. The present chapter will explore his ideas on the kind of education he believed should be provided in the years of adult life. It will examine its aims and purposes, the range of programmes that he believed ought to be taught, and the kind of pedagogic methodology he recommended for their successful implementation. These issues will be the concern of this opening section. The next section will explore his thinking on institutionalised higher education, giving particular attention to the role and functions of the university and similar centres of higher learning and scholarly research. The third and fourth sections will examine two of the major functions he believed adult and continuing education should aim to serve: the promotion of religious tolerance and understanding between all men, and finally, the promotion of peace and harmony amongst the nations of the world. In these latter sections the emphasis will lie both on the kinds of values that should be disseminated in educational programmes designed to promote ecumenicity and peace and on the means through which he suggested this could be most effectively achieved.

The integration of education with the totality of life experiences was the guiding principle in Comenius's conception of the aims and processes of adult education. Essentially, he saw it as the application of the fruits of formal learning to the non-formal conditions of everyday life. This is the primary objective defined for the School of Manhood in the *Pampaedia*: 'The whole reward of wisdom lies in prudent use of life,' he declares. 'Men must therefore be taught how to apply the collective light of their wisdom to all the tasks of life, so that they cope with good and evil on their journey and cannot fail to reach a perfect ending.'[4] Using a metaphor originally employed by the second century physician, Claudius Galenus, he compares the man whose theoretical knowledge has not yet been tested out in the conditions of life itself to a sailor whose knowledge of navigation is drawn from books rather than seafaring experience: 'The man of theory without practice is like a sailor taught from a book, who sits on a stool without a care in the world making fine pictures of harbours, rocks, headlands . . . and eventually makes a fine job of steering his ship through a kitchen or over a table-top. But if he puts out to sea at the helm of a trireme, he will come to grief on the rocks that he previously knew so well.'[5] What he advocates therefore is a process of education that differs fundamentally from that of the conventional school by virtue of its overwhelming concern with the integration of learning and social experience, of theoretical knowledge and practical life-related activities:

> The whole of life is a school, as we have seen in the preceding chapters. This applies especially to the middle period of full strength, as the previous ages with their schools of infancy and boyhood were only steps leading up to this, where failure to progress would mean stepping backwards, especially as many things still remain to be learned, and learning comes not through mere preliminary action but through serious activity.
>
> The lower schools through which the student passes might have taught him a great deal, but that which he now enters surpasses them in serious handling of real situations and a variety of human associations for the rest of his lifetime.
>
> One writer made a good point when he said: 'I have derived much learning from my tutors, more from my classmates, but most of all from my pupils,' as though modelling others we are modelled ourselves, and through working we become skilled in our work. At this stage everyone becomes a member of a particular group in school, church, state, or even at home, and all will serve as regular instructors in any activity that has to be undertaken in their circle. The true scholastic method models us through modelling and makes us experts in our work through constantly putting theory into practice; and as that practice in schools is undertaken only for the sake of exercise and is to some extent performed by students in an atmosphere of play-acting, it cannot produce such true and serious progress as when full maturity is exercised in a serious setting.[6]

This life-related education was to be conducted in a manner consistent with the liberal pedagogic methods advocated by Comenius for all modes of education, whether formal or non-formal. Essentially, the whole process was directed towards the fostering of the potentiality for self-education he believed was present in every student. 'The method adopted in this school should be that of soliloquy, with every student on attaining manhood speaking to himself and formulating all his own problems for solution,' he writes in the *Pampaedia*.[7] The curricular and pedagogic policy he advocated involved a sensitive balancing of formal and non-formal approaches. While, for example, he would not restrict students to a prescriptive programme of studies at this level, he clearly recognised the need for substantive content nonetheless and saw the whole process as continuous with the formal educational activities of conventional schooling:

> The school of manhood indeed allows more freedom by not restricting students to particular books and masters. Yet as every

man's vocation will now be his school, it is essential that each individual should personally serve his family and himself as master, book and school combined by supplying them with examples, precepts, and continuous exercises. Nevertheless as it is beyond doubt that two eyes see more than one, and as no one is too sensitive to accept some advice from a friend, whether living or dead, I am adding a paragraph on this subject.

The regrettable custom prevailing in some nations of abandoning books on leaving school and as it were throwing off their fetters compels me to protest and take a moment to consider the folly, the ill-effect and the iniquity of it all. You would surely say that a craftsman sharpening an axe and then throwing it away was acting like a fool. What could be more damaging than to wish to lose all the reward of so many years of toilsome labour? You will lose it if you do not continue your study. (In this respect failure to make progress means falling back.) Could anything be more iniquitous for a craftsman who has been learning to practise a craft as a means of livelihood than to neglect it thereafter?[8]

Comenius envisaged three types of curriculum content for the adult school. It would consist, firstly, of what he called 'the book of the mind', a term signifying the classical disciplines of philosophy, literature, language, history, science etc.; secondly, it would consist of what he called the 'book of the world', signifying practical, life-related studies such as economics and nature study, or vocational studies such as arts and crafts and home economics; and thirdly, it would include the study of scripture and theology which he saw as the natural integrating focus for all educational pursuits.[9] While providing as fully as possible for individual freedom and choice, he insisted nonetheless that measures be taken to ensure the curriculum was intellectually challenging, authoritative and stimulating, and saw a decisive role for the teacher in the whole process. Advising strongly against random or directionless study habits, he clearly saw a need for guidance in the purposeful choice of subject-matter on the part of adult students. Quoting Seneca's 'The man who is everywhere is nowhere,' he urges a careful, well-informed selection of books for study, defining specific criteria for the whole process:

As for the choice of books, this is necessary because there is an infinite number of them, and it is impossible to read all that are available even in a modest library. If Cicero complained of his own age that books of poetry were so numerous that even twice the allotted span of life would not be enough for the reading of lyric poetry, what are we to say of our own era when so many Latin poets of the highest merit have been forthcoming, such as Virgil,

Horace, Ovid and Claudian, and such an immense flood of writers on history, philosophy, medicine, law, theology, etc. that even if one lived a thousand years it would be impossible to read through the thousandth part of our libraries.

What must be done, then, since no book is so bad (in the opinion of Pliny) that it does not contain some element of good? My answer is: We shall act as a man of moderation and wisdom usually does when he attends a sumptuous banquet. We shall look at everything, if it is our pleasure, and we shall choose for our purpose a sample of the very best, firstly because there is no need to spend our time on many when the springs of light appear, and secondly because it is harmful to be distracted by variety. . . . 'The man who is everywhere is nowhere,' says Seneca. I conclude that it is almost impossible for a man who reads many books to escape the crackle of odd opinions or the jangle of idle repetitions.

Books should therefore be selected (1) according to the purpose of the reader, political works for the politician, theological for the theologian, medical for the doctor, with the addition of one or two universal books; (2) according to their reputation for outstanding wisdom or prudence or eloquence ancient and modern; (3) according to their clarity. Reading obscure books is a waste of time, unless they are believed to contain some remarkable underlying mystery.[10]

Some of the most insightful guidance provided by Comenius on this whole matter occurs in the passages from the *Pampaedia* where he gives specific pedagogic advice on the conduct of the reading process. His approach is entirely consistent with his enlightened treatment of reading pedagogy in the texts devoted to language education in the primary and post-primary school. He urges students to read for meaning, advocating a process of assimilative and critical comprehension, requiring a close, perceptive and thoughtful engagement of reader and text. He urges the reader towards careful and intelligent evaluation of content, suggesting a number of practical measures that should be taken to ensure its fullest possible assimilation into the realm of individual experience, so that it can be made meaningful in the context of everyday life:

> *How should books be read?* (1) Always attentively, (2) taking selections and extracts, (3) with a view to their practical application. This means that we should get into the habit of using books not as cradles or litters for self-indulgence but as vehicles or ships to take us on our way. You must never take a book in hand but for the single purpose of making yourself more intelligent or wiser or better in some respect; and you must not lay it down until you have gleaned from it some new understanding or fuller virtue.

Also, we should never put an author aside after reading him without selecting his literary flowers and committing them to our beehives and adapting them for some present or future use.

Selections and extracts are necessary when reading authors, and they depend on a keen critical faculty recognising what to select or reject, as human writings almost invariably contain a mixture of good and bad, falsehood and truth, harmful and useful. We should do well to copy the example of bees, which suck the honey from flowers and leave the poison. Prudence must determine your selection to give you good reason for your approval or disapproval, and this will mean constant reference to the source of light from which the author obtains his explanations or proofs. For if he proves anything through *sense*, you must apply your own sense to the same thing to determine whether it is correct, or if through reasoning you must inwardly reflect to see if your reasoning comes to the same conclusion, or if through *testimony*, you must consult the same witness as he quotes and ask yourself whether he makes his statement in the same words and with the same meaning. If anything fails to pass this test, it may be rejected by passing it over completely or by treating it as doubtful and suspending judgement or by openly refuting what is openly false or by abominating what is blasphemous.

Extraction is necessary for passages that you would not wish to forget, because man is seldom if ever blessed with the kind of memory that can reproduce facts at will unless they have been duly stored away in his personal treasury, by which I mean the collection of common passages or Pandectae where you include anything useful that you have learned and keep it for reference as occasion requires.[11]

A central concern of the adult school, as conceived by Comenius, was its integration of education with working life. He saw a vital need for incorporating vocational training—at that time consisting mainly of various types of apprenticeship—within the framework of a broad liberal education. This was the fundamental purpose of the adult school. Initially, he emphasised the importance of work in making life purposeful: 'The basis of long life is not to live in idleness but always to engage in useful work,' he writes in the *Pampaedia*. 'For the idle life means constant night and slumber, the busy life means daylight and wakefulness. Idleness is like burying a man alive. Therefore the idle man is like the dead.'[12] Seeing work as the central and most consistently demanding of all life's activities, he considered it essential that healthy moral attitudes be developed towards it if life was to be truly self-fulfilling and meaningful. In a section of the *Pampaedia* entitled 'Life is Work' he writes: 'Everyone should believe that he has been brought into the world by the Heavenly

Father to do some kind of work in His vineyard or His fields or in business, and that this daily work constitutes his whole life.'[13] (His words have ironic connotations at a time when mass unemployment is seen as an inevitable and unavoidable feature of developed economies and millions of young people face the prospect of a lifetime of enforced idleness despite their best efforts to obtain work.)

The broader function of adult education, he suggests, however, is to give vocational matters their appropriate place within the framework of the religious, spiritual, moral and intellectual concerns that he believed should constitute a good general education at any stage in life. He quotes Seneca on the need to view all aspects of life, including the vocational, from a holistic perspective. 'We make mistakes because we are all thinking about parts of life and no one considers it as a whole. Therefore in your wisdom think of it as a whole, view it from beginning to end and recognise the means to the end.'[14] His advice on career choice is that it be 'honourable in regard to one's good name and reputation', 'useful in respect of physical sustenance' and 'pleasant, if possible, that is peaceful and agreeable.'[15] Ultimately, however, he insists the career itself must be conducted in accordance with the convictions of faith. It must be seen, he says, as a means to the service of mankind and thereby as a means to the service of God. It must be informed by the moral-spiritual beliefs which alone can make life meaningful:

> Everyone in his particular career should say, 'Whether I become a servant of God's word or a doctor or a magistrate or a humble citizen or a craftsman or a merchant, I am ready to serve God and men. (Any one who acts otherwise and does not profess as his end the service of God through service to men is failing to understand his vocation or abusing it and thereby seriously obstructing his own advancement.) 'For so long as I make it my serious intent to serve God in all that I do, my reward will await me here and to eternity, and my vocation will be my way to the kingdom,' as the Apostle Paul declares in Colossians, III, 24 and 1 Timothy II, 15. This is a great consolation, and rightly so, to all men of every vocation, even the humblest. For such is the glory of our eternal Father that in His house no vocation is too mean and contemptible to give him pleasure and earn from him the crown of life. In a word, we must at this stage choose the One Thing Needful, and it should be needful to the community more than to yourself. For we are not born for ourselves alone.[16]

Comenius defines the aims of adult education in the same terms, its function being to ensure that all of life's activities are informed by moral and spiritual perspectives. In the *Pampaedia* he writes: 'Everything in life

should be arranged for the benefit of our future life just as everything
that happens in our mother's womb has some bearing on our present
life. . . . The goal of life is the peace of old age and then of eternity.'
'There is one universal rule for the whole realm of practical wisdom,' he
adds: 'Do the things that in the hour of your death you will wish to
have done.' All decisions relating to life must be taken, therefore, in the
light of their final significance: 'The wise man must in all circumstances
look to the end, the means and the mode of your action. You should
wish the end for its own sake, the means only as they lead to the end.'[17]
While seeing the fostering of an awareness of man's ultimate destiny as
the most essential function of the adult school, he warns nonetheless that
considerations of this nature should not lead to stressful, morose or
anxiety-creating self-reflection:

> No one, therefore, if he is wise, will be so committed to practical
> life as to leave himself no time for meditation for refreshing of his
> spirit and invigoration of his mind. Nay, my good man, you must
> daily remember (1) your original creation in the image of God and
> your proud domination over all other creatures; (2) your first lapse
> through turning your back upon God, an error never to be repeated;
> (3) your first summons to God's tribunal with the words 'Adam,
> where art thou?' a summons that you will not escape if in any way
> your faults are repeated; (4) the promise of grace and pardon that
> makes you desire steadfastly to trample Satan under your feet; (5)
> the penalty meantime imposed on you (ordained for you to pay as
> the price of your redemption), of toil in the sweat of your brow, so
> that you submit to it willingly, relieved that the thunder of the curse
> strikes not at yourself, but at the earth because of you; (6) the
> sending of the Redeemer through whose act of atonement on your
> behalf you are justified through faith, and to secure justification
> you must be constant in faith and pray for increase of it. . . .
>
> Everyone should be earnest in the words of his vocation and
> offer prayer to God, but should guard against undue anxiety. Cares
> that weigh too heavily on the mind should be committed to God,
> even if you see that something could be done better than you are
> doing it. It is not for you to wish for more than has been granted
> to you. It is better that you should offer prayer in these words: 'O
> God, have pity on my works, and take me not away until I have
> completed all that Thou hast assigned to me and that I have under-
> taken to Thy glory. And endure me not again if I prove worthless,
> so that I may not live to meet punishment and shame but may
> make way for better men.' In the meantime you must press on with
> whatever is within your power. For, in the words of Ecclesiastes
> IX, 10, 'there is no work, nor device nor knowledge nor wisdom in

the grave whither thou goest.' The poet Ovid says: 'So long as strength and age allow, endure your toil. Presently silent-footed old age will cripple you.'[18]

Not surprisingly, Comenius saw a particular need for an education focussed on the eternal or the hereafter in the years of retirement and old age. 'As old age is part of this life, it is therefore part of our school and is itself a school,' he declares in the section of the *Pampaedia* entitled 'The School of Old Age.' 'It must have its teachers, its precepts, its exercises and studies and its learning to assist the old in their progress through life.' 'Old age,' he writes, 'is not a tomb nor a complete cessation of work but is part of life and since our whole life consists of labour old men will discontinue their labour not to take to a life of ease and idleness, but to turn their backs on the past and drive ever faster along the remaining road that leads to the end of their course and the happy attainment of their goal.'[19] Citing Plato's 'Philosophy is the contemplation of Death,' he defines the goal of education in old age as the fostering of an easeful and hope-informed acceptance of the inevitability of life's end and the prospect of eternal happiness to which it leads:

> On this subject, Seneca put it very well when he said, 'As a young man I used to think how to live well: now in my old age I am thinking how to die well.' Surely this will be perfect wisdom, 'to consider their latter end,' with God as witness (see Deuteronomy XXXII, 29). Although it is right to do this from early infancy, it cannot be taken so seriously in early manhood when the novelty of things in the world and their pleasing variety and the hope of further life are wonderful distractions to the mind. But it can and ought to be done in old age. It *can* be done, because the noise of business is dying down and the senses are sick of it. It *ought* to be done, because while there is no thought for the past but only for the present and future, old men, unless they are out of their minds, already have death in view. Is there anything better to think about than how to embrace death even if it comes unexpectedly? Plato's definition of philosophy is most appropriate here, when he says 'Philosophy is the contemplation of death.' Certainly the best part of philosophy is to have learnt to die, meaning to die well. Death needs no skill; it will come by itself. But to die well is the art of arts.
>
> As the more distant goals are better, the most distant ought to be the best; and the old man should be obliged not simply to learn how to die, but to know how to pass through death into the last stage of all, eternity itself. There is truth in the saying 'Life is movement, death is rest.' A man's death does not bring about his end but at most removes him to another place, leading not to the

resignation of his mind or his desires or his endeavours but to still further striving. And in what direction? Towards eternity itself, which contains the furthest limit of existence. Death is only the point or hinge on which eternity turns.[20]

Once again, Comenius recommends three familiar methods for education at this stage in life: the methods of 'example, precept and practice'.[21] By the term 'example' he signifies the heritage of wisdom appropriate to education at all stages in life, i.e. the traditions of literature, history, science and philosophy—in this instance designated the accumulated wisdom of 'all those who have passed wisely through this earthly school before us.' 'Precepts,' he suggests, are to be drawn mainly from the scriptures and related studies in theology and sacred literature. 'Practice', he suggests, should consist in regular reflection on moral and religious truths: 'As men sink deeper into old age they will cultivate religion and morals more keenly and will have time to concentrate upon the good mind, not only for their own sakes to preserve a blameless conscience or to achieve it at last, but also for the good of others, to leave behind the greatest congregation of true students of wisdom, sincere worshippers of God, and excellent citizens of their fatherland.'[22] He insists that all this be conducted in a spirit of cheerful, optimistic acceptance of the inevitability and imminence of death: 'Decrepit old men are faced with the task of embracing Death and in her company entering a new and immortal life. To accomplish this successfully they must on no account fear death as worldly men do. You were not afraid of birth. . . . Just as in all innocence you entrust to your Creator the place, time and manner of your birth, so with full knowledge and consent you must entrust him with your death.'[23] Most of all, he insists, the old must prepare for death through their active and relentless pursuit of virtue, goodness and truth:

> In particular, they must constantly bear in mind the advice of Solomon in his great wisdom (at the end of his old age he had confessed and recovered from the errors of a dissolute life) when he said, 'Whatsoever thy hand findeth to do, do it with thy might. For there is no work nor device nor wisdom in the grave whither thou goest' (Ecclesiastes IX, 10), also the memorable words of Christ our Lord, who was still working and teaching towards the end of his life, as he proceeded to the noble work of healing the man who had been blind from birth, 'I must work the works of him that sent me while it is day.' (John IX, 4). This was clearly meant for us to imitate, for he turned to his disciples and added, 'The night cometh when no man can work.'
>
> Horace's well-known line, 'Release the ageing horse in good time,' should also apply, but on the understanding that life's ploughing-

season has already been honourably completed. To make its completion possible, every kind of helpful facility should be employed. 'We
must plunge into the middle, lest we may be too late in coming to
the end,' said Cicero. Therefore if any old man becomes aware that
he is too widely involved in the business of life, he should begin to
shorten his sails on his approach to harbour. As his whole life's
course of learning consisted of right wisdom, right speech and right
action, the highest grade of this study ought to achieve (1) pure
wisdom, which means acknowledging and reforming the errors of
life, (2) pure speech, which means supplying others with good advice,
(3) pure action, which means doing only that which befits candidates
for immortality. In a word, old men should now only engage in
serious action, express only salutary advice, and think only holy
thoughts. The closing year does not play with blossoms, but gives
forth fruit, and not soft fruit like strawberries or cherries, but solid
and lasting fruit; and such is the appropriate fruit for the last stage
of life. 'An old man learning his alphabet is a sorry sight,' said
Seneca. Therefore an old man learning his words is also a sorry
sight, an eloquent babbler with no work to do.[24]

Some sense of the significance of Comenius's writings on adult education
can be gained by comparing him briefly with two notable and influential
figures in the field from more recent years: the nineteenth century Danish
educator, Bishop Abel Grundtvig and the twentieth century Jewish
philosopher, Martin Buber. Comenius anticipated much of what Grundtvig
exemplified as the functions of adult education in his pioneering work in
the Danish folk schools—long since a model for adult and continuing
education in various societies throughout the world. Like Comenius,
Grundtvig was deeply concerned at the corrupting power of chauvinistic
nationalism—the excesses of which he had witnessed in the war with
Russia in the 1860s as Comenius had similarly witnessed it in the barbar-
ities of the Thirty Years War—and both men saw a particular role for
adult education in purging society of its contaminating influences. Both
men saw the work of the adult school as a means towards the reawak-
ening of the spiritual and cultural traditions of their people and both
recognised the need to give it full institutional status to ensure it was
regarded with the same degree of seriousness as the more formal modes
of education provided in conventional schools. Both therefore insisted
that a substantial curriculum, consisting of the traditional disciplines of
philosophy, history, literature, science etc., be taught in the adult school.
To ensure that this was conducted effectively each man sought to develop
pedagogic procedures appropriate to education at this stage in life, stressing the need for informal, spontaneous but nonetheless formative and
productive contact between teacher and learner. Their profound sense of

the importance of the whole enterprise contrasts strikingly with the frivolous and superficial concept of adult education currently in vogue in several contemporary western societies.

Buber shared with Comenius and Grundtvig a sense of the potential of adult education as a means to spiritual and cultural formation and sought to provide it along these lines for the masses of immigrants that came flooding into Israel in the aftermath of the Holocaust.[25] He too devised a curriculum for the adult school that gave appropriate representation to the religious, cultural and historical traditions of his people. Where he advanced most significantly on both Comenius and Grundtvig was in his development of a sophisticated andragogy for the advancement of the whole process—though much of what he proposed was already present in its basic forms in Comenius's pedagogic writings. What Buber devised became the basis of the andragogic methodology further developed by his disciple, Paulo Freire, and implemented with extraordinary success in the great literacy campaigns of the 1970s and 80s, and in community education projects throughout the world ever since. What they all shared with Comenius was a commitment to the ideal of universal education, for the effective realisation of which they saw the provision of education on a lifelong basis as an essential pre-requirement. Regrettably, while much has been achieved in the expansion of educational opportunity everywhere in recent years, the provision of lifelong education as a universal right remains largely an unrealised dream, particularly if seen in the enlightened terms in which it was conceived originally by Comenius and articulated in his major pedagogic writings.

2. THE IDEA OF THE UNIVERSITY

As was mentioned previously, substantial evidence exists to support the long-standing tradition that Comenius was offered the Presidency of Harvard College in 1641, five years after its foundation. In a volume of commemorative essays, published in 1942, the President of Harvard, James B. Conant, spoke of the University's 'peculiar indebtedness to Jan Comenius' and described him as 'the principal authority on education in Europe' in his time. 'He conferred a double benefit on education,' Conant wrote, 'first by his impatience with mere traditionalism and pedantry, and secondly by his own important and original contributions to the principles of education.' 'The spirit of Comenius,' he said, 'should make possible in every generation that fresh envisaging of educational problems which he, against overwhelming odds, forced upon his contemporaries.'[26] Conant's tribute illustrates the remarkable status enjoyed by Comenius in the field of higher education as well as in the sphere of conventional schooling. As has already been shown, his writings significantly influenced the founding of the Royal Society in 1668, an institution which became a model for centres of academic research throughout the world in subsequent years. And though himself a graduate of Herborn—a non-degree awarding institution—Comenius maintained strong contacts throughout his life with various European universities. They included Oxford, Leyden, Heidelberg, Amsterdam and Prague. (Despite some strains between the Unitas Fratrum and Charles University in Prague, Comenius himself had a close relationship with that institution, as Josef Polisensky has shown in an essay published by Charles University icn 1990).[27]

All of this suggests the need to undertake a close examination of Comenius's conception of the aims and goals of higher education and particularly of the nature and role of the university as a centre for higher learning and research. The concept of the university outlined in Chapter XXI of *The Great Didactic* and in Chapter XII of the *Pampaedia* derives directly from the ideal of pansophic learning described in several of his major writings. The pansophic ideal emphasises the indivisible unity and wholeness of all knowledge and points especially to the spiritual-moral focus on which all its complex modes must converge. It will be recalled that in *The Great Didactic* Comenius saw the fostering of learning, morality and piety as the primary concern of all educators and that he saw this as the means ultimately for the moral regeneration of all mankind. This remains the all-embracing goal of the university and provides the moral and epistemic justification for the ideal of integrated knowledge he considered it the particular function of the university to maintain.

That whole vision is given its full philosophical justification in the *Via Lucis*, a work comparable to later studies such as Newman's *Idea of a University* for its original and farseeing vision of the nature and scope of higher learning. The aim of pansophic learning, Comenius declares, is the search for the unity of all knowledge and truth—a unity manifested in its interrelatedness, its radical order and integrity. Intellectual enquiry, he suggests, is essentially a quest for the harmony inherent in all that exists, a search for unifying meaning. The significance of all modes of knowledge would have to be defined in terms of their place in the universal order: the temporal would have to be related to the intemporal, the finite to the infinite. In dedicating the work to the 'Members of the Royal Society' he praised them for 'bringing real philosophy to a happy birth,' for 'bringing the light of Natural Philosophy from the deeper wells of truth,'[28] by the latter signifying their linking of the empirical to the transcendental—the crucial principle by which all their research was guided and the full significance of which it sought to unfold. 'To Cause a Thing, by Whatever Size it May be, to Be seen as a Whole'—that is the primary aim of the whole process of intellectual illumination, he says. 'Present the thing as a whole to the organs of sight, and they will see it whole. So if you show to the intellect, whatever you do show to it, as a whole (from one end of it to the other, from its beginning to its end, from top to bottom and from right to left)—if you do this, the intellect cannot but perceive it as a whole.' If, he adds, a 'Thing is to Be Seen Distinctly', the thing 'must be shown, not merely as a whole and generally, but in all and each of its parts, from the largest to the most minute.'[29] Translated into a conception of aims for higher learning, this represents primarily a balancing of general and specialised modes of enquiry, the latter becoming fully meaningful only by virtue of its recognition of the significance of specialised knowledge in the universal order of truth. That principle is succinctly conveyed in this passage from the *Via Lucis*:

> I said in the last place, that General and Special subjects ought to be taught, and I will now add, even those of the most special nature, as far as possible. For it is in these, and not in the general subjects, that knowledge of things and the use of knowledge consist. And the greater the number of highly specialised kinds of knowledge a man possesses (provided he has them exactly and not from hearsay) the richer the harvest he reaps from his science. But (we must remember that) specialised kinds of knowledge, in as much as in themselves they have a quality of aloofness and isolation, must in the interest of order be brought together into certain universal groups.[30]

The university therefore would have to promote specialised knowledge and training within the framework of a liberal education embracing the range of humane, scientific and sacred disciplines traditionally considered essential for the full and balanced development of all human potentialities. This liberal concept of learning would ensure, in turn, that all learning would find its ultimate focus in the sphere of moral and spiritual truth. All learning, all modes of enquiry must be morally and spiritually informed, Comenius repeatedly insists throughout the *Via Lucis* and other related works. In the *Pampaedia* he condemns certain 'philosophers of old' (the Cynics) who 'made unscrupulous use of philosophising to the point of neglecting morals.'[31] He quotes the words of Cicero and St. Paul, the first on the innate human propensity towards the quest for truth that exists in all men, the second on the moral nature of that quest, i.e. its ultimate orientation towards the Good: '"Inquiry into truth is the special attribute of man," said Cicero. If it is an attribute, it should be inseparable from human nature. The saying, "Prove all things; hold fast that which is good," must be accepted as applying to the whole human race."'[32]

All this is particularly brought into focus in his treatment of the study of science, the major new force in scholarly learning that had emerged in the seventeenth century. As was pointed out in an earlier chapter,

Comenius—a scientist of considerable stature himself—saw all scientific enquiry as ultimately pointed towards the discovery of God through the contemplation of material creation—a position he held in common with Bacon and several other scientific scholars of the time. 'To know more of God's creation is to increase in love of the Creator'—this was his motto, J.L Paton wrote. 'There were many,' Paton said, 'who were afraid that this new science men were gaining from the "interrogation of Nature" would clash with Revelation. Comenius welcomed it with open arms as itself a new revelation. Contrary to tradition it was, but "Christ called himself not Tradition but Truth." If he and his message are truth, then every increase of knowledge can be used to enrich the truth that rests on Him.'[33] Zdenek Kučera has described Comenius as simultaneously a realist and a transcendentalist: 'Comenius's THEOLOGUMENON is dialectical,' he writes. 'The objective bears the signum of the non-objective, uses the objective as its medium. Profane matters reveal in the medial context sacral depth, and reflect the light of eschata. . . . This synergy of God and man is the root of Comenius's synthesis of the old universalism—newly interpreted eschatologically—with modern empiricism, conceived noetically and ontologically in historically functional connections.'[34] It was his deep religious awareness, a modern scientist has written, that enabled Comenius to 'see the dangers of the pursuit of knowledge for individual enrichment.' He spoke of his appreciation of the 'coherence of religion and science'—a coherence that was widely recognised in the seventeenth century:

> To us, still confused by the nineteenth century conflicts between Religion and Science, it is difficult to see the extremely close relation which existed in the seventeenth century between mystical 'experimental' Christianity, hard practical self-help, and experimental science. Yet a study of the personalities of the seventeenth century scientists shows all these elements present and indeed the combination is the keynote of Puritanism—in the conversions of men like Boyle, Pascal and Steno, and in the poetry of Milton and Marvell. The two roots of modern science, the study of Nature and of human trades, both appeared as eminently religious objects to the Puritan, the first because it would reveal the glory and wisdom of Divine Providence, the second because it could only lead to an increase of sobriety and godly industry.[35]

The great tragedy of the present age, another scientist, J.G. Crowther,[36] has written, is that science has lost its way, being directed neither to spiritual ends, as it was in the seventeenth century, nor even towards the benefit of mankind as a whole whose welfare it purports to serve. Science, he says, has simply become an instrument of capitalist production. He calls for a reappraisal of its aims, especially in the context of higher learning and scholarly research. The significance of Comenius's work, he writes, is that it argues so convincingly for the location of scientific enquiry in a wider scheme of learning, embracing the whole range of humane and sacred studies, and that he saw the university and comparable institutions of higher learning as having a crucial role in effecting this fusion. The well-documented rift between Descartes and Comenius is particularly significant in this context, their disagreement clearly pointing to the dichotomy of secular and sacred learning that has proceeded inexorably since the seventeenth century. Their meeting at Leyden in 1642 was essentially a confrontation between two conflicting views of the nature of intellectual enquiry. Jaroslav Panek has described the meeting in a recent study:

> While Comenius defended a link between science and faith, Descartes denied the authority of the Bible in his philosophical considerations. In his approach to nature, he was undoubtedly less influenced by tradition and showed greater consistency in concentrating on a mechanistically understood movement of matter. He proceeded from the optimism of natural science and from the idea that everything may be expressed in quantitative terms. Next to him, Comenius appeared old-fashioned and his thinking was burdened by Biblical authorities, mysticism, and mediaeval scholasticism. However, in contrast to Descartes, who exactly grasped and depicted partial natural phenomena, Comenius retained his sense of the comprehensiveness of nature, of the dynamics of history, and of the creative character of the human being. When the two scholars parted—politely but coolly—a wall of mutual lack of understanding remained between them. Comenius felt uneasy about the consequences of Descartes' philosophy. His concern was justified because while Cartesianism opened the door to modern, technological civilisation, it deprived man of his human qualities and turned him into a component of a rigid world that could be expressed in mathematical formulae.[37]

Comenius's subsequent description of Cartesianism as a 'haven for the godless' and 'the most malignant of all philosophies' vividly conveys his fear of the consequences of this dichotomous rift at the heart of intellectual enquiry.[38] His apprehension was shared by Wilhelm Leibnitz who wrote approvingly of his (Comenius's) dream of a world where scientific and mathematical enquiry would be seen to complement all other modes of thought, both sacred and secular. In a celebrated couplet Leibnitz declared: 'Tempus erit, quo te Comeni, turba bonorum./ Factaque, spesque tuas, rota quoque ipsa colet.' ('The time will come,

Comenius, when hosts of noble minded men will honour/What thou hast done, honouring as well the dream of thy hopes.'[39] It is the realisation of that dream that Radim Palouš, the current Rector of Charles University, identifies as the primary goal for higher education in the modern age. In an eloquent commemorative tribute, published for the 400th anniversary of Comenius's birth in 1992, he wrote:

> Comenius has been emerging in the world of learning in ever novel ways and with an ever stronger impact—at first as an inventor of a method for teaching languages, then as a master of the universal *ars docendi*, later as a theoretician in the field of education, and in our century as a philosopher opposed to the Cartesian dichotomy dividing All into *res cogitans* and *res extensa*, and finally now and for the future as a thinker offering a unified philosophical-theological approach to the created world in its entirety, and not only that: also a theoretical view in unity with the practice of life and human fortunes, making into one ontological questioning and answering, epistemological heuristic and agatalogical-moral listening, calling for one single responsibility—the responsibility of all people and every individual for the common drama which is called 'the world.'

> The basic characteristic of the crisis of our times is the end of modern spirituality marked by a technico-scientific approach to All: on the one hand a 'scientific', i.e. cold, unconcerned aloofness of scientists examining objects, on the other hand technological endeavour to control and to exploit. All human endeavour had been taking on, gradually and ever more, the character of anthropocentrism-oriented domination because even scientific objectivity, however much it strove for concreteness, with great success, posited a separate observation point of the scientist-explorer, situated in some 'God-like position.' This 'humanistic' (or perhaps better 'hoministic') orientation was naturally manifested evermore both in the system of values and in the entire living style. Man has lost what Comenius and many with him called 'nexus hypostaticus', fundamental link, man's bond with God as a being among the other creatures, as a partner among-fellow beings in the created world, the most important among them as 'imago Dei', entrusted with the role of a careful manager co-responsible for the destiny of the world. Man has freed himself from this relationship and has taken the position of a ruler who, either stupidly or in a more ingenious way, intends to exploit the world only and solely for his own purposes, or succumbs to fatal passivity of indifferent whirling in rushing senselessly through space and time.

> Comenius's voice calls on us to live such a human life which is neither the former nor the latter variant mentioned above, neither

an anthropocentric dictate to the world nor resignation to blind meaninglessness of fate. Mankind's passage through the modern era is certainly a significant experience which has produced many positive fruits but also harsh and bitter experiences. But quite possibly, it is thanks to tears that we are only now capable of comprehending that hopeful chresis offered by Comenius, meaning acceptance of mankind's belonging to the world family, and at the same time calling for a great world 'culture', that responsible cultivation of the 'garden' of All, care for the common fate of the earth—our motherland, of that whole community of beings whose drama we have the honour and the task to live and to create together.[40]

It is significant that Palouš defines 'chresis' as an ideal not merely signifying the unity of all knowledge and truth, but as one embracing the corresponding obligation of all men to take responsibility for the welfare of their fellowmen. 'What is this "unum" in the spirit of Comenius?' he asks. "Let us express it by the word culture. We now have in mind the verb "collere"—to cultivate, and thus we do not mean any complete and enclosed grown product, but care, that which requires contribution, participation. Human life, the life of the whole world, is not something complete that is given, a fateful automaticity, a mechanically flowing gravitation of processes, but shared participation, effective concern to ensure that "everything turns out well."'[41] Elaborating on this concept of 'chresis' in another essay from the same collection, Miloslav Bednár contrasts the Platonic concept of 'paedaia' with the Comenian ideal of '*pam* -paedaia'. Seeing the 'former as simply signifying the intellectual search for truth, he points to the manner in which that process is transformed by Comenius into a universal moral responsibility:

Comenius's radical democratisation of Plato's educational concept stems from the requirement that every man should live in accordance with his principal human purpose, which is to learn the truth and to live guided by it. In his Pampaedia, which is pedagogic in the sense of his all-reforming philosophy of upbringing and education, Comenius—in the spirit of his democratic approach—draws consequences from the then usual, but originally ancient conception of man (Philo of Alexandria, Plotinus), or of the human soul as a mirror reflecting the totality of things back to its source. Comenius obviously knew this idea from the works of Cusanus in Pinder's anthology, Speculum Intellectuale. The conception of man as a mirroring focus of the cosmos is a prerequisite for the possibility of a philosophically conceived education which provides meaningful knowledge of everything to all. Thus Comenius deduces from the traditional philosophical conception of man, dialectically developed

by Hegel two centuries later, radical democratic educational consequences, and continues the Czech Reformation tradition in this way.
It is here that the irreplaceable importance of Comenius's CHRESIS
becomes fully clear, as an adequate and unforced way of leading
everyone to the realisation of man's innate destiny in the above-
mentioned sense. In Comenius's conception, the full achievement of
this educational ideal is identical with a world-wide reform of individual and political life, a reform which turns both individual and
political life from the head to the legs, i.e. from the previous semi-
education of values relativism and narrow egotism, individual and
political life is turned towards its overall spiritual purpose. In
Comenius's reform version, Plato's ideal becomes the concern of all.[42]

The concept of 'unum' further implies the ideal of cultural continuity,
by virtue of which all knowledge is related to its roots in the entire heritage of culture and truth. Man's knowledge of himself and the universe
he inhabits can only be fully realised, Comenius suggests, through his
understanding of the historical processes that have shaped his consciousness. The illusion of progress, of pure contemporaneity, of truth as
disclosed in the here and now—the illusion of a pure science isolated
from other modes of cultural enquiry—derives from man's isolation from
his own past, his isolation from the continuum of historical time in which
the present is embedded. The pansophic ideal requires that all new knowledge be fully located in the intellectual and cultural traditions from which
it has emerged. What is most significant about the ideal, as Dagmar
Čapková has shown, is not primarily its range and comprehensiveness,
but its affirmation of a basic methodological principle: the principle of
knowing as a reaching towards wisdom manifested as the 'unum,' i.e. the
focus where all truths converge. In a recent essay she writes:

> European scholars began to express considerable interest in
> Comenius's pansophy after the publication of his *Janua Linguarum*
> and *Prodromus Pansophiae* (the first edition of which appeared in
> 1637 under the title *Praeludia*). At the end of the 1630s, Hamburg
> Professor A. Tassius wrote to Comenius's friend Hartlib in England
> that the whole of Europe was excited by Comenius's pansophic and
> didactic views. Pansophy was expected to help unify the fragmented
> contents of school education, or unify the results of human knowl-
> edge in general; these were the objectives of the efforts of English
> scholars around Hartlib, an important organiser of scientific contacts
> between a number of European and non-European countries. But
> Comenius later sought much more, and he devised a broader and
> deeper application of pansophy. When it became evident that
> Comenius's pansophy is not only 'omniscience' designed to unify

human knowledge, but that it is a kind of universal wisdom, and that it has a broader and deeper methodological functiton—i.e. to unify and integrate all human activities, both theoretical and practical, both material and spiritual, into a new cultural whole, as Comenius explained it in his later writings—views concerning pansophy began to change and polarise, up to its rejection.[43]

From all of this comes a conception of higher learning as predominantly a quest for the unity of all knowledge and truth. As the institution designed to promote this ideal, the university, Comenius suggests, must possess the resources to ensure its effective realisation. It must have 'learned and able professors of all the sciences, arts, faculties and languages who can impart information to all the students on any subject,' he writes in *The Great Didactic*.[44] Its curriculum, he declares in the *Pampaedia*, must ensure the concentration of all learning 'into one tree', so as to emphasise its essential integrity:

> The purpose here is to take all the learning acquired through the senses, through reasoning and through divine testimony and concentrate it into a tree of one human omniscience, since perfect reasoning results in the pure understanding of things, and perfect exercise of the will in choosing the best things, and perfect use of the faculties in expert handling of all things.
>
> Therefore youths who are now accustomed to the bonds of reasoning must be promoted to this school: so that without laborious argument they may be able to speak on many subjects and take action readily and wisely with their wide understanding and their ability to see the light wherever it is to be found.
>
> Ludovicus Vives wrote these lines in his *Palace of Laws*: 'Grow, ye virtues, and let manhood flourish! Lo! the field is open to men's minds; favour is assured for the deserving, and industry meets with due reward. Be lifted up on high, ye illustrious souls, blessed with a share of the divine spirit! Pursue your goal to the goal of distinction.'[45]

The concept of the university put forward by Comenius embraces three interrelating objectives: teaching, research, and vocational or professional training. 'What is an academy?' he asks in the *Pampaedia*. '(1) A permanent assembly of wise men, (2) a central library for books of every available kind, (3) a factory for wisdom, busily occupied in earnest, realistic and continuous exercises.'[46] There should be one such institution, he says, in every nation or every sizeable province; it should 'have residences or colleges where all students concentrate on wisdom, segregated from craftsmen and merchants and the general public.'[47] He envisages conditions in which students would conduct their activities in seclusion from the bustle and busy-ness of everyday life. At one point in the *Pampaedia* he writes: 'They ought to be shielded like Nazarites of God from the bustle of the world and the company of the common people, living a simpler and more reasonable life and wearing simpler clothing, as befits leaders of men turning their backs on the conventional folly of the world and showing the way to reform.'[48] He revised his thinking on this latter issue in later years and saw significant merit—particularly for the teaching of science—in siting universities in large cities and towns, close to the 'bustle of the world and the company of common people.'

The three main types of activity in which Comenius believed universities should be engaged are designated in the *Pampaedia* as, respectively: pansophic studies (formal academic study), pambiblia (independent research) and panetoimia (vocational training).[49] The pansophic curriculum was to be a broad introductory programme of liberal studies that would be taught to all students. (It strongly resembles first year courses in liberal studies taught in many European universities, especially in France, until quite recently). Comenius recommended that the programme be taught through the use of 'epitomes' or succinct distillations of classical texts that would lead the students eventually to conduct independent study of these texts themselves.[50] He outlines the method in this passage from *The Great Didactic*:

> We said that every class of author should be read in the University. Now this would be a laborious task, but its use is great, and it is therefore to be hoped that men of learning, philologers, philosophers, theologians, physicians etc., will render the same service to students as has been rendered to those who study geography by geographers. For these latter make maps of the provinces, kingdoms, and divisions of the world, and thus present to the eye huge tracts of sea and land on a small scale, so that they can be taken in at a glance. Painters also produce accurate and lifelike representations of countries, cities, houses, and men, no matter of what size the original may be. Why, therefore, should not Cicero, Livy, Plato, Aristotle, Plutarch, Tacitus, Gellius, Hippocrates, Galen, Celsus, Augustine, Jerome etc. be treated in the same way and epitomised? By this we do not allude to the collections of extracts and flowers of rhetoric that are often met with. These epitomes should contain the whole author, only somewhat reduced in bulk.
>
> Epitomes of this kind will be of great use. In the first place it will be possible to obtain a general notion of an author when there is no time to read his works at length. Secondly, those who (following Seneca's advice) wish to confine themselves to the works of one writer (for different writers suffer different dispositions), will be

able to take a rapid survey of all and to make their choice in accordance with their tastes. Thirdly, those who are going to read the authors in their entirety will find that these epitomes enable them to read with greater profit, just as a traveller is able to take in the details of his journey with greater ease, if he have first studied them on a map. Finally, these abstracts will be of great use to those who wish to make a rapid revision of the authors that they have read, as it will help them to remember the chief points, and to master them thoroughly.[51]

Comenius further recommended that a wide range of pedagogic strategies be employed for the teaching of the pansophic programme. He suggested they include formal lectures, structured seminars, public disputations, the presentation and defence of dissertations, and the organisation of projects for independent study. (All are described in Chapter XXXI of *The Great Didactic*).[52] In the sphere of natural philosophy or science he emphasised the need for practical experimentation. He stresses the importance of this in the following passage from the *Pampaedia*, citing the authority of Bacon in support of his views:

So much for the theoretical exercises in Pansophia. When these are completed, Pansophia must be put into practice in a course of experiments—hence my argument for siting the academy in a capital city, seething with practical business of every kind. Philosophers must agree that it is better to be closely associated with practical experiments within the academies themselves than to spend their lives in abstract theoretical speculations and bewildering discussions without practice. This is undoubtedly true. Proofs of every kind should be established at this stage by personal sight and touch to reach mechanical certainty of knowledge.

   Francis Bacon was right when he said: 'It is esteemed a kind of dishonour unto learning to descend to inquiry or meditation upon matters mechanical. . . . So it cometh often to pass, that mean and small things discover great, better than great can discover the small.' Then he adds: 'But if my judgement be of any weight, the use of history mechanical is of all others the most radical and fundamental towards natural philosophy; such natural philosophy as shall not vanish in the fume of subtile, sublime, or delectable speculation, but such as shall be operative to the endowment and benefit of man's life.' In fact, in Book III, Chapter 4, after saying 'I hold it not possible that the formal causes of natural objects will ever be invented by that course of invention which hath been used in the past (by natural philosophers),' he adds 'in regard that men (which is the root of all error) have made too untimely a departure and too remote a recess from particulars, and have devoted themselves wholly to their own meditations and arguments.'[53]

Side by side with the provision for liberal learning is a strong emphasis on independent research, described by Comenius as an 'exercise in pambiblia'. He advises researchers to be selective in their reading—'both in period and subject-matter'—and, on a practical level, suggests that 'the first reading should be rapid, using summaries and abridgements, followed by more detailed reading of selected passages.'[54] Predictably, he reminds researchers that the ultimate significance and meaningfulness of all knowledge is to be sought in the sphere of religious faith, rather surprisingly citing Descartes' *Contra Voetium* in support of this. 'Note,' he tells them, 'where he . . . concludes that since almost all human writings are commentaries on the books of God, the wisest men will be those who are nurtured on God's books with little influence from those written by men.'[55]

In his treatment of professional training Comenius stressed the importance of developing it within a broad framework of liberal studies. He recommended that universities provide efficient and systematic training in areas such as medicine, law and theology, urging a system whereby professors would train and examine students through a continuous and closely integrated process of teaching and assessment. 'The professor,' he says, 'should expound them [his topics] in the morning, and examine the students in the afternoon on: (1) the meaning of every point or the true state of a controversy, (2) the arguments to be used in proof. (3) The student should be plied with objections until he knows how to solve the problem.'[56] While insisting that access to university education be open to all, he recognised the need for selection, largely because of the professional dimension of education at this level, and recommended that it be on the basis of academic merit and vocational aptitude. The methods of selection for entry to professional courses that he advocated—in this instance involving written examinations—are again broadly similar to those now generally in use.

An interesting adjunct to Comenius's definition of the three main functions of the university is his recommendation that higher studies be complemented by travel—'a most enriching experience if wisely arranged.' He advised students to travel firstly in their own countries—urging that it not be 'undertaken casually for trivial purposes' but 'for the purpose of increasing wisdom'—and suggested that this should be followed by extensive travel in other countries. The following passage indicates how seriously he wished the whole process to be taken by students:

As for things he will see, he will regard everything that is rare or unusual as well worth visiting, whether nature's handiwork, such as mountains, cliffs, the Pillars of Hercules in Spain, Scylla and Charybdis in Sicily and also fiery Mount Etna, or products of human skill like gardens and famous buildings, some still upstanding, others ancient and lying in ruins.

But he should be much more concerned with the various products of human wisdom: Colleges of learning, senates and tribunals, temples and monasteries, the consistories of the church (especially when they are actually engaged in teaching, judging, deliberating, discussing, etc.), arsenals, money-markets and places of exchange, theatres and spectacles, wherever produced, wedding ceremonies, funerals, feasts and anything which contrasts with the custom of his fatherland.[57]

The essential character of the Comenian university, therefore, consists in its integration of three functions—teaching, research and professional training—a synthesis that gives it a special relevance for the present time with so much evidence of new institutions, frequently styling themselves as universities, coming into being without the balance of functions traditionally considered essential for a proper education at this level. He would almost certainly have deprecated the fashion for highly specialised institutes, especially in the technical/technological sphere, that is currently in vogue, as he would have denounced the trend towards the separation of research from teaching in higher education which has also been occurring, frequently with state encouragement, in many countries in recent years. Both trends run counter to his concept of the higher institute as an agency for the promotion of the fundamental values of our civilisation. Central to that whole vision was his concept of the scholar as a spiritual pilgrim seeking to bring order and meaning to the problems and crises of his age. The pilgrim-narrator of the *Labyrinth*, as two Czech historians have written, is Comenius's prototypical image of the scholar: 'The pilgrim type of Comenius's *Labyrinth* has its analogy in the European renaissance humanist culture where the author took a direct model from. Not only in literature, but in the whole of renaissance culture, the pilgrim–intellectual constantly looks for himself in the changing essence of life's conditions, and what's more, even more substantial, the contradiction of social conditions (coincidentia oppositorum) continually forces him to choose and discern what he should do according to his own conscience and what he should avoid when the social convention and practice is not in agreement with the norm.'[58] It is the role of the scholar-educator to find meaning in periods of intellectual, social and spiritual crisis, to restore order where confusion and chaos exist. The kind of men who should be chosen to dedicate themselves to the task of promoting 'universal light' are described by Comenius in the *Via Lucis*. In that work he envisages the establishment of a universal College of

Light, a worldwide convocation of scholars, through which all could combine their energies in the promotion of humanitarian values and ideals:

> For this task fit men will be chosen from the whole world, men of quick and industrious temper, of piety, warmly devoted to the welfare of the people, taken indifferently from laymen engaged in public affairs and ecclesiastics; these must be set, as it were, in a watch-tower to look out for the well-being of mankind, and to see every possible way, means or occasion of seeking whatever will be beneficial to all men, of developing what they find, and of protecting what they have developed against corrupting influences.
>
> When I say men, I mean that many are needed: one man or a few men can do nothing in so great a matter. 'The multitude of the wise is the welfare of the world.' Clearly it is beyond the power of one man to undertake teaching of this universal range, especially if it is intended not for one people or for one Church, but for the world, and if through it the benefit not of one year or of one age, but of all posterity, is to be consulted. We need, then, an alliance of a great number of men, who with united effort and continuous labour shall seek to serve the best interests of men as long as men exist.[59]

In the *Panorthosia* this whole notion is given practical expression in the concept of a network of colleges—Comenius mentions existing institutions such as the Academia dei Lincei in Italy, the College des Roses in France, the Fruchtragender in Germany—which would pool their talents to form a universal convocation of scholars devoted to the dissemination of pansophic ideals. Again, he insists that only the ablest and wisest be entrusted with the task of scholarship: 'Care must be taken to choose these select men from among the best, i.e. the wisest of the wise. . . . Only then will the members of the College of Light in truth and in deed be what Seneca called philosophers: teachers of the human race.'[60] The functions of the College of Light are specified in detail in the following passage from the work:

> It will be their task to direct relations between mind and being, that is to say, to guide human omniscience that it may not exceed its bounds nor fall short, nor err from its path, in any of its degrees, conditions or cases; to extend the dominion of the human mind over things and promote the light of wisdom among all nations and minds, always for the higher and better. This College could also be called the Teacher of the human race, the Heaven of the Church and the Luminary of the world.
>
> They will have to pay attention

    (i) To themselves, as the ministers to the Light;
   (ii) To the light itself, to be refined and diffused by their works;
  (iii) To the schools, as the workshops of light;
   (iv) To the heads of the schools, as the light-bearers;
    (v) To teaching methods, as the purifiers of light;
   (vi) To books, as the vessels of light;
  (vii) To the printers, as the makers of these vessels;
 (viii) To the new language, as the finest vehicle of the new light;
   (ix) To the other colleges, as assistants in spreading light every-
        where;
    (x) To Christ Himself, the fountain of light.[61]

A further function envisaged by Comenius for the College of Light was
the promotion of educational reform through the active intervention of
scholars in the process of policy-making and through their initiation and
monitoring of change in all branches of the schooling process. Special
emphasis is given in the *Panorthosia* to the potential influence of scholars
in the sphere of pedagogic reform. 'In particular,' he writes, 'they will
pay attention to the methods of teaching used by this, that or the other
man in educating young people; whether they lead their charges to the
fixed goal along the right road, over level ground, gently and pleasantly;
or whether they will afflict them, dragging them by circuitous ways,
along rough roads and over thorns. For even God Himself, taking pity
on young people, has shown at last how all schools can be made into
playgrounds; therefore we cannot suffer any school to continue to be like
a grindstone or a house of torment for souls.'[62] Ultimately, however, the
primary function of the institute of higher learning, as Comenius saw it,
remained the conduct and propagation of scholarly research, both through
independent study, teaching and the active pursuit of political, social or
educational reform. The whole process is described eloquently in this
passage from the *Panorthosia*:

    Then they will pay attention to the light of wisdom itself, which
    they are to make shine in beauty over all the variety of things and
    their universality, to clarify and purify, and to spread effectively
    over all nations to the ends of the earth. For just as the sun in the
    sky was not born and given to any one region alone, but rises for
    all men, turning towards the south and back towards the north and
    lighting up all things around; so the sun of the mind, wisdom,
    rising already now with such splendour, should not belong to one
    or even to a few peoples, but should follow its orbit over the whole
    human race; these apostles of the light will see and provide for this;
    thus they will be the brightest light-bearers, bringing the light of
    the dawn to the darkness of the peoples of the world, until such

time as the sun of justice Himself, Christ, shall rise. And wherever the sun has already risen, they will take care that no darkness of the mind should return to darken the daylight of the Church, that no little star of partial knowledge already shining in the firmament of the Church should cease to shine, and even less that the sun of the Church itself, or the moon, should decline; for the Lord shall be its everlasting light, as has been promised. (Isaiah, IX, 20)[63]

Amongst the more prominent functions envisaged by Comenius for educators at this level were two specific processes of reform, both of which were concerned with the promotion of peace and understanding between all men. The first was the promotion of religious tolerance through the active pursuit of ecumenical ideals—a need acutely felt in the aftermath of the religious wars of the sixteenth and seventeenth centuries. The second was the promotion of more harmonious relations between the peoples and nations of the world through the fostering of the spiritual and cultural values he considered essential for the attainment of genuine and lasting peace. Each will be discussed in some detail in the two remaining sections of this chapter.

3. EDUCATION AND ECUMENICITY

At the time of writing, the news media carry reports almost on a daily basis of intersectarian conflict in various places throughout the world, most prominently, Northern Ireland, the Middle East, Nagorno-Karabakh, and various provinces of the former state of Yugoslavia. More than three thousand people have died violently in the conflict between Protestant and Catholic communities in Northern Ireland since the latest phase of sectarian conflict began there in the late 1960s. The long-standing divisions between Muslims and Jews in Palestine continues, as it has for over one hundred years, despite various attempts to bring about peace, and it seems certain to lead to prolonged instability in the region, despite slowly emerging proposals for a political solution, involving the creation of a semi-autonomous Palestinian state. Christians and Muslims are locked in embittered conflict in Nagorno-Karabakh, a Christian enclave in the predominantly Islamic state of Azerbaijan. This conflict has also cost thousands of lives and seems set to continue for years to come. The world has been horrified by the deadly encounters occurring between Orthodox Christians, Catholics and Muslims in Bosnia, Serbia and Croatia since the breakup of the federation of Yugoslavia in the late 1980s. The country has seen some of the most barbaric atrocities that have occurred in Europe since the horrors of the Nazi regime of more than forty years ago.

These are merely some contemporary instances of the evils and long-
term consequences of religious bigotry and intolerance—consequences of
which Comenius warned repeatedly in his writings more than three
centuries ago. The problem remains as acute and intractable now as it
was in the aftermath of the religious wars of the post-Reformation period
and still requires radical initiatives of the kind that Comenius proposed
if its corrupting influence is ever to be healed. It will be recalled from a
brief discussion of this issue in an earlier chapter that the ideal of religious
tolerance was central to the teachings of the Moravian movement and was
defended to the point where Comenius urged his followers that its promotion was more important even than the survival of the Unitas Fratrum
itself. Exemplification of the virtues of fellowship and brotherhood were
considered the mark of the genuine Christian by the Moravians and
denominational rivalry was seen as being profoundly in conflict with
this. Uniquely among Christian denominations, they placed the ideal of
brotherhood, tolerance and charity even above their own future as a
religious communion, a position greatly facilitated by the non-dogmatic
character of their teachings. As one historian has written: 'The aim of
Church Unity was so deeply held to, that it was affirmed that Moravian
existence as a separate body must disappear in the interests of the wider
unity of the people of God.'[64]

The Moravian Brethren, like the Tolstoyan communities two centuries
later, saw sectarian intolerance as a virulent corruption of the essential
teachings of Christ and saw theological doctrine as being wholly subordinate to their overruling commitment to brotherly love. In their eyes,
many Christian communities had failed this most basic test of the sincerity
of their faith, and they saw dogmatism and theological rationalism as
having much to do with this. In the movement's non-dogmatic and
unambiguous defence of the simple truths of scripture Comenius saw a
model for the promotion of religious tolerance on a global scale. As a
Czech historian, Jiřina Popelová, has written: 'Some domestic solutions
to human affairs filled Comenius with pride, and throughout his life
served him as an example for a universal arrangement of things. This
applies to religious tolerance, whose model Comenius found in the so-
called Czech Confession, which was an arrangement on settling religious
conditions in Bohemia and which he contrasted with the German
Confession, i.e. with the Augsburg Confession, whose principle "cuius
regio eius religio" was condemned by Comenius as being forcible and
conscience oppressing.'[65] That the law of love was the motivating force
in all his own activities is clearly evident from this passage in the *Unum
Necessarium*:

> I have said that all the endeavours of my life hitherto were similar
> to the care of Martha for the Lord and his disciples; motivated by

love, indeed, for I am not conscious of anything to the contrary. For cursed be every hour and every moment of whatever labour spent on anything else! That includes, according to my conviction, even those things about which some accused me of innovations. Thus, for instance, it includes my didactic labours, to which I have devoted myself and to which I have given many years [of work], desiring to free the school and young people from very difficult labyrinths. But despite that, some supposed that it did not comport with my theological profession, as if Christ had not connected the two things: 'Feed my sheep, and feed my lambs,' entrusting both to his beloved Peter. But I render my grateful thanks to my eternal love—Christ—who inspired my heart with this love for his lambs, and allowed me to bring the matter as far as it had been brought . . . and although these [my] counsels have not hitherto been heard and schools have not ceased to wander in their labyrinths, still I hope and firmly expect from my God that they all will be utilised in accordance with my request when the winter of the Church is past, the rain is over and gone, the flowers appear on the earth, and the time of grafting the trees has come (Song of Solomon 2). And God shall give his flock shepherds according to his own heart, who shall not feed themselves but the flock of the Lord.[66]

Comenius's reference to his didactic labours in this passage clearly includes his efforts to turn the Churches towards ecumenicity—a process he saw as essentially educational, its concern being to re-educate believers in the simple truths of scriptural Christianity. As was earlier intimated, he attributed much of the dissension between the Churches to the rationalistic and abstract character of their interpretations of the scripture text. Writing about the need for religious renewal on the part of all the Christian Churches in *Haggaeus Redivivus*, he urged them to abandon 'theological quarrelsomeness' and strive to rediscover the fundamentals of Christ's teaching.[67] That message is repeated in *The Bequest of the Unity of Brethren* and is the cornerstone of his appeal in that work to all the Churches to sink their differences and commit themselves in a spirit of love to the reaffirmation of the *essentials* of Christ's teachings:

To all Christian Churches together I bequeath lively desire for unanimity of opinion and for reconciliation among themselves, and for union in faith, and love of the unity of spirit. May the spirit which was given me from the very beginning by the Father of spirits be shed upon you all, so that you would desire as sincerely as I did the union of all who call upon the name of Christ in truth! And may God give you wisdom to discern the distinction between the things fundamental, instrumental and accidental, as He gave me to perceive. For then ye all would know what things are or are not worthy of zeal, and which are worthy of greater or less zeal, so that ye would avoid all zeal which is without knowledge, and brings no edification, but rather destruction to the Church. On the other hand, that ye may know where to show the fiercest zeal, so that for the glory of God ye may be ready in your fierce zeal to lay down your lives! O, that ye may all be truly desirous of the genuine experience of God's mercy, and the true participation in the merits of Christ, and the genuine experience of the most sweet inward gifts of the Spirit which are attained through a true faith, true love, and a true trust in God, for in these the essence of Christianity is to be found! . . . . Furthermore, I wish that all ye who count yourselves members of the one house of the Church might also form a single house of God which would be well ordered and united, and in it one single household living under one single law of God, helping each member in concord and love. For as the body has many members, yet each serves the other to grow and increase in unity; so might the time come when the Christian Church and at the same time the angels might sing: 'Behold, how good and pleasant it is for brethren to dwell together in unity!'[68]

It was this search for the fundamentals of Christian teaching that Comenius considered the chief goal of ecumenicity. 'Every Christian should not look at him who teaches but at what he teaches and compare it with the scriptures,' he writes in *Haggaeus Redivivus*.[69] The true Christian follows the word of the scriptures in a spirit of faith, the faith that transcends reason, he declares through the medium of dramatic dialogue in *The Sorrowful*, a work written in the terrible aftermath of the defeat of the Moravian Protestants at the White Mountain in 1620.[70] In the opening section of the dialogue, Comenius, the Man of Sorrow, faces the personified characters of Reason and Faith and debates a dilemma long ago articulated in the Old Testament by Job: how evil appears to triumph despite the repeated scriptural affirmation of the omnipotence of God. Like Job, Comenius concludes that for the Christian believer the only response to this dilemma is to trust wholly in God's love ('I know that my Redeemer liveth, etc.')[71] He urges this kind of trust in God's love on the warring religious sects, seeing this as the only pathway to understanding and peace. 'God grant,' he writes in the *Bequest*, 'that all Thy sons may learn to pray with David: "Let simplicity and uprightness preserve me."'[72] In his Epilogue to *The History of Lasitius*, written in the midst of the devastation that followed the Peace of Westphalia of 1648, he urged the defeated Brethren to continue to give witness to their beliefs by showing charity and tolerance towards their co-religionists, despite the massive injustices they had sustained in the enforcement of the Peace.

(Roman Catholicism was declared the official religion of Bohemia and Moravian Protestants were denied the rights accorded reformist believers in the German states.) Christians, he says, are distinguished not by the intellectual sophistication of their teachings, but by the love, tolerance and understanding which inspires all their actions. 'Let us follow after the things which make for peace,' he cries:

> Now then, beloved brethren, let us not cease to be an example to our evangelical brethren, showing them that the perfection of the Gospel does not consist in the loftiness of the senses, or in the difference of questions and in the readiness to examine them this or that way, or as the holy father Hilarius says, God does not call us to heaven asking us smart questions, but moved by the holy love delivered unto us, which suffereth long, is kind, envieth not, vaunteth not itself, is not puffed up, does not behave unseemly, thinketh not evil, beareth all things, believeth all things, hopeth all things. (1. Cor. 13). And that it is more profitable to humbly know things than proudly know them, or fearfully believe than curiously assert or rebelliously resist and violently defend such imperfection of all of us, where we know only in part and prophesy in part (Ibid. V. 9). Let us show, that we believe in the Apostles' Creed, that, if a man is not content with the teaching which is according to godliness, he is proud, knowing nothing but doting about questions and contentious of words whereof cometh envy, strife, railings, evil surmisings etc. and again he is a man of God, who avoids such things and follows after righteousness, godliness, faith, love, patience, meekness (1. Tim. 6, 3, 4, 5, 11). If we believe so with all our heart, let us follow after the things which make for peace, and the things wherewith one may edify another with all that call on the Lord out of a pure heart. (1. Tim. 2, 22).[73]

Pointing to the radicality of Comenius's message of religious tolerance, Miroslav Hroch has written: 'The idyllic conditions of religious tolerance, many times upset, as known in Bohemia, was at that time in Europe an absolute exception and it is possible that just this fact (and life experience) made it difficult for many Bohemian educators to understand contemporary Europe.'[74] Any criticism of the dominant Roman Catholic Church was considered heresy in the Hapsburg dominated regions of Europe, and was usually punished accordingly. Comenius did not shirk the responsibility of criticising all the Churches for their betrayal of Christ's message, seeing this as a fundamental condition for the fostering of the ecumenical spirit and the first step in re-educating Christians on their responsiblity to show tolerance and charity in their dealings with each other. He did not refrain, for instance, from condemning the English and Scottish

Puritans for their fanaticism; though they belonged to a communion very close to his own, he criticised them severely for their intolerance and bigotry. In the *Bequest* he describes them as having made 'a sad and derogatory exhibition of themselves' and 'as having defamed Thy name among their fellows.'[75] His most impassioned criticism, however, is directed at the Roman Catholic Church—the Hapsburg Church that had cruelly and relentlessly persecuted the Bohemian Brethren. He called on it to repent of its misdeeds:

> Thou hast been our mother, but hast become a step-mother, yea, even a wild she-boar which licks the blood of her young ones. I wish thee that thou mayest recall thyself in thy old age and repent, and leave the Babylon of thy abominations. To which end I bequeath thee—if perchance it might aid thee—my own example of honouring God who remembered us in the days of our former backwardness, and leaving the darkness of thy idolatry, thou mayest follow the light of His Word.[76]

Reviewing the history of the Christian Churches on this whole issue, Comenius saw previous attempts at religious reform as having failed, largely because of the limited and partial nature of what was proposed. In the *Panorthosia* he writes: 'All the reformations of the Church up to the present time (originated by Wiclef, Hus, Luther, Calvin, Menno, Socinus, and even several times by the Pope) were just the first act of healing the blind man by Christ (Mark 8, 19.22. 23); now it is necessary to have a perfect and universal reformation, which would represent the second act of Christ's healing, by which the blind man was restored to sight, so that he saw everything clearly.' Only when a total renewal of institutional Christianity—guided by the teachings of scripture—is attempted, will unity and peace be in sight, he writes. 'Only then,' he declares, 'will come true the saying of the Song of Songs, "My dove is but one."'[77] He calls for a complete reform of all the Christian churches, such as had never been attempted before. For a seventeenth century Churchman, this was an extraordinarily enlightened and far-seeing vision, but one that was not destined to be taken truly seriously until more than three centuries after it was first given expression:

> We ask for a full reformation of the Churches; for such has never been before, although in the past centuries efforts have been made to reform the Christian Church, but only locally and diversely according to the various local conditions, without any universal idea or regard to it. For the Roman Pope and his faithful have several times tried to reform, but what? The order which lay in ruins, and manners. But it was only a superficial and mediocre thing and not

too useful, and it happened that everything had always fallen into a greater confusion than before. It was Hus who began his reform more ardently. But what did he reform? Principally the worldly government in the things spiritual. What about Luther? Mainly the doctrine regarding the justification by faith and what is connected with it, but he forgot all about the ecclesiastical discipline to be used as an antidote against the misuse of the teaching of the Gospel. What about his follower, Calvin? Mainly the article of the Lord's Supper and superstitious ceremonies left over by the papacy. Not even others who considered it to be their duty to try to do something for the reform of the condition of the church, did not set to work in any other way than that they endeavoured to purify some parts of religion. Up to the present time no reformation has been so complete as is expected by God (Isa. 26, 17).[78]

It might be objected that what Comenius proposed was impossibly idealistic for the conditions of seventeenth century Europe, and unlikely to be achieved even in the supposedly more favourable conditions of the present time, following the climate of ecumenical endeavour created by Vatican II. Comenius fully realised the enormity of the obstacles that lay in the way of Christian unity, but he saw the aspiration towards perfection as an essential manifestation of the spirit of faith, something intrinsic in its very nature, and therefore as an ideal to be striven for by every believing Christian. In the *Panorthosia* he declared: 'Suppose that, as some have recently written, Rome or Constantinople is irreconcilable, that Calvinism or Lutheranism (i.e. local teaching) is irreconcilable—yet Christianity shall not be irreconcilable, if Christ be the reconciler. He is the only one, he is the truth itself and he will not be able to disagree with himself; neither shall we who are connected with him in all points.'[79] It is in this spirit of total trust in Christ that he addressed his Admonition to the Churches, advising that they were obliged, by virtue of their common faith, to strive earnestly to bring about unity amongst their followers by every means at their disposal:

> Open your eyes, Christian people, and learn to know that except for the foundation of the unity there is no cohesion, for everything easily breaks down. In all things (of nature, handicraft and morals) the only basis of prosperity is unity. Every thing must relate to it, viz. the first and the last, the highest and the lowest, the right and the left. So that all be moved, if one of them is moved. According to this idea God created the earth and all individual things on earth; for example, the body of any animal or even of any plant whose all individual parts relate to, and are connected with, one another by means of uninterrupted ties. To this idea it is necessary

to reduce every society including the Church. For wherever there is multiplicity, there is confusion if the multiplicity is not made one by means of the order. If unity breaks up, there is no other possibility than that the multiplicity diffuses. For it is impossible for the multiplicity which is not connected with the bond of unity, not to fall into discord, from discord into strifes, and from strifes into perdition.[80]

The mechanism by which Comenius saw these ideals being realised was a body, similar in many ways to the College of Light, which would assume responsibility for the process of educational and institutional renewal necessary to create the conditions for Christian unity.[81] In the *Panorthosia* he envisages an 'Oecumenical Consistory' whose function it would be to bring the Churches together to explore the ways by which they could resolve their differences and unite around their common Christian heritage. 'It will be the task of the Oecumenical Consistory to ensure that all the bells of the horses and all the pots, etc., should be "Holiness unto the Lord" (Zechariah, XIV. 20) and that "There shall be no more utter destruction, but Jerusalem shall be safely inhabited. (V. 11)"'[82] The functions of the Consistory are set out in detail in Chapter XVIII of the *Panorthosia*. They consist mainly of the identification and propagation of the fundamental teachings of Christianity and the fostering of the spirit of tolerance and charity amongst all believers:

> It will be their duty to see that the ties between the soul and God remain undisturbed for all degrees and conditions of men and in all cases; that is to say, to see that the reign of Christ is preserved in the Church and that the communion of the faithful throughout the world is maintained and continued without reproach by the subordination of all the members of the Church to a single head, Christ. The consistory could as well be called a universal presbytery, the synedrion of the world, the vigils of Sion etc.
>   It will be their duty to pay attention to:
>   (i) Themselves, as those who lead others to piety;
>   (ii) Faith and piety themselves, that they may be ever more purified and infused throughout the Church;
>   (iii) Churches and all sacred gatherings, as workshops of piety;
>   (iv) The heads of the Church, as the guardians of piety;
>   (v) The art of painting the heavens and laying the foundations of the earth, and whether it is rightly used by all;
>   (vi) Sacred books, as the pillars of piety;
>   (vii) Those who write, distribute and use these books;
>   (viii) Acts of piety, the most glorious adornment of Christianity, particularly the virtue of charity;

(ix) The other two tribunals, as helpers in the Lord's work;
(x) Finally, the Holy Ghost, the inner teacher of piety, the only source of true enlightenment, the comforter who protects us for eternity.[83]

Education by example, a key Comenian pedagogic principle, is seen as a prominent function of the Consistory: 'Their primary task must be—since all who lead the Church in the name of Christ have been called the "light of the world" and the "salt of the earth"—to endeavour to become the leaders of the elect, the salt of salts and the light of lights; that is to say, to be pure and undefiled in all ways, holy and unblemished, true lambs and doves, the most pious of men. . . . '[84] He saw a particular responsibility for this body in the monitoring and supervision of the affairs of the different Churches, its main objective being to organise their activities in a spirit of active co-operation and to suppress any tendencies towards prejudice or judgemental behaviour in their dealings with their sister Churches. They will ensure, he writes 'that no man should be shocked by anything his fellow has done, should scorn him and turn aside from him, nor that he should judge others and excommunicate them from the Church, giving opportunity for schism.'[85] The Consistory, he suggests, should actively prevent tendencies towards dogmatism or authoritarianism on the part of any of its member Churches, seeing the voluntary practice of faith as the hallmark of genuine Christianity, its essence consisting in the freedom of individual conscience. 'This aim will be achieved,' he writes, 'by allowing the whole garden of the Church to blossom with voluntary piety without coercion, that is to say without the key of priestly discipline, as far as possible; if this is not possible, then by means of the key.'[86] A particularly significant feature of the whole proposal is its clear separation of the functions of Church and State. Comenius insists that no laws be promulgated which would either duplicate, or be in conflict with, those made by the civil authorities. He also urges that Church laws be defined only after a consensus is reached by the entire Consistory:

> They will give their earnest attention to see that no partial ecclesiastical rules come into being side by side with the secular, and against them, for this would offer opportunity for dissent and schism. If a Church or an ecclesiastical teacher observes something useful, let him put it before the Consistory for their opinion, first the Consistory at home, national; and then, if it is a matter of greater difficulty, the World Consistory. If they see the thing is good, they will give their approval, and the matter will gain greater weight and usefulness than if it has been tested only by private opinion. The sum of this recommendation is this: apostolic approval should be treated as sacrosanct, that the spirit of the prophets are subject to

the prophets (1 Corinthians, XIV. 32); and no thought, opinion, habit or custom should be the private property of any individual, but all things should be public and universal; that the garment of Christ (which is the outer and inner form of his Church) be without seam, woven from the top throughout.[87]

Comenius's Consistory of the Churches, like the projected College of Light, has never been realised. The World Council of Churches, founded in the present century, is the nearest attempt that has been made to bring Christians together through a worldwide organisation. Its agenda, however, was much narrower than that proposed by Comenius and the refusal of one of the largest communions, the Roman Catholic Church, to participate, has rendered it largely ineffectual as an agency for Christian unity. In any event, the establishment of such a world-wide body was only one means that Comenius foresaw for the promotion of the values of ecumenicity. To a large extent, he saw these being achieved through the kind of non-formal, life-related education that was described in the opening section of this chapter. Furthermore, he saw the promotion of the goal of religious tolerance and brotherhood as part of a much wider process: the resolution of conflict and the promotion of harmony and peace in *all* the affairs of mankind. In the *Unum Necessarium* he saw the obstinacy of his fellow Christians in the face of his pleas to sink their differences on matters of faith as merely a symptom of the deeper propensity towards conflict inherent in man's nature:

> This obstinacy of Christians one to another, and the hitherto vain efforts of various men to reconcile them, caused me to consider and to hope that it would be easier to heal the whole than the part; to give the whole body a common medicine, than to apply a plaster only to the head or the foot, or the side. That is, I began to concentrate my desire upon an endeavour to reconcile the whole human race (which is out of harmony with things, with each other, and with God) and to seek ways and means how to accomplish this project.[88]

The goal of ecumenicity would have to be pursued therefore in the context of an all-embracing quest for peace amongst men, involving every facet of their lives. This would require a radical renewal of political, social and moral, as well as religious, values—a total and all-inclusive peace process—such as the Unitas Fratrum had sought continuously to bring about in the five centuries of its existence. The nature of this whole process will be explored in the forthcoming section.

If we regard Christianity, in the sense of its founder, as a religion of love, we are faced with the problem how to understand that Christians, Churches and States have for centuries, for nearly two thousand years, preached the love and charity enjoined by Christ but have little observed them in practical life. Thus the violence done to Hus and his martyr's death became the starting-point of the Hussite wars and the religious wars of Europe. This terrible experience soon aroused amongst us a campaign against war. The most consistent champion of war against war was Chelčický, the founder of the Church of the Czech Brethren, or, as it is called in England and America, the Moravian Church. Comenius adopted, in modified form, Chelčický's idea of absolute non-resistance to evil. He therefore proclaimed the idea of ever-enduring peace. . . . In practice this effort meant love and devotion to one's own nation and language and at the same time love and charity towards all other nations. Comenius himself provides a splendid example of how it is possible to harmonise nationality and international sentiment. Exiled from his native land under the policy of vengeance pursued by the Hapsburgs, he wandered from country to country and gained for his cause and for his nation the sympathies of those countries, not by mere political propaganda, but by the fact that he worked in all and for all.[89]

So wrote Thomas G. Masaryk, the first President of Czechoslovakia, in a tribute delivered in 1928 to 'commemorate the tricentenary of the departure of J.A. Komenský (Comenius) from his native country.' Masaryk's words were reechoed by Edward Beneš, his successor as President in 1942. 'Komenský,' Beneš wrote, 'had a premonitory apprehension of peace ideals far beyond his time; through his universal genius he had a European and a world consciousness even in the first half of the seventeenth century. In spite of his burning Czech patriotism he was always a good European and a man whose sympathies were world-embracing.'[90] At a UNESCO Conference held in Delhi in 1956 Comenius was described as 'one of the first proponents of the ideas that have inspired UNESCO since its founding,'[91] and a year later at the World Peace Council he was eulogised for giving expression to 'ideas of peace and human brotherhood which have enriched the cultural heritage of all mankind.'[92]

These are some indications of the significance accorded to Comenius's writings on the subject of peace and of the continuing relevance of his personal witness to its pursuit as a practical manifestation of his Christian faith. Significantly, both Masaryk and Beneš drew attention to the origins of Comenius's pacifist beliefs in the traditions of Moravian Christianity.

Masaryk saw him as being imbued with the spirit of Chelčický's teaching on non-resistance to evil, though in a less absolute form than Chelčický had conceived it. Beneš similarly describes him as being in the same mould as 'the great national philosopher, Petr Chelčický, who four centuries before Tolstoy gave expression to his ideas regarding universal peace, self-sacrifice and the religious life of the individual and the nation.'[93] Ernest Barker, in a political analysis of the contemporary relevance of these ideals, spoke of Comenius as 'an extension as well as an expression of the native and original genius of the Bohemian Brethren.' He spoke of the Moravian pacifist tradition as embracing both the values of millenarianism and modernism. 'I cannot,' he writes, 'but celebrate its first figure, Petr Chelčický, a Tolstoy before Tolstoy and a Quaker before George Fox, the leader of the advanced reforming party among the Hussites in the latter half of the fifteenth century. By himself he might have led the Brethren whom he founded into a desert of millenarianism; but the Unitas Fratrum with the steady and solid sense inherent in the Czechs, and with a Czech gift for order and organisation, settled down into a middle way which reconciled the aspirations of millenarianism with the needs of modernism.'[94]

Throughout its history the Moravian Church gave witness faithfully and consistently to the pacifist ideals of scriptural Christianity. For 350 years its members practised complete pacifism, vigorously defending their right to refuse to participate in all military activity, whatever its cause or purpose. The first breach in this tradition—albeit a minor one—occurred in 1803 when some members felt obliged to join a popular militia to defend England against an expected Napoleonic invasion. Their action was condemned by the elders of the Church and an Act of Parliament of July 24, 1803 upheld the right of members to exemption from military service. Their teachings on this issue were tested once again during the American Civil War when members, both North and South, felt themselves obliged to support the national cause—again, with extreme reluctance—on the grounds that they had a responsibility to uphold the laws of the State. The First World War saw some members joining both the British and German armed forces—on the same grounds of discharging their duty towards the State—though by this stage their Church treated the issue as a matter for individual conscience, while still insisting on the inherently pacifist character of Christian teaching as enunciated in scripture.[95]

Comenius's writings reflect both the consistency and the complexity of Moravian tradition on this issue. Throughout his life he insisted that pacifism is inherent in the message of the scriptures, particularly in the Sermon on the Mount as recounted in the Gospel of St. Matthew. The passages from the *Labyrinth* in which he condemned violence and denounced the whole institution of soldiery were considered briefly in an earlier chapter. 'It is monstrous,' he declared, 'to wear a coat of mail over a surplice, a helmet over a barret, to hold the word of God in one hand, a sword in the other; to carry Peter's keys in front and Judas's wallet behind.'[96] The work evokes the horror and barbarism of war, denouncing its whole culture of death and destruction. Yet, as Miroslav Hroch has shown, Comenius faced some major personal dilemmas on this issue when he found himself welcoming the support of friendly Protestant nations for the defence of his fellow-countrymen in the face of the massive persecution they had to endure in the period of the Thirty Years' War and later. On this whole matter, he says, 'Comenius's position was full of conflict. He was a sincere pacifistic Christian whose innermost human interest made him a war agitator. He was a patriot, who was forced to look for a replacement for his lost country. These constant clashes of principle and reality had already made it impossible to approach the world other—after all—than as a labyrinth.'[97] While insisting on the fundamental truth of the Christian injunction towards non-violence as articulated in the scriptures, Comenius recognised the huge difficulties of adhering to this in practice and simply encouraged his followers to trust wholly in God's grace in their efforts to follow this most demanding of all of Christ's teachings. This is the message of Chapter 48 of the *Labyrinth*, entitled 'The Godly Have Peace on all Sides':

> Therefore neither the desire for anything nor the loss of anything causes the true Christian suffering. If someone smites him on the right cheek, he cheerfully turns to him the other one also. And if one disputes with him about his cloak, he lets him have his coat also. He leaves everything to God, his witness and judge, and feels assured that all these things will, in the course of time, be revised, amended, and at last justly decided.[98]

It is instructive to compare Comenius's position on this issue with that of one of his chief religious and philosophical mentors, Desiderius Erasmus. Both men questioned the moral validity of the long-standing Church doctrine of the just war. Traditionally, the teaching had been that war is just if its objective is the defence of a just cause and the eventual restoration of peace. Generally, the doctrine required the minimum employment of force and the humane treatment of the victims of the conflict. In reality, as Erasmus argues in *The Complaint of Peace*, both sides in a war regard their cause as just and consequently no absolute criteria can be applied to determine where the balance of moral validity lies. Like Comenius, he condemned the Churches for associating themselves so closely throughout their history with the conduct of war. This passage from the *Complaint* is close to the spirit of the *Labyrinth* in

its impassioned condemnation of war and of the leading role played by
Christians in supporting it throughout their history. The personified
figure of Peace speaks of the profound contradiction underlying the behaviour of a Christian engaging in violent conflict for supposedly moral ends:

> How can it be consistent to salute the people with the words 'Peace
> be with you' and at the same time to be exciting the whole world
> to bloody war—with the lips to speak peace and with the hand, and
> every power of action, to be urging on havoc? Dare you describe
> Christ as a reconciler, a Prince of Peace, and yet palliate or com-
> mend war with the same tongue? Which, in truth, is nothing less
> than to sound the trumpet before Christ and Satan at the same
> time. Do you presume, reverend sir, with your hood and surplice
> on, to stimulate the simple, inoffensive people to war, when they
> come to church expecting to hear from your mouth the gospel of
> peace? Are you not apprehensive lest what was said by those who
> announced the coming of Christ, 'How beautiful are the feet of
> him that bringeth glad tidings of peace; who bringeth tidings of
> good, who bringeth tidings of salvation!' should be reversed, and
> addressed to you in this manner: 'How foul is the tongue of priests
> exhorting to war, inciting to evil, and urging men to destruction.'
> Think of the incongruous idea, a bloody priest! . . .
>   Chaplains follow the army to the field of battle; bishops preside
> in the camp, and, abandoning their churches, enlist in the service
> of Bellona. . . . The unfeeling mercenary soldier, hired by a few
> pieces of paltry coin to do the work of a man-butcher, carries
> before him the standard of the Cross; and that very figure becomes
> the symbol of war, which alone ought to teach everyone that looks
> at it, that war ought to be utterly abolished. What hast thou to do
> with the Cross of Christ on thy banners, thou blood-stained soldier?
> With such a disposition as thine; with deeds like thine, of robbery
> and murder, thy proper standard would be a dragon, a tiger, or a
> wolf. That Cross is the standard of him who conquered, not by
> fighting, but by dying; who came, not to destroy men's lives, but
> to save them.[99]

'There is scarcely any peace so unjust but it is preferable, upon the
whole, to the justest war,' Erasmus declares at a later point in this work.
Addressing the question of how peace is to be maintained, he responds
at two levels. Firstly, he affirms the primary importance of faith and
trust in God's grace; secondly, he affirms the necessity of individual self-
reform as a condition for social and political reform 'How then is peace
to be secured?' he asks. 'It is from the corrupt passions of the human
heart that the tumults of war arise,' he says. 'Firm and permanent peace

is not to be secured,' he writes, 'by marrying one royal family to another, nor by treaties and alliances made between such deceitful and imperfect creatures as men. . . . No, the fountains from which the stream of this evil flow must be cleansed.'[100] This is the same message as that conveyed by the Pilgrim in the *Labyrinth*. He speaks eloquently at the end of that work of the peace that comes from a life lived in accordance with the teachings of Christ—the 'peace that passeth understanding': 'The godly have not only simple peace within them, but also joy and pleasure, which flow to their hearts from the presence and feeling of God's love.' He speaks of the inner peace that is made possible by the self-purifying power of grace: 'This is that sweetness that the world understandeth not; this that sweetness that he who once tasted it strives for at any risk; this that sweetness from which no other sweetness can separate us, no bitterness drive us away, and from which no bitterness, not even death, can turn us away.'[101] This same theme is reiterated in the sections of the *Via Lucis* where Comenius puts forward his proposals for a world forum of nations that would create the conditions for international peace. The following passage is from the section of the penultimate chapter where he unfolds his vision of world harmony and order achieved through moral and spiritual reform. The pursuit of peace, he says, must begin with the individual and the community before it can be extended into the relations of peoples and nations:

> Means ought to be in just proportion to their ends; and we must not expect that a great thing will be had at a small cost. A large harvest demands a larger number of reapers, and of sickles, many granaries and enough time for the work. . . . If they have in their hands the instruments of harmony as their sickles, and bestow the proper diligence each one upon his own place, then what we see at the time of the corn harvest in all lands, will with God's help be brought to pass—within a few days we shall see the fields reaped, and the barns filled and the desires of the farmers satisfied. Just as in a great city, if before some festival the Head of every family see to it that his own house and the part of the street which fronts it is swept out, the whole city in a single day is, as we know, cleansed and made bright; so if every man who has been brightened by the divine light does his duty among his own folk and among his neighbours—and this we cannot see anywhere now, or if it is done at all it scarcely begins to be evident anywhere—then the waste places will be turned into gardens of God, as the divine oracles foretell.[102]

Side by side with his insistence on faith and individual self-reform as the conditions for the advancement of peace, Comenius recognised the need for just laws to guarantee that it is properly maintained. In his essay,

'Jurisprudence in Comenius's Times' Valentin Urfus has emphasised
Comenius's links with the great philosopher of law, his fellow Puritan,
Hugo Grotius. He points to strong similarities in their background and
beliefs: 'They both were torn out of their original milieu, they both spent
large parts of their lives as uprooted exiles, and both moved in almost the
same geographical and political regions. These are not the only parallels,
and other points of contact exist: their close religious positions, their
deep and resolute inward personal convictions, and finally the fact that
despite different social background and social status, they both belonged
to late humanistic and topically humanitarianism-oriented intelligentsia.'[103]
Comenius wholly approved of Grotius's insistence that civil law be
founded on the principles of morality inherent in the natural law, as is
evident in his writings on the creation of a new world order. Urfus
explains:

> Like Comenius, Grotius was ahead of his time, and exceeded his
> subjective intentions. His work revealed new horizons beyond which
> it was possible to regard law in a different way than previously, as a
> phenomenon determined by the human naturalness which—as
> Grotius emphasised—forces man to be sociable. Therefore the law
> which asserts itself in this sociability is necessarily a law that can be
> comprehended and determined by reason. . . .
>   Existing literature has shown that Comenius had some knowl-
> edge of jurisprudence and its roots dating back to the mediaeval
> adaptation of Roman law. His knowledge was not knowledge in the
> specialised sense of the term. In a number of passages in his works,
> he has critical observations about jurisprudence, some going as far
> as rejecting it. This is undoubtedly an expression of the utopian
> aspects of Comenius's thinking. His approach is not too different in
> those places where he writes in a positive way about law and juris-
> prudence. Like other Utopians, he is trying to formulate—often with
> excessive attention to details—ideal rules by which interhuman
> relationships should be guided. It is certainly possible to agree with
> those who stress that in Comenius's works, this reform-oriented
> complex of various principles goes hand in hand with his belief
> that there would be only minimum law in society.[104]

As the passage suggests, Comenius's concept of justice reached much
further than the narrow confines of the enforcement of law, however
humanely the latter was conceived. Clearly recognising that the origins
of violence are to be traced to social injustice and inequity, he called
repeatedly for radical social reform as a condition for the promotion of
peace. In *The Angel of Peace* where he addressed the Dutch and English
super-powers at the Breda Conference—urging them to end their war-

making and to consider terms for the conclusion of peace—he spoke of the need to re-appropriate material wealth amongst their poverty-stricken subjects, both at home and in their colonies abroad, as a condition for the creation of lasting peace. He urged them to provide for the educational, social and material needs of those whom they had 'mercilessly exploited for material gain.'[105] On another occasion he addressed a pamphlet to the people of Leszno, condemning the practice of isolating those stricken by fever from normal society. It was customary at the time to drive victims of plague from their homes, forcing them to spend their last days in the forests and mountains, ostracised from their communities. Comenius called on the citizens of Leszno to end this practice and to respond to the plight of their fellowmen in a spirit of Christian compassion and brotherly love. (The prejudice experienced by these plague stricken victims has been compared by one historian to that directed at AIDS sufferers at the present time.)[106] In his pamphlet Comenius said:

> We have seen how the inhabitants behave towards those people who were struck by the plague as God's visitation. And since we regarded this to be too serious and at variance with the Word of God, and too different from the way we behave towards such persons, some of us spoke out against it, expressing our views of the matter and pointing out our customs. . . . But when the sick, with boils and sores, are treated worse than criminals, is it the right conduct? No, it is nothing but cruelty, because criminals are kept warm, given food and drink, allowed to receive visitors who talk to them and can even do something for them; their offences are carefully considered, as is the punishment they deserve. Criminals are permitted to defend themselves, and are allowed to prove their innocence. Priests may visit criminals, serve their needs and be with them at the time of death. Is it right to give harsher treatment to good people, pious, who have done no wrong but who, served God and the community well, and lived in honesty? Is it right to drive them away or to confine them, to mistreat them by hunger, thirst and cold, not to permit doctors, priests and servants to visit them, and to drive away all who would visit them or nurse them? And thus this brief report on the pestilence should make it clear to all that when we Czechs care for the people stricken by the plague in a Christian manner, and when we tend to their needs, we are not guilty of any unseemly audacity or recklessness. Therefore we ask you all, dear Christians and brothers, not to abhor us for our deeds of mercy which we do for plague-stricken people, thus offending not only us but even more God.[107]

He recognised that all this would require radical changes in attitudes towards the poor and oppressed in all societies. The fostering of such attitudes would be one of the aims of the process of life-long education that was described earlier in this chapter. Comenius saw a further role, however, for a world-wide forum of peace-makers, comparable in its aims and structure to the College of Light and the Oecumenical Consistory. Such a body, he said, would seek to heal the divisions created by militant nationalism; it would seek to promote the spirit of peace amongst all nations, propagating the virtues of brotherhood, advancing the rule of law, and striving to eliminate injustice everywhere. Its functions are set out in the following passage from the *Panorthosia*:

> It will be their task to watch over human wisdom in governing themselves through all degrees and conditions, or even cases (which may happen) to maintain undisturbed human society with all its business, on all sides. In other words, to lead the propagation of justice and peace from nation to nation all over the world. It could be called the Directorate of the powers of the world, the Senate of the earth, or the Areopagus of the world; the directors themselves could be best called the Eirenarchs of the kingdoms (the supreme arbiters of peace); Cicero called the Roman Senate *orbis terrae consilium*, but the name would be more appropriate for the Dicastery of the world.
>
> Going into greater detail, their tasks will be to pay strict attention to:
>   (i) Themselves, as the criterion and example of justice;
>   (ii) Justice itself, in all ranks of human society;
>   (iii) In particular the courts of justice and institutions of government, as the seat of justice;
>   (iv) Judges, as the priests of justice;
>   (v) The juridical procedure employed by this man or that;
>   (vi) The laws of the books setting out the law;
>   (vii) The interpreters of the laws, the commentators or notaries;
>   (viii) Measures, weights, coins, public ways etc. as instruments of public equity and security;
>   (ix) The other two tribunals, as helpers in guarding order;
>   (x) Finally God Himself, the eternal defender of justice.[108]

In addition to its legal and organisational functions, Comenius also envisaged an explicitly educational role for the Dicastery in the promotion of peace. Again he emphasises the importance of teaching by example. In the *Panorthosia* he writes: 'Their first duty will be to be themselves first and foremost such as they are to teach others to be: just on all sides, peace-loving, pleasant, loyal; a true bond binding human society, true magnets drawing all men and all things to the pole of peace, living columns and supports of all order in the human race.'[109] Side by side with this, he urged them to seek actively to resolve conflict wherever it occurred until all war should have ceased and the Christian vision of harmony would be fulfilled:

> But it will not be enough for them to set an example of adamantine loyalty and to instil the love for it unto all other men; they must pay attention to the way the counsels of peace are universally followed. Thus they will be the foremost defenders of the common weal, to prevent wars, tumults and bloodshed from returning, or the occasion for them; that all such things should rather be buried in eternal oblivion. Standing thus on the look-out they will not stand watch only over the peace of one nation, or each only over his own, but over the peace of the whole world, building eternal barriers to war everywhere, that before the world comes to an end the primeval state of the world may return, peaceful in all ways, as Christ (Luke, XVII 26.27) and the Apostle (I Thessalonians, V. 3) prophesied.[110]

As the passage indicates, the creation of truly liberal democracies, the promotion of justice, equality and freedom, would always remain central to the promotion of lasting peace. A Czech historian, Jaroslav Pánek, sees this as the essence of Comenius's message to the modern world: 'After a life filled with disillusionment, he offered to mankind an optimistic prospect towards peace and unity through a democratic system of inter-human relations and equality of nations. This prospect, which by far transcended Comenius's own times, has lost nothing of its attraction even at the threshold of the third millennium.'[111]

VIII

CONCLUSION:
COMENIUS IN PERSPECTIVE

The unity and integrity of Comenius's educational thought has been emphasised repeatedly throughout this work. It remains now to reaffirm the degree to which this derived from the liberal Christian faith that informed all his activities from his childhood in Moravia to his last years as an exile in Amsterdam in the closing decades of the seventeenth century. He was first and foremost an ardent disciple of the teachings of Christ, deriving his understanding of the aims and purposes of human life and all its activities from the Christian celebration of the uniqueness and freedom of the individual person. He saw this attested in its purity only in the Christian scriptures and these consequently became the focus of all his thoughts and activities, being the ultimate reference point from which all his beliefs and ideas were validated and confirmed. From this primary affirmation of the uniqueness and freedom of the individual person emerged his belief in the necessity for universal education and his corresponding affirmation of the need for the radical pedagogic, curricular and institutional reforms he considered essential to make it a practical and realisable goal. From this same source sprang both his conviction that education should be conceived as a life-long process and his sense of the importance of its non-formal as well as its conventional modes to ensure the realisation of the ideal of a full and balanced education for all. From this also derived his call for a liberal balancing of academic, scholarly and professional activities in the sphere of higher learning, side by side with his pleas for the advancement of knowledge in conditions that would ensure the meaningful integration of all its secular and spiritual modes. From his Christian convictions finally there emerged a radical reconception of the potentiality of education to bring about fundamental social reforms, especially in the spheres of justice, tolerance and peace—the implications of which have acquired particular urgency in the conditions and circumstances of the present age.

The Christian spirit that informs his writings could be described as simultaneously 'liberal' and 'radical'. The term 'liberal' is used, quite simply, to signify a profound commitment to the promotion and enhancement of individual freedom. It is used to signify a 'freedom for' rather than a 'freedom from'. The term is not used in its classical connotation as indicating a freedom attained primarily through the development of intellectual potentiality, nor in the empiricist sense of a freedom signifying release from external restriction or authority. It is used to indicate a freedom manifested in the wholeness of being, a freedom seen not as a goal in itself, but as the means to the realisation of what this wholeness implies. Freedom, Comenius believed, is fulfilled through altruism, brotherhood and love, through selfless devotion to the service of mankind and thereby to the service of God. Reasserting this as the central message of Christ, he emphasised the primacy of conscience as the sole arbiter of the rightness or wrongness of all thought and action and the primary existential manifestation of the freedom inherent in man's nature. He stressed the obligation on every individual to exercise responsibility in accordance solely with the dictates of conscience, i.e. a conscience informed and illuminated by the ultimate authority that exists on all matters of Christian belief: the words of Christ himself as recorded in the scriptures.

His radicalism consists in his reassertion of the original Christian message as one profoundly concerned not only with the promotion of individual freedom but also with the closely related ideals of tolerance, justice and peace. Seeing these aspects of Christian teaching as having been severely distorted by the sectarian institutions claiming their roots in scriptural Christianity, he sought to reaffirm the radical manner in which they were enunciated by Christ himself and the apostles. He warned repeatedly of the evils of religious dogmatism, bigotry and intolerance, having himself witnessed some of its most horrific manifestations in the events of the Thirty Years' War. Seeing sectarian conflict as a virulent corruption of the essential message of the scriptures, he insisted theological doctrine be subordinated always to the promptings of individual conscience, illuminated only by the words of the scriptures. He called for nothing less than a universal reformation of the Christian Churches—a far more wide-ranging reformation than was advocated by Wycliff, Hus or Luther—insisting the Churches had failed through fifteen centuries of history to promote the simple teachings enunciated by Christ and recorded in the Gospels.

His Christianity was radical in two further senses: its inherent pacifism and its concern for the implementation of the Gospel teachings on justice and social reform. The Churches' advocacy of, and active support for, violence and war throughout its history was seen by Comenius as a further manifestation of its corruption of the original teachings of Christ. The doctrine of non-resistance to evil espoused by the Moravian movement was a reassertion of this teaching and, despite some exceptions—including some well documented deviations from this teaching by Comenius himself—was adhered to faithfully by the members of the Church throughout five centuries of its existence. Comenius, like his predecessors in the Moravian movement, recognised the inherent contradictions of the just war theology and urged his followers to abide by the Gospel injunction not to resist evil, trusting in God's grace to enable them to live in accordance with Christ's message of peace. The key to its achievement, he insisted, is the inner peace that comes from penitence, humility and prayer, together with faith in the infinity of God's love and in its limitless potentiality for the transformation of a fallen mankind. Seeing that violence derives in most instances from injustice and inequity, he considered the pursuit of social reform an essential condition also for the creation of peace. Thus he urged the equitable distribution of material wealth, emphasised the importance of the community spirit and urged that radical changes in attitude be fostered towards the poor and oppressed in all societies—seeing all this as an authentic manifestation of the practice of Christian love. Social reform, he insisted, begins with the spiritual transformation of the individual person and is achieved primarily, not through political or revolutionary change, but through faith, penitence, humility and the practice of active love.

Given the centrality of Christianity in his educational thought, it was entirely appropriate that he should emphasise the need to integrate all aspects of the educational process around the basic principles of the Christian faith. All modes of learning, he said, should be illuminated by religious and moral concerns, the conjuncture of knowledge, virtue and piety being the cornerstone of the whole process. All would have to be subordinated to an overriding commitment to the ethico–religious formation of the individual person. Comenius, however, saw the concept of education as the means to ethico–religious formation as carrying a corresponding obligation to make the whole process accessible to every individual, regardless of social origin, family background, intellectual ability or religious creed. In the Christian affirmation of the uniqueness of every man and the sanctity of all human life he recognised a corresponding commitment to the cause of universal education, i.e. the provision of the means to the attainment of wisdom for all and the radical renewal of the pedagogic, curricular and institutional processes necessary to make this a realisable prospect, not merely a naive and utopian dream.

'He was the first great democrat among educational thinkers,' declared Edward Beneš[1], the President of Czechoslovakia immediately before the years of communist rule. Oskar Kokoschka, the Austrian born painter with close ties to Czechoslovakia, pointed to the specifically Christian character of Comenius's democratic beliefs.[2] (Kokoschka painted an inspiring portrait of Comenius, showing him, together with President T.G. Masaryk, as jointly symbolising the independent spirit of the Bohemian people.) In a commemorative essay on Comenius, he wrote: 'Although arguments of an unmistakable, if crude scientific materialism were already heard, most of his contemporaries believed with Comenius in religion as revealed to all human beings, the consequence of which is the essential equality of men. The existing order, outlasting its time had come into opposition, in Protestant and Catholic countries alike, with this Christian principle of the human dignity of the individual.'³ Kokoschka spoke of Comenius's revivification of the Gospel teachings on equality fifteen centuries after they were first enunciated and, significantly, spoke of the unfulfilled nature of this vision even by the middle of the twentieth century: 'Three centuries later the world still suffers misery and chaos,' he wrote, 'because Comenius, the man with the message of universal brotherhood in knowledge and love, failed.' 'To-day,' he declared, 'we need more than ever the faith of Comenius in the talents latent in man.'⁴

The liberal-Christian character of Comenius's vision of democratic education is vividly conveyed in these words of Kokoschka's. He points to the Christian view of education, in the terms in which Comenius conceived it, as one which is intrinsically radical and egalitarian. All men, Comenius declared, deserve access to the way of light, to the wisdom comprehending both reason and faith that leads to God. He denounced ignorance as the darkness of man's unawareness of his destiny. 'He who knows not that he is ill cannot heal himself,' he cried.⁵ All men, he declared, have the inborn potentiality for light, for the wisdom that comes from knowledge and faith. All, he insisted, are educable. But crucially, he saw the innate capacity for knowing as an undeveloped potency, requiring appropriate pedagogic fostering for its mature development. The ideal of universal education could be realised only through pedagogic, curricular and institutional reforms sufficiently radical to accommodate the great diversity of learning needs amongst those unlearned masses whom he sought to give access to its rewards.

At the heart of Comenius's proposals for pedagogic reform lies the doctrine of 'learning through experience.' This also is the issue on which his writings have been most frequently misrepresented and misunderstood, particularly by pragmatists and Marxists from whom his work has received most consistent attention in the present century. Man, he says, is 'naturally a learning being,'⁶ possessing within his own nature all the resources necessary for the attainment of wisdom. The image of the seed, growing towards maturity from its own innate resources, was his favourite metaphor for this whole process. All knowledge, he insisted, begins with sense perception—'nothing exists in the mind that has not previously existed in the senses.'⁷ Learning, he argued, must be fostered initially through the medium of multi-sensory experience and appropriate pedagogic strategies must be designed to achieve this. It must be allowed to proceed by way of direct observation, experiment and the spontaneous powers of discovery and enquiry that are present in every child from birth. But he ultimately saw learning and knowing as the perception of the order and harmony of all that exists and spoke of that order as comprehending the interrelated spheres of the material and the spiritual, the physical, hyperphysical and metaphysical realms of being— all constituting a unified and harmonious whole. The perception of the reality of each is the means, he said, to the perception of the other spheres to which it is inextricably linked. The perceptions of sense, he insisted, are the means to the perception of the realms of reality transcending the sensual and the material. He saw learning, therefore, as a progression from the finite to the infinite, from the material to the spiritual, from nature to God. The truths made known through sense immanently disclose the truths of the spirit, of the intemporal and the infinite. Empirical knowl- edge, he argued, is the gateway to the non-empirical, to the ultimate reality of the spiritual—all of which indicates a very different conception of the whole doctrine of learning through experience than the naturalistic version promoted both by pragmatist and Marxist thinkers.

This concept of experience was at the root of his understanding of the whole relationship of the teacher and the learner and it accounts for a critical balance in the relationship that has, by and large, been followed by subsequent liberal educators like himself, but has been severely distorted by modern 'progressive' thinkers such as Dewey, Piaget and others. While he argued that the 'seeds of learning' are present in all men, Comenius insisted that the process of growth, while being essentially free and spontaneous, must nonetheless be guided carefully and systematically by the teacher. In the first instance, he saw readiness, or the potentiality for learning, as something that can itself be fostered through effective and resourceful teaching and he provided detailed guidance on how this was to be done. Secondly, he argued that the teacher has a responsibility to ensure that learning is guided towards the perception of the inter- relating orders of being, and towards the comprehension of the spiritual truths through which all experience becomes ultimately meaningful. The teacher, he said, should possess the pedagogic competence ('he should be master of the necessary techniques')[8] which would enable him to guide the process of learning in his pupils purposefully and meaningfully towards the integrated harmony of knowledge, wisdom and faith he considered to be its ultimate fulfilment.

This emphasis was maintained by Comenius without any sacrificing of his commitment to allow the course of learning to follow its natural progress in every child. Learning, he insisted repeatedly, could progress only through the learner's own motivational resources, this being the internal dynamic empowering the whole process—a dynamic manifested empirically as the personal pleasure and fulfilment to be derived from the learning experience itself. He spoke of the 'facility, ease and rapidity'[9] of learning as being largely dependent on this and urged all teachers to create the conditions to ensure that learning was an enjoyable and self-fulfilling activity in the highest possible degree. Thus he described teaching as an 'assimilation of the processes of art to the processes of nature,'[10] the teacher's directive functions being exercised always with due sensitivity to the needs and interests of the individual learner. 'Nothing is difficult for the willing pupil,' he declared. 'Man can only be taught by the halter that comes from his own heart.'[11] And while he insisted that learning always be an ordered and disciplined process, he saw this as being achieved voluntarily and consensually in the non-coercive conditions he envisaged as essential for its proper fostering in the school classroom.

What he advocated therefore was a sensitive balancing of the principles of authority and freedom in the practical conduct of the education process. That balance is evident not only in his conception of the interrelationship of teaching and learning, but also in his corresponding conception of the relationship of the learner to the curriculum. Here again it can be shown that his innovative thinking was conceived in the context of beliefs and convictions that lie centrally within the Judaeo-Christian tradition, while being oriented towards the reaffirmation of a spirit of individual freedom he saw as being an essential feature of that tradition. Essentially, his concern was to accommodate both the individual interests of the child and his/her need for access to the realms of knowledge and meaning necessary for the kind of personal fulfilment implied in his fundamentally Christian beliefs about the nature and destiny of mankind. While he insisted that the curriculum be stimulating, intellectually and imaginatively—and he himself designed some remarkably attractive textbooks to achieve that objective—he also emphasised the need for order, depth and substantiveness in the subject-content made available to every child. He urged the careful classification and sequencing of subject-content, advocating a highly structured curriculum at all stages of the schooling process to ensure 'ease and rapidity in learning' and to ensure depth and facility of understanding in the highest possible degree.

The curriculum was to be integrated around the moral-spiritual principles which he saw as the ultimate focus of all truth, the source from which all knowledge was finally rendered meaningful. A genuinely liberal—or self-liberating—curriculum, he said, would be one where the primacy of moral-spiritual principles was visibly affirmed by virtue of the hierarchical structuring of all knowledge around this primary and all-embracing focus. As in the case of his pedagogic theories, his position here was once again determined ultimately by his metaphysical and religious beliefs. In this he differs fundamentally from progressive thinkers of later years who, discarding the traditions of Judaeo-Christian belief, eventually discarded the historical and cultural traditions of curriculum practice as well. Comenius insisted the curriculum would be one where

the *range* of subject-matter was sufficiently comprehensive to ensure the
pupil gained access to the spheres of moral and spiritual truth *by way* of
the diversified modes of knowledge and wisdom through which those
ultimate orders of truth are disclosed. The harmony and unity of the
universe would have to be directly experienced by all pupils in terms of
its diversified but interrelated manifestations in the received traditions of
knowledge and truth. Those traditions he saw as being embodied in the
historically sanctioned classical curriculum, which became the basis of
what he advocated for adoption in all school classrooms. For the pre-
school stage he advised a programme of planned learning activities in the
spheres of religion, language, number, art, music and nature study. For
the primary school he advocated the standard basic curriculum, consisting
of vernacular studies, mathematics, religion, music, art, history and geography, nature study and physical education. The secondary curriculum
he proposed was essentially an evolution of the classical trivium and
quadrivium, with detailed subject-content being specified for each of the
disciplines.

The liberal and innovative manner in which Comenius conceived of
curricular and pedagogic practice can be demonstrated from two areas
where his ideas have proved most influential: the spheres of ethico-
religious and linguistic education. While his thinking on ethical and
religious education was clearly rooted in the Judaeo-Christian tradition,
he demonstrated the compatibility of that tradition with an entirely liberal
and learner-centred view of the educational process. His ethics were
founded on the paradoxical, though essentially complementary, principles
of the absolute character of moral truth and the radical freedom of ethical
choice or decision-making as dictated solely by the inner imperatives of
conscience, illuminated only by an individual interpretation of the scriptures. Thus he avoided the pitfalls of moral relativism in his conception
of the nature of moral truth, while fully recognising the conditions of
individual freedom in which ethical decisions must be grounded. In the
context of school practice he urged the application of the doctrine of
learning through experience for the realisation of each of these goals.
'Virtue,' he declared, 'is practised by deeds, not by words'; 'the virtues
are learned by constantly doing what is right.'[12] He emphasised the
altruistic context in which a Christian approach to moral education must
be fostered, again stressing the need for ethical behaviour to be developed
experientially. 'For love,' he said, 'is the special virtue of Christians. . . .
We are not born for ourselves alone.'[13]

This interrelating emphasis on virtuous and altruistic behaviour is the
basis of his fusion of the goals of moral and religious education. Both
were focussed ultimately on the fostering of the spirit of selfless love, the
altruistic service by each of the needs of his fellowman. 'It is true
Christianity,' he said, quoting St James, 'to express faith by works.'[14]

That propensity towards active love (which he saw as a universal potentiality) was to be fostered through scripture study, meditative reflection and prayer—all under the guidance and direction of the teacher, in the non-dogmatic style that was typical of the teaching traditions of the Moravian Church. Two radical propositions determined Comenius's approach to all this: one, the conviction that Christianity is primarily not a body of doctrine, but a way of life, modelled on the simple truths of Christ's teachings, and deriving its authority only from the scripture text; two, the related conviction that the religious spirit is to be fostered through the practical implementation of those teachings in the everyday conditions of life itself. The scriptures became the mainstay therefore of the religious curriculum, their narrative excitement and simplicity being especially suited for the learner-centred methods that Comenius advocated. Stressing the profound humanistic principles that lie at the root of Christ's teachings, he urged the practical application of those teachings in the ordinary conditions of life, providing detailed pedagogic guidance on how this was to be actively promoted by the teacher. Religious education, he insisted, should aim to achieve a dual fulfilment: self-fulfilment through freedom and self-fulfilment through love. The universal potentiality for love could be realised only in conditions of freedom. That crucial conjuncture of love and freedom was central to his conception of the process of moral and religious education. It remained central to the educational ideals promoted by later educators in the liberal Judaeo-Christian tradition— such as Leo Tolstoy and Martin Buber—while being conspicuously absent from the writings of educators in the progressive movement from John Dewey onwards.

That Comenius's Christian convictions were totally compatible with a liberal view of education—were in fact the source and ultimate justification of this—can be illustrated further from his theories of linguistic formation. Like all liberal educators, he saw the attainment of literacy as the key to educability and therefore to the fulfilment of the goal of universal education. Seeing cultural liberation as the basis of self-liberation, he devised methods of fostering literacy as a foundation for all the modes of development he considered necessary for the full realisation of individual potentiality. His emphasis on the importance of vernacular proficiency, and on the learner-centred pedagogy that he considered most appropriate for its development, were revolutionary in an age when Latin was the cornerstone of education in most of the schools of Europe. His balancing of the principles of spontaneity and readiness with purposeful pedagogic formation, his thinking on matters such as motivation, the developmental stages in language growth, the role of sense experience, the place of the imagination and play-related activities, anticipated some of the most significant developments in modern thinking on the nature of linguistic formation. Centuries before writers such as Vygotsky and Bruner, he recognised in particular the necessity of developing oral-aural proficiency as a foundation for all language learning. That principle has only been properly recognised in theories of language pedagogy since the 1960s, the whole process being dominated before then by the development of reading and writing competence. Comenius saw the importance of developing oral-aural competence in the years of pre-school education and devised a fully developed pedagogy and curriculum for that critical stage in every child's education. Favouring an ordered curriculum and a high level of active intervention by the teacher, his methods closely anticipate the post-Piagetian interactive pedagogy now widely favoured for linguistic development in the years of infant and early primary education. All this was rooted in a conception of the nature of experience and of the process of individual self-fulfilment that was located centrally, if unconventionally, within the cultural and metaphysical traditions of Christian belief.

Those same traditions underpin his thinking on higher and adult education. His concept of the aims and function of the university marked a significant departure from the mediaeval-classical model of higher education, insofar as he conceived of it as primarily an instrument for the furtherance of pansophic learning. Stressing the indivisible unity of all knowledge, and the spiritual-moral focus around which all its modes must converge, he defined the whole process of scholarly learning as ultimately a quest for the principles which give order and meaning to all life and existence. Thus he warned of the dangers of excessive specialisation, particularly in the realm of scientific enquiry, if it were to result in a divorcing of secular knowledge from the spheres of the spiritual and the ethical where its ultimate meaningfulness would have to be determined. Liberal learning, by this conception, would have to involve a meaningful integration of the secular and the spiritual, the empirical and transcendental. The importance of this conception can scarcely be over-emphasised and it seems appropriate to dwell briefly on some of its implications. It has a special bearing on contemporary problems, such as the widespread scandal of ecological destruction and the equally widespread abuses of nuclear energy, both of which are due largely to the single-minded pursuit of scientific enquiry, regardless of its moral and social consequences. The President of the Czech Republic, Václav Havel, has commented in a recent work on the dangers of this unbridled and amoral pursuit of science for its own sake. His words echo the warnings of his cultural and spiritual predecessor:

> Our attention, therefore, inevitably turns to the most essential matter: the crisis of contemporary technological society as a whole, the crisis that Heidegger describes as the ineptitude of humanity face to face with the planetary power of technology. Technology— that child of modern science, which in turn is a child of modern

metaphysics—is out of humanity's control, has ceased to serve us, has enslaved us and compelled us to participate in the preparation of our own destruction. And humanity can find no way out: we have no idea and no faith, and even less do we have a political conception to help us bring things back under human control. We look on helplessly as that coldly functioning machine we have created inevitably engulfs us, tearing us away from our natural affiliations (for instance from our habitat in the widest sense of that word, including our habitat in the biosphere) just as it removes us from the experience of 'being' and casts us into the world of 'existences'. This situation has already been described from many different angles and many individuals and social groups have sought, often painfully, to find ways out of it (for instance through oriental thought or by forming communes). The only social, or rather political, attempt to do something about it that contains the necessary element of universality (responsibility to and for the whole) is the desperate and, given the turmoil the world is living in, fading voice of the ecological movement, and even there the attempt is limited to a particular notion of how to use technology to oppose the dictatorship of technology. 'Only a God can save us now,' Heidegger says, and he emphasises the necessity of 'a different way of thinking,' that is, of a departure from what philosophy has been for centuries, and a radical change in the way humanity understands itself, the world and its position in it.[15]

Another contemporary Czech writer, the novelist, Ivan Klíma, speaks of the widely held illusion in contemporary society that all life and existence is ultimately explicable through science. 'It occurred to me,' one of his characters reflects, 'how man strayed off his path by deifying himself, that man can behave arrogantly not only by deifying his own ego and proclaiming himself as the finest flower of matter and life, but equally when he proudly believes that he has correctly comprehended the incomprehensible or uttered the unutterable, or when he thinks up infallible dogmas and with his intellect, which wants to believe, reaches out into regions before which he should lower his eyes and stand in silence.'[16] The demon of the age, Havel cries in 'Six Asides About Culture,' is positivistic science. Divorced from ethics, religion and art, it has survived the demise of its cultural offspring, Marxism. Ultimately, he writes, it represents a greater threat to individual freedom and morality than the totalitarian nightmare of the communist years:

> The civilisation of the new age has robbed old myths of their authority. It has put its full weight behind cold, descriptive Cartesian reason and recognises only thinking in concepts.

I am unwilling to believe that this whole civilisation is no more than a blind alley of history and a fatal error of the human spirit. More probably it represents a necessary phase that man and humanity must go through, one that man—if he survives—will ultimately, and on some higher level (unthinkable, of course, without the present phase), transcend.

Whatever the case may be, it is certain that the whole rationalistic bent of the new age, having given up on the authority of myths, has succumbed to a large and dangerous illusion: it believes that no higher and darker powers—which these myths in some ways touched, bore witness to, and whose relative 'control' they guaranteed—ever existed, either in the human unconscious or in the mysterious universe. Today, the opinion prevails that everything can be 'rationally explained', as they say, by alert reason. Nothing is obscure—and if it is, then we need only cast a ray of scientific light on it and it will cease to be so. . . .

To this day, we cannot understand how a great civilised nation—or at least a considerable part of it—could, in the twentieth century, succumb to its fascination for a single, ridiculous, complex-ridden *petit bourgeois*, could fall for his pseudo-scientific theories and in their name exterminate nations, conquer continents, and commit unbelievable cruelties. Positivistic science, Marxism included, offers a variety of scientific explanations for this mysterious phenomenon, but instead of eliminating the mystery, they tend rather to deepen it. For the cold 'objective' reason that speaks to us from these explanations in fact only underlines the disproportion between itself—a power that claims to be the decisive one in this civilisation—and the mass insanity that has nothing in common with any form of rationality.[17]

All of this points to the profound relevance of the Comenian ideal of integrated learning and to the importance of his view that the university has a responsibility to see that all modes of learning and enquiry are informed by the moral and spiritual principles that will ensure they are employed for the betterment of humankind. Simultaneously a realist and a transcendentalist, he saw the synergy of the spiritual and the secular as the stabilising force in all intellectual enquiry and the mainstay of scholarly research if it is truly to serve the needs of mankind. Rejecting the idea of research as the pursuit of knowledge for its own sake, he argued convincingly that knowledge must always be morally informed and thereby directed towards the service of the common good. His ideal, as Radim Palouš, the Rector of Charles University, has shown in an important collection of commemorative papers, was the *unum* or *chresis*, the *nexus hypostaticus* or integrity of all truths—moral, spiritual, scientific, humanistic—which is ultimately manifested as the responsibility of all men for the common fate of mankind. It implies particularly a responsibility on the part of all those engaged in the pursuit of knowledge to ensure their activities are always conducted towards morally desirable goals. This shared responsibility, to be exercised by scholars and laymen alike, is, Palouš says, the essential element in the radical vision of Christian democracy unfolded by Comenius.[18]

Equally relevant to the needs of the present time is his concept of the university as an institution embracing three main functions: teaching, research and professional training. All three, he said, should be promoted in a balanced and orderly combination. This ideal has become increasingly relevant with the growth and proliferation recently of highly specialised training colleges, especially in the scientific-technocratic sphere, which lack the balance of disciplines traditionally considered essential for institutions designating themselves universities. The curriculum Comenius envisaged was to embody the liberal principles earlier described. He insisted, for instance, that instruction in the professional disciplines, such as medicine and law, be combined with programmes of humane and sacred studies in the same way that this was to be done at the earlier stages of schooling. He provided some enlightened guidelines on the nature of university teaching, advocating a mixture of formal lecturing, seminar discussion and various forms of independent activity, such as project work and laboratory experimentation. He offered some innovative ideas also on assessment at university level, seeing it as essentially a continuous process, embracing the entire time-span of the academic year.

Liberal Christian values again determined his approach to non-formal education. His conception of education as a life-long process followed logically from the universal ideal. His assertion of the right of all men to have access to education necessitated its reconception as a process reaching beyond the formal conventions of schooling. The vital principle here again was his location of all learning within the integrating framework of moral and spiritual formation. It was the all-informing presence of ethico-spiritual values which would define the ultimate meaningfulness of the whole process, he said. Ethico-religious formation, therefore, became the focus and centre of all the educational activities he envisaged for the years of adult life. Correspondingly, he insisted on the need for pedagogic reform to make all this a realisable goal. Anticipating Buber, Freire and other innovators in the sphere of adult and community education, he conceived a learner centred pedagogy that was designed to meet the particular needs of adult students, its main objective being the fostering of the potentiality for self-education present in all men. He further anticipated modern thinkers in his insistence that substantial subject-content be provided for education at this level. The curriculum he advocated for this stage of education was again the classical model, embracing all the major sacred and secular disciplines, though he insisted on the need to relate it to the practical circumstances of everyday life in a far greater degree than is possible in conventional schooling.

Recent events in Eastern Europe have brought the relevance of Comenius's ideas on social justice sharply into focus and they point to their strong potential significance in the reappraisal of the whole process of social and political change that is now occurring. Throughout his life Comenius projected a radical vision of social reform on matters such as the sharing of material goods, the service of the poor, the sick and the oppressed, and above all, the proper provision for the educational needs of all sectors of society. 'For every man will understand that the welfare of each individual depends on the welfare of all,' he declared.[19] He urged the rich to take responsibility for the needs of the poor and called on the more prosperous nations of the world to assist those less fortunate than themselves—all in a spirit of Christian compassion and love. He saw his vision of social reform as being achieved, however, not through radical political change, but through a process of self-reform initiated by every individual in the privacy of his own conscience and made effective by each in the circumstances of daily life. The fallenness and corruptibility of mankind require that social reform begin with the moral transformation of the individual person, he said. This is a recurring theme in *The Great Didactic*, the *Labyrinth* and the *Pampaedia*. 'The tendency towards evil is the innate character of all the descendants of Adam,' he cries in the *Pampaedia*.[20] Mankind is corrupt and diseased, needing the healing powers of the spirit, its best hope being the transformation to be attained through faith, penitence, humility, selflessness, and trust in the infinite power of God's grace.

Much of this was reechoed by some of Comenius's most distinguished fellow-countrymen in the harsh and inhuman conditions that existed in Eastern Europe in the years of communist rule. In their work they sought to give voice to a new vision of social reform that could replace the discredited hopes of the collectivist ideology which brought unparalleled suffering to their people throughout the greater part of the present century. Particularly prominent amongst those engaged in this whole process have been several notable Czech writers such as Havel, Kundera, Klíma and Skvorecky. It seems appropriate that the continuing relevance of Comenius's writings should be illustrated finally from the work of these writers.

Skvorecky in *The Miracle Game* has spoken explicitly of the Comenian vision of world peace and harmony as embodying the only truly realisable ideal of genuine social reform. Reflecting in the novel on the events of the Russian Revolution, he speaks of the mass brutalisation that resulted from its much vaunted emancipation of the proletariate. 'You cannot have revolutionary terror without sadism,' one of his characters cries.

'And I can't accept sadism, for any end,' he concludes.[21] Reflecting on the attempt to give 'socialism a human face' during the period of the 'Prague Spring', another of his characters invokes Comenius's vision of Christian brotherhood as offering the only true prospect of reform. 'I realised,' he says, 'that cruelty begets cruelty, revenge begets revenge, and that if all of us want to extricate ourselves from the situation into which the years of Stalinism cast us, we . . . must shake hands not only with Communists, but also with our former guards and torturers. Only in a state of general reconciliation, the kind that Comenius spoke about so long ago, is there hope for the Czechoslovak experiment.'[22]

Like Skvorecky, Milan Kundera, in *The Unbearable Lightness of Being*, attributes the evils of humanist socialism to the collectivist ideology which inspired and sustained it throughout its recent history. 'Behind all occupations and invasions lurks a more basic, pervasive evil and the image of that evil was a parade of people marching by with raised fists and shouting identical syllables in unison,' Sabina says, as she describes the Soviet occupation of Czechoslovakia in 1968.[23] Echoing the Grand Inquisitor sequence from *The Brothers Karamazov*, she speaks of a tendency to take refuge in the collective as being inherent in the nature of man himself. Havel has emphasised the same point in his essay, 'The Power of the Powerless.' 'There is obviously something in human beings which responds to this system,' he writes, 'something they reflect and accommodate, something within them which paralyses every effort of their better selves to revolt.'[24]

Of the communist poet, Jarovil, Kundera remarks in *Life is Elsewhere*: 'His monstrosity is potentially contained in all of us. It is in me. It is in you. It is in Rimbaud. It is in Shelley, in Hugo. In all young men, of all periods and regimes. Jaromil is not a product of communism. Communism only illuminated an otherwise hidden side, it released something which under different circumstances would merely have slumbered in peace.'[25] The desire for collective security, side by side with the humanist dream of earthly bliss, lies behind the universal quest for a social utopia. As Klima has written: 'People search for images of paradise and cannot find anything other than images from this world.'[26] The moral nihilism which springs from a purely humanist quest for self-fulfilment is eloquently expressed in this passage from his novel, *Love and Garbage*:

> Perhaps there is within us still, above everything else, some ancient law, a law beyond logic, that forbids us to abandon those near and dear to us. We are dimly aware of it but we pretend not to know about it, that it has long ceased to be valid and that we may therefore disregard it. And we dismiss the voice within us as foolish and reactionary, preventing us from tasting something of the bliss of paradise while we are still in this life.

We break the ancient laws which echo within us and we believe that we may do so with impunity. Surely man, on his road to greater freedom, on his road to his dreamed-of heaven, should be permitted everything. We are all, each for himself and all together, pursuing the notion of earthly bliss and, in doing so, are piling guilt upon ourselves, even though we refuse to admit it. But what bliss can a man attain with a soul weighed down by guilt? His only way out is to kill the soul within him, and join the crowd of those who roam the world in search of something to fill the void which yawns within them after their soul is dead. Man is no longer conscious of the connection between the way he lives his own life and the fate of the world, which he laments, of which he is afraid, because he suspects that together with the world he is entering the age of the Apocalypse.[27]

Havel, like Comenius—whom he quotes in support of his vision of ethico-social and political reform—affirms the need to ground the whole process in the exercise of individual responsibility, conducted in conditions of social and political freedom. 'Any existential revolution', he writes, 'should provide hope of a moral reconstitution of society, which means a radical renewal of the relationship of human beings to what I have called the "human order" which no political order can replace. . . . In other words, the issue is the rehabilitation of values like trust, openness, responsibility, solidarity, love.'[28] Social reform, he insists, is a moral, not a political issue, primarily; the morality of personal relationships is the condition on which social and political reform depends. And interpersonal morality depends, in turn, on the exercise of individual responsibility in accordance with the dictates of conscience. In an eloquent passage from 'Politics and Conscience' Havel describes the power of individual conscience to effect moral, social and political change, seeing it as the ultimate guarantor of individual freedom:

It is becoming evident that truth and morality can provide a new starting point for politics and can, even today, have an undeniable political power. The warning voice of a single brave scientist, besieged somewhere in the provinces and terrorised by a goaded community, can be heard over continents and addresses the conscience of the mighty of this world more clearly than entire brigades of hired propagandists can, though speaking to themselves. It is becoming evident that wholly personal categories like good and evil still have their unambiguous content and, under certain circumstances, are capable of shaking the seemingly unshakable power with all its army of soldiers, policemen and bureaucrats. It is becoming evident that politics by no means need remain the affair of professionals and that one simple electrician with his heart in the right place, honouring something that transcends him and free of fear, can influence the history of this nation.[29]

That this is a thoroughly hopeful vision of man's future is made clear by Havel in his essay, 'The Politics of Hope.' Differentiating between optimism and hope, he sees the former as merely the expectation of success, while the latter, he says, is an inner certainty, based on faith. 'Hope,' he writes, 'is definitely not the same thing as optimism. It is not the conviction that something will turn out well, but the certainty that something makes sense, regardless of how it turns out. . . . Either we have hope within us or we don't; it is a dimension of the soul, and it's not essentially dependent on some particular observation of the world or estimate of the situation.'[30] The source of hope is faith in God, trust in the infinity of God's grace. 'I feel,' he continues, 'that its deepest roots are in the transcendental, just as the roots of human responsibility. . . . It is this hope, above all, which gives us the strength to live and continually do new things, even in conditions that seem as hopeless as ours do, here and now.'[31] If faith is the source of hope, individual conscience is its voice, as Havel further explains in one of the most moving passages from his *Letters to Olga*. Whose is the voice, he asks, which calls him to responsibility:

It is again that to which, through all my relationships, I alone relate and to which, through all my responsibilities, I alone am ultimately responsible: the mysterious 'voice of Being' that reaches my 'I' from 'outside' more clearly (so clearly that it is usually described as coming 'from above') than anything else, but which, at the same time—paradoxically—penetrates to a deeper level than anything else, because it comes through the 'I' itself: not only because I hear it in myself, but above all because it is the voice of my own being, torn away from the integrity of Being and thus intrinsically bound to it, of my own being considered as my deep-seated dispositions (developed or betrayed in one way or another), of my sense of rootedness and orientation, of my direction, task and meaning, of my true and unique human limitation and fulfilment. . . .

This 'partner,' however, is not standing beside me; I can't see it nor can I quit its sight: its eyes and voice follow me everywhere; I can neither escape it nor outwit it: it knows everything. Is it my so-called 'inner voice', my 'superego', my 'conscience'? Certainly I hear it calling me to responsibility, I hear this call within me, in my mind and my heart; it is my own experience, profoundly so, though different from the experience mediated to me by my senses. . . .

Who, then, is in fact conversing with me? . . . Someone who 'knows everything' (and is therefore omniscient) is everywhere (and therefore omnipresent) and remembers everything; some one who, though infinitely understanding, is entirely incorruptible, who is, for me, the highest and utterly unequivocal authority in all moral questions and who is thus Law itself; someone eternal, who through himself makes me eternal as well, so that I cannot imagine the arrival of a moment when everything will come to an end, thus terminating my dependence on him as well; someone to whom I relate entirely and for whom, ultimately, I would do everything.[32]

Havel's words in this letter epitomise the values that lie at the heart of the vision of human self-fulfilment disclosed by Comenius in his literary, religious, philosophical and educational writings. The primacy of conscience and the supreme importance of ethico-religious ideals have been shown throughout this present study to be the all-informing principles in Comenius's work. He too was a lone voice, denouncing tyranny and corruption, proclaiming the Gospel message of love, sustained only by the inner certainty of his faith and the conviction that good will always triumph over evil in the end. The vision disclosed in his writings is one that is intrinsically Christian, by virtue of its consistent and authentic affirmation of the values of love, truth and freedom. It is a vision that was embodied in the spiritual and cultural traditions of Bohemia from Hus to Havel, but is one which, self-evidently, has a profound and compelling relevance for the whole of humankind.

NOTES

Where English translations of Comenius's writings are available, these are the texts that are cited in the references which follow. This is the case with virtually all of his purely educational writings. In cases where an English translation was not available, the Latin original is cited; most of the Latin texts were consulted in university libraries in Oxford, Cambridge, London and Dublin. In the case of texts not available in these libraries references relate to the Collected Works of J.A. Comenius (*Veškeré Spisy*) consulted by the author in the Comenius Pedagogic Library (*Státní Pedagogická Kninovna Komenského*) in Prague. A new collected edition of the works of Comenius, *Opera Omnia*, has been in preparation since 1969; at the time of writing twenty volumes from a projected edition of twenty-seven have been published by Academia Publishers in Prague. References to this edition are given also where appropriate.

CHAPTER I

1 Václav Havel, *Open Letters, Selected Prose, 1963–1990* (edited by Paul Wilson) (London: Faber and Faber, 1991), p. 39
2 See, for example, the Preface to the three-volume edition of *Opera Didactica Omnia* produced by the Comenius Institute in Prague in 1957. The following passage is typical of the selective nature of Marxist interpretations of Comenius's work. Ignoring the fundamentally religious orientation of his writings, it suggests that his ideas found their highest fulfilment in the egalitarian, but entirely secularist, educational policies adopted by the socialist government that came to power in Czechoslovakia in 1948: 'After three centuries in his native country, there arise the conditions that will make possible the realisation of his [Comenius's] most daring plans. The socialist society realises the unified school system from the primary school up to the highest school standard, as Komensky has proposed it; in the socialist society all children are given a general education without any discrimination of sex, social origin and property as it was Komensky's idea.'

3 See Capková references in the bibliography. See also essay by Čapková in J. Pešková (editor) *Homage to J.A. Comenius* (Prague: Charles University, 1991).
4 See, for example, Jiřina Popelová, 'Comenius as a Czech National Figure and as a World Figure' in *Universita Karlova J.A. Komenskému 1670–1970* (Prague, 1970), pp. 13–30.
5 See Jean Piaget, Introduction to *John Amos Comenius, 1592–1670, Selections* (Paris: UNESCO, 1957).
6 Daniel Murphy, *Martin Buber's Philosophy of Education* (Dublin: Irish Academic Press, 1988); *Tolstoy and Education* (Dublin: Irish Academic Press, 1992).
7 Martin Buber, *Between Man and Man* (London: Fontana Books, 1979), p. 117.
8 David Remnick, *Lenin's Tomb* (London: Viking, 1993), p. 173.
9 J.A. Comenius, *Pampaedia* (Dover: Buckland Publications, 1986) *Panglottia* (Shipston-on-Stour, Drinkwater, 1991); *Panorthosia* (Sheffield Head Press, 1993). All were translated and edited by A.M.O. Dobbie.
10 J.A. Comenius, *De Rerum Humanorum Emendatione Consultatio Catholica* (Prague: Czechoslovak Academy of Sciences, 1966).

CHAPTER II

I am especially indebted to the following sources for biographical information on Comenius:

Čapková, Dagmar. *Jan Amos Komensky*, 1592–1670 (Prague: Institute for Informatics in Education, 1991).

Dietrich, Veit-Jakobus, *Johann Amos Comenius* (Hamburg: Rowholt, 1991).

Heyberger, Anna. *Jean Amos Comenius* (Paris, 1928).

Hofmann, Franz. *Jan Amos Komensky* (Berlin, 1963).

Jakubec, Jan. *Johannes Amos Comenius* (Prague, 1928).

Keatinge, M.W. *The Great Didactic of John Amos Comenius*, Part I (London: A & C. Black, 1910).

Kozík, Frantisek. *Comenius* (Prague: Orbis, 1981).

Krasnorski, A.A. *Jan Amos Komenski* (Moscow, 1953).

Laurie, S.S. *John Amos Comenius* (Cambridge University Press, 1899).

Lochman, Jan Milic. *Comenius* (Freiburg-Hamburg, 1982).

Lordkipanidze, D.O. *Jan Amos Komenski*, 1592–1670 (Moscow, 1970).

Monroe, W.S. *Comenius and the Beginnings of Educational Reform* (London: Heinemann, 1900).

Panek, Jaroslav. *Joan Amos Comenius, 1592–1670* (Prague, Orbis, 1991).

Rood, W. *Comenius and the Low Countries, 1656–1670* (Amsterdam, Van Gendt, 1970).

Spinka, M. *John Amos Comenius: That Incomparable Moravian* (University of Chicago Press, 1943).

Turnbull, H.H. *Hartlib, Dury and Comenius* (London: 1947).

Young. R.F. *Comenius in England* (Oxford University Press, 1932).

1 See Spinka, *J.A. Comenius*, p. 24; Jakubec, *J.A. Comenius*, p. 13; Dagmar Čapková, *Jan Amos Komensky* (Prague: 1991), p. 9. In an interview conducted in September 1993 Dr. Dagmar Capkova informed this author that she believed the probability was that Comenius had been born in a field and was subsequently reared in the towns of Nivnice and Uhersky Brod.

2 Jan Amos Komensky, *The Labyrinth of the World and the Paradise of the Heart* (trans. Count Lutzow) (London, 1905), p. 59.

3 G.W. Keatinge (editor), *The Great Didactic of John Amos Comenius* (London, A.C. Black, 1910), pp. 79–80.

4 J.A. Comenius, *A Reformation of Schools Designed in Two Excellent Treatises* (Menton: Scholars' Press, 1969), p. 46.

5 Jan Amos Komensky, 'Letters to Heaven,' in *Veškeré spisy* (Brno, 1914), XV, pp. 1–25. *Opera Omnia*, Vol. 3 (Prague: Academia, 1969 ff.)

6 Jan Amos Komenský, 'The Impregnable Fortress in *Veškeré spisy*, XV, pp. 69–91. *Opera Omnia*, Vol. 3.

7 Jan Amos Komenský, 'The Sorrowful' in *Veskeré spisy*, XV, pp. 93–180. *Opera Omnia*, Vol. 3.

8 Ibid., p. 99.

9 See Note 2 above.

10 Jakubec, *J.A. Comenius*, p. 19.

11 Ibid., pp. 21–2.

12 Jan Amos Komensky, 'Centrum Securitatis' in *Veškeré Spisy*, XV, pp. 377–465. *Opera Omnia*, Vol. 3.

13 Johannes Amos Comenius. *Opera Didactica Omnia*, 3 vols. (Prague, 1957).

14 Johannes Amos Comenius. *Janua Linguarum Reserata* (trans. T. Horn) (London: 1673). Also in *Opera Didactica Omnia*, Vol 1. (Prague, 1957).

15 R.F. Young. *Comenius in England*, pp. 27–8.

16 *A Reformation of Schools*, pp. 59–60.

17 Spinka, p. 54.

18 Keatinge, *The Great Didactic*, pp. 20–5, 29–30, 40–1.

19 Ibid., 111. Jakubec, J.A. Comenius, pp. 26, 37.

20 J.A. Comenius. *A History of the Bohemian Persecution from the Beginning of Christianity in the Year 894 to the Year 1632* (London, 1650)

21 J.A. Comenius. *Praxis Pietatis* (Brno, 1922), *Opera Omnia*, Vol. 4.

22 *Veškeré spisy*, XVII, 157–260. *Opera Omnia*, Vol. 2.

23 Ibid., p. 208.

24 Ibid., p. 209.
25 *Veškeré spisy*, XVII, pp. 449–487. *Opera Omnia*, Vol. 8.
26 Ibid., I, pp. 48–129.
27 J.A. Comenius. *Janua rerum reserata* (Leyden, 1681). *Opera Omnia*, vol. 14.
28 See Note 4 above.
29 Keatinge, *The Great Didactic*, p. 31.
30 *Veškeré spisy*, I, pp. 131–304. *Natural Philosophy Transformed by Divine Light* (English translation) (London, 1651).
31 *Veškeré spisy*, I, p. 343.
32 *A Reformation of Schools*, p. 66.
33 Spinka, *J.A. Comenius*, p. 68.
34 See *Veškeré spisy*, I, 389–433; also *A Reformation of Schools*, Part II.
35 *Veškeré spisy*, I, pp. 403–4.
36 Jan Kvačala, *Korrespondence J.A. Komenského* (Prague, 1897), I, pp. 51 ff.
37 Young, *Comenius in England*, p. 40.
38 Ibid., p. 39.
39 J.A. Comenius, 'Dedicatory Letter to the Royal Society, *Via Lucis* (ed. Campagnac) (Liverpool University Press, 1938), p. 4.
40 Young, *Comenius in England*, p. 65.
41 Ibid., p. 42.
42 Ibid.
43 Introduction to *Opera Didactica Omnia*, Part II.
44 Thomas Fuller, *The Church History of Britain* (Oxford, 1845), V, p. 387.
45 See Note 39 above.
46 Introduction to *Opera Didactica Omnia*, Part II.
47 *Via Lucis*, p. 152.
48 Ibid., p. 163.
49 Ibid., pp. 172–3.
50 Ibid., pp. 42–4, 202–3.
51 Cotton Mather, *Magnalia Christi Americana* (New Haven, 1820).
52 Eduard Beneš (editor), *The Teacher of Nations* (Cambridge University Press, 1942), p. 40.
53 *Via Lucis*, pp. 10–11.
54 Young, *Comenius in England*, pp. 49–50.
55 Ibid., pp. 49–50.
56 Keatinge, *The Great Didactic*, pp. 51–2.
57 J.A. Comenius, *Linguarum methodus novissima* (Lezsno, 1648), *Veškeré spisy*, Vol. VI. Opera Omnia, Vol. 15. Chapter X of this work was re-published as *The Analytical Didactic* (trans. Vladimir Jelinek (Chicago University Press, 1953).

58 J.A. Comenius, *De dessidentium in rebus fidei christianorum reconciliatione hypomnemata* (Leszno, 1643). Opera Omnia, Vol. 20.
59 J.A. Comenius *De regula fidei judicium duplex* (Amsterdam, 1658). Opera Omnia, Vol. 20.
60 Spinka, *J.A. Comenius*, pp. 102–3.
61 J.A. Comenius, *De Rerum Humanorum Emendatione Consultatio Catholica* (Prague: Czechoslovak Academy of Sciences, 1966).
62 Patera, A. (editor) *J.A. Komenského Korrespondence* (Prague, 1892).
63 J.A. Comenius, *The Bequest of the Unity of Brethren* (trans. Spinka) (Chicago: National Union of Czechoslovak Protestants, 1940), pp. 22–3.
64 Ibid., p. 26.
65 Ibid., p. 28.
66 Ibid., p. 31.
67 Spinka, *J.A. Comenius*, pp. 114–18.
68 *Bequest of the Unity of Brethren*, pp. 28–9.
69 J.A. Comenius, *Independentia aeternarum confusionum origo* (Leszno, 1650). Opera Omnia, Vol. 20.
70 Keatinge, *The Great Didactic*, pp. 70–1.
71 *Schola Philosophiae Delineatio, Opera Didactica Omnia*, III.
72 *Praecepta morum in usum juventutis collecta, Opera Didactica Omnia*, III.
73 *Leges scholae bene ordinate, Opera Didactica Omnia*, III, pp. 784–803.
74 Spinka, *J.A. Comenius*, pp. 129–30.
75 Ibid.
76 *Schola ludus sed encyclopaedia viva, Opera Didactica Omnia*, Vol. III.
77 J.A. Comenius, *Orbis Pictus* (facsimile edition edited by J.E. Sadler) (Oxford University Press, 1968). (Original title of Nuremberg edition was *Orbis Sensualium Pictus*. Later editions generally use the shorter title.)
78 Ibid., pp. 89–95.
79 Keatinge, *The Great Didactic*, p. 79.
80 V.I. Strahov, 'John Amos Comenius's "The World of Sense-Things in Pictures" and Modern Democratic Education,' Seventh European Conference of Directors of Educational Research Institutions, Nitra, Czechoslovakia, October, 1992 (Strasbourg, Council of Europe, 1992).

81 Kvačala, *Korrespondence*, II, pp. 263–86.
82 *Opera Didactica Omnia*, III, Appendix.
83 *Panegyricus Carolo Gustavo* (Leszno, 1655). *Opera Omnia*, Vol. 13.
84 Keatinge, *The Great Didactic*, p. 86.
85 Ibid., p. 87.
86 *Opera Didactica Omnia* (Amsterdam, 1657).
87 Preface to *Opera Didactica Omnia*.
88 *Lux in tenebris* (Amsterdam, 1657). *Opera Omnia*, Vol. 24.
89 *Continuatio admonitionis fraternae* (Amsterdam, 1669). *Opera Omnia*, Vol. 21. Sections 39–59 in English translation in Young, *Comenius in England*, pp. 25–52.
90 *Gentis felicitas* in Kvačala, *Korrespondence*, II, pp. 263–86. Opera Omnia, Vol. 13.
91 *Novi testamenti epitome* (Nuremberg, 1658) *Opera Omnia*, Vol. 22; *Confessio aneb pocet z viry* (Amsterdam, 1662). *Opera Omnia*, Vol. 8.
92 *De bono unitatis et ordinis disciplinaeque ac obedientiae* (Amsterdam, 1660). *Opera Omnia*, Vol. 8. *An Exhortation of the Churches of Bohemia to the Church of England* (trans. Joshua Tymarchus) (London, 1661).
93 *Bibliorum turcicorum dedicatio* in Patera, *Korrespondence*, p. 284. *Opera Omnia*, Vol. 22.
94 *Angelus pacis ad Legatos pacis Anglos et Belgas Bredam missus* (1667). *Opera Omnia*, Vol. 13.
95 Spinka, *J.A. Comenius*, p. 146.
96 *Unum necessarium* (Amsterdam, 1668; Prague, 1920). *Opera Omnia*, Vol. 18.
97 Ibid., p. 267.
98 See Note 61 above.
99 Laurie, *J.A. Comenius*, pp. 94–5.
100 *Unum necessarium*, p. 178.

CHAPTER III

I am indebted to the following sources for details of the history of the Moravian Church:

Hamilton, J.T. *A History of Moravian Missions in the Eighteenth and Nineteenth Centuries* (London, 1901).

Holmes, John Beck. *Historical Sketches of the Missions of the United Brethren* (London, 1827).
Hutton, J.E. *A History of Moravian Missions* (London: Moravian Publications Office, 1928).
Hutton, J.E. *A Short History of the Moravian Church* (London: Moravian Publications Office, 1897).
Mellows. F.H. *A Short History of Fairfield Moravian Church* (Manchester: Fairfield, 1977).
Senft, E.A. *Les Missions Moraves* (Paris, 1890).
Schulze, Adolf. *Abrisz einer Geschichte der Brüdermission* (Berlin, 1901).
de Schweinitz, Edmund. *The History of the Unitas Fratrum* (Bethlehem, Pennsylvania: Moravian Publication Office, 1885).

1 J.E. Hutton, *A Short History of the Moravian Church*, p. 192.
2 Following the arrival of a large number of Brethren from Moravia in 1740 it was decided the Church should thenceforward be named the Church of the Moravian Brethren. See Hutton, *A Short History*, p. 178.
3 The kingdom of Bohemia consisted of two main provinces, roughly corresponding to the states of Bohemia and Moravia in the contemporary Czech Republic.
4 The Chiliasts believed the end of the world was near and that the righteous should prepare for their predestined salvation. The Adamites' main objective was to recreate the innocent state of mankind as it existed in the Garden of Eden. They abandoned the wearing of clothes and appeared naked at their prayer meetings. The Picards rejected the doctrine of transubstantiation and eventually joined with the Taborites, with whom they enjoyed a large following throughout Bohemia.
5 The Waldenses had come to Bohemia from Italy and set up communities who modelled themselves on the lives of the early Christians. Being strict pacifists, they totally rejected violence and shared their material resources communally, seeing the accumulation of wealth and property as evil and sinful.

6 The name came from the village of Chelcic in Southern Bohemia where Chelcicky was born in 1390.

7 Gregory was buried in Brandys, a town near the Moravian frontier where Comenius found refuge from the Hapsburg forces after the defeat at the White Mountain in 1621.

8 Luke of Prague, born in 1483, was a graduate in theology from Charles University, Prague.

9 This followed the criticism by Descartes that he had 'confused secular and sacred knowledge'. Comenius exonerated himself before the Synod at Leszno. See Chapter II, section 2.

10 Blahoslav was deeply respected throughout Bohemia as a religious historian and theological scholar.

11 See Chapter II, section 5.

12 Hutton, *A History of Moravian Missions.*

13 J.A. Comenius, *The Bequest of the Unity of Brethren*, pp. 26–8.

14 For a discussion of Luther's Letter to the Councillors see Heinrich Bornkamm, *Luther in Mid Career* (London: Darton, Longman and Todd, 1983), pp. 138–142. For a discussion of the Sermon see H.G. Hailie, *Luther: A Biography* (London: Sheldon Press, 1980).

15 Bornkamm, op. cit., p. 140.

16 Ibid., p. 141.

17 Ibid.

18 See R. Quick, *Essays on Educational Reformers* (New York, Appleton, 1893). For an analysis of Comenius's knowledge of earlier educational reformers see J. Pešek and M. Svatoš, 'The Czech Education Before the White Mountain and Comenius's Didactics' in J. Pešková (editor) *Homage to J.A. Comenius* (Prague: Charles University, 1991), pp. 73–82.

19 N. Hans, *Comparative Education* (London: Routledge and Kegan Paul, 1967), p. 152.

20 Comenius, *The Bequest of the Unity of Brethren*, pp. 28–9.

21 'L'ordre des Escholes de Genevé reveu et augmente par ordnance des nostrés Seigneurs syndiques et Conseil l'an 1570'. See Keatinge, *The Great Didactic*, p. 129.

22 Ibid., p. 121.

23 A.M.O. Dobbie (ed). *Comenius's Pampaedia or Universal Education* (Kent: Buckland Publications, 1986), pp. 133–4.

24 Hans, *Comparative Education*, p. 153.

25 Ibid., p. 155.

26 Comenius, *The Bequest of the Unity of Brethren*, p. 29.

27 Young, *Comenius in England*, p. 65.

28 John Brinsley, *A Consolation for Our Grammar Schools* (ed. E.T. Campagnac) (Liverpool, 1917).

29 See Chapter II, Section 3.

30 See G.H. Turnbull, *Hartlib, Dury and Comenius* (Liverpool, 1947).

31 S.S. Laurie, *John Amos Comenius: His Life and Educational Works* (Cambridge University Press, 1899), pp. 6–7.

32 François Rabelais, *The Heroic Deeds of Gargantua and Pantagruel* (London: Dent, 1933), pp. 37–8.

33 See Keatinge, *The Great Didactic*, p. 107.

34 Rabelais, *Gargantua and Pantagruel*, pp. 162–5.

35 Robert Recorde, Preface to *The Grounde of Artes* (London, 1561). See Keatinge, *The Great Didactic*, p. 107.

36 Text of *De Pueris Statim ac Liberaliter Instituendis* is given in W.H. Woodward, Desiderius Erasmus: Concerning the *Aim and Method of Education* (Cambridge University Press, 1904). See p. 204. See also L.K. Born, *The Education of a Christian Prince by Desiderius Erasmus* (New York: Columbia University Press, 1936); J.A. Froude, *Life & Letters of Erasmus* (New York: Scribner, 1894); J. Mangan, *Life, Character and Influence of Desiderius Erasmus* (New York: Macmillan, 1927); R.H. Murray, *Erasmus and Luther: Their Attitude Toward Toleration* (London: Society for Promoting Christian Knowledge, 1920).

37 *De Civilitate Morum Puerilium* in Woodward, *Desiderius Erasmus*, p. 73.

38 H.G. Good, *A History of Western Education* (New York: Macmillan, 1847), p. 150. See also M. Sobotka, 'J.A. Comenius and Philosophy in His Time' in J. Pešková, Homage to *J.A. Comenius* (Prague: Charles University, 1991).

39 Woodward, *Erasmus*, pp. 208–9.

40 Ibid., p. 211.

41 Ibid., pp. 213–14.
42 Ibid., p. 264.
43 G.E. Hodgson, *The Teacher's Montaigne* (Edinburgh: Blackie, 1915), pp. 130–1.
44 Ibid., p. 146.
45 Ibid., p. 130.
46 Ibid., p. 87.
47 F. Watson, *Vives on Education* (Cambridge University Press, 1913), p. cxiv.
48 Ibid., pp. cxiv–v.
49 J.A. Comenius, *Via Lucis* (trans. E.T. Campagnac) (London: Hodder & Stoughton, 1938), p. 173.
50 W.S. Monroe, *Comenius and the Beginnings of Educational Reform* (London: Heinemann, 1900), p. 16.
51 Ibid., p. 23.
52 Ibid.
53 Ibid., p. 25.
54 Ibid.
55 S.S. Laurie, *John Amos Comenius: His Life and Educational Works* (Cambridge University Press, 1899), p. 19. This work examines the influence of Bacon on Comenius and provides substantial readings from Bacon for comparison with parallel texts by Comenius. For the complete texts of Bacon's work see Novum Organon (ed. Thomas Fowler) (Oxford, 1878); The Advancement of Learning (ed. G.W. Kitchin) (London: Dent, 1962); The New Atlantis (ed. G.M. Smith) (Cambridge, 1900).
56 Laurie, op. cit., p. 16.
57 Ibid., p. 19.
58 Monroe, *Comenius and the Beginnings of Educational Reform*, p. 28.
59 Ibid.
60 Francis Bacon, *The Advancement of Learning* (ed. Arthur Johnston) (Oxford: Clarendon Press, 1974), pp. 78–83.
61 Ibid.
62 Laurie, *John Amos Comenius*, p. 26.
63 Keatinge, *The Great Didactic*, Part II, p. 7.
64 S.J. Curtis, *A Short History of Educational Ideas* (Slough: University Tutorial Press, 1953), p. 171.
65 Karl von Raumer, *Geschichte de Pädagogik* (Gütersloh, 1882). Cited in Laurie, *John Amos Comenius*, pp. 39–40.
66 Ibid.
67 Ibid.
68 Ibid.
69 Ibid.
70 Ibid.
71 Ibid.
72 Keatinge, *The Great Didactic*, Part II, p. 7.
73 Ibid.
74 F.E. Held, *The Christianopolis of John Valentine Andreae* (New York: Oxford University Press, 1916). A good deal of attention is given to the education of young children in *The Christianopolis*. This would explain its attraction for Comenius.
75 J.H. Alsted, *Encyclopaedia Scientiarum Omnium*, II, p. 287.
76 Ibid., p. 281.
77 Ibid., p. 273.
78 Curtis, *A Short History of Educational Ideas*, p. 173.

CHAPTER IV

1 J.A. Comenius, *The Labyrinth of the World and the Paradise of the Heart* (ed. Count Lutzow) (London: Dent, 1895), p. 68.
2 Ibid., p. 74.
3 Ibid., p. 76.
4 Ibid., pp. 76–7.
5 Ibid., p. 100.
6 J.A. Comenius, *Via Lucis* (London: Hodder and Stoughton, 1938), pp. 124–5.
7 Ibid. p. 123.
8 Ibid., p. 124.
9 G.W. Keatinge, *The Great Didactic of Comenius* (London: Black, 1910), p. 27.
10 *Via Lucis*, pp. 30–1.
11 *The Great Didactic*, p. 12.
12 Ibid., p. 13.
13 *Via Lucis*, p. 88.
14 Ibid., pp. 86–7.
15 Ibid., p. 4.
16 Ibid., p. 115.
17 Ibid.
18 Ibid., pp. 121–2.
19 *The Great Didactic*, p. 38.
20 Ibid., pp. 36–8.
21 *Comenius's Pampaedia* (ed. A.M.O. Dobbie) (Kent: Buckland Publications, 1986), p. 32.
22 Ibid., p. 15.
23 *Via Lucis*, p. 69.
24 Ibid., pp. 80–2.

25 Ibid., p. 6.
26 Ibid., p. 8.
27 Ibid., p. 2.
28 *The Great Didactic*, p. 41.
29 *Pampaedia*, p. 27.
30 *The Great Didactic*, p. 47.
31 Ibid., Part II, p. 4.
32 Ibid., p. 66.
33 *Via Lucis*, p. 175.
34 *Pampaedia*, p. 19.
35 *Via Lucis*, p. 131.
36 Ibid., p. 130.
37 *Pampaedia*, p. 31.
38 *The Great Didactic*, p. 67.
39 *Pampaedia*, p. 19.
40 *The Great Didactic*, p. 52.
41 Ibid., pp. 52–3.
42 Ibid., p. 61.
43 Ibid.
44 Ibid., p. 62.
45 *Pampaedia*, p. 62.
46 *The Great Didactic*, pp. 63–4.
47 Ibid.
48 Ibid., pp. 81–2.
49 J.A. Comenius, *Panorthosia* (trans. A.M.O. Dobbie) (Sheffield Head Press, 1993). Ch. XXII.
50 *Via Lucis*, p. 138.
51 Ibid., p. 163.
52 Ibid., pp. 164–5.
53 *Pampaedia*, p. 58.
54 Ibid., p. 59.
55 *The Great Didactic*, p. 259.
56 *Pampaedia*, p. 108.
57 Ibid.
58 Ibid., p. 109.
59 Ibid., pp. 108–9.
60 Ibid., p. 112.
61 *The Great Didactic*, p. 266.
62 Ibid., pp. 266–7.
63 *Pampaedia*, p. 127.
64 Ibid.
65 *The Great Didactic*, Chapter XXX.
66 *Pampaedia*, p. 145.
67 Ibid.
68 *Via Lucis*, p. 3.
69 *The Great Didactic*, p. 42.
70 Ibid.
71 Ibid., pp. 43–4.
72 *Via Lucis*, p. 24.
73 *Pampaedia*, p. 27.
74 R.M. Hutchins, *The Learning Society* (Penguin Books, 1967), p. 12.
75 *Via Lucis*, pp. 12–14.
76 *Pansophiae Prodromus* in *A Reformation of Schools*, pp. 65–76.
77 *Pansophiae Diatyposis* (Danzig, 1643). Published in English as *A Patterne of Universall Knowledge* (trans. J. Collier) (London 1651). Sections XV–XIX. *Opera Omnia*, Vol. 14.
78 *The Great Didactic*, p. 93.
79 J.A. Comenius, Preface to *Physicae ad lumen divinum reformatae synopsis* in *Veškéré spisy*, I, 131–304. *Opera Omnia*, Vol. 12. Translated in English as *Naturall Philosophie Reformed by Divine Light: Or a Synopsis of Physics* (London: 1651).
80 *The Great Didactic*, p. 106.
81 Ibid., pp. 139–40.
82 *Pampaedia*, p. 40.
83 *Via Lucis*, pp. 17–19.
84 *The Great Didactic*, pp. 88–90.
85 Ibid., p. 52.
86 Ibid., p. 53.
87 J.A. Comenius, *The School of Infancy* (trans. W.S. Monroe) (London: Isbister, 1897), p. 12.
88 J.A. Comenius, *The Analytical Didactic* (Trans. Vladimir Jelinek) (Chicago University Press, 1953). p. 112.
89 *The Great Didactic*, p. 123.
90 See L. Vygotsky, *Thought and Language* (Cambridge, Mass.: MIT Press, 1962). See also J. Bruner, 'Vygotsky: A Historical and Conceptual Perspective' in *Language and Literacy*, Vol. I (ed. N. Mercer) (Open University Press, 1988), pp. 86–98.
91 *The Great Didactic*, p. 124.
92 Ibid., pp. 151–2.
93 Ibid., p. 180.
94 *Pampaedia*, p. 65.
95 Ibid., p. 89.
96 Ibid., p. 91.
97 Ibid., p. 93.
98 *The Analytical Didactic*, Axiom CLXVI.
99 *Pampaedia*, p. 89–90.
100 Ibid., p. 80.
101 *Pampaedia*, p. 120.
102 J.A. Comenius, *Outline of a Pansophic School (Delineatio)*, *Opera Didactica Omnia*, III, pp. 35–60.
103 *Pampaedia*, p. 80.
104 Ibid., pp. 80–81.

105 Ibid., p. 92.
106 *The Great Didactic*, pp. 112–13.
107 Ibid., p. 112.
108 Ibid., pp. 137–8.
109 *The Analytical Didactic*, Axiom, XXXIV.
110 *The Great Didactic*, p. 96.
111 *The Analytical Didactic*, Axiom CXLVIII.
112 *Outline of a Pansophic School*, pp. 32–9.
113 *Pampaedia*, pp. 93–4.
114 Ibid., p. 90.
115 *Via Lucis*, pp. 132–3.
116 *Pampaedia*, p. 83.
117 *The Great Didactic*, pp. 154–5.
118 *The Analytical Didactic*, Axiom XXXIV.
119 *Pampaedia*, p. 97.
120 *The Great Didactic*, pp. 175–6.
121 Ibid., pp. 176–7.
122 *Pampaedia*, p. 93.
123 Ibid.
124 *The Analytical Didactic*, Axioms CLXVI–CLXXIV.
125 *Pampaedia*, p. 31.
126 *The Great Didactic*, p. 86.
127 *Pampaedia*, p. 101.
128 *The Great Didactic*, p. 249.
129 *The Analytical Didactic*, Axiom CLXXXVI.
130 Ibid., XLIX.
131 *Pampaedia*, p. 50.
132 *The Great Didactic*, p. 70.
133 *Via Lucis*, p. 7.
134 Ibid., pp. 5–7.
135 *Pampaedia*, p. 74.
136 *Via Lucis*, p. 144.
137 *Pampaedia*, p. 68.
138 *The Great Didactic*, p. 118.
139 Ibid., p. 151.
140 Ibid., p. 153.
141 *Pampaedia*, p. 15.
142 *Via Lucis*, pp. 39–40.
143 Ibid.
144 Ibid., pp. 118–19.
145 Ibid., p. 120.
146 Ibid., pp. 120–1.
147 *The Great Didactic*, p. 186.
148 Ibid., p. 187.
149 *Homage to J.A. Comenius*, p. 147.
150 Ibid.
151 Ibid., pp. 148–9.
152 Ibid., p. 157.
153 Ibid., p. 158.

154 *The Great Didactic*, Chapter XXVIII. *Pampaedia*, Chapter IX.
155 *Homage to J.A. Comenius*, p. 159.
156 *Pampaedia*, pp. 152–3.
157 *Pampaedia*, Chapter IX. *The Great Didactic*, Chapter XXIX.
158 *The Great Didactic*, p. 267.
159 Ibid., pp. 268–9.
160 Ibid., p. 270.
161 Ibid., p. 272.
162 *Pampaedia*, p. 140.
163 Ibid., p. 141.
164 *Homage to J.A. Comenius*, pp. 160–1.
165 *The Great Didactic*, pp. 274–5.
166 *Pampaedia*, p. 147.

CHAPTER V

1 *The Labyrinth*, pp. 223–4.
2 F. Dostoevsky, *The Brothers Karamazov* (trans. Garnett) (London: Landsborough, 1958), p. 224.
3 *Tolstoy on Education* (trans. Wiener) (Chicago University Press, 1967), p. 182.
4 Boris Pasternak, *Doctor Zhivago* (London: Collins and Harvill, 1958), p. 49.
5 *Via Lucis*, p. 115.
6 *The Great Didactic*, p. 14.
7 *Pampaedia*, p. 15.
8 *The Moravian Church: Background, Belief and Practice* (Manchester: Fairfield, n.d.), p. 2.
9 *The Labyrinth*, p. 224.
10 Ibid., pp. 223–4.
11 Ibid., pp. 234–5.
12 Ibid., pp. 226–7.
13 F.H. Mellows, *A Short History of Fairfield Moravian Church* (Fairfield, 1977), pp. 12–13.
14 *The Labyrinth*, p. 116.
15 Ibid., pp. 227–8.
16 Ibid., p. 230.
17 *Unum Necessarium*, pp. 178–82.
18 Ibid.
19 *Via Lucis*, pp. 210–11.
20 The Gospel of St. Matthew, V, 39.
21 Mellows, *A Short History of Fairfield Moravian Church*, p. 12.
22 *The Labyrinth*, p. 111.
23 Ibid., pp. 133–5.
24 *Via Lucis*, p. 26.

25 *The Labyrinth*, pp. 207–8.
26 Ibid., pp. 241–2.
27 Ibid., pp. 245–6.
28 Ibid., pp. 229–31.
29 *Via Lucis*, p. 131.
30 *The Brothers Karamazov*, p. 145.
31 *Via Lucis*, p. 164.
32 F. Dostoevsky, *The Brothers Karamazov*, p. 210; L. Tolstoy, *Anna Karenina*, (trans. Garnett) (London: Heinemann, 1977) pp. 236–7; Tolstoy, *Resurrection* (trans. Maude) (Moscow: Progress, 1972), p. 520.
33 *The Great Didactic*, p. 12.
34 *Via Lucis*, p. 10.
35 *Pampaedia*, p. 52.
36 *The Labyrinth*, pp. 205–6.
37 *Pampaedia*, pp. 52–3.
38 *The Labyrinth*, p. 114.
39 Ibid., pp. 199–200.
40 Ibid., pp. 218–19.
41 Ibid., pp. 118–19.
42 The Gospel of St. Matthew, VI, 5.
43 *The Labyrinth*, p. 206.
44 *Via Lucis*, p. 124.
45 Ibid., p. 123.
46 Ibid., pp. 121–2.
47 *The Labyrinth*, p. 115.
48 Ibid., p. 206.
49 *Via Lucis*, p. 91.
50 Ibid., p. 24.
51 Ibid., p. 118.
52 Ibid., pp. 134–5.
53 *The Great Didactic*, p. 211.
54 Ibid., p. 212.
55 *Pampaedia*, p. 46.
56 *Via Lucis*, p. 135.
57 *Pampaedia*, p. 51.
58 *Via Lucis*, pp. 54–5.
59 *The Great Didactic*, p. 215.
60 *The Labyrinth*, pp. 109–110.
61 *The Great Didactic*, p. 213.
62 Ibid., pp. 214–15.
63 Ibid., pp. 212–13.
64 Ibid., p. 215.
65 Ibid., p. 214.
66 *Pampaedia*, p. 99.
67 *The Great Didactic*, pp. 262–3.
68 Ibid., p. 262.
69 *Pampaedia*, p. 120.
70 Ibid.
71 *The Great Didactic*, p. 268.
72 Ibid., p. 270.

73 *Pampaedia*, p. 132.
74 Ibid., pp. 131–2.
75 *The Great Didactic*, p. 275.
76 Ibid., p. 276.
77 Ibid., p. 278.
78 *Pampaedia*, p. 149.
79 Ibid.
80 Ibid.
81 Ibid., p. 150.
82 *The Great Didactic*, p. 226.
83 Ibid., p. 218.
84 Ibid.
85 Ibid., pp. 225, 228.
86 *The Brothers Karamazov*, pp. 49–50.
87 *Pampaedia*, p. 46.
88 Ibid., pp. 98–9.
89 *The Great Didactic*, p. 219.
90 Ibid., pp. 219–20.
91 Ibid., p. 219.
92 *The Great Didactic*, pp. 218–30; *Pampaedia*, pp. 110–16, 133–36, 151–2.
93 *The Great Didactic*, pp. 223–4.
94 *Tolstoy on Education* (ed. Wiener), pp. 307–8.
95 *The Great Didactic*, p. 224.
96 Ibid., pp. 225–6. See M. Buber, 'The Man of Today and the Jewish Bible' in *Israel and the World* (New York: Schocken, 1963). See also D. Murphy, *Martin Buber's Philosophy of Education* (Dublin: Irish Academic Press, 1988), pp. 119–28.
97 Ibid., p. 263.
98 *Pampaedia*, pp. 115–16.
99 Ibid., pp. 121–2.
100 *The Great Didactic*, p. 268.
101 *Pampaedia*, pp. 133–4.
102 Ibid., pp. 134–5.
103 Ibid., p. 138.
104 Ibid., p. 136.
105 *The Great Didactic*, p. 275.
106 Ibid., pp. 277–8.
107 *Pampaedia*, p. 151.

CHAPTER VI

1 *The Great Didactic*, p. 205.
2 J.A. Comenius, *Methodus Linguarum Novissima, Opera Didactica Omnia*, Vol. II. Chapter X of the *Methodus* was published as *The Analytical Didactic* (ed. Vladimir Jelinek) (University of Chicago Press, 1953).

3 J.A. Comenius, *Orbis Pictus* (Facsimile of the first English edition of 1659) (Edited by B.W. Alderson) (Introduced by John E. Sadler) (Oxford University Press, 1968), pp. 97–8.
4 *The Great Didactic*, p. 112.
5 Ibid.
6 Ibid., pp. 119–20.
7 Ibid., pp. 123–4.
8 *Pampaedia*, p. 89.
9 *The Great Didactic*, p. 114.
10 Ibid., p. 84.
11 Ibid., p. 87–8.
12 Ibid., p. 185.
13 *Orbis Pictus*, p. 21. *Analytical Didactic*, Axiom LXXXIII.
14 J.E. Sadler, Introduction to *Orbis Pictus*, pp. 21–2.
15 Jean Piaget, 'The Significance of John Amos Comenius at the Present Time' in *J.A. Comenius, 1592–1670, Selections* (edited by J. Piaget) (Paris: UNESCO, 1957), pp. 15–17.
16 See J.E. Sadler, *Comenius and the Concept of Universal Education* (London: Allen and Unwin, 1960), p. 155.
17 Piaget, 'The Significance of J.A. Comenius', p. 17.
18 J. Pešková (editor), Homage to *J.A. Comenius*, pp. 237–9.
19 *Pampaedia*, p. 94.
20 Ibid., pp. 94–5.
21 Ibid., pp. 65–6.
22 *The Great Didactic*, p. 296.
23 Ibid., pp. 296–7.
24 *Pampaedia*, p. 71.
25 *The Bequest of the Unity of Brethren*, p. 36.
26 *Theatrum universitatis rerum* in *Vēškere spisy*, I, pp. 48–129. *Opera Omnia*, Vol. 1.
27 *The Bequest of the Unity of Brethren*, p. 36.
28 Jiřina Popelová, 'Comenius as a Czech National Figure and a World-Wide Figure' in *Universita Karlova J.A. Komenskému, 1670–1970*, (Praha: Universita Karlova, 1970) p. 28.
29 R. Mulcaster, *Positions I* cited in J.E. Sadler, *Comenius and the Concept of Universal Education*, pp. 143–4.
30 H. Woodward, *A Light to Grammar and a Gate to Science* cited in Sadler, op. cit., p. 144.

31 P. Coustel, *Rules for the Education of Children* cited in H.C. Barnard, *The Little Schools of Port-Royal* (Cambridge University Press, 1913), p. 119.
32 W. Ratke, *Memorial* cited in R.H. Quick, *Essays on Educational Reformers* (London: Longmans, Green, 1904).
33 *The Great Didactic*, p. 261.
34 See A.K Halliday, *Explorations in the Functions of Language* (Oxford University Press, 1974); A. Wilkinson, *Spoken English* (University of Birmingham, 1965), *The Foundations of Language* (Oxford University Press, 1971).
35 *The Great Didactic*, p. 259.
36 Ibid., pp. 203–4.
37 *Pampaedia*, p. 84.
38 Ibid.
39 Piaget, 'The Significance of J.A. Comenius,' p. 20.
40 *The Great Didactic*, pp. 176–7.
41 J. E. Sadler, Introduction to *Orbis Pictus*, pp. 21–2.
42 Piaget, 'The Significance of J.A. Comenius', p. 21.
43 Ibid.
44 See D. Ausubel, *The Psychology of Meaningful Verbal Learning* (New York: Grune and Stratton, 1963), *Educational Psychology: A Cognitive View* (New York: Holt, Rinehart and Winston, 1978); J. Bruner, *Toward a Theory of Instruction* (Harvard University Press, 1967), *The Process of Education* (Harvard University Press, 1977), *Actual Minds, Possible Worlds* (Harvard University Press, 1986); P. Bryant, *Perception and Understanding in Young Children* (London: Methuen, 1974); G. Brown and C. Desforges, *Piaget's Theory: A Psychological Critique* (London: Routledge and Kegan Paul, 1979); M. Donaldson, *Children's Minds* (London: Fontana, 1978), *Sense and Sensibility* (University of Reading, 1989).
45 Bruner, *Toward a Theory of Instruction*, p. 41.
46 Ibid., p. 29.
47 See *The Analytical Didactic*, (Methodus, Ch. X), pars. 7–8, 58–59.
48 *Pampaedia*, pp. 84–5.
49 Ibid., pp. 116–17.
50 Ibid., p. 118.
51 Ibid.

52 Ibid., pp. 118–19.
53 *The Great Didactic*, pp. 264–5.
54 *Orbis Pictus*, p. 93.
55 *Pampaedia*, p. 140.
56 See *Tolstoy on Education* (ed. Wiener), pp. 270–90. See also Daniel Murphy, *Tolstoy and Education* (Dublin: Irish Academic Press, 1992), pp. 142–9.
57 V.I. Strahov, 'John Amos Comenius's "The World of Sense Things in Pictures" and Democatic Education', Seventh European Conference of Directors of Educational Research Institutions, Nitra, Czechoslovakia, October, 1992 (Strasbourg: Council of Europe, 1992.
58 *The Great Didactic*, p. 270.
59 *Pampaedia*, p. 146.
60 *Continuatio admonitionis fraternae de temporando caritate zelo* (Amsterdam, 1669), par. 109. *Opera Omnia*, Vol. 21.
61 *Schola Ludus* in *Opera Didactica Omnia*, Vol. III.
62 *Pampaedia*, pp. 145–6.
63 Ibid., p. 148.
64 Ibid., p. 146.
65 Ibid., p. 147.
66 *The Great Didactic*, p. 79.
67 Ibid., p. 264.
68 *Orbis Pictus*, pp. 89–92.
69 J.E. Sadler, Introduction to *Orbis Pictus*, pp. 52–5.
70 Charles Hoole, *A New Discovery of the Old Art of Teaching Schoole* (ed. E.T. Campagnac) (Liverpool, 1917).
71 J.E. Sadler, Introduction to *Orbis Pictus*, p. 69.
72 J.A. Comenius, *Orbis Pictus* (edited by C.W. Bardeen) (New York, 1887).
73 *Orbis Pictus*, pp. 186–7.
74 Ibid., pp. 112–13.
75 Ibid., pp. 410–11.
76 Ibid., pp. 99–100.
77 *Janua linguarum reserata*, (trans. T. Horn) (London: 1673), Chapter XXI, pars 241–8.
78 Ibid., Chapter XXXIV, pars 406–8.
79 Strahov, op. cit., p. 2.
80 Ibid.
81 J.A. Comenius, *The School of Infancy* (ed. W.S. Monroe) (London: Isbister and Co., 1897), p. 50.

82 P.W. Zwerling, *Nicaragua: A New Kind of Revolution* (Wesport, Conn., Lawrence Hill, 1985), p. 76.
83 Piaget, 'The Significance of J.A. Comenius,' p. 25.
84 Paulo Freire, *Pedagogy of the Oppressed* (Penguin Books, 1972).
85 *Via Lucis*, p. 103.
86 Ibid., pp. 104–5.
87 Ibid., p. 130.
88 *Pampaedia*, p. 38.
89 *Pampaedia*, pp. 24–5.
90 See Sadler, *Comenius and the Concept of Universal Education*, p. 147.
91 *Via Lucis*, p. 180.
92 Sadler, op. cit., pp. 147–8.
93 Ibid.
94 *Via Lucis*, pp. 179–80; *Panglottia* (ed. A.M.O. Dobbie), VII, 3.
95 *Panglottia*, III, 6. On this issue some important research has appeared recently. See, for example, Napsal Radko Pytlík, 'Comenius and Semiotics' in *Comenius Redivivus* (Prague: Vydala Agentura Fajma, 1992), pp. 63–69.
96 *Via Lucis*, p. 186.
97 *Pampaedia*, p. 145.
98 *Via Lucis*, p. 142.
99 Paulo Freire, *Pedagogy of the Oppressed* (Penguin, 1972); *Cultural Action For Freedom* (Penguin, 1972).
100 *Via Lucis*, p. 186.

CHAPTER VII

1 *Pampaedia*, p. 33.
2 Ibid., p. 13.
3 Ibid., p. 19.
4 Ibid., p. 165.
5 Ibid., p. 164.
6 Ibid.
7 Ibid., p. 165.
8 Ibid., pp. 165–6.
9 Ibid., p. 166.
10 Ibid., pp. 166–7.
11 Ibid., pp. 167–8.
12 Ibid., p. 179.
13 Ibid., p. 168.
14 Ibid., p. 173.
15 Ibid.
16 Ibid., p. 174.
17 Ibid., p. 175.

18 Ibid., p. 177.
19 Ibid., p. 181.
20 Ibid., p. 183.
21 Ibid., p. 188.
22 Ibid., pp. 186–7.
23 Ibid., p. 189.
24 Ibid., p. 187.
25 Daniel Murphy, *Martin Buber's Philosophy of Education* (Dublin: Irish Academic Press, 1988) pp. 199–203.
26 Beneš, *The Teacher of Nations*, p. 40.
27 J. Polišensky, 'Antonín Gindely and Jaroslav Goll on the Life and Work of J.A. Comenius' in Pešková, *Homage to J.A. Comenius*, pp. 62–73.
28 *Via Lucis*, p. 3.
29 Ibid., p. 93.
30 Ibid., p. 127–8.
31 *Pampaedia*, p. 51.
32 Ibid., p. 37.
33 J.L. Paton, 'Comenius as a Pioneer of Education in Beneš, *The Teacher of Nations*, p. 16.
34 Zdenek Kučera, 'Comenius: A Theologian of Universality' in Pešková, *Homage to J.A. Comenius*, p. 195.
35 J.D. Bernal. 'Comenius's Visit to England and the Rise of the Scientific Societies in the Seventeenth Century' in Beneš, *The Teacher of Nations*, p. 33.
36 J.G. Crowther, 'The Social Relations of Science in the Seventeenth and Twentieth Centuries' in Beneš, *The Teacher of Nations*, p. 76.
37 Jaroslav Pánek, *Joan Amos Comenius: Teacher of Nations* (Prague: Orbis, 1991), pp. 41–2.
38 Ibid., p. 52.
39 Ibid., p. 69.
40 R. Palouš, Introduction to *Homage to J.A. Comenius* (edited Pešková), pp. 11–12.
41 Ibid.
42 M. Bednář, 'Comenius's Idea of Pampaedia and Plato's Conception of Paedeia' in *Homage to J.A. Comenius*, pp. 141–2.
43 D. Čapková, 'The Importance of Slovakia for the Preservation of the Comenian Tradition and for the Knowledge in his Work in the Czech National Renascence' in *Homage to J.A. Comenius*, p. 202.

44 *The Great Didactic*, p. 281.
45 *Pampaedia*, p. 153.
46 Ibid., p. 154.
47 Ibid., p. 155.
48 Ibid.
49 Ibid., p. 155–9.
50 *The Great Didactic*, pp. 282–3.
51 Ibid.
52 Ibid., pp. 283–4.
53 *Pampaedia*, p. 157.
54 Ibid., p. 159.
55 Ibid.
56 Ibid.
57 Ibid., p. 161.
58 J. Petráň and L. Petráňová, 'An Autobiographical Statement of the Young Comenius in his Labyrinth of the World' in *Homage to J.A. Comenius*, p. 33.
59 *Via Lucis*, pp. 167–8.
60 J.A. Comenius, *Panorthosia* in *J.A. Comenius, 1592–1670, Selections* (edited by J. Piaget) (Paris: UNESCO, 1957), pp. 160–1.
61 Ibid., pp. 162–3.
62 Ibid., p. 164.
63 Ibid., p. 163.
64 F.H, Mellows, *A Short History of Fairfield Moravian Church*, p. 13.
65 Popelová, op. cit., p. 29.
66 *Unum Necessarium*, pp. 178–9.
67 J.A. Comenius, *A Perfect Reformation*, An Anthology Selected by Amadeo Molnár, with an Introduction by J.L. Hromádka (Prague: Comenius Faculty of Protestant Theology, 1957), p. 16.
68 *The Bequest of the Unity of Brethren*, pp. 29–31.
69 *A Perfect Reformation*, p. 35.
70 'Truchlivý' in *Veškeré spisy*, XV, pp. 93–180.
71 Ibid.
72 *The Bequest of the Unity of Brethren*, p. 29.
73 *A Perfect Reformation*, pp. 20, 38–9.
74 M. Hroch, 'The World As A Labyrinth' in *Homage to J.A. Comenius*, p. 26.
75 *The Bequest of the Unity of Brethren*, p. 29.
76 Ibid., p. 23.
77 *A Perfect Reformation*, p. 51.
78 Ibid., p. 50.
79 *A Perfect Reformation*, p. 53.
80 Ibid., pp. 65–6.

81 *Panorthosia* (ed. Piaget), pp. 160–3.
82 Ibid., p. 159.
83 Ibid., p. 173.
84 Ibid., pp. 173–4.
85 Ibid.
86 Ibid., p. 175.
87 Ibid., pp. 176–7.
88 *Unum Necessarium*, pp. 181–2.
89 Jan Jakubec, *Johannes Amos Comenius* (Foreword by T.G. Masaryk) (Prague, 1928), pp. 4–5.
90 Beneš, op. cit., p. 6–7.
91 Pánek, op. cit., p. 74.
92 Ibid.
93 Benes, op. cit., p. 8.
94 Ibid., p. 82.
95 Mellows, op. cit., pp. 80–1.
96 *The Labyrinth*, p. 33.
97 Hroch, op. cit., p. 30.
98 *The Labyrinth*, p. 241.
99 D. Erasmus, *The Complaint of Peace* (ed. Alexander Grieve) (London: Headley, 1917), pp. 44–5, 48–9.
100 Ibid, pp. 54, 57.
101 *The Labyrinth*, pp. 245–6.
102 *Via Lucis*, pp. 228–9.
103 V. Urfus, 'Jurisprudence in Comenius's Times' in *Homage to J.A. Comenius*, p. 97.
104 Ibid., p. 101.
105 *The Angel of Peace* (trans. W.A. Morison) (London: 1944), p. 56.
106 J. Neuwirth, 'Comenius and the Plague in Leszno' in *Homage to J.A. Comenius*, p. 106.
107 Text of Address given in Neuwirth, pp. 108–11.
108 *Panorthosia* (edited J. Piaget), pp. 168–9.
109 Ibid., p. 169.
110 Ibid., pp. 169–70.
111 Pánek, op. cit., p. 67.

CHAPTER VIII

1 Beneš, *The Teacher of Nations*, p. 14.
2 Oskar Kokoschka, 'Comenius, the English Revoluthion and our Present Plight' in Beneš, *The Teacher of Nations*, pp. 61–70.

3 Beneš, *The Teacher of Nations*, p. 63.
4 Ibid., p. 65.
5 *The Great Didactic*, p. 12.
6 Ibid., p. 42.
7 Ibid., p. 106.
8 *Pampaedia*, p. 80.
9 See *The Great Didactic*, Chs. XVII–XIX.
10 Ibid., p. 112.
11 *Pampaedia*, p. 93.
12 *The Great Didactic*, p. 213.
13 Ibid., pp. 214–15.
14 Ibid., pp. 225, 228.
15 Václav Havel, *Living in Truth* (London: Faber and Faber, 1986), pp. 114–5.
16 Ivan Klíma, *Love and Garbage* (Harmondsworth: Penguin, 1990), p. 109.
17 Václav Havel, *Open Letters* (London: Faber and Faber, 1991), pp. 286–7.
18 Radim Palouš, 'The World of Comenius' in *Homage to J.A. Comenius* (ed. Pešková) (Prague, 1991), pp. 11–12.
19 *Via Lucis*, p. 131.
20 *Pampaedia*, p. 52.
21 Josef Skvorecky, *The Miracle Game* (London: Faber and Faber, 1991), p. 376.
22 Ibid., p. 391.
23 Milan Kundera, *The Unbearable Lightness of Being* (London: Faber and Faber, 1984), p. 100. See also Joseph Brodsky, 'The Post-Communist Nightmare,' *New York Review of Books*, January, 1994, pp. 28–30.
24 Havel, *Open Letters*, p. 144.
25 Milan Kundera, *Life is Elsewhere* (London: Faber and Faber, 1986), p. 310.
26 Klíma, *Love and Garbage*, p. 221.
27 Ibid., p. 192.
28 Havel, *Open Letters*, p. 210.
29 Ibid., pp. 270–1.
30 V. Havel, *Disturbing the Peace* (London: Faber and Faber, 1990), pp. 181–2.
31 Ibid.
32 V. Havel, *Letters to Olga* (London: Faber and Faber, 1988), pp. 344–5.

BIBLIOGRAPHY

A complete bibliography of primary and secondary works by and about Comenius would run to several thousand items. The following list, therefore, is necessarily selective and is confined to works dealing specifically with education—those by Comenius himself and those by scholars who have undertaken biographical or analytical studies of his work. It includes other works only insofar as they have some bearing on Comenius's educational thought.

Adamson, J.W. *Pioneers of Modern Education, 1600–1700* (Cambridge University Press, 1921).

Barker, Donald, G. 'A Hierarchical Grouping of Great Educators,' *Southern Journal of Educational Research*, 11, 1, 1977, pp. 23–30.

Beneš Eduard. (editor), *The Teacher of Nations* (Cambridge University Press, 1942).

Blodgett, J.H. 'Was Comenius Called to the Presidency of Harvard?' *Educational Review*, VII, 1898.

Brickman, William W. 'Jan Amos Comenius (1592–1670), Cosmopolitan Citizen and Ecumenical Educator,' *School and Society*, CXXXXVIII, 1970, pp. 437–9.

Butler, Nicholas Murray. *The Place of Comenius in the History of Education* (Syracuse, New York, 1892).

Caravolas, Jean. 'Comenius et la didactique des langues modernes,' *Canadian Modern Language Review*, XVI, 1, 1984, pp. 13–21.

Capková, Dagmar. "Comenius: An Alternative,' *Paedagogica Historica*, XXVII, 2, 1992, pp. 187–97.

—— 'J.A. Comenius's "Orbis Pictus" in its Conception as a Textbook for the Universal Education of Children,' *Paedagogica Historica*, X, 1, 1970, pp. 5–27.

—— *Jan Amos Komensky*, 1592–1670 (Prague: Institute for Informatics in Education, 1991).

—— 'Pre-School Education in the Work of J.A. Comenius,' *International Journal of Early Childhood*, II, 1, 1970, pp. 1–7.

Cole. P.R. *A Neglected Educator: Johann Heinrich Alsted* (Sydney: Australia, 1910).

—— *A History of Educational Thought* (London, 1931).

Comenius, Johannes Amos. *The Analytical Didactic* (trans. Vladimir Jelinek) (Chicago University Press, 1953).

—— *The Angel of Peace* (trans. W.A. Morrison (London: 1944)

—— *The Bequest of the Unity of Brethren* (trans. J. Spinka) (Chicago: National Union of Czechoslovak Protestants, 1940).

—— *Continuatio admonitionis fraternae de temporando caritate zelo* (Amsterdam, 1669). *Opera Omnia*, Vol. 21. (Prague, 1969 ff.).

—— *The Great Didactic* (G.W. Keatinge) (London, A.C. Black, 1910).

—— *Janua Linguarum Reserata* (trans. T. Horn) (London: 1673). *Opera Omnia*, Vol. 11.

—— *The Labyrinth of the World and the Paradise of the Heart* (trans. Count Lutzow) (London, 1905).

—— *Opera Didactica Omnia*, 3 vols. (Prague, 1957).

—— *Opera Omnia*, 27 Vols. (in progress) (Prague, 1969 ff.)

Comenius, Johannes Amos. *Orbis Pictus* (Facsimile of the first English edition of 1659) (Edited by B.W. Alderson) (Introduced by John E. Sadler) (Oxford University Press, 1968)

—— *Pampaedia* (edited by A.M.O. Dobbie) (Dover: Buckland Publications, 1986).

—— *Panglottia* (edited by A.M.O. Dobbie) (Shipston-on-Stour, Drinkwater, 1991).

—— *Panorthosia* (Edited by A.M.O. Dobbie)(Sheffield Head Press, 1993).

—— *A Perfect Reformation*, An Anthology Selected by Amadeo Molnár, with an Introduction by J.L. Hromádka (Prague: Comenius Faculty of Protestant Theology, 1957.

—— *A Reformation of Schools Designed in Two Excellent Treatises* (Menton: Scholars' Press, 1969).

—— *The School of Infancy* (trans. W.S. Monroe) (London: Isbister, 1897).

—— *Unum Necessarium, Opera Omnia*, Vol. 18.

—— *Via Lucis* (ed. E.T. Campagnac) (Liverpool University Press, 1938).

Curtis, S.J. and Boultwood, M.E.A. *A Short History of Educational Ideas* (Liverpool: University Tutorial Press, 1953).

Dietrich, Veit-Jakobus, *Johann Amos Comenius* (Hamburg: Rowohlt, 1991).

Dircks, H. *A Biographical Memoir of Samuel Hartlib* (London, 1865).

Dobinson, C.H. (editor). *Comenius and Contemporary Education* (Hamburg: UNESCO, 1970).

Fischer, M. *Die Unterrichtsmethode des Comenius* (Köln, 1983).

Good. H.G. *A History of Western Education* (New York: Macmillan, 1955).

Gundem, Bjorg B. 'Vivat Comenius: A Commemorative Essay on Johann Amos Comenius, 1592–1670,' *Journal of Curriculum and Supervision*, VIII, 1, Fall 1992, pp. 43–55.

Heyberger, Anna. *Jean Amos Comenius (Komensky): sa vie et son œuvre d'educateur* (Paris, 1928).

Heydorn, H.J. (editor) *Jan Amos Comenius: Geschichte und Aktualität 1670–1970* (Abhandlungen: Glashütten, 1971).

Hofmann, Franz *Jan Amos Komensky* (Berlin, 1963).

—— *Jan Amos Comenius. Lehrer der Nationen* (Köln, 1976).

Hornstein, Herbert *Weisheit und Bildung, studien zur Bildungslehre des Comenius* (Düsseldorf, 1968).

Hutton, J.E. *A History of Moravian Missions* (London: Moravian Publications Office, 1928).

—— *A Short History of the Moravian Church* (London: Moravian Publications Office, 1897).

Jakubec, Jan. *Johannes Amos Comenius* (Prague, 1928).

Juva, Vladimir & Monatova, Lili. 'Quarante Ans de Developement de la Pedagogie Prescolaire en Tchecoslovaquie et ses Perspectives,' *International Journal of Early Childhood*, XXI, 1, 1989, pp. 1–10.

Kozík, Frantisek. *Comenius* (Prague: Agencia De Prentis Orbis, 1981).

Krasnorski, A.A. *Jan Amos Komenski* (Moscow, 1953).

Kratochvil, J. (editor) *Jan Amos Komensky a moderni pedagogika* (Stuttgart, 1971).

Krotky, Etienne. *La Pensée éducative de Comenius*, (3 vols.) (Paris, 1983).

Kvačala, Jan. *Korrespondence J.A. Komenského* (2 vols.) (Prague, 1898, 1902).

—— *Johann Amos Comenius: sein leben und seine Schriften* (Berlin, 1982).

Laurie, S.S. *John Amos Comenius* (Cambridge University Press, 1899).

Lochman, Jan Milic. *Comenius* (Freiburg-Hamburg, 1982).

Lordkipanidze, D.O. *Jan Amos Komenski, 1592–1670* (Moscow, 1970).

Matthews, Albert. 'Comenius and Harvard College,' *Publications of the Colonial Society of Massachusetts*, Vol. XXI, 1919.

Michel, Gerhard. 'Die Bedetung des "Orbis Sensualium Pictus" für Schulbucher im Kontext der Geschichte der Schule', *Paedagogica Historica*, XXVIII, 2, 1992, pp. 235–51.

Michel, G. und Schaller, K. (editors). *Pädagogik und Politik* (Comenius Colloquium, Bochum, 1970) (Ratingen, 1972).

Monroe, W.S. *Comenius and the Beginnings of Educational Reform* (London: Heinemann, 1900).

—— *Comenius, the Evangelist of Modern Pedagogy* (Boston, 1892).

Odlozilík, O. 'Comenius and Christian Unity', *Slavonic Review*, IX, 1930.

Olsen, Edward G. 'Standing on the Shoulders of Pioneers,' *Community Education Journal*, V, 6, 1975, pp. 8–12.

Palouš, Radim. *Die Schule der Alten. J.A. Comenius und der Gerontagogik* (Kastellaun, 1979).

Pánek, Jaroslav. *Joan Amos Comenius: Teacher of Nations* (Prague: Orbis, 1991).

Patera, A. *J.A. Komenského korrespondence* (Prague, 1892).

Patočka, Jan. *Jan Amos Komensky.* (2 vols.) (Bochum, 1981).

—— *Die Philosophie der Erziehung des J.A. Comenius* (Paderborn, 1971).

Pešková, Jaroslava. (editor) *Homage to J.A. Comenius* (Prague: Charles University, 1991).

Piaget, Jean. (Editor) *John Amos Comenius, 1592–1670, Selections* (Paris: UNESCO, 1957).

Pleskot, Jaroslav. *Jan Amos Komensky's Years in Fulnek* (Prague, 1972).

Pope, James D. 'Comenius Speaks to Modern Man,' *School and Society*, CXXXXVIII, 1970, pp. 440–5.

Pytlík, Napsal Radko. *Comenius Redivivus* (Prague: Vydala Agentura Fajma, 1992).

Quick, R.H. *Essays on Educational Reformers* (New York: Appleton, 1903).

Riemek, Renate. *Der andere Comenius* (Darmstadt, 1969).

Rood, W. *Comenius and the Low Countries, 1656–1670* (Amsterdam, 1970).

Rössel, Hubert. *Wörterbuch zu den tschechischen Schriften des J.A. Comenius* (Münster, 1983).

Rusk, Robert R. *The Doctrines of the Great Educators* (London: Macmillan, 1967).

Sadler, J.E. *Comenius and the Concept of Universal Education* (London: Allen and Unwin, 1960).

Schaller, Klaus. *Comenius* (Darmstadt, 1973).

—— *Jan Amos Komensky. Wirkung eines Werkes nach drei Jahrhunderten* (Heidelberg, 1970).

de Schweinitz, Edmund. *The History of the Unitas Fratrum* (Bethlehem, Pennsylvania: Moravian Publication Office, 1885).

Schurr, Johannes. *Comenius: Eine Einführung in die Consultatio Catholica* (Passau, 1981).

Spinka, M. *John Amos Comenius: That Incomparable Moravian* (University of Chicago Press, 1943).

Steiner. Martin. 'J.A. Comenii Opera Omnia,' *Paedagogica Historica*, XXVIII, 2, 1992, pp. 309–14.

Strahov, V.I. 'John Amos Comenius's "The World of Sense-Things in Pictures" and Modern Democratic Education,' Seventh European Conference of Directors of Educational Research Institutions, Nitra, Czechoslovakia, October, 1992 (Strasbourg, Council of Europe, 1992).

Turnbull, H.H. *Hartlib, Dury and Comenius* (London: 1947).

Ulich, Robert. *A History of Educational Thought* (New York: American Book Company, 1945).

Universita Karlova J.A. Komenskému 1670–1970 (Prague, 1970).

Weitz, S.E. *Johann Amos Comenius, 1670–1970* (Köln, 1971).

Young. R.F. *Comenius and the Indians of New England* (London, 1929).

—— *Comenius in England* (Oxford University Press, 1932).

INDEX